# Dreamweaver MX: Advanced PHP Web Development

**Gareth Downes-Powell**

**Tim Green**

**Allan Kent**

**Bruno Mairlot**

**George McLachlan**

**Dan Radigan**

Published by glasshaus Ltd,
Arden House,
1102 Warwick Road,
Acocks Green,
Birmingham,
B27 6BH, UK

Printed in the United States
ISBN 1-904151-19-1

# Dreamweaver MX: Advanced PHP Web Development

## Cover Image

The cover image for this book was created by Don Synstelien of http://www.synfonts.com, co-author of the glasshaus book, "Usability: The Site Speaks For Itself".
You can find more of Don's illustration work online at http://www.synstelien.com.

glasshaus

**labor-saving devices for web professionals**

# Trademark Acknowledgments

# Credits

**Authors**
Gareth Downes-Powell
Tim Green
Allan Kent
Bruno Mairlot
George McLachlan
Dan Radigan

**Technical Reviewers**
Aaron Richmond
Dave Gibbons
Nancy Gill
David Powers
Dino Hadzibegovic
Dan Price
Shefali Kulkarni
Rick Stones
Drew McLellan
Midhun James
Martin Honnen

**Proof Reader**
Agnes Wiggers

**Commissioning Editor**
Simon Mackie

**Lead Editor**
Matt Machell

**Technical Editors**
Alessandro Ansa
Dan Walker

**Publisher**
Viv Emery

**Project Manager**
Sophie Edwards

**Production Coordinators**
Rachel Taylor
Pippa Wonson

**Production Assistants**
Paul Grove
Tina Ramwell

**Cover**
Dawn Chellingworth
Natalie O'Donnell

**Indexer**
Adrian Axinte

# About the Authors

## Gareth Downes-Powell

Gareth Downes-Powell has been working in the computer industry for the last twelve years, primarily building and repairing PCs, and writing custom databases. He branched out onto the Internet five years ago, and started creating web sites and custom web applications. This is now his main area of expertise, and he uses a variety of languages including ASP and PHP, with SQL Server or MySQL backend databases.

A partner in Buzz inet, *http://www.buzzinet.co.uk/*, an Internet company specializing in web design and hosting, he uses a wide range of Macromedia products, from Dreamweaver MX through to Flash and Director, for custom multimedia applications. Gareth maintains http://ultradev.buzzinet.co.uk/ as a way of providing support for the whole Macromedia UltraDev and MX Community. There, he regularly adds new tutorials and custom written extensions to this rapidly expanding site.

Gareth enjoys keeping up with the latest developments, and has been providing support to many users, to help them use UltraDev and Dreamweaver MX with ASP or PHP on both Linux and Windows servers. Rarely offline, Gareth can always be found in the Macromedia forums (news: forums.macromedia.com), where he helps to answer many users questions on a daily basis.

## Tim Green

Tim Green is a full-time IT Consultant, eBusiness/B2B Advisor and CEO of The Rawveg Consultancy (*www.rawveg.org*). Beginning his working life as a COBOL and Assembly Language programmer, he moved into web application development in 1996, after dabbling in numerous other careers, from acting to being a chef.

A contributing developer to PHAkT, an implementation of PHP for UltraDev 4, Tim now concentrates on the development of PHP utilities for Dreamweaver MX, and has released a shopping cart management system, IntelliCART MX, to critical acclaim.

*Contributing to this book has been a very rewarding experience; I'd like to thank the whole author and review team for their dedication and hard work. It has been an honor to work with you. Thanks also go to my good friend, Bruno, who never ceases to be a source of inspiration, and thanks too to the Extension Development Community as a whole, as without them, I would never have got involved.*

*Last, but never least, I'd like to thank my wife Becky. Without her support and guidance I would never have done any of this. You're the spark that brings the light babe, thanks.*

## Allan Kent

Allan has been programming seriously for the last 9 years and other than a single blemish when he achieved a diploma in COBOL programming, is entirely self taught. He runs his own company where they try to make a living out of making a lot of noise and playing Quake. When that doesn't work they make a lot of noise while doing development and design for an ad agency. Allan lives in Cape Town, South Africa with his girlfriend and 4 cats.

## Bruno Mairlot

Bruno Mairlot specialises in developing implementations of network and Internet protocols with PHP and MySQL. He began his working life as the founder of a web site development and network services company four years ago, then moved on to work with other companies, but always working mainly as a web site developer and security consultant for the Web.

Along with Tim and Gareth, Bruno is a contributor to the Dreamweaver and PHP community, and is part of the management team of the community site http://www.udzone.com. He is the author of a project that aims to give users a powerful MySQL administration console in Dreamweaver as an extension. He works as a consultant for a Belgian company.

*Writing this book has been a tremendous and exciting experience, but wouldn't have been possible without the help of many people. First and foremost person I would like to thank my friend Tim Green. His support and enthusiasm on this project has helped me more than I could say. Thanks Tim. Next, my thanks go to my soul mate, Pascale. I couldn't have written any of this book without her being at my side, encouraging me and supporting me. I would also like to thank Simon Mackie from glasshaus, who did a tremendously good management job.*

*Special thanks go to my colleague and friend, Con Dorgan, who helped me during my working hours and gave me a lot of suggestions for the book.*

## George McLachlan

George lives in Bothwell, a small village 12 miles south of Glasgow. He is a part time PHP developer, and a full time student, currently studying Software Engineering at Strathclyde University. He was one of the beta testers for Dreamweaver MX and is a member of Team Macromedia. George is a regular contributor in the Macromedia newsgroups. He is a strong supporter of the Open Source movement, and when time permits, tries to provide feedback to the PHP QA team.

*http://www.experimentalmonkey.co.uk*

## Dan Radigan

Dan Radigan has been working in the Internet industry for 7 years. He's currently working as a lead on the Dreamweaver team at Macromedia in the Quality Assurance department. He started the project for PHP integration in Macromedia UltraDev 4 which later became PhAkt. He also led the design of the PHP Server Model in Dreamweaver MX.

Dan spends most of his development time in PHP spread across the Windows, Macintosh, and Linux builds. His main areas of interest are server-side graphics and object-oriented programming in PHP. He also spends a considerable amount of time investigating how Dreamweaver can be extended to handle the latest in PHP technology.

*Contributing to this book has been a both an honor and pleasure. First, I'd like to thank the Dreamweaver MX team for the opportunity to work with some of the best and brightest folks I know. I'd also like to thank Chris Denend and Randy Edmunds for always challenging me technically. I'd like to also thank my family and friends for their encouragement and support. And hats off to all at glasshaus for their patience and flexibility!*

# Table of Contents

Table of Contents

iv

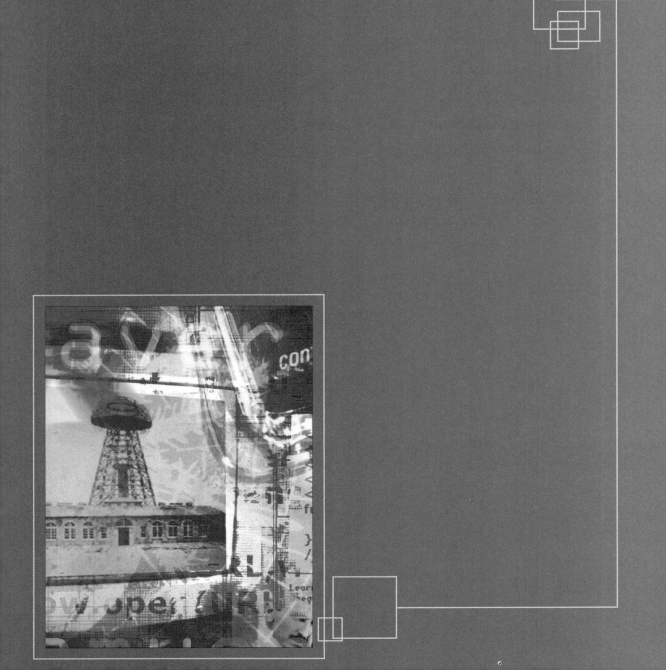

# Introduction

PHP is one of the most popular server-side scripting languages. Its wealth of features and the fact that it is free make it a popular choice for the web professional. It is used everywhere on the Web, from small e-commerce sites to global portals like Yahoo.com. The introduction of the PHP server model in Dreamweaver MX brought a new group of people to building dynamic web sites with this technology.

The code that Dreamweaver produces allows you to create rich database-driven sites. But the PHP created by server behaviors can only take you so far. Eventually you will have urgent need of a piece of functionality that just isn't available through server behaviors. What do you do then?

That's where this book comes in.

First we'll take you through the basics of hand coding, getting you up to speed with the PHP language and the features in Dreamweaver MX that help make it easy (including how to make your own server behaviors).

Then we'll focus on some of the powerful features of PHP. We'll show you how to use dynamic graphics to produce charts and graphs, construct Flash movies on the fly, process an XML news feed, generate e-mail, and manipulate the file system.

Finally we'll show you how to put this new-found knowledge to work with two case studies. The first, an online training log, will show you how you can use your new PHP skills to enhance existing Dreamweaver-produced code. The second will take you through the process of building a content management system, giving you valuable insight into coding PHP and providing you with a useful application to customize.

## Who's This Book for?

This book is for the web professional who has mastered the basics of the PHP server model in Dreamweaver MX, and seeks to learn more about the language behind it.

It assumes you are already familiar with using the PHP server behaviors to interact with a MySQL database.

Though this book stands on its own, it is the ideal companion volume for those who have read our earlier book *Dreamweaver MX: PHP Web Development*, (Gareth Downes-Powell, et al., glasshaus, ISBN 1904151116) and want to expand their knowledge of hand coding and PHP functions.

## What Do I Need to Begin?

The book assumes you already have the following applications set up on your machine (or available to you): Dreamweaver MX, a web server, PHP, and MySQL.

If you don't yet have these, we recommend you install the following:

- The trial version of Dreamweaver MX, found at: *http://www.macromedia.com*
- Apache 1.3.27, available at *http://httpd.apache.org*
- MySQL, available for download at *http://www.mysql.com*
- PHP, which can be downloaded from *http://www.php.net*

If you are using Mac OS X, we recommend you visit *http://www.entropy.ch/software/macosx/,* where Marc Liyanage maintains installation packages for PHP and MySQL.

Certain chapters may also require the installation of additional PHP modules, where this is necessary we have noted it in the text, and given instructions.

# Style Conventions

We've used a number of styles in the book to help you understand what's going on.

We've used the **important words** style to flag up new or important subjects.

*Screen Text* is used to indicate anything you'd see on the screen, including URLs.

New blocks of code are in this code foreground style:

```
<html>
<body>
<script language="JavaScript">

  var myCalc = 1 + 2;
  document.write("The calculated number is " + myCalc);

</script>
</body>
</html>
```

If we're amending a script, perhaps adding in a new line or making changes to an existing one, then we use the code background style for the code that you've already seen together with the foreground style to highlight the new code:

```
<html>
<body>
<script language="JavaScript">
  var userEnteredNumber = prompt("Please enter a number","");
  var myCalc = 1 + userEnteredNumber;
  var myResponse = "The number you entered + 1 = " + myCalc;
  document.write( myResponse);
</script>
</body>
</html>
```

To talk about code within text we use this `code in text` style, which is also used for filenames like `myFirstJavaScript.htm`.

*Asides to the current discussion are presented like this.*

*Essential not–to–be–missed information appears like this.*

## A Note About Code Formatting

We've tried to make the code as easy to read as possible. This does mean that there is sometimes whitespace in the scripts that would break the code if you used it exactly as it is printed. For example, this JavaScript code:

```
        output+="<a href=\""+getPageName(pages[i][j])+".html\" class=\"page\"
title=\""+pages[i][j]+"\">";
```

will look like this in the book:

```
        output+="<a href=\""+getPageName(pages[i][j])+".html\" class=\"page\"
                title=\""+pages[i][j]+"\">";
```

The code in the download is without the whitespace.

# Support/Feedback

Although we aim for perfection, the sad fact of book publication is that a few errors will slip through. We would like to apologize for any errors that have reached this book despite our efforts. If you spot such an error, please let us know about it using the e-mail address *support@glasshaus.com*. If it's something that will help other readers then we'll put it up on the errata page at *http://www.glasshaus.com*.

This address can also be used to access our support network. If you have trouble running any of the code in this book, or have a related question that you feel that the book didn't answer, please mail your problem to the above address quoting the title of the book, the last 4 digits of its ISBN, and the chapter and page number of your query.

# Web Support

Feel free to go and visit our web site, at *http://www.glasshaus.com*. The example code for this and every other glasshaus book, can be downloaded from our site.

# 1

- PHP syntax

- Variables and operators

- Coding style

**Author: Allan Kent**

# PHP Syntax

## Introduction

In this chapter we'll start by taking a look at variables in PHP and how we can use them, along with some more advanced subjects you may not have known about. We'll then take a more detailed look at the kinds of things you can store in variables by looking at the various PHP variable types. PHP has a number of pre-defined variables that you can access, and we'll see what kind of information you can find in them. Once we have dealt with variables we'll move on to looking at the building blocks of the PHP language: operators. Lastly, we'll see how we can organize our code and make it more presentable, reusable, and easy to read.

## The PHP Escape Tags

Before we begin, let's quickly look at how we escape from HTML and into PHP. When PHP parses your page, it looks for a set of special tags that tell it that the code between these tags is PHP, and should be evaluated as such. PHP provides four options for these tags. These are show in the following table.

| Opening Tag | Closing Tag |
|---|---|
| `<?php` | `?>` |
| `<script language="php">` | `</script>` |
| `<?` | `?>` |
| `<%` | `%>` |

The first method, `<?php` and `?>`, is the preferred way of escaping PHP code. It is what Dreamweaver MX uses, and what the code in this book will use. The first and second methods are available on all PHP installations, no matter how they have been set up. The third option, `<?` and `?>`, is only available if it has been enabled with the `short_open_tag` directive in the `php.ini` file. Be careful of using this method as it is also a valid tag in XML. The fourth option is the ASP style of escaping, and will only be available if enabled via the `asp_tags` directive in your `php.ini` file.

Something else we need to cover right up front is the **assignment operator**. We'll get into operators and what they do in more detail after we've covered variables, but we'll be using the assignment operator in all of our examples when looking at variables, so we need to know what it is.

The assignment operator is what you would know as the equals sign, "=". What we mean by "assignment" is that whatever expression is on the right-hand side of the assignment operator, is evaluated, and the result is assigned to whatever is on the left-hand side of the assignment operator. Therefore, in PHP, "=" means "is set to" rather than "equals".

Let's look at an example:

```php
<?php $chapterNumber = 1; ?>
```

We've assigned the value of 1 to the variable `$chapterNumber` (i.e. `$chapterNumber` *is set to* 1).

# Variables

Simply put, a variable is a way of temporarily storing a piece of data. For instance, an amount of money, a person's name, or the current date. Variables have a name, by which we refer to them, and a value (the data that we're currently storing in that variable).

In PHP we indicate a variable by prefixing its name with a `$` symbol. Therefore if we wanted a variable called `theDate`, we would indicate it in PHP code as `$theDate`.

There are two things that you need to keep in mind when naming your variables. The first is that variable names are case-sensitive. This means that if you assign two variables, `$theDate` and `$thedate`, PHP will see them as two *separate* variables. This is a common pitfall for new programmers (or people who are coming from a Visual Basic or ASP background).

The second thing to bear in mind when naming your variables, is to give them valid names. PHP has some limitations when naming variables. They aren't restrictive, but you need to be aware of them.

● Variable names must start with an underscore or a letter

● Variable names can only contain numbers, letters, underscores, or the ASCII characters with codes from 127 to 255.

Examples of valid variable names are things like `$theDate`, `$_Date`, or `$the_date`, while invalid variable names include things like `$01_user` (variable name starts with a number), or `$_the-Date` (variable name contains a minus symbol).

# Variable Types

When we speak about variable types, we are talking about the kind of data that is being stored in the variable. Some programming languages, like Java, require the programmer to specify the type of data that the variable will hold, and will only allow data of that type to be stored as the value of that variable thereafter. PHP is not so picky. In PHP, the variable type is determined at runtime by PHP itself. Therefore, if you set the value of a variable to a numeric value, the variable type will be assigned as the most appropriate of the numeric variable types available, to hold that value. Similarly if you set the value to a string, such as a person's name, the variable type will be set to a string. PHP can also change the variable type at runtime, as needed, to prevent data loss (more on this later).

PHP supports eight variable types. The four most common (also known as **Scalar** types) are:

- boolean
- integer
- floating-point
- string

You then get two variable types that can store a number of other types, and are thus known as **compound types**:

- array
- object

Lastly there are two special types:

- NULL
- resource

We'll take a look at each of these in more detail.

## Boolean

The Boolean variable type is the easiest to understand. Boolean specifies a state of either True or False. This is equal to yes or no, on or off.

To create a variable of type Boolean, you can assign a value of True or False to the variable name:

```
$firstChapter = TRUE;
```

PHP will now see the variable $firstChapter as a Boolean type that has the value of True. It is worth noting that in the case of Booleans, the values of True and False are not case-sensitive, so we can also assign Boolean values in the following way:

```
$lastChapter = False;
```

However, for the sake of consistency and good programming practice it is worth deciding on a single way of writing `True` and `False` and sticking to it.

When a PHP language construct requires a Boolean variable and you pass it a variable of a different type, PHP will convert the value that you have passed it into a Boolean variable (although the value of the original variable passed remains unchanged). For this purpose, values of `0`, `Null`, empty strings, and empty objects are all considered `False`: anything else is considered `True`. Don't worry if this doesn't make sense yet, just keep it in mind for when we cover control structures.

## Integer

An integer is any positive or negative whole number, and therefore any whole number that we assign as the value to a variable results in that variable having a type of integer.

```
$chapterNumber = 1;
```

`1` is a whole number and so `$chapterNumber` now has a type of integer. You can also assign values using the octal and hexadecimal notation. For example:

```
$pageNumber = 0x3D;
```

The maximum size of integer that you can store in an integer variable type depends on the platform PHP is running on, but is normally stored as **32 bits signed**. For those of you that have no idea what that means, it's from about -2 billion to +2 billion.

You might be wondering what happens if you perform some kind of math on your integer variable, which then returns a fraction or non-whole number. Alternatively, what happens if you assign a value that is too large for the integer variable type to handle? Well, as we said earlier, if this happens, PHP automatically converts your integer variable type to a float. Let's look at floats now.

## Floating Point

A floating point number is any number that has a decimal point or a fractional part. As we said earlier, PHP will automatically convert your integer types to a float type if the value that you are storing in the variable exceeds the bounds of the integer variable type. The size of the float variable type is also platform-dependent, but it's around 1.8E380 – that's $1.8 \times 10^{380}$.

As with any other variable, PHP will automatically determine the type of the variable when you assign a value to it:

```
$basketTotal = 386.76;
```

Just as you could use octal and hexadecimal notation to assign an integer value to a variable, you can use scientific notation to assign a floating point number to a variable:

```
$smallValue = 1.5E-8;
```

# String

A string is a series of characters, exactly like the line of text you are reading. There are 256 characters that are valid as characters in a string (PHP does not yet support Unicode), and there are three ways of specifying the value of a string variable:

1   Single quotes

2   Double quotes

3   Heredoc syntax

## Single Quotes

Assigning any value enclosed in single quotes will define the variable type as a string:

```
$chapterTitle = 'PHP Syntax';
```

If you want to include a single quote in your string, you will need to **escape** it, by preceding it with the backslash character:

```
$filmTitle = 'Angela\'s Ashes';
```

## Double Quotes

Assigning a value enclosed within double quotes also defines the variable type as a string, but by using double quotes you can now have what's known as **variable expansion** within your string. The best way to demonstrate this is by way of an example:

```php
<?php
$chapterTitle = 'PHP Syntax';
$message = "The chapter you are currently reading is $chapterTitle";
echo $message;
?>
```

When we assigned the string $message, it was enclosed in double quotes. PHP therefore looks through the string and sees if there are any variable names within the string. In this case there is: $chapterTitle. PHP expands $chapterTitle for us to its full value, and substitutes that value in place of the variable name. When we echo $message we therefore get:

*The chapter you are currently reading is PHP Syntax*

For expanding more complex expressions we have to make use of the curly braces within the string. Consider if, for some reason, we wanted to enclose the title of the chapter with underscore characters. Your initial suspicion might be to try something along the lines of:

```php
<?php
$chapterTitle = 'PHP Syntax';
$message = "The chapter you are currently reading is _$chapterTitle_";
echo $message;
?>
```

but when we try this piece of code, all we get as output is:

*The chapter you are currently reading is _*

This is because the underscore character is a valid character for use in a variable name and so PHP sees the variable name as `$chapterTitle_`. No such variable exists, so PHP expands the `$chapterTitle_` variable to an empty string and "outputs" the empty string. The solution to this is to use curly braces around the variable name:

```php
<?php
$chapterTitle = 'PHP Syntax';
$message = "The chapter you are currently reading is _{$chapterTitle}_";
echo $message;
?>
```

This will now result in the output we were after.

*The chapter you are currently reading is _PHP Syntax_*

When using double quotes, there are a number of additional escape characters that you can include in the string. The most common ones that you will encounter are shown in this table:

| Escape character | | Returns |
|---|---|---|
| \\ | Backslash | \ |
| \" | Double quote | " |
| \r | Carriage Return | ASCII character 13 |
| \n | Newline | ASCII character 10 |
| \t | Tab | ASCII character 9 |
| \$ | Dollar | $ |

## Heredoc syntax

Heredoc syntax behaves in exactly the same way as double-quoted strings, but because you do not use the double quotes to delimit the string, you can safely use double quotes in your text. Heredoc syntax starts the string with <<< and an identifier, and then closes the string with the same identifier and a semi-colon. The closing identifier must be on its own line, at the start of the line, and be the only thing that appears on that line. Here's an example:

```
$strHeredoc = <<<HEREDOC
Heredoc syntax behaves in exactly the same way as double-quoted strings, but because
you do not use the double quotes to delimit the string, you can safely use double
quotes in your text. Heredoc syntax starts the string with <<< and an identifier,
and then closes the string with the same identifier. The closing identifier must be
on its own line and the only thing that appears on that line. Here's an example
HEREDOC;
```

If you use Heredoc syntax, however, you will find that Dreamweaver MX does not know how to understand it, and may render it incorrectly in Code View. For example, if you enter the above code into Dreamweaver MX's Code View, you will see that it fails to treat the single quote in `Here's` as being escaped, and highlights the words `do`, `as` and `string` as reserved words – as, indeed, it does the opening `<<<` sequence. For this reason alone you may wish not to use Heredoc syntax.

Windows users should also take special note that if their editor includes a carriage return at the end of a line, the Heredoc syntax will not work. Most decent text editors will allow you to save your files in UNIX format, which does not include a carriage return at the end of the line: only a newline character.

## Array

As we said earlier, arrays are what are known as compound types because they can be made up of more than one type of variable. An array is a list or collection of values that are stored within, and referred to, by a single variable name. You can access individual values within the array by specifying the **index** of the value within the array, or by using any keys that may exist for the values within the array. *Chapter 2* will cover arrays in detail.

## Object

An object, like an array, is also a compound type. The difference is that, whereas the array was merely a collection of data, the object can not only store data, but can also contain specific methods that allow you to work with the data stored within the object. *Chapter 4* deals specifically with object-oriented programming and will cover objects and their classes in far more detail.

## NULL

The `Null` data type is special and is used when a variable has no value. A variable can be of type `Null` if:

- It has been assigned the value of `Null`

- It has not been assigned any value

- It has been destroyed using the `unset()` function

For example:

```
$password = NULL;
```

Like `True` and `False`, `Null` is also case-insensitive. Note that, when assigning the values of `True`, `False` or `Null` to a variable, enclosing the value in quotes will assign the value as a string. The line of code:

```
$password = "NULL";
```

...will assign `$password` the string `"NULL"`, not the special type `Null`.

## Resource

A resource type is a special variable and contains a reference to an external resource. A resource is something that is created and used by specific PHP functions. The most frequent type of resource that you will encounter is the resource handle that is returned when making a connection to a database. We will come across other resource type variables in *Chapter 12, Creating graphics with PHP*, and *Chapter 13, Using Flash with PHP*.

# Pre-defined variables

The PHP language provides a number of pre-defined variables that you can access from within your script. All of the pre-defined variables are automatically global in scope.

## $GLOBALS

If we define a function within PHP, the function will not know about all the variables that have been defined in the script that is calling it. $GLOBALS is an associative array that we can use to contain all the variables and their values that we want to have global scope within the script. By defining a variable as global in scope, we make the variable and its value available to any functions that we may call within our script at any point. We will deal with functions in more detail towards the end of this chapter.

## $_SERVER

The $_SERVER array contains any variables that we may have received from the web server itself. The contents of this variable depends on the web server that you are using, but you should at least have those that are specified by the CGI 1.1 specification (*http://hoohoo.ncsa.uiuc.edu/cgi/env.html*). Some of the more common ones that you may come across and use within your scripts are show in this table:

| | |
|---|---|
| PHP_SELF | The filename of the current script. This is relative to the document root. This is useful if you want to create a link that refers to the current script. |
| HTTP_ACCEPT | The contents of the Accept: header will typically include values such as: image/gif, image/x-xbitmap, image/jpeg, image/pjpeg, */* |
| HTTP_ACCEPT_ENCODING | The contents of the Accept-Encoding: header would include values such as gzip or deflate. By checking that the browser can accept gzip-encoded documents, we can use gzip to compress the output from our script and send the compressed version to the browser to speed up the download time. |
| HTTP_USER_AGENT | This is a string that specifies the user agent or browser that the person is using to access your page Internet Explorer 6 on Windows XP comes out as "Mozilla/4.0 (compatible; MSIE 6.0; Windows NT 5.1)" while Mozilla 1.1 on the same machine returns "Mozilla/5.0 (Windows; U; Windows NT 5.1; en-US; rv:1.1) Gecko/20020826" |

| | |
|---|---|
| REMOTE_ADDR | The IP address of the person that is viewing this page. |
| REQUEST_METHOD | The method used to request the current script: GET, HEAD, POST or PUT. |
| HTTP_REFERER | The address of the page that referred the browser to the current page. |

These pre-defined variables contain their values as associative arrays. You will learn more in *Chapter 2* about associative arrays, but we will quickly look at how you can access these variables. To get to the value of the HTTP_USER_AGENT variable in the $_SERVER array, you specify it as $_SERVER['HTTP_USER_AGENT'], for example, when viewing a page with Internet Explorer 6 on a Windows XP box, the code:

```php
<?php
 echo $_SERVER['HTTP_USER_AGENT'];
?>
```

…returns:

*Mozilla/4.0 (compatible; MSIE 6.0; Windows NT 5.1)*

# $_GET

The $_GET array contains any name/value pairs that were passed to the script as part of the query string (appended to the URL).

As an example, create the file showvars.php in your web server's web root directory, which contains the following (the print_r() function simply displays information about a variable and its contents):

```php
<pre>
<?php print_r($_GET); ?>
</pre>
```

Now call the showvars.php script from your browser with a URL similar to:

*http://localhost/showvars.php?firstName=Allan&lastName=Kent*

Using the URL above, this outputs the following result:

*Array*
*(*
 *[firstName] => Allan*
 *[lastName] => Kent*
*)*

In the same way as our example in the previous section accessed the values of the `$_SERVER` array, we can do the same for the `$_GET` array:

```php
<?php
 echo $_GET['firstName'];
?>
```

Before we go any further it is worth noting a considerable change that took place in the PHP language from version 4.1.0 to version 4.2.0. Prior to version 4.1.0 the variables `$firstName` and `$lastName` would have been automatically available to you in `showvars.php` and you wouldn't have had to access them via the `$_GET` array, as you do now. In PHP version 4.1.0 the language provided a set of variables that contained any values of variables that came from the web server, the web server environment, or from any user input. These are the `$_SERVER`, `$_GET`, and as we will see later, the `$_POST` and `$_COOKIE` arrays. Since PHP version 4.2.0 these arrays are the only way to access the information passed to the PHP script by default: you can no longer access these values directly.

## $_POST

`$_POST` is exactly like `$_GET` except it contains the values of any name/value pairs that have been passed using the HTTP `POST` method. Typically this would be the content of forms.

Alter `showvars.php` to look like this:

```php
<pre>
<?php print_r($_POST); ?>
</pre>
```

To show this in action, we are going to have to be a bit more inventive than before because we cannot simply call the page directly. We have to submit some values to it via a form. Create a file named `myform.html`.

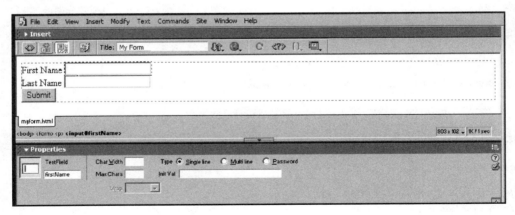

First, set the Action of the form to `showvars.php` and make sure that the `method` is set to POST.

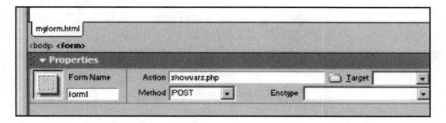

Next, set the `id` of the text fields to `firstName` and `lastName` respectively.

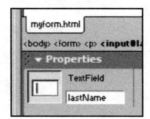

If you take a look at the Code View of the form you should see something like this:

```
<!DOCTYPE HTML PUBLIC "-//W3C//DTD HTML 4.01 Transitional//EN">
<html>
<head>
<title>My Form</title>
<meta http-equiv="Content-Type" content="text/html; charset=iso-8859-1">
</head>

<body>
<form name="form1" method="post" action="showvars.php">
  <p>First Name
    <input name="firstName" type="text" id="firstName">
    <br>
    Last Name
    <input name="lastName" type="text" id="lastName">
    <br>
    <input type="submit" name="Submit" value="Submit">
  </p>
</form>
</body>
</html>
```

Previewing your form, you should see something like this:

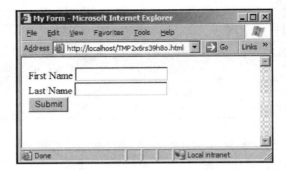

Fill in the fields and submit the form. `showvars.php` will load and display the values it was passed:

Dreamweaver MX also gave the `Submit` button a value, and this is reflected in the array of POST variables.

## $_COOKIE

Any cookies that the user's web browser sends to the server, are available to you in the `$_COOKIE` array. To demonstrate how this works, alter `showvars.php`, thus:

```
<pre>
<?php print_r($_COOKIE); ?>
</pre>
```

Then create a new script called `setcookie.php` that contains the following code:

```
<?php
setcookie("advDWMX","Advanced Dreamweaver MX");
?>
<html>
<head>
<title>Untitled Document</title>
<meta http-equiv="Content-Type" content="text/html; charset=iso-8859-1">
```

```
</head>
<body>
<a href="showvars.php">Continue</a>
</body>
</html>
```

First we set a cookie called `advDWMX` and we give it the value of `Advanced Dreamweaver MX`. We then link to the `showvars.php` page, which will show our newly created cookie. You would retrieve the value of this cookie in PHP via `$_COOKIE['advDWMX']`.

## $_FILES

The `$_FILES` array is a special array that is only available if you have allowed the user to upload a file using a `POST` form in your page. Handling file uploads is beyond the scope of this chapter, but we will cover it in more detail in *Chapter 8*.

## $_ENV

The `$_ENV` array contains the **environment variables** and their values for the system that is hosting PHP. This provides a similar list of values as you would get if you typed `set` in a DOS prompt under Windows. Again, these variables will be different depending on the platform PHP is hosted on.

## $_REQUEST

This array contains any variable that has been sent to the script from any kind of user input. This array will therefore include the contents of the `$_GET`, `$_POST`, `$_FILES`, and `$_COOKIE` arrays.

## $_SESSION

`$_SESSION` is an associative array of any session variables and their values. A session in PHP is a way of preserving data so that we can carry it from one page's scripts to another. The `$_SESSION` array is only available if you have initialized a session with the `session_start()` function. We won't give away too much here, because you'll be dealing with sessions in far more detail in *Chapter 11*.

### A Note on Pre-Defined Variables

Before we end our look at the pre-defined variables, we need to take a look at how Dreamweaver MX handles these arrays. If you look at the PHP toolbar (Under the *PHP* tab in the *Insert* dialog), you will notice that there are four buttons on the left-hand end, for *Form Variables*, *URL Variables*, *Session Variables*, and *Cookie Variables*.

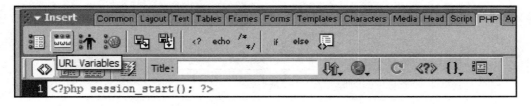

19

If you insert these into your page you'll get the following code for each of them respectively:

```php
<?php $HTTP_POST_VARS[]; ?>

<?php $HTTP_GET_VARS[]; ?>

<?php $HTTP_SESSION_VARS[]; ?>

<?php $HTTP_COOKIE_VARS[]; ?>
```

Prior to PHP version 4.1.0, these were associative arrays that were used instead of $_POST, $_GET, $_SESSION, and $_COOKIE. These arrays were not automatically global in scope, so in order to use them in any functions, you had to use the keyword global within the function.

These older arrays are now **deprecated**, meaning they may stop being supported in some future version of PHP. Dreamweaver uses them, however, in order to achieve a maximum range of compatibility. Until an update or new version of Dreamweaver MX is released, you will have to add the newer arrays by hand or create them as code snippets.

# Operators

Operators are crucial to the PHP language. They are a set of symbols that tell PHP to *do* something. As well as the arithmetic operators, we will also have a look at string and comparison operators.

## Arithmetic Operators

The arithmetic operators are the old favorites that you learned at school:

| | | |
|---|---|---|
| + | Addition | Adds the values on either side of the operator. |
| - | Subtraction | Subtracts the value on the right from the value on the left. |
| * | Multiplication | Multiplies the values on either side of the operator together. |
| / | Division | Divides the value on the left by the value on the right. |
| % | Modulus | Divides the value on the left by the value on the right and returns the remainder: 10 % 3 would result in a value of 1. 3 goes into 10 three times (9) with a remainder of 1. |
| ++ | Increment | Adds 1 to the value: `$chapterNumber = 1;` `$chapterNumber++;` after this code has run, $chapterNumber will have a value of 2. |
| -- | Decrement | Subtracts 1 from the value. |

The increment and decrement operators can be placed either before or after the variable they act on. When it is before the variable, as in `--$chapterNumber;`, it is called a **pre-decrement** and the decrement is done before the variable is used. When after the variable name it is called a **post-decrement** and the decrement is done after the variable is used. Consider these two examples:

```php
<?php
 $a = 10;
 $b = $a++;
 echo $b;
?>
```

...and :

```php
<?php
 $a = 10;
 $b = ++$a;
 echo $b;
?>
```

In the first example, we are using a post-increment, therefore the value of $a is incremented *after* the value is assigned to $b. $b is therefore set to 10. In the second example we are using a pre-increment, and the increment takes effect on $a *before* the value of $a is assigned to $b. $b in the second example is therefore set to 11.

## String Operators

As you might expect the string operators work with strings and string variables. There are only 2 operators that deal with strings, so this will be really easy. The first one is the concatenating operator, and its symbol is a period or full stop ".".

This operator concatenates, or joins together, two strings or string variables. If we had two string variables and wanted to join them together into a single string, we would use the operator as follows:

```php
$bookTitle = 'Dreamweaver MX: Advanced PHP Web Development';
$chapterTitle = 'PHP Syntax';
$fullName = $bookTitle . ', ' . $chapterTitle;
```

In the last line, we've used the assignment operator, two concatenation operators, some variables, and a string. What we're saying, is: join the contents of $bookTitle to the contents of $chapterTitle with a comma, and assign the result into a new variable called $fullName. After that piece of code has run, $fullName will contain:

*Dreamweaver MX: Advanced PHP Web Development, PHP Syntax*

Take a look at the following line of PHP:

```php
$chapterTitle = 'PHP Syntax';
```

What would we do if we wanted to add something onto the end of that? We could do something like:

```
$chapterTitle = $chapterTitle . ', Chapter 1';
```

which would add `, Chapter 1` onto the end of the current value of `$chapterTitle` and assign the new value back to `$chapterTitle`. This probably seems like a roundabout way of doing it, though. Luckily we have the second string operator to help us, the **concatenating assignment operator**. Although it's a mouthful to say, it's actually just what we need. We can rewrite our previous line as:

```
$chapterTitle .= ', Chapter 1';
```

where `.=` is our new concatenating assignment operator. What it does is concatenate the value on the right onto the value on the left.

At this point it is worth mentioning that, if necessary, PHP will do automatic type conversion. What this means is that if you use an arithmetic operator on two variables, and one variable is a string, PHP will convert the string to a float or integer for the purpose of performing the calculation.

```
$strNumber = "10";
$fltNumber = 3.8;
$Result = $strNumber + $fltNumber;
```

Because we are performing an arithmetic addition between a string and a float, the result will be a float (with a value of `13.8`, in this example). Next, try this example:

```
$strNumber = "10";
$fltNumber = 3.8;
$Result = $strNumber.$fltNumber;
```

Here, `$Result` is a string: `"103.8"`. `$fltNumber` (`3.8`) is converted to the string `"3.8"` and concatenated onto the end of the string `"10"`. A very important point to note is that the initial types of the variables that are used in the operation remain unchanged – at the end of the operation `$strNumber` is still a string and `$fltNumber` is still a float.

## Comparison Operators

Comparison operators allow you to compare two values. These operators will be extremely useful to you in *Chapter 2* when you will use these comparisons to make decisions in your code.

Comparison operators always compare 2 things with one another and, depending on their values and the comparison that is being made, will either return `True` or `False`.

| == | Equal | Will return `true` if the two values are equal. |
|---|---|---|
| === | Identical | Will return `true` if the two values are equal and *of the same type*. |
| != | Not equal | Returns `true` if the two values are not equal. |
| <> | Not equal | `<>` is the same as `!=` |
| !== | Not identical | Returns `true` if the two values are not the equal or not the same type. |
| < | Less than | Returns `true` if the value on the left is less than the value on the right. |
| > | Greater than | Returns `true` if the value on the left is greater than the value on the right. |
| <= | Less than or equal to | Returns `true` if the value on the left is less than or equal to the value on the right |
| >= | Greater than or equal to | Returns `true` of the value on the left is greater than or equal to the value on the right |

In the previous section we mentioned that PHP will automatically convert variables to the same type in order to perform string and arithmetic operations on them. This is also true in the case of the comparison operators. If you are comparing two variables that are of different types, PHP will convert them both to the same type in order to compare them. If either of the operands are Boolean or float, PHP will convert the other operand to Boolean or float as well. This is where the `===` and `!==` operators are important, as they compare the values and types of the variables at the same time. Be careful when using these operators for comparing strings, though, as you may get strange results – rather, use the `strcmp()` function.

There are some operators that we have not taken a look at, for example the logical and array operators, but these will be covered in *Chapter 2* when you look at flow control and arrays.

# Coding Style

Until now, Dreamweaver MX probably created the majority of the code that you made. In this book we will be spending most of our time learning how to code for ourselves, so before we get too far along that road we need to spend some time and look at how we can make things easier for ourselves.

Writing code is a lot like creating a newspaper. (This might seem a bit strange, but bear with me for a moment.) The language of the newspaper is like the language that you are programming in. Even though each newspaper may be written in English, each newspaper *editor* and *writer* will have their own style of writing and their own way of putting their story across.

For the most part, we can understand what they are trying to say, but each newspaper is laid out in a similar, but slightly different way. This is the problem. Some of them have news bars down the side with adverts across the top, some of them choose to have no news bar and only run full page images with a headline on the front page. If you picked up a different newspaper from the one that you usually read and wanted to find the weather, you wouldn't find it as easily as you could in your normal paper.

It is for this reason that we talk about coding style. Everyone has their own style and way of laying out their code; if you're the only person who's ever going to read your code, then that's OK. For small projects, if you've only got 50 lines of code, it's not going to take you too long to find a specific line. However, start getting to 200 or more lines of code and you may begin to struggle to find things.

If you ever work in an environment where other people need to look at your code, you'll find it difficult to understand one another's code and fix it if you all use different styles. In short, you'll be back in the situation where everyone is used to a different newspaper layout.

We'll look at 2 areas of style that will make it easier for both yourself and for others to read, understand, and find their way around your code. The first area covers coding conventions. The second part is code organization.

## Code Conventions

Code conventions deal primarily with the aesthetic side of programming. They make things easy to read, easy to understand, and easy to maintain. We'll look at four specific areas: naming variables, using braces, indenting code, and adding comments.

### Naming Variables

I'll be honest with you, I'm the last person you'd have expected to be evangelizing about naming variables, but I've been reformed. A few years ago, I wrote a series of reports for the management at the place I was working and they wanted them changed and a few things added. I didn't really have time, so somebody came up with the bright idea of me teaching *management* how to write these reports themselves, so they wouldn't have to bother me about it. Great idea – no more report writing for me. As things often happen, the couple of days before the scheduled teaching I was a bit busy, so I didn't really have time to prepare anything. No problem I thought, I'll just fire up one of the reports, take them through it, and I'll be free.

I arrived at the training room, fired up my PC, and opened the first report on the overhead screen projector And there they were my variables: `$woohoo1`, `$woohoo2`, `$woohoo3`, and so on. It had been a while since I last worked on this report and I had no idea what these variables were for, what values they were supposed to hold, or where they would be used in the code. Needless to say, I carried on in my role as the management's report-writer.

The point of this story is this: meaningful variable names act as reminders and clues to what's going on in your code. `$woohoo1` means nothing to me now, nor did it mean anything to the people sitting in front of me reading the code, on that fine morning. It may have been blatantly obvious to me at the time I wrote the code, but this was a month (and many lines of code) later. Whatever was going through my mind at the time of `$woohoo1` is lost forever.

So use something descriptive that has meaning, and will mean that *same thing* in 6 month's time. For instance, if you were writing a shopping basket application, don't use a variable name like `$total`. Try and be a bit more descriptive: `$total` what? Total cost? Total number of items in the basket? Total idiot?

```
$basketTotalValue
$basketTotalItems
```

Another thing to keep in mind when creating a number of variables that all relate to the same thing, is that it is often easier, and makes more sense, to keep these values in an array or object. We will cover arrays and objects in detail later in the book.

You'll notice also that I've used a mixture of case in naming my variables. This is what is known as **Hump Back Notation** (among other names) because of way the uppercase letters form humps, like humpback bridges, in the text. There are a number of ways of going about it. You could use uppercase for every word that makes up the variable name, as in:

```
$BasketTotalValue
```

...or use uppercase for all the initial letters except the first one (this is commonly referred to as **Camel Case Notation** – again, presumably, as an allusion to humps):

```
$basketTotalValue
```

The second option is more popular amongst programmers. Whichever you choose, stick to it, and it'll make your code neater and easier to read.

Something else you could do to make your code more readable is to prefix each variable name with a short code that specifies the type of value that the variable holds. Although PHP assigns types for you, it's always a good idea to show what sort of value you expected a variable to hold. That way, you can test to see if it actually does hold that value. This will allow you to see at a glance whether a specific variable is supposed to hold a string, an integer, or an object.

Using the previous above, we know that the total value of the basket could well have a decimal point in it, so the variable would be a float. We therefore name the variable accordingly:

```
$fltBasketTotalValue
```

Or if we had a variable that stored the customers' name, that would be a string:

```
$strCustomerName
```

The short three-letter prefixes help show what a variable should contain if all is well.

## Using Braces

Braces (curly brackets), are used in PHP to surround blocks of code in control structures and functions. Don't worry for now if you don't know what a control structure is, we'll be looking at those in *Chapter 2*. Even though in most cases you would have to use braces in your control structures, there will be cases where you can get away without using them. Here's a hint: Don't. It'll make your code look messy and if you come along later and change that piece of code, you could break it. That being said, there are two ways of approaching braces; don't worry if you don't understand the code we present here, you'll cover it all during the course of the book. For now, just look at what the code looks like, aesthetically.

```php
<?php
while ($rowCustomers = mysql_fetch_array($rsCustomers)) { $strFirstName =
$rowCustomers['cust_fname'];
$strLastName = rowCustomers['cust_lname']; }
?>
```

Compare that block of code with the following block:

```php
<?php
while ($rowCustomers = mysql_fetch_array($rsCustomers)) {
 $strFirstName = $rowCustomers['cust_fname'];
 $strLastName = rowCustomers['cust_lname'];
}
?>
```

Notice how there is no code following the opening brace {, and that the closing brace } is on a line of its own. Looks a lot neater don't you think? The other method of laying out that block of code is to have the opening brace on a line of its own like the closing brace:

```php
<?php
while ($rowCustomers = mysql_fetch_array($rsCustomers))
{
 $strFirstName = $rowCustomers['cust_fname'];
 $strLastName = rowCustomers['cust_lname'];
}
?>
```

Either of these last two techniques is fine, but whichever one you choose, stick with it.

## Indenting code

If we take a look at the following block of code:

```php
<?php
while ($rowCustomers = mysql_fetch_array($rsCustomers)) {
$strFirstName = $rowCustomers['cust_fname'];
$strLastName = rowCustomers['cust_lname'];
if ($strFirstName=='Allan') {
$fltBasketTotalValue = 0;
$boolIncludeFreeBooks = TRUE;
}
}
?>
```

it's a little bit difficult to see what starts and ends where. This is because every line starts on the first column. What we can do is indent the code blocks within the control structures. In that way we will be able to see what code goes where:

```php
<?php
while ($rowCustomers = mysql_fetch_array($rsCustomers)) {
    $strFirstName = $rowCustomers['cust_fname'];
    $strLastName = rowCustomers['cust_lname'];
    if ($strFirstName=='Allan') {
        $fltBasketTotalValue = 0;
        $boolIncludeFreeBooks = TRUE;
    }
}
?>
```

In this example we can see which control structure the closing brace applies to, in each case. This gets very important when you start nesting them!

Dreamweaver MX has a helpful feature built into it called **Balance Braces**. If you position your cursor in Code View just after an opening brace and choose *Balance Braces* from the *Edit* menu, Dreamweaver MX will select all the code from the current opening brace up to its corresponding closing brace. You can quickly see if you have omitted a brace somewhere along the line with this feature.

## Adding comments

Adding comments to your code is another very useful thing you can do to help yourself out. Like naming your variables properly, commenting your code is going to help you or any one else who may have to come back later and make changes to your code. When you write a piece of code, you always understand why it is that you've coded something in a particular way, but this is not always obvious to someone else and you'll probably forget, yourself, over time. Comments act as helpful reminders, and explain what's going on.

There are two ways of adding comments to your code: one method for adding a single-line comment, and one for adding multiple lines.

### Single-line comments

Single-line comments are added by putting a double forward slash (//). Anything after this point up to the end of that line becomes a comment. In Code View, Dreamweaver MX responds to this by coloring the line that you have commented out in orange. This line of code will not be executed by PHP:

```php
$perpage=10;          //How many threads to be shown...

//create a dummy array with relevant values for certain DB fields necessary on first itteration
//of the threading loop
$row=array("msg_id" => 0, "haschild" => 1, "first" => 1, "limit" => $perpage, "start" =>$start);

//Connect to the database
$db=Connect() or die("Unable to connect to database server");
```

Notice that you can begin a comment on a line that already has some code on it: you just can't have any more code after the comment starts.

### Multi-line comments

If you need to add a large block of comments, it would be tedious to add // to the beginning of each line. A better method would be to use the /* and */ characters. There is a button to comment code in this way on the *PHP* tab of the *Insert* panel in Dreamweaver:

```
/*
This next section of code loops through the list of all
available customers, pops their first and last names into
variables and then checks to see if their first name is
Allan.  if so, the order is free and the customer also receives
some free books.
*/
while ($rowCustomers = mysql_fetch_array($rsCustomers)) {
  $strFirstName = $rowCustomers['cust fname'];
```

The characters /* signify the start of a comment block, while */ signify the end of it.

## Code Organization

Now that we've dealt with the aesthetic side of writing our code, we need to look at ways of organizing it so that we can find things easily when we need to.

### Include files

Many applications that you write will have some settings. A common example of this is if you are connecting to a database in your application. In order to connect to your database you're going to need to know the hostname of the machine where the database is, the username and password required to log in, and the name of the database itself. Now imagine you have 30 or 40 PHP pages or scripts in your application and each one connects to the database at some point. If your database name or password changed, you'd have to go and change that password in each of the 40 pages. To make our lives easier we can just store that information in a separate file, and reference it from each of our pages that connects to the database. When we create a database connection in Dreamweaver MX, it automatically creates just such a file for us in the process. These files are stored in the /Connections/ folder and are named after the connection name that we created.

So, if we created a connection called *dwmx*, the following file is saved as /Connections/dwmx.php.

```php
<?php
$hostname_dwmx = "localhost";
$database_dwmx = "dwmx";
$username_dwmx = "dwmxuser";
$password_dwmx = "dwmxpassword";
$dwmx = mysql_pconnect($hostname_dwmx, $username_dwmx, $password_dwmx) or
die(mysql_error());
?>
```

Then in the PHP page, Dreamweaver MX uses the `require_once()` function to insert this code into our page:

```php
<?php require_once('Connections/dwmx.php'); ?>
```

After this line of code, the variables that have been declared within `dwmx.php` are available to be used:

```php
mysql_select_db($database_dwmx, $dwmx);
```

If we had to change our password it would be a simple matter of altering the `/Connections/dwmx.php` file and the changes would filter through to all of our PHP scripts that included it.

There are four functions that we can use to include files into our page. `include()` and `require()` are identical, except that if the file is not found, `include()` will generate a warning, while `require()` will result in a fatal error. `include_once()` and `require_once()` are similar, but have the additional functionality that, if the code that is being included or required has already been inserted once, it will not be inserted a second time.

## Functions

Functions are very useful code structures for grouping together repetitive blocks of code. If you have a piece of code that you are using over and over again, instead of retyping it each time you need it, you could move it all into a function and just call the function. Functions are also great for writing utility pieces of code. Say you needed to convert a temperature from Celsius to Fahrenheit – you could insert the formula straight into your page where you needed to do the conversion, but it would be neater and more effective if you wrote a function to do the conversion, and then just called the function. That way you could call the function from any point in your code without having to duplicate the actual code to do the conversion.

Let's take a look at what I mean:

```php
<?php
// grab the current temperature from the currentTemp form field
$fltCurrTempCel = $_POST['currentTemp'];
// convert the temperature to fahrenheit
$fltCurrTempFah = (1.8 * $fltCurrTempCel) + 32;
?>
```

As it stands, if we wanted to convert another temperature to Fahrenheit, we would have to use the same formula in our code again, `(1.8 * temp in Celsius) + 32`. The formula in itself isn't very informative, and it would be better if we could call a function called something like `mkFahrenheit()`, for example.

Let's write such a function. The first thing to know about functions is that they can take things called **arguments**. An argument is any piece of information that you want to give to the function to work with. In our case we will need to tell our function what the value of the temperature is that we want to convert, otherwise how would it know? The second thing we need to know is that a function can **return** a value. In our example we would want to know what the converted temperature actually is. Here's the function:

```
function mkFahrenheit($Celsius) {
 return (1.8 * $Celsius) + 32;
}
```

The first line contains our function definition: we start with the keyword `function`, so that PHP knows we are declaring a function here. Immediately afterwards we give the function a name. This is what we will be calling from our script to do the actual conversion. The bit in brackets after the function name holds the arguments that we will pass to the function. What we are telling the function here is that the value that it gets in the brackets is known as `$Celsius`.

The next line does the actual conversion. Notice that we use `$Celsius` in our formula, since this is the name of the variable within that function that holds the value of the temperature. We say that the variable is **local in scope**, meaning that every time the `mkFahrenheit()` function is called, a variable `$Celsius` is created and initialized, and assigned with the value passed to the function as the argument. The `return` keyword in front tells PHP to send the resulting value back to whatever code called the function.

Let's see how we would actually call the function:

```
// grab the current temperature from the currentTemp form field
$strCurrTempCel = $_POST['currentTemp'];
// convert the temperature to fahrenheit
$fltCurrTempFah = mkFahrenheit($strCurrTempCel);
```

We replace the formula for calculating the temperature with the name of the function that we declared, and include the temperature in Celsius in the brackets as the argument to the function.

We've used our assignment operator to assign the value of the function `mkFahrenheit()` to the variable `$fltCurrTempFah`. The value of the function is whatever is returned by the function. Notice also the type conversion that takes place: `$strCurrTempCel` is retrieved from the `$_POST[]` array as a string, but `$fltCurrTempFah` is calculated as a float.

By default, arguments to functions are **passed by value**. What this means, is that the value of the variable, rather than the variable itself, is passed to the function. If we alter or modify the value passed to the function, it will not affect the value of the variable outside of the function. For instance:

```
<?php
function addOne($value) {
 return ++$value;
}
$amount = 10;
$newAmount = addOne($amount);
echo $amount.'<br/>'.$newAmount;
?>
```

results in the output:

*10*
*11*

The original value of `$amount` is not affected by the function. We can, however, ensure that it is. This is known as passing the value **by reference**. We use the `&` operator to achieve this:

```php
<?php
function addOne(&$value) {
  return ++$value;
}
$amount = 10;
$newAmount = addOne($amount);
echo $amount.'<br/>'.$newAmount;
?>
```

The value of `$amount` is affected by the code in the function because a direct reference to it was passed to the function. We can see this from the output:

*11*
*11*

Because of this behavior, passing large arrays of data by value could cause your code to run slowly or create unnecessary overhead on the server. In such a case you would want to pass the values by reference.

That's really all there is to it. You can put any code that you want inside the function and call it whenever you need to. By using arguments as placeholders for actual values, you can make your functions as generic as you like. Something to keep in mind, is that any variables inside your function, either declared or passed through as an argument, are available only within that function. Similarly any variables that have not been declared within your function, are not available inside the function. In the script:

```php
<?php
function mkFahrenheit($Celsius) {
return (1.8 * $Celsius) + 32;
}
// grab the current temperature from the currentTemp form field
$fltCurrTempCel = $_POST['currentTemp'];
// convert the temperature to fahrenheit
$fltCurrTempFah = mkFahrenheit($fltCurrTempCel);
?>
```

...the variables `$fltCurrTempCel` and `$fltCurrTempFah` don't exist, as far as the `mkFahrenheit()` function is concerned.

And once the function has finished running, the `$Celsius` variable no longer exists either. Variables only exist within their own scope, within your code. The only exceptions to this rule are the pre-defined variables that we looked at earlier in the chapter. These are automatically global in scope and you can access them from anywhere within your functions.

If you wanted to create a variable with global scope, you would do so within the function that needed to access that variable. Take the following code as an example:

```php
<?php
function mkFahrenheit() {
 global $fltCurrTempCel;
 return (1.8 * $fltCurrTempCel) + 32;

}
// grab the current temperature from the currentTemp form field
$fltCurrTempCel = $_POST['currentTemp'];
// convert the temperature to Fahrenheit
$fltCurrTempFah = mkFahrenheit();
?>
```

This piece of code does the same thing as the previous one, except that we are not passing the Celsius value as an argument to the function. Instead we are making the variable $fltCurrTempCel global in scope, so that the function can access its value and use it. This example relies on our Celsius temperature being stored in a variable called $fltCurrTempCel and therefore it is not very reusable.

### Built-in Functions

PHP comes with many built-in functions, and these will be introduced throughout this book. Where a function's syntax is being explained we will use the form:

```
boolean thisfunction (int parameter1 [, int parameter2])
```

This means that the function thisfunction returns a variable that is of type boolean, and it takes one argument called parameter1 and an optional argument called parameter2, both of which are integers. So when we actually use the function, we might type:

```
thisfunction(5, 6)
```

## Summary

In this chapter we covered a number of areas of PHP that will form a base for the chapters that follow.

We started off by looking at variables; what they are, how we can use them, and what the different types of variables are. We ended off that section by taking a look at the pre-defined variables that PHP makes available to us.

We then took a quick look at the various operators that we have to manipulate the values of variables. We covered the arithmetic, comparison, and string operators

Then we finished the chapter off by looking at some elements of good coding style. In this section we discussed variable-naming conventions, using braces, indenting code, and adding comments – all methods which will make our code more readable and easier to understand. We also discussed how to organize our code better, by moving sections of code into include files and using functions to group repetitive code and chunks of utility code.

**PHP Syntax**

# 2

- Control structures
- Arrays

**Author: Gareth Downes-Powell**

# Decision Making, Loops, and Arrays

In this chapter, we will look at the control and decision-making structures that let us create code that can react to the data it receives from the user, and follow different paths, based on certain conditions being either true of false. We will also look at the different types of loop structures, why they are useful, and how to apply them.

We'll then look at **Arrays**, examining both single, associative arrays, and two-dimensional arrays. Using practical examples, you will learn how to dynamically sort arrays, compact arrays so they can be stored in a single database field, and then reconstruct the array afterwards.

## Control Structures

Control Structures form the very heart of a PHP script. Without control structures, a script would just be a static sequence of commands, only capable of executing the same procedure every time they were run, and unable to "react" to changes in the data being used. Control structures allow your code to make decisions, and to take different paths, depending on predefined conditions.

Open Dreamweaver MX and create a new PHP page in order to try the examples in this chapter.

### Decision Making

The first structure we're going to look at is the if structure. This is one of the most widely used PHP commands, as it allows you to only execute certain sections of code if a condition is met.

## The if Statement

The first structure we'll look at is the `if` statement. It allows you to execute a section of code, depending on whether the result of a condition is true or false. In its simplest form, an `if` statement consists of code similar to this:

```php
<?php
if ($weather == "rain") {
    echo "Don't forget your Umbrella !";
?>
```

When this code is run, the PHP processor uses `==`, known as the **comparison operator**, to compare the value stored in `$weather` with the string `"rain"`. The `==` comparison operator checks if the values are equivalent. If they are, then the message *" Don't forget your Umbrella !"* is output. We can use the following comparison operators:

| Operator | Description | Example | Result if $value = 15 |
|----------|-------------|---------|------------------------|
| == | Equal To | $value == 10 | false |
| != | Not Equal To | $value != 10 | true |
| < | Less Than | $value < 10 | false |
| > | Greater Than | $value > 10 | true |
| <= | Less Than or Equal To | $value <= 10 | false |
| >= | Greater Than or Equal To | $value >=10 | true |

In the previous example, only a single code statement was executed if the condition was `True`. While this is useful, most of the time you'll want to execute a block of code, rather than a single statement. To do this we add curly braces to the code. An opening brace denotes the start of the code block, and a closing brace denotes the end of the code block. Using braces, we'll now expand our previous example:

*Its important to note, that unlike some other languages such as VBScript, PHP uses the `==` operator to check whether two values are equal. A single = sign assigns a value, and it's a common mistake to confuse the two.*

```php
<?php
if ($weather == "rain") {
    echo "Don't forget your Umbrella !\n";
    $rainyDays = $rainyDays + 1;
    echo "There have been " . $rainyDays . " days of rain this month";
}
?>
```

*It's worth noting that you don't need to use a semicolon after an opening or closing brace.*

Now if $weather is equal to "rain", the script will print *"Don't forget your Umbrella"*, but it will also add 1 to the variable $rainyDays, and then print *"There have been 10 days of rain this month"* (or whatever value is stored in $rainyDays when the code is run).

## else

The else statement is used to run some code when the condition in an if statement evaluates to False. It's used with the if statement so that you can execute one block of code if the condition is True, and a different block of code if the condition is False.

```php
<?php
if ($weather == "rain") {
    echo "Don't forget your Umbrella !\n";
    $rainyDays = $rainyDays + 1;
    echo "There have been $rainyDays days of rain this month";
} else {
    echo "You don't need your umbrella today\n";
    $sunnyDays = $sunnyDays + 1;
    echo "There have been $sunnyDays sunny days this month";
}
?>
```

Again, we can expand our previous example, and include an else statement :

Now, let's assume that before we run this code, $rainyDays has a value of 9, and $sunnyDays has a value of 11. If $weather is equal to "rain" it will print:

*Don't forget your Umbrella !*
*There have been 10 days of rain this month*

However, if $weather doesn't equal "rain" (if it has *any* other value, in fact) it will print:

*You don't need your umbrella today*
*There have been 12 sunny days this month*

## else if

The last part of this control structure is else if, which can be used if we have more than two actions that can be taken. Let's change the example slightly to show the else if statement at work.

```php
<?php
if($weather=="sun") {
    echo "It's a lovely Sunny Day";
} else if ($weather=="rain") {
    echo "It's Raining again";
} else if($weather=="wind") {
    echo "It's a Windy Day today";
} else {
    echo "The weather report says there will be $weather today";
}
?>
```

else if allows you to add multiple conditions to the structure, so you can cover a range of possible values for the variable you are checking. If $weather is equal to "sun", our script prints out:

*It's a lovely Sunny Day*

...if $weather is equal to "rain", it prints:

*It's Raining again*

...and if $weather is equal to "wind":

*It's a Windy Day today*

The last part, which is an else statement, handles anything else that might be in the variable $weather. If $weather was equal to "snow", for instance, then the code would print:

*The weather report says there will be snow today.*

Putting all the parts of the structure together allows you to create complex statements that can handle many different data values, and perform different actions accordingly.

## More Complicated Expressions

You're not limited to using a single expression in the if / else / elseif statements before. By using Boolean operators, you can use more than one expression to control the program flow. The Boolean operators you can use are:

| Symbol | Description |
| --- | --- |
| && | AND |
| \|\| | OR |
| ! | NOT |

### AND - &&

When you use the AND function in an expression, the expression will only evaluate to True, if both parts of the expression are true. For example, imagine we were building a site for an Internet bookstore, and are creating the postage options for the user once they have selected their books.

There are two options, *Next Day Delivery* or *Standard Delivery*. However the former can only be offered if the customer has ordered less than 5 books and the time the order is placed is prior to the 3pm cut-off time (15:00 hours). We can code this using the AND condition:

```
<form name="form1" id="form1" method="post" action="">

<?php if($totalBooks < 5 && $hour < 15) { ?>
    <input type="radio" name="postMethod" value="1" /> Next Day Delivery
<?php } ?>
    <input type="radio" name="postMethod" value="0" /> Standard Delivery
</form>
```

Note that we have "sandwiched" the HTML code within the PHP `if` structure. The HTML in between the PHP will only be sent to the browser if the PHP expression evaluates as `True` and will be ignored if the expression is `False`. The expression is only `True` if *both* of our rules are matched; in all other cases, the result is `False`. So, the form that the customer sees only has the *Next Day Delivery* option if these criteria are met, otherwise only *Standard Delivery* is made available.

## OR - ||

After seeing how the AND statement above works, you probably already have an idea of the behavior of the OR function. OR is denoted by ||. As the name suggests, the result of an OR statement is `True`, if either the first condition or the second condition is `True` (or if both conditions are true, of course). The result is only `False` if both conditions are false.

Going back to our bookstore example, we could have a situation where the customer is given a 10% discount if they buy ten books or more, or spend over a hundred dollars. This could be coded as:

```php
<?php
if($bookTotal >=10 || $total > 100){
    $total = $total * 0.9;
}?>
```

Now, if `$bookTotal` is 10 or more, or `$total` is greater than 100 dollars (or both conditions are true), the discount will be applied. If both criteria are true, it will still only apply the discount once.

## Putting It All Together

Although all the examples we've seen so far have been relatively simple, you can put them all together to allow complex decisions to be made depending on many different variables. For instance, you can use more than one AND or OR operator in an `if` statement, or you can combine the two. For example, at our bookstore all customers who spend over 100 dollars or buy ten or more books, and have a loyalty card, get the cheapest book free. This could be coded as shown below.

```php
<?php
if (($hasLoyalty == 1)  && ($bookTotal>=10 || $total > 100)) {
    $total = $total - $cheapest;
}
?>
```

In the example above we have two conditions:

```
($hasLoyalty==1) && ($bookTotal>=10 || $total > 100)
```

First, the expressions in brackets are evaluated to either `True` or `False`. These two results are then used in the final AND operation. It is important to use brackets round each sub-expression in the main expression, so that the calculations are carried out in the correct order. Some operators have higher precedence over others, meaning they are calculated first. You can find the complete order in which operations are carried out in the online PHP manual at:

*Note, that although not always essential, it's a good practice to put each expression in brackets, so that the parameters are checked in the correct order. It also makes the expression easier for us to read.*

*http://www.php.net/manual/en/language.operators.php#language.operators.precedence*

So if our book buyer has a loyalty card, and buys ten books or more or spends over £100, the expression becomes:

```
(true) && (true)
```

We know that for the AND operator, if both expressions are true, then the result will also be `True`, and so the code that follows is run, which deducts the cost of the cheapest book (which would already have been obtained from a shopping cart, for example):

```
$total = $total - $cheapest;
```

You can also nest `if` / `else` / `else if` statements, as in the example below:

```php
<?php
if($hasLoyalty==1) {
    echo "Thank you, we have applied your Loyalty Card Discount";
} else {
    if($total >100){
        echo "As your total is more than £100, you are entitled to a loyalty card";
    }
}
?>
```

Here, if the customer already has a loyalty card, we send a message telling them their loyalty discount has been applied to their order total. If the customer doesn't have a loyalty card, but spends more than 100 dollars, then we print a message telling them they are entitled to a loyalty card.

*When you're adding a new* `if` / `else` / `else if` *structure, it's best to type the commands first, complete with braces, as shown below:*

```php
<?php
if ($x > 10)
        {
        }
else
        {
        }
?>
```

*You can then go back and fill in the required code. Adding the braces first is a good habit to get into, as they're easy to forget, which causes errors. Another good habit is to indent each control structure, as shown above, so that you can easily see the flow of the program.*

## switch

Imagine we are calculating the cost of a customer's order for a company that sold T-shirts over the Web, and the cost of the T-shirt is determined by its size. This could be done with a series of `if` statements as shown on the next page.

```php
<?php
$total = 0;
$size = "medium";
if ($size == "small"){
    $total = $total + 10;
} elseif ($size == "medium"){
    $total = $total + 15;
} elseif ($size=="large"){
    $total = $total + 20;
} elseif($size=="extra-large"){
    $total = $total + 25;
}
echo "Current Total is $total";
?>
```

However, we could use the `switch` statement instead, as in:

```php
<?php
$total = 0;
$size = "medium";
switch($size){
    case "small":
        $total = $total + 10;
        break;
    case "medium":
        $total = $total + 15;
        break;
    case "large":
        $total = $total + 20;
        break;
    case "extra-large":
        $total = $total + 25;
        break;
}
echo "Current Total is $total";
?>
```

Both methods do the same thing, but `switch` makes the code easier to follow. However it can only deal with different values in a single variable: as we've seen, the `if` structure can deal with more complex expressions.

The reason we need a `break` statement in each `case` is because, even if the PHP processor finds a positive match in one of the `case` statements, it will carry on executing the other `case` statements, right to the end of the `switch` block. Using `break` stops this from happening.

For example if you tried the following:

```php
<?php
$count=0;
switch ($count) {
    case 0:
        print "count equals 0 ";
    case 1:
        print "count equals 1 ";
    case 2:
        print "count equals 2 ";
}
?>
```

…it would display:

*count equals 0 count equals 1 count equals 2*

This happens because the first `case` evaluated as `True`.

This is clearly not what we want. Using the `break` statement at the end of each `case` code block, as in our previous example, would tell the PHP processor to break out of the `switch` structure, so that only *count equals 0* is output.

### Switch Default

There is also a built-in `case` statement you can use with the `switch` structure, which is called if no match is found in any of its preceding `case` statements. Imagine that were now working out the post and packing for our T-shirts, coded as in the example below.

```php
<?php
$shirtTotal = 8;
$postage = 0;
switch($shirtTotal){
    case 1:
        $postage = 2.50;
        break;
    case 2:
        $postage = 3.50;
        break;
    case 3:
        $postage = 5.00;
        break;
    default:
        $postage = 10.00;
}
echo "Postage and Packing Total = $postage";
?>
```

The `default` code gets executed if none of the previous `case` statements match the given variable (which is true in the above example).

The `default` statement must always be the last one in the `switch` structure, since all the other matches have to be tried first. Note that in the previous example, the number with each case statement has no quotes round it, as these are not necessary when matching numbers. Quotes are needed around the value to be matched if you're matching text.

# while and do...while

Now that we've looked at the `if` statement, we're going to look at the `while` structure. Whereas the `if` statement runs if an expression is `True`, `while` is used for an expression where the state will change to `False` at some point, but will run your code while the expression remains `True`.

## while

`while` statements are the simplest type of loop in PHP, and tell the PHP processor to repeat a piece of code while an expression is `True`. As an example, look at the following block of code:

```php
<?php
$count = 1;
while($count<10){
    echo $count . " ";
    $count++;
}
?>
```

When this code is run, the following output will be displayed.

*1 2 3 4 5 6 7 8 9*

First the PHP processor checks to see if `$count` is less than 10. If it is, then the code inside the braces is run. This code prints the value of `$count`, and then increments `$count` by 1. When `$count` reaches 10, the expression `$count < 10` is no longer `True`, and so the loop is broken out of.

As with the `if` / `else` / `else if` structures, we can also use more complex expressions containing `&&`, `!`, or `||` operators.

When you use a `while` loop, you need to ensure that your code actually modifies the variable in the `while` condition in a way that will allow it to eventually evaluate as `False`. Consider this next example (but do not try running it):

```php
<?php
$count = 1;
while ($count < 10 ) {
    echo $count;
}
?>
```

When this code is run it would form an endless loop, continuously printing the value of `$count`, which will always be 1, so it's important to modify the variable being tested in the code that is being run, so that the `while` loop eventually stops at some stage, that is, the condition becomes `False`.

Decision Making, Loops, and Arrays

## do... while

The main difference between a do... while loop and a while loop is that the condition comes at the end of the loop, as shown in the next example.

```php
<?php
$count = 1;
do {
    echo $count . " ";
    $count++;
} while ($count > 2)
?>
```

When this code is run, the following output will be printed to the screen.

*1*

Since the expression comes at the end of the loop, the value of $count, 1, is guaranteed to be printed at least once, even if the condition evaluates as False when it is checked – as in this example. When the condition *is* checked and found to evaluate as False, the loop is halted. To summarize: in any do.. while loop the code is always run at least once, whereas in a while loop, the code may never be run at all.

## for Loops

for loops are extremely useful. The syntax is shown below.

```php
for ( expression1 ; expression2 ; expression3 ){
}
```

expression1 is run at the start of the loop, expression2 is then evaluated, and if it is True then the code in the loop is run, if it's False then the loop stops. expression3 is run at the end of every iteration of the loop. A working example is shown below.

```php
for ($count = 1 ;   $count < 10 ; $count++ ) {
    echo $count . " ";
}
```

When this code is run, first $count is set to the value 1. The second expression is then evaluated: since $count = 1, which is less than 10, it evaluates as True, and so the loop is run. The value of $count is printed to the screen. Then the third expression is then evaluated, and the variable $count is incremented by one. $count now equals 2. The second expression is re-evaluated, $count < 10, and, as $count is still less than 10, the expression again returns True. The value of $count is printed to the screen and another 1 is added to $count making it 3, and so on, until $count = 10. When this condition is met, the loop is halted. So, here's the output:

*1 2 3 4 5 6 7 8 9*

As the second expression, `$count < 10`, is evaluated before the code in the loop is run, when `$count` finally does reach `10`, and the expression evaluates to `False`, the loop is broken out of and the value of `$count` is not printed. So, although `$count` does eventually reach `10`, this value is never output.

## Nesting for Loops

As with other control structures we've mentioned so far, you can also build nested `for` loops, putting one loop inside another, as shown in this next example:

```php
<?php
for($firstNumber=1 ; $firstNumber <= 12; $firstNumber ++){
    // Print Title i.e. 1 Times Table, 2 Times Table etc
    echo "<br />";
    echo $firstNumber. " Times Table <br /><br />";
    for($secondNumber=1 ; $secondNumber <=12; $secondNumber ++){
        // Prints body of table e.g. 1 x 1 = 1, 1 x 2 = 2 etc
        $result = $secondNumber * $firstNumber;
        echo $firstNumber . " x " . $secondNumber . " = " . $result . "<br />";
    }
}
?>
```

This example prints out the times tables from 1 to 12 to the screen. The outer loop (which uses the variable `$firstNumber`) holds the number of the times table being printed. It goes from 1 to 12, executing the inner loop each time. At the beginning of each outer loop, we see the title of the current times table – for example:

*1 Times Table*

The inner loop (using variable `$secondNumber`) then prints out each line of the times table, inserting a line break (`<br />`) after each one, for example:

*1 x 1 = 1*
*1 x 2 = 2*
*..*
*..*
*12 x 11 = 132*
*12 x 12 = 144*

So whilst the code in the outer loop runs 12 times (once for each table from 1 to 12), the code in the inner loop runs 144 times (12 times each inner loop, while the outer loop is, itself, called 12 times).

## Special Commands

There are also two special commands, and these change the way the previous two loops work. In certain circumstances, you might not want all the code in a loop to be run, or you might want to end the current iteration, without ending the whole loop, which is where these commands are used.

## break

The break command works with each of the loops we've seen so far, and stops the current loop, even if the loop expression is still True. Let's see an example.

```php
<?php
for ($count = 1; $count<10; $count++) {
    echo $count . " " ;
    if ( $count == 5){
        break;
    }
}
?>
```

The example above, when run, will print the following to the screen.

*1 2 3 4 5*

Although the for loop is set to run while $count is less than 10, when $count gets to 5 the code in our if structure is executed, and breaks out of the loop. Note that the 5 is printed to the screen, because the if structure, and the subsequent break, come after the echo command.

We can break out of more than one loop if we want to. break can accept an optional numeric parameter, which contains the number of loop structures to be halted. If used without the optional parameter, it will only break the current loop, but if we provide the break command with the number of loops to break out of, it will halt this number of consecutively nested loops, working outwards. An example may help clarify things. Let's go back to the code we used to print the times tables from 1 to 12.

```php
<?php
for($firstNumber=1 ; $firstNumber <= 12; $firstNumber ++){
    // Print Title i.e. 1 Times Table, 2 Times Table etc
    echo "<br />";
    echo $firstNumber . " Times Table <br /><br />";
    for($secondNumber=1 ; $secondNumber <=12; $secondNumber++){
        if($firstNumber == 4){
            // Don't Print 4 Times Table
            break;
        }elseif($firstNumber ==6){
            // If $firstNumber = 6 then stop completely
            break 2;
        }
        // Prints body of table egg 1 x 1 = 1, 1 x 2 = 2 etc
        $result = $secondNumber * $firstNumber;
        echo "$firstNumber x $secondNumber = $result <br />";
    }
}
?>
```

Open a page in Dreamweaver MX and try this code. You'll see that this time, only the times tables from 1 to 5 are printed, minus the 4 times table. This is because when $firstNumber equals 4, the break command in our if structure is run, and this stopped the loop that would otherwise print the 4 times table. However, because the code to print the title of the times table is executed before the if statement, the label *4 Times Table* is still printed out.

When $firstNumber comes around to 6, the break 2 command in the else if is executed. First the inner loop, and then the outer loop, are broken out of. Although its title is output, the 6 times table never gets printed, and nor do all the other times tables up to 12. Try changing the value you give break to 3: you'll see this has no effect. Essentially break is a fairly blunt weapon, in that it will break its way out of loops until it has either broken out of as many as instructed, or it has simply run out of loops.

## continue

The other special command we can use with loops, is the continue command. Take a look at the following example.

```php
<?php
for($count = 1; $count < 10 ; $count++ ){
    if($count==5){
        continue;
    }
    echo "$count ";
}
?>
```

This example will print the following to the screen.

*1 2 3 4 6 7 8 9*

As we would expect, it has printed numbers from 1 to 9, except that the number 5 is missing. This is due to the continue command being run when $count was equal to 5. The continue command tells the PHP processor to stop the current iteration of the loop, and move to the next one. So unlike the break command, which stops the loop entirely, the continue command just stops the current iteration, and then the loop carries on as normal. As with the break command, continue can also accept an optional numeric parameter, indicating the level of loops to continue. Again we can see this with a modification to our times tables example.

```php
<?php
for($firstNumber=1 ; $firstNumber <= 12; $firstNumber ++){
    // Print Title i.e. 1 Times Table, 2 Times Table etc
    echo "<br />";
    echo "$firstNumber Times Table <br /><br />";
    for($secondNumber=1 ; $secondNumber <=12; $secondNumber ++){
        if($secondNumber == 4){
            // miss out 4 x ? each time
            continue;
        }else if($firstNumber==6){
```

```
                  //miss out whole of 6 times table, by continuing both loops.
                  continue 2;
            }
            // Prints body of table egg 1 x 1 = 1, 1 x 2 = 2 etc
            $result = $secondNumber * $firstNumber;
            echo "$firstNumber x $secondNumber = $result <br />";
        }
    }
?>
```

This time you can see that in each times table, the line *4 x...* is missing. Also, the whole 6 times table is gone, except for its label.

The *4 x...* line is missing, because each time the variable $secondNumber in the inner loop equals 4, the continue statement is run and the PHP processor skips the code in the inner loop, moving straight to the next iteration (i.e. $secondNumber == 5).

As we can see, like break, the continue command can take an optional numeric value. In our example, the 6 times table is missing entirely because when variable $firstNumber in the outer loop equals 6, the continue 2 command is run, and the PHP processor skips not just the code in the inner loop, but also the code in the outer loop and starts a new iteration of the outer loop with $firstNumber equal to 7.

# Arrays

Variables are useful, but they can only hold a single piece of data at a time. Arrays are used to store a number of related elements, in one group, as if they formed part of a table. Say we had a shopping cart on an e-commerce site; if you had three items in the shopping cart, then price[1] could be used to represent the price of the first item in the shopping cart, while name[1] could identify its name. The members of the array are known as **elements** and the value inside the square braces identifies the position in the array that the element occupies, and is known as the **index**. Each index identifies an individual element. Although in the example we just discussed, price[1] and name[1] are not *implicitly* related to each other, by storing everything about the items in our shopping cart in arrays, we can ensure that the values for each item all share a common index value in the overall logic of our shopping cart application. This can create opportunities for some useful short cuts, as we shall see.

## Creating an Array

There are a number of different ways to create an array, and we'll take a look at each one, since each is useful for certain jobs. First we'll create an array containing the names of a number of different web languages.

```
<?php $languages = array("PHP","ASP","XML","JavaScript","HTML"); ?>
```

We now have an array, which contains five elements, each holding the names of one of the languages above. Arrays are zero-based, meaning that their index values always start at zero. To reference an element in an array, we use its index:

```
$array[index value]
```

For example if we want to print values from our array above, we could use:

```php
<?php
$languages = array("PHP","ASP","XML","JavaScript","HTML");
echo $languages[0] . "<br />";
echo $languages[1] . "<br />";
echo $languages[2] . "<br />";
?>
```

When run, this code will print the following to the browser:
*PHP*
*ASP*
*XML*

We can also create an array by explicitly specifying the index for each element as we add the data, as shown in this example:

```php
<?php
$languages[0] = "PHP";
$languages[1] = "ASP";
$languages[2] = "XML";
$languages[3] = "JavaScript";
$languages[4] = "HTML";
?>
```

This creates an array identical to the one we made previously, containing the names of some web languages. It's important to notice that, because index numbers start at zero, the index of the last element in an array is always one less than the number of elements in the array.

We can also create an array and add elements to it, using the following notation

```php
<?php
$languages[] = "PHP";
$languages[] = "ASP";
$languages[] = "XML";
$languages[] = "JavaScript";
$languages[] = "HTML";
?>
```

Note that we do not need to specify an element number. Each time we add an element, the array is automatically expanded, with the new element placed into the next available position. This can be extremely useful when you do not know how many items an array is going to hold. Again, the array we create here is identical to the two arrays we made previously.

The last method we can use to create an array, allows us to assign our own element index, using a string value instead of a number. We can see this in action in the following example.

```php
<?php
$languages = array("first" => "PHP", "second" => "ASP", "third" => "XML", "fourth"
=> "JavaScript", "fifth" => "HTML");
?>
```

Here data is assigned to the array in the format `index => data, index => data`, etc. This is what is known as an **associative array**, Note that it's important that each string index you use is unique; you cannot assign the same index to more than one item. To access the array data, we use the index of the element we want to access:

```php
<?php
$languages = array("first" => "PHP", "second" => "ASP", "third" => "XML", "fourth"
=> "JavaScript", "fifth" => "HTML");
echo $languages["first"] . "<br />";
echo $languages["third"] . "<br />";
?>
```

When run, this code would produce the following in the browser:

*PHP*
*XML*

which are the two pieces of data stored with indexes of `"first"` and `"third"`. The above notation is best used when you're creating an array for the first time. If you're adding data to an existing array, the following is better:

```php
<?php
$languages["first"] = "PHP";
$languages["second"] = "ASP";
$languages["third"] = "XML";
$languages["fourth"] = "JavaScript";
$languages["fifth"] = "HTML";
?>
```

An advantage of string indexes is that it's easier to see which element has which index when you are reading through your code. Note that although the array was created with string-indexed elements, the numeric indexes still exist. You can still use position numbers to refer to each element. For example `$Languages["first"]` in the example above can be referred to as `$languages[0]`, since it is at the first position in the array. Elements in an associative are numbered sequentially, in the order in which they were added to the array.

## Using Arrays

So far we've looked at creating arrays, and reading the data by providing the index of the element we want to access. However, in most cases we don't reference arrays by explicitly providing the numeric index value, but rather store the index value dynamically in a variable, `$variable`, say, and referring to the element via the notation `$languages[$variable]` (to use our previous example).

For example, if we are using an array to hold shopping cart data, the array is going to be a different size for each customer depending on how many items they have bought. This is where loops come in. We can use a loop to go through the array from the first element to the last element, and work on each of the pieces of data stored in the array as we do so. Before we can do this, however, we need to know how many elements are stored in the array, using the count() command.

## count($array)

The count() command tells us how many elements are in an array. For example if we modify one of the examples above to:

```php
<?php
$languages[] = "PHP";
$languages[] = "ASP";
$languages[] = "XML";
$languages[] = "JavaScript";
$languages[] = "HTML";
echo "There are " . count($languages) . " elements in the array";
?>
```

when you run this code you'll see the following printed to the browser:

*There are 5 elements in the array*

Now that we know how many elements our array contains, we can use a loop to work through the array, one element at a time, and process the data the array holds.

*Note that* count() *returns the actual number of elements in the array, but to access the last element in the array based on this number, you would have to deduct 1, because arrays are zero-based.*

## Using a for Loop to Process an Array

As a simple example, take a look at the following code, to loop through the array and print each value to the browser.

```php
<?php
$languages = array("PHP","ASP","XML","JavaScript","HTML");
$arrayCount = count($languages);
for( $count = 0 ; $count < $arrayCount ; $count++ ) {
    echo "Element $count is " . $languages[$count] . "<br />";
}
?>
```

When run, this code prints the following to the screen:

*Element 0 is PHP*
*Element 1 is ASP*
*Element 2 is XML*
*Element 3 is JavaScript*
*Element 4 is HTML*

Decision Making, Loops, and Arrays

In the code above, we first set up an array that holds the data, and fill it with values. Next, we use the `count()` command to find out how many elements are in the array, so `$arrayCount` will be 5, as there are five elements. Next we use a `for` loop, using a count variable `$count`, to loop through the array and print out the values. Notice that we check for `$count < $arrayCount`, because the last item in the array has an index of `$arrayCount-1`, as we noted earlier. If we used `$count <= $arrayCount` instead, the loop would iterate a sixth time, and since we only have five elements, the last line would just return:

*Element  is*

## A New Form of for Loop: foreach

There is another type of control structure, which we're going to look at now. It's very similar to the `for` structure we looked at earlier, but `foreach` is specifically designed for working with arrays. Here is the format of a `foreach` command:

```
foreach($array as $value){
    statement
}
```

`foreach` automatically loops through the array from the first element to the last element, and on each iteration of the loop `$value` holds the value of the current element. We can see how this is used in this next example.

```php
<?php
$languages = array("PHP","ASP","XML","JavaScript","HTML");
foreach($languages as $value){
    echo "Element is $value<br />";
}
?>
```

This code will print the following to the screen:

*Element is PHP*
*Element is ASP*
*Element is XML*
*Element is JavaScript*
*Element is HTML*

This result is very similar to what we got from the `for` loop previously, but uses less code, and you don't have to find out how many elements are in the array before you use it. You can also use `foreach` to display the index value of each element as well as the element data, using this sort of notation:

```
foreach($array as $index => $data){
    statement
}
```

To show this, we'll modify one of the previous examples, which created an array with a string index and a value. The modified code is shown in the example opposite.

```php
<?php
$languages = array("first" => "PHP", "second" => "ASP", "third" => "XML", "fourth"
=> "JavaScript", "fifth" => "HTML");
foreach ($languages as $index=>$data){
    echo $index . " element is " . $data . "<br />";

}
?>
```

When this code is run, the following output is printed to the screen:

*first element is PHP*
*second element is ASP*
*third element is XML*
*fourth element is JavaScript*
*fifth element is HTML*

This is extremely useful when then the array's string index has a meaning, in addition to the data.

## Checking That a Variable Is an Array

When we work with an array, we need to be sure that it contains some elements to work with. PHP

```php
is_array($array)
```

contains a simple command for this, the format of which is shown below:

`is_array()` returns `True` if the variable is an array, and `False` if the variable is not an array. The example below shows `is_array()` in action.

```php
<?php
$languages = array("first" => "PHP", "second" => "ASP");
$test = "test";
if(is_array($languages)){
    echo "languages is an array <br />";
} else {
    echo "languages is not an array <br />";
}
if(is_array($test)){
    echo "test is an array <br />";
} else {
    echo "test is not an array <br />";
}
?>
```

Here is what we get when we run this code.

*languages is an array*
*test is not an array*

This allows us to quickly and simply check whether a variable is an array, before we process it.

## Two-Dimensional Arrays

Now we've looked at single-dimension arrays, where each element of the array holds one value only, we're going to look at two-dimensional arrays, which are quite literally arrays of arrays! As we've seen earlier, an array lets us hold a group of related data, for example an array for a book could hold the title, author, number of pages, ISBN number etc. A two-dimensional array is an array that contains other arrays, so for example you could have an array that is the stock list for a bookshop, where each element is an array containing details about each book.

As an example, we're going to create an array containing a number of book arrays. First we'll create the individual book arrays. Open a new PHP page, and add the following code to the page body.

```php
<?php
// Create arrays containing Book Details
$bookArray1 = array("name"=>"PHP Web Development", "price"=>"28.99",
"isbn"=>"1904151116");
$bookArray2 = array("name"=>"Practical XML for the Web","price"=>"27.99",
"isbn"=>"1904151086");
$bookArray3 = array("name"=>"Content Management Systems","price"=>"20.99",
"isbn"=>"190425106x");
?>
```

This creates three separate arrays, holding details for three different books. The array is associative, in that the index is defined, as well as the actual data. We know from earlier in the chapter, that if we want to read the name of the book from `$bookArray1` we could use the following code:

```php
<?php
echo $bookArray1['name'];
?>
```

When run, this would print *PHP Web Development*.

We're now going to create a new array, and add each of our `bookArrays` as an element. Add the following code to your page, after the previous example code:

```php
<?php
// Create array of Book Arrays
$allBooks[0] = $bookArray1;
$allBooks[1] = $bookArray2;
$allBooks[2] = $bookArray3;
?>
```

We now have an array called `$allBooks`, where each element is itself an array of book details. Imagine we wanted to find the name of the second book. We would use the following format:

```php
<?php
echo $allBooks[1]['name'];
?>
```

Add this new code block to your page, and view the page in a browser. The following should be printed to the screen.

*Practical XML for the Web*

which is the name of the book in $bookArray2, which is stored in element 1 of the $allBooks array.

As this is just a simple introductory example we manually created the $bookArray arrays containing the book details. In a real-life situation, you would normally pull the arrays from a database table, an XML document, or even pull live data from another web site.

# Array Navigation Commands

In this section were going to look at some commands which help you to navigate through an array. We've already seen that we can navigate through an array using a `foreach` loop. We're now going to look at the other PHP commands that allow you to navigate through the values in an array.

## Using an Array Pointer

Each array that you create contains an internal pointer to the current element being worked on. When you first create an array, the internal pointer is at the beginning of the array, that is, element 0. To read the value of the element being pointed to by the array's internal pointer, we use the PHP `current()` command, which we will look at now.

### current()

To see `current()` in action, take a look at the following code which sets up a simple array, and then uses the `current()` command to show the value of the element being pointed to by the internal pointer.

```
<?php
    $languages = array("zero" => "PHP", "one" => "XHTML", "two" => "CSS");
    echo current($languages);
?>
```

When you run this code, it will display *PHP*, because the array has just been created and the internal pointer points to $array["first"], which is the first position, and contains the string *PHP*.

### next()

As the name suggests, the `next()` command moves the array's internal pointer forward by one, so that it points to the next element. When you use the `next()` command, as well as moving the internal pointer forward by one, it returns the value that the pointer currently points to. As an example, if we run the following code:

```
<?php
    $languages = array("zero" => "PHP", "one" => "XHTML", "two" => "CSS");
    echo next($languages);
?>
```

the output will be *XHTML*. First the array is created, and so the internal pointer points to position 0 which holds the value PHP. We then advance the pointer by one using the next() command, which returns the value at position 1 (equivalent to string index "one"), which is XHTML.

## prev()

The prev() command does the opposite of the next() command, and moves the internal pointer backwards by one to point to the previous element. If we change the example above to the following

```php
<?php
    $languages = array("zero" => "PHP", "one" => "XHTML", "two" => "CSS");
    echo next($languages) . "<br />";
    echo prev($languages);
?>
```

when this code is run it will print *XHTML* and then *PHP*. First the internal pointer is at position 0, and we use the next() command to move it forward by one to position 1 (equivalent to the "second" string index) and print the value, *XHTML*. We then use the prev() command to move the internal pointer backwards by one to position 0 and return the value stored there: *PHP*.

## end()

The end() command moves the internal pointer to the last element of the array. So the following code would return *CSS*, as the internal pointer is moved to the last element, index position 2, which contains the value CSS.

```php
<?php
    $languages = array("zero" => "PHP", "one" => "XHTML", "two" => "CSS");
    echo end($languages);
?>
```

## reset()

The reset command is the opposite of the end() command. It sets the internal pointer back to the start of the array. This can be seen with the following code:

```php
<?php
    $languages = array("zero" => "PHP", "one" => "XHTML", "two" => "CSS");
    echo end($languages) . "<br />";
    echo reset($languages)
?>
```

This will output *CSS* first, which is the last element in the array, and then it will print *PHP*, as the internal pointer is set back to the first element in the array.

# list()

The `list()` command assigns to a number of variables the values from an array in one operation. For example, have a look at the code below.

```php
<?php
    $array = array("PHP","XML","CSS");
    list ($first,$second,$third) = $array;
        echo "The value of the first variable is " . $first . "<br />";
        echo "The value of the second variable is " . $second . "<br />";
        echo "The value of the third variable is " . $third . "<br />";
?>
```

When run this outputs:

*The value of the first variable is PHP*
*The value of the second variable is XML*
*The value of the third variable is CSS*

As we have assigned to the variables `$first`, `$second`, and `$third` the values from the array elements. They are assigned in the order in which they appear in the array. Each variable is matched to a position in the array, so `$first` is assigned the value at index position 0, `$second` is assigned the value at index position 1, and `$third` is the value at index position 2. If we wanted to ignore the second value, we just use a comma to act as a placeholder to indicate we wanted to skip over that element.

```php
<?php
    $array = array("PHP","XML","CSS");
    list ($first,,$other) = $array;
        echo "The value of the first variable is " . $first . "<br />";
        echo "The value of the other variable is " . $other . "<br />";
?>
```

This outputs "*The value of the first variable is PHP*", then "*The value of the other variable is CSS*". If we hadn't put the extra comma in our `list()` command, the output would have been "*The value of the first variable is PHP*" and "*The value of the other variable is XML*".

# each()

The `each()` command is used to return the current value of the element pointed to by the internal pointer, then advance the internal pointer by one. If the `each()` command is used on the last element of the array, it will return `False`. We can use this behavior to loop through an array, as shown here.

```php
<?php
    $array = array(1,2,3);
    while (list ($key, $val) = each ($array)) {
        echo "Index[".$key."] = ".$val;
}
?>
```

This will output:

*Index[0]=1 Index[1]=2 Index[2] = 3*

We use the `each()` command to read each element of the array, and the `list()` command to assign the values returned from the `each()` command into the variable `$key` and `$val`. At the end of the array, each is `False`, so the `while` loop ends.

# Sorting arrays

In this section we look at the commands available for sorting through an array. This section is split into two, we'll look at sorting normal arrays first, and then we'll move on to sorting associative arrays.

### sort()

The sort command sorts an array into alphabetical or numerical order. For example, the following code sets up an array of numbers in no particular order. It then sorts the array, printing out the new order.

```php
<?php
    $array = array(34,24,36,15);
        sort($array);
        foreach($array as $element){
                echo $element . " ";
        }
?>
```

When the code is run, it outputs:

*15 24 34 36*

which shows that the array has been correctly sorted. If we used words and numerical values, the words are sorted in alphabetical order, and then the numbers sorted in numerical order. For example the code below sorts an array containing words and numbers.

```php
<?php
    $array = array(34,fred,24,harry,36,15);
        sort($array);
        foreach($array as $element){
                echo $element . " ";
        }
?>
```

When the code is run, it will output:

*fred harry 15 24 34 36*

### rsort()

The `rsort()` command works in the same way as the `sort()` command above, but sorts an array in the reverse order. For example the code below uses `rsort()` to sort an array of the names of this book's authors.

```php
<?php
    $array = array("dan","allan","gareth","bruno","george", "tim");
        rsort($array);
        foreach($array as $element){
                echo $element . " ";
        }
?>
```

This will display the names in the following order:

```
tim george gareth dan bruno allan
```

which shows they have been sorted in reverse alphabetical order.

## Sorting Associative Arrays

Next we're going to look at sorting associative arrays. If we used the normal sort commands we've already looked at on an associative array, the data in the array would lose the association to its string indexes of the data they are supposed to refer to. The commands we are going to look at now sort the array and make sure that the link between the data and its index is maintained.

### asort()

The asort() command is used to sort an array's elements into numerical or alphabetical order, whilst keeping the links between the index and the data. We can see this in the following example:

```php
<?php
    $array = array("dibnah"=>"fred","prince"=>"harry","king"=>"george");
        asort($array);
        foreach($array as $index=>$data){
                echo "index[" . $index . "] " . $data . "<br />";
        }
?>
```

This will output the following:

*index[dibnah] fred*
*index[king] george*
*index[prince] harry*

This shows that the array has been sorted, and the links between the indexes and their data maintained.

### arsort()

Again, the rsort() command is used to sort an associative array into reverse order, and again keeping the links between the indexes and the data intact. For example, try the following code:

```php
<?php
    $array = array("dibnah"=>"fred","prince"=>"harry","king"=>"george");
    arsort($array);
    foreach($array as $index=>$data){
            echo "index[" . $index . "] " . $data . "<br />";
    }
?>
```

This returns the following:

*index[prince] harry*
*index[king] george*
*index[dibnah] fred*

And again you can see that the array is now sorted in reverse alphabetical order, with the links between the data and indexes intact.

## Sorting an array by Index

As well as sorting an array by its data, we can also sort an array by the array's indexes.

### ksort()

In the code below, we set up a simple array and then sort the array by the values in the indexes rather than the actual data.

```php
<?php
    $array = array("dibnah"=>"fred","prince"=>"harry","king"=>"george");
    ksort($array);
    foreach($array as $index=>$data){
            echo $index . ": " . $data . "<br />";
    }?>
```

When run, this code will output the following:

*dibnah: fred*
*king: george*
*prince: harry*

The array has been alphabetically sorted by its index strings.

### krsort()

The krsort() command reverses the effects of the ksort() command; it sorts the array by its indexes, but this time in reverse order. If we change the example above to:

```php
<?php
    $array = array("dibnah"=>"fred","prince"=>"harry","king"=>"george");
    krsort($array);
    foreach($array as $index=>$data){
            echo $index . ": " . $data . "<br />";
    }?>
```

it will output the following data which shows the array has been alphabetically sorted by its indexes in reverse order.

*prince: harry*
*king: george*
*dibnah: fred*

# Converting Arrays to Strings and Back Again

Arrays and databases go hand in hand, and often a database table is used to populate an array; similarly array data can be stored in an database table. For example, in our previous shopping cart example, each row of the main book array would be written to a row in a database table, along with some identifying value to keep all the rows related.

Sometimes if you have small arrays, you might not want to use a row in the database table for each element in the main array, and would instead prefer to store the whole array information in one table row. Let's take a look at a couple of PHP commands that help us achieve this.

## implode()

The first command we're looking at is the `implode()` command. This is used in the following format:

```
implode(separator, array)
```

The command puts all of the elements in an array into a single string, with each value separated using the separator given (separators consisting of one or more characters – ", " or ":", for example). Open a new PHP page and enter the following code:

```
<?php
$authorArray = array("Bruno Mairlot", "Gareth Downes-Powell", "Tim Green");
$authors = implode(", ",$authorArray);
echo $authors;
?>
```

When viewed in a browser we see the following output:

*Bruno Mairlot, Gareth Downes-Powell, Tim Green*

The authors string can now be stored in a single database field, rather than needing a separate record for each entry.

### Using implode() with Associative Arrays

If you are using an associative array, where each element's index has a meaning as well as the data, we need to use a `foreach` loop to compact both the index and the data into a string, as shown in the following example code.

```php
<?php
$bookDetails = array("name"=>"PHP Web Development", "price"=>"28.99",
"isbn"=>"1904151116","type"=>"php");
foreach($bookDetails as $index => $data){
        $book[] = $index . "=" . $data;
}
$bookString = implode(", ",$book);
echo $bookString;
?>
```

This code first sets up an array, $bookDetails, assigning an index and a value. Next we use a foreach loop to cycle through the array, combine the index and tag into a single string, and then add that string to a new array, $book. We then use the implode() command to transfer the array into a string.

When the above code is viewed in a browser, the following output is seen:

*name=PHP Web Development, price=28.99,isbn=1904151116, type=php*

As this is a string, it can be stored in a single field of a database table.

Now that we know how to compress an array into a single string, we also need a way to take the string and recreate the original array, which we do with the explode() command.

# explode()

The explode() command isn't as exciting as it sounds, but it is very useful. explode() is essentially the opposite of the implode() command, and takes a string with values separated by a common separator, and turns it into an array. The explode() command uses the following format:

```
explode(separator, string)
```

Again, the separator can consist of more than one character, as long as it is common to each separator. First, we will look at creating a simple array, which has no specific indexes. We'll take the output from our first implode() example above, and turn it back into a string, using the following code:

```php
<?php
$bookAuthors = "Bruno Mairlot, Gareth Downes-Powell, Tim Green";
$authors = explode(", ",$bookAuthors);
foreach($authors as $author){
    echo $author . "<br />";
}
?>
```

First we set up a string containing the output of our previously imploded array. We then used the explode() command, to split $bookAuthors, using the separator ", ". Lastly, we use foreach to cycle through each element of the newly created $authors array, and print each value.

When this code is viewed in a browser, the following output is displayed:

*Bruno Mairlot*
*Gareth Downes-Powell*
*Tim Green*

This shows that a new array has been created from the string.

## Using explode() with an Associative Array

Again, as with the `implode()` command, we have to add some extra code to recreate an associative array from a string. If we take the output from the earlier `implode()` example which was:

*name=PHP Web Development, price=28.99, isbn=1904151116, type=php*

we are now going to turn this back into an array. The first step is to split the string by the common separator `"`  `"`, and create an array. We can do this with the following code:

```php
<?php
$bookDetails = "name=PHP Web Development, price=28.99, isbn=1904151116, type=php";
$book = explode(",",$bookDetails);
foreach($book as $detail){
    echo $detail . "<br />";
}
?>
```

When viewed in a browser the code above creates the following output:

*name=PHP Web Development*
*price=28.99*
*isbn=1904151116*
*type=php*

So we're halfway there: each book detail becomes an element in the $book array, but the index tags and data still need to be split. Change the code to read like this:

```php
<?php
$bookDetails = "name=PHP Web Development, price=28.99, isbn=1904151116,
type=php";
$book = explode(",",$bookDetails);
foreach($book as $detail){

    $singleDetail = explode("=",$detail);
    $newDetails[$singleDetail[0]] = $singleDetail[1];
}
foreach($newDetails as $index=>$data){
    echo $index . " : " . $data . "<br />";

}
?>
```

In the code above, we first split the string `$bookDetails` into an array `$book`, using the ",  " as a separator. We now have an array, `$book`, which contains the data in the form `"tag=data"` for each element. We now cycle through this array, and split each of its elements again, using "=" as a separator. This creates a new array, `$singleDetail`, where `index[0]` is the tag, and `index[1]` is the data. We then add these to another new array, `$newDetails`, in the format `$newdetails[tag] = data`. Finally we loop through our `$newDetails` array and print the index and data to the screen.

When the code is viewed in a browser, you will see the following output:

*name : PHP Web Development*
*price : 28.99*
*isbn : 1904151116*
*type : php*

and we can see that we now have an exact copy of the array we imploded in the previous example.

## Using explode() to Split a Date

`explode()` can be used in many different situations, and is an extremely useful command. Here we'll look at using `explode()` to quickly and easily split a date, so that it can then be rearranged into a different date format.

If you've ever tried to store a date in a MySQL date field, you'll know that it uses the format yyyy-mm-dd, but a date typed in by a user in the UK, for instance, will be in the format dd/mm/yyyy. The date can't be stored in the database in this format, though, so we need to rearrange it to the MySQL format, which is where `explode()` comes in. Take a look at the following code:

```php
<?php
$userDate = "20/09/2002";
$dateArray = explode("/",$userDate);
?>
```

Here we have a date in the format dd/mm/yy. We use the `explode()` statement to split the data by "/", and put the pieces into `$dateArray`.

In the above example, the data held in `$dateArray` will be as follows:

$dateArray[0] = days (20)
$dateArray[1] = months (09)
$dateArray[2] = years (2002)

Now that we have the date split, we can rearrange it in any format, with any separator. Change the example code above to read:

```php
<?php
$userDate = "20/09/2002";
$dateArray = explode("/",$userDate);

$americanFormat = $dateArray[1] . "/" . $dateArray[0] . "/" . $dateArray[2];
$mysqlFormat = $dateArray[2] . "-" . $dateArray[1] . "-" . $dateArray[0];

echo "The date in British Format is: " . $userDate . "<br />";
echo "The date in American Format is: " . $americanFormat . "<br />";
echo "The date in MySQL Format is: " . $mysqlFormat . "<br />";
?>
```

Here we have rearranged the date to US and MySQL formats. When the page is viewed in a browser, the output will show:

*The date in British Format is: 20/09/2002*
*The date in American Format is: 09/20/2002*
*The date in MySQL Format is: 2002-09-20*

As you can see, although it maybe not an obvious choice, the `explode()` command makes converting between different date formats very easy.

# Summary

In this chapter, we first looked at different types of control and decision-making structures. We used these to make sure that sections of code only ran if certain conditions were true, and we looked at combining expressions to make more complicated conditions.

We then looked at loops, and the different types of loop structures available to us. Next we looked at arrays, and learned how we could use loops to read through the arrays and process their elements, and how to make more complicated two-dimensional arrays.

Finally we looked at how to compress arrays, so they can be stored in a single field in a database table, and how to recreate the original arrays from the compacted strings. Lastly, we looked at using array commands to make formatting a date easy, converting it between different formats, in particular the MySQL date format.

# 3

- Error handling
- Code debugging
- Sources of help

**Author: Gareth Downes-Powell**

# Error Handling

No matter how talented or experienced a programmer is, they will probably have to face code errors at some stage of a project; and the more complex the system, the more likely it is to go wrong somewhere. In this chapter we will look at strategies for avoiding – or at least minimizing –errors, and making sure your code runs smoothly. By following good coding practices, such as commenting and indenting your code, you can avoid syntax errors; by using techniques such as anticipating errors, and designing your code to handle them, you can make your code a lot more robust. Following the principles set out in this chapter will save you a lot of development time and help you write code that can cope even with unexpected external events, such as the loss of a network connection, without falling over.

**Debugging** is the process of identifying and removing syntactical and logical errors from the code. This is one area where Dreamweaver MX can really help the web developer: we can configure Dreamweaver MX to create the optimal working environment within which common syntactical errors such as forgetting to close a bracket, can be easily avoided.

There are several different types of error, some more serious than others. With PHP, we can set an **error-reporting level** so that, for example, it only reports serious errors. We can also creating a custom error handler which takes over from the default PHP error handler, and displays a more informative error message, which can be formatted with CSS.

When errors occur, it can be useful to log the errors in a log file to help diagnose the problem, in this chapter we will look at how we can do this, and also how we can have PHP send us an e-mail every time an error occurs. We will also look at MySQL errors, and how to get more information about them when they occur. We finish by looking at a number of debugging tips, and also at sources of help and advice.

Before we get started looking at the different error types and what can cause them, we're first going to configure Dreamweaver MX to make working with code easier.

# Configuring the Dreamweaver MX Environment

Dreamweaver MX has several features that can make coding PHP a lot easier. It is worth spending a little time configuring it so that we have an optimal environment in which we can work, making the time we spend coding more productive.

The first setting we're going to look at is the font settings for the Dreamweaver MX Code View. If you have your Windows desktop set to a high resolution, you'll probably find that the default font size is too small to read comfortably, so we're take a look at how to increase its size, to make it easier to read.

## Code View – Changing the Default Font Size

From the main Dreamweaver MX menu bar, select *Edit -> Preferences*, or alternatively press *Ctrl + u*:

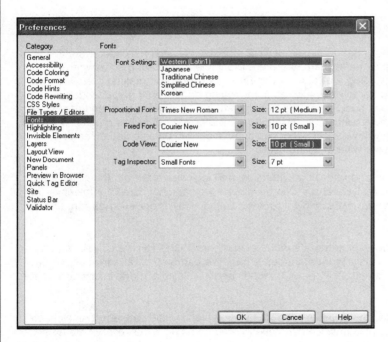

From the *Preferences* window that appears, select *Fonts*, as shown in the screenshot. Here you can change the default fonts and sizes that Dreamweaver MX uses to display text. Second from the bottom is the *Code View* font setting: you can change this to make the font size larger.

## Configuring Code View

There are some useful settings for the Dreamweaver MX Code View, which may not be turned on by default. In *Code View*, click on the last icon in the Dreamweaver MX Document tool bar; this is shown overleaf with its drop-down menu activated:

## Word Wrap

*Word Wrap* is useful if you have a small monitor and you spend a lot of time scrolling sideways through the code to see the end of a line. It reformats the code so that lines that are normally off the edge of the screen are wrapped round and started on the next line.

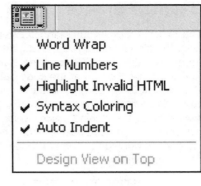

## Line Numbers

If you haven't already got the *Line Numbers* option turned on, it's a good idea to do so. Having Dreamweaver MX display line numbers alongside your code makes it much easier to locate the line of code where PHP reports an error.

## Highlight Invalid HTML

This should also be turned on because it quickly shows you if there is any invalid HTML markup in the page, and if there is, it is highlighted. If you've created some PHP script that outputs HTML and the result didn't turn out as you expected, you can save the page in the browser, load it back into Dreamweaver MX, and Dreamweaver MX will highlight any invalid markup.

## Syntax Coloring

*Syntax Coloring* should be selected if it isn't already. This assigns different font colors to different parts of your code, depending on whether the line is a code instruction, or a variable, and so on. With *Syntax Coloring* on you can quickly spot errors: if a line of code isn't colored in the color you would expect, you should inspect it closely and see if, for example, a set of quotation marks is missing from the end of a string.

## Auto Indent

*Auto Indent* is another option that should be turned on. This option tells Dreamweaver MX to automatically indent your code, which allows you to easily see the flow of the script, and allows you to follow through the different code blocks.

Note that you can also use the *Indent* and *Outdent* options in the *Edit* menu on the main Dreamweaver MX menu, to indent and outdent sections of your code manually, for example if you load in HTML code from another package that hasn't been formatted.

```php
<?php
    for($i=1;$i<10;$i++){
        echo $i;
    }
?>
```

## Balance Braces

The *Balance Braces* command, located in the *Edit* menu on the main Dreamweaver MX menu bar, is used to help you debug your code, and ensure that every opening brace, {, has a closing brace, }.

As an example that illustrates the *Balance Braces* command, create a new PHP page, and switch to *Code View*, then enter the code below, which sets up a simple `for` loop.

Click next to echo `$i;` to place the current insertion point there. Select *Edit -> Balance Braces*, and you will see that all the code between the two braces is highlighted, as in the following screenshot:

Now remove the closing brace, which is on line 10 in the screenshot above. Once again place the current insertion point next to echo `$i;` and select *Edit ->Balance Braces*. This time you will see that the code is not highlighted indicating that the braces are unbalanced (that is, an opening brace and no closing brace).

```
1   <html>
2   <head>
3   <title>Untitled Document</title>
4   <meta http-equiv="Content-Type" content="text/html; charset=iso-8859-1">
5   </head>
6   <body>
7   <?php
8       for ($i=1;$i<10;$i++) {
9           echo $i;
10      }
11  ?>
12  </body>
13  </html>
14
```

For small, simple code blocks like the above example, it's pretty easy to see where a brace is missing. However if you have more complicated code, with different levels as shown below, it's much harder to spot where a brace is missing, although the indenting makes it slightly easier.

When faced with a block of code like the one above, start with the innermost loop, and work outwards through the different code structures. Using the *Balance Braces* command at each level, you'll quickly find where a brace is missing, which is a closing brace in the above example. We can see this in the following screenshot , which shows the section highlighted by the *Balance Braces* command:

```
<?php
    for($i=1;$i<10;$i++){
        while($i > 6){
            if ($i == 8){
                echo $i . " is 8 <br>";
            } else {
                echo $i . " is not 8 <br>";
                if ($i >8){
                    echo $i . " is equal to 8 <br>";
                }


        // should be a closing brace here
        // to close brace opened by the code
            // if ($i == 8);
    }
    if ($i==3){
```

```
              echo $i . " is equal to 3 <br>";
        }
    }
?>
```

```php
<?php
  for($i=1;$i<10;$i++){
      while($i > 6){
          if ($i == 8){
              echo $i . " is 8 <br>";
          } else {
              echo $i . " is not 8 <br>";
              if ($i >8){
                  echo $i . " is equal to 8 <br>";
                  }

          // should be a closing brace here
          // to close brace opened by the code
             // if ($i == 8);

          }
      if ($i==3){
          echo $i . " is equal to 3 <br>";
      }
  }
?>
```

In the screenshot you can see that the area highlighted is from the start of the else statement, to the closing brace for the while statement, and these are not matched, so a bracket is missing in that block. The screenshot also shows how much easier it makes it to find the problem with proper indentation.

# PHP Error Types

The Dreamweaver MX code environment has been optimized to make our job much easier, now we can try to get a deeper understanding of the types of errors we can get. These are split into three main categories:

- Syntax errors
- Runtime errors
- Logic errors

We will take a look at each category separately.

## Syntax Errors

Syntax errors are caused by entering the code incorrectly so that it is incomprehensible to the PHP parser. There are two basic causes of syntax errors:

- Incorrect code syntax: for example, where a semicolon is omitted, or forgetting to close a set of braces
- Typos: for example, misspellings of variable names

If we enter the code below as a simple example:

```
8   <?php
9       echo "This line will cause a Syntax Error ! <br>"
10      echo "When it's viewed in a browser";
11  ?>
```

When viewed in a browser, the above code will display something similar to the following:

*Parse error: parse error, unexpected T_ECHO, expecting ',' or ';' in test.php on line 10*

You can see in the above output that the PHP parser is reporting line 10 as the source of the error. This is because although the missing semicolon should be at the end of line 9, the parser has to process line 10 before it can be sure that the semicolon is missing, and so PHP reports line 10 as the error

> *Often, when you see an error such as the one above, it's worth reading backwards through the last couple of lines of code before the line where the error is reported, because often the error lies in the preceding lines, as was the case in the previous example.*

Another common example of a syntax error in the code is omitting a closing brace, as the following code sample illustrates:

```
1   <html>
2     <head>
3       <title>Untitled Document</title>
4       <meta http-equiv="Content-Type" content="text/html; charset=iso-8859-1">
5     </head>
6     <body>
7       <?php
8         test();
9         function test(){
10            echo "This is an example of a missing brace.";
11
12      ?>
13    </body>
14  </html>
```

As you can see, there is a closing brace missing from the function, which we would expect to find on line 11.

However, when this code is viewed in a browser, the following output is shown:

*Parse error: parse error, unexpected $ in test.php on line 14*

This time the PHP parser carries on until the end of the file looking for the closing brace, and because it never finds one, an error message is given that shows the line the PHP parser finished on, which in the above example is line 14.

PHP is case-sensitive, so a common cause of syntax errors is the use of incorrect case for variables, function names, and so on. The variable `$myvariable`, for example, is completely different from the variable

*Bear in mind that this is a very short snippet of code, in the real world your PHP scripts are likely to be hundreds of lines long. If you omit a brace, the PHP parser will report that the error occurred on the very last line of your code. As we mentioned above, you can avoid this problem by taking advantage of Dreamweaver MX's Balance Braces function.*

`$myVariable`. Following the coding practice of using a consistent naming convention will go a long way towards reducing this problem, for example if a variable name contains two words, you could decide to always start the second word with a capital letter, for example, `$myVariable`. When you choose a naming convention, be sure to stick to it throughout the entire project. Although you are free to create your own standard, there is an example standard at: *http://utvikler.start.no/code/php_coding_standard.html*

## Runtime Errors

Runtime errors, as the name suggests, occur when your script is running. These errors can be hard to track down, as more often than not, they're down to external factors, and not actually your script itself.

For example, your site could run fine for months, and then suddenly die one day because the server's hard disk becomes full. Or your script could fetch information from an external site, and that site goes down, and consequently takes down your script with it.

" *How you handle errors is directly linked to your online reputation* "

Although it's impossible to think of every single eventuality, before you build your script you need to think about the main things that your script will rely on, such as free disk space, or data from another site's server. When you have listed these, it will be possible to make the script robust by incorporating error checking, so if an external factor does fail, your script can print an informative message and close properly, rather than just dying and leaving the user with no idea what's gone wrong.

How you handle errors is directly linked to your online reputation; users are likely to be much more forgiving if they know what has happened and receive a message to try again later for example, than if the screen just goes blank and the user has no idea what's going on. In the latter case, it's unlikely the user will ever return to your site. On the other hand, if you can maintain a professional image when things go wrong, you can still keep the user's trust despite the failure. Don't leave anything to chance, and try to imagine as many possible scenarios as you can. Even if you give clear instructions to a user, for example indicating a field can only accept numbers, you're guaranteed to get a least one person entering text into the field. Never trust data that is entered by a user, and validate all of the user's input to ensure that it's in the format that is expected. This can stop errors occurring, it makes your site more robust, and also increases security.

## Logical Errors

Logical errors are relatively difficult to identify. They occur when your PHP code is valid, and the syntax is correct, but the code doesn't actually do what you intended it to do.

```php
<?php
$test = 1;
while($test = 10){
    echo "10";
}
?>
```

As a very simple example, take a look at the code below, but **do not** try to run it:
Apparently, this code first sets the variable `$test` to 1, then has a loop which runs only when the variable is 10, so, in theory, the loop shouldn't be run and nothing should be outputted. However when this code is run in a browser, you get an endless stream of 10s, and your browser may even lock up.

This happens because we made a basic and common mistake of using `while($test = 10)` instead of `while($test == 10)`. We wanted to compare the variable `$test` to see if it was equal to 10, and then print the code if it is. However, with PHP the sign for equality is `==`, and as a result when our code is run in our erroneous code, `$test` is *assigned* the value of 10 and so the condition becomes true. The code then goes into an endless loop and never sends the closing HTML markup to the browser.

If you frequently forget to use `==` to test for equality, and instead use a single `=`, there is a technique which you can use, which can make finding these errors easy called **reverse testing**.

## Reverse Testing

Normally, when you test a variable in an expression, you would use this condition:

```php
while($test == 10)
```

As we've seen before, if we mistakenly enter a single equals sign instead of two equals signs to test for equality, the code is valid and still runs but causes problems in our scripts. This is where reverse testing comes in, and relies on the fact that the above expression can also be written as:

```php
while(10 == $test)
```

This is exactly the same expression, and does exactly the same thing, except we've written it the other way round. However, if when typing this we make a mistake and type a single equals sign, as in the code below:

```php
while(10 = $test)
```

when this code is run, the PHP processor tries to assign the value of the variable `$test` to the number 10, which of course cannot be done, and so the script is stopped and the error is reported along with the line number, and we can go straight to it and fix it.

Using the reverse testing notation means that if we do make a mistake, it won't slip through unnoticed, and the PHP processor stops the script and alerts us before any problems are caused.

# Error Types

So far, we've looked at the standard PHP error messages that occur when something goes wrong. While these are fairly informative to the developer, they can be meaningless to your end users, and displaying them can make your site look unprofessional. Often when the error is printed to the screen, your page layout will become corrupted and the site won't display as it was intended to.

PHP has a solution to this problem; it allows us to override the default error messages, and instead run our own custom error handler that can give a more user-friendly error and make sure that the entire page formatting remains intact. This can be a major decider as to whether a user comes back to your site again in the future.

Before we look at building our own custom error handlers, we first need to look at the PHP error types. These help categorize different errors, and help determine where the error occurred, so that we can then deal with it in the correct manner.

## Standard Error Types

There are twelve standard error types, and these are shown in the following table.

| Constant | Value | Description |
|---|---|---|
| E_ERROR | 1 | Fatal Run Time Error |
| E_WARNING | 2 | Non Fatal Run Time Warning |
| E_PARSE | 4 | Fatal Compile Time Parse Error |
| E_NOTICE | 8 | Non Fatal Run Time Warning |
| E_CORE_ERROR | 16 | Fatal Error that occurs during the PHP Engine startup |
| E_CORE_WARNING | 32 | Not Fatal Warnings that occur during the PHP engine startup |
| E_COMPILE_ERROR | 64 | Fatal Compile Time Error |
| E_COMPILE_WARNING | 128 | Non Fatal Compile Time Warning |
| E_USER_ERROR | 256 | Fatal User Generated Error |
| E_USER_WARNING | 512 | Non Fatal User Generated Warning |
| E_USER_NOTICE | 1024 | Non Fatal User Generated Notice |
| E_ALL | 2047 | Represents all of the above options |

These error types fall into these three categories:

- Notices – Non-Fatal. These are used to display messages to the user about things that might be a problem, such as using a variable that isn't defined. These are only really useful during the site development, and should be turned off when the site goes "live".

- Warnings – Non-Fatal. These are used to display warnings. These are more serious than notices, and indicate that PHP found a problem, but it was able to recover from the error and carry on running the script.

- Errors – Fatal. Errors are problems that PHP cannot recover from, and the script is forced to stop running.

*You will also notice that we use the terms **Fatal**, and **Non-Fatal**. Fatal means that the script stops running, whereas Non-Fatal means that PHP can recover, and can continue running the script.*

The error types are referred to by the name constant in the table above. So if you wanted to tell PHP you were interested in fatal errors in your script, you would use E_ERROR. If you wanted to refer to all the error types at once, you would use E_ALL, which saves you having to type in all the names of the error types.

Telling PHP to only respond to certain types of error is called setting the Error-Reporting Level, and we're now going to look at this in detail.

## Error-Reporting Levels

Setting a custom error message tells PHP to only respond to certain error types, and to ignore other types such as notices or warnings, which don't stop your script from running. If you run your own server, you can set the error-reporting level by editing your `php.ini` file, and editing the error-reporting directive, which we'll be looking at in more detail later in this chapter.

If you don't run your own server, and you're using shared hosting, for example, so you can't access the servers `php.ini` file, you can set the error-reporting level for your scripts locally, using the PHP `error_reporting()` function. This means that the custom error-reporting level you set will be applied to the script that it's defined in only. The format for the `error_reporting()` function is shown below:

```
error_reporting (E_ALL);
```

You can include any of the error type constants as parameters, and the following operators:

| Description | Symbol |
|-------------|--------|
| AND | & |
| OR | | |
| NOT | ~ |

In *Chapter 2*, we looked at the various logical expressions you can use, such as AND, OR, and NOT. When we use the logical operator NOT with error reporting, it tells PHP not to include an error type in an expression.

Using these expressions and the error type constants, you can set different levels of response to any errors that occur. The usual default error-reporting level is:

```
E_ALL & ~ E_NOTICE
```

This tells PHP to respond to all errors, warnings, and notices, except those of the type E_NOTICE. Note that you cannot use ~ on its own, you need to use & ~, which when read in English would say "AND NOT". If you only wanted to respond to actual errors, you could use:

```
E_ERROR & E_CORE_ERROR & E_COMPILE_ERROR & E_USER_ERROR
```

Normally, you would have E_NOTICE excluded from the error-reporting level, because it displays extra messages warning you if a variable hasn't been specifically defined, for example. While this can be useful when you're developing a site, once you have the code finished and the site is ready to go live, you would turn off notices so that they are not shown to the user. Because of their non-serious nature, they can safely be ignored.

## Setting Error-Reporting Levels

Now that we've seen how to create the expression for the error_reporting() function, we're now going to look at using it to set a new error-reporting level.

First, take a look at the following piece of code:

```php
<?php
for($loopCount = 1; $loopCount < 10; $loopcount++){
    echo "Current Count is: " . $loopCount;
}
?>
```

This should create a for loop, which runs while the variable $loopCount is between 1 and 9. However, if you look closely at the for expression, you'll see that the variable $loopCount is never incremented, because we've accidentally typed $loopcount instead (with lowercase c), which is a completely different variable. This means that the above code will actually run in a never-ending loop (so it's advisable not to try the above code!).

Now, although the above is an endless loop, the code is still valid, and so PHP runs it without question. However, if we set the current error-reporting level to show all errors, warnings, and notices, as in the following code:

```php
<?php
error_reporting(E_ALL);
for($loopCount = 1; $loopCount < 10; $loopcount++){
    echo "Current Count is: " . $loopCount;
}
?>
```

when the script is run, we receive the following output:

*Notice: Undefined variable: loopcount test.php on line 9*

This warns us that `$loopcount` is undefined, and so has possibly been spelt incorrectly, and we can then go back and correct the error.

It's useful to turn on all error reporting when you actually develop the site, so you can see warnings such as the one above, and then once the site is built you can turn the error reporting back down to a lower level.

A useful technique is to store the error-reporting level in a variable, and temporarily change it to a higher level as the following code sample illustrates:

```php
<?php
    $newLevel = E_ALL;
    $oldLevel = error_reporting($newLevel);
    echo "Old Error Reporting Level was : " . $oldLevel . "<br>";
    echo "New Error Reporting Level is : " . $newLevel . "<br>";
    echo "<br>";
    for($loopCount = 1; $loopCount < 5; $loopCount++){
        echo "Current Count is: " . $loopCount . "<br>";
    }
    echo "<br>";
    $newLevel = $oldLevel;
    $oldLevel = error_reporting($newLevel);
    echo "Old Error Reporting Level was : " . $oldLevel . "<br>";
    echo "New Error Reporting Level is : " . $newLevel . "<br>";
?>
```

This code sets a new error-reporting level of `E_ALL`, and assigns the old error-reporting level to the variable `$oldLevel`, and prints out the new and old error-reporting values. We then run a small loop, and swap the error-reporting level back to what it was when the script started, and again print out the new and old values. When this code is run, you should see this output:

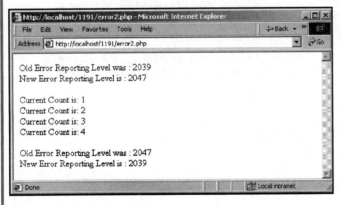

As you've probably noticed, the PHP processor uses numerical values to represent the error type constants, that is, 2047 instead of `E_ALL`. This is a throwback to earlier versions of PHP that used numerical values to set the error-reporting level. These values have now been deprecated, and it's best to use the error type constants to ensure your code works as intended in all future versions of PHP. When expressions are used to create an error-reporting level, the numeric value is calculated. For example the error-reporting level `E_ALL & ~ E_NOTICE` would be calculated as 2047 – 8 which equals 2039. The numerical equivalents of the error constants are shown in the table at the start of this section.

78

# Setting Error Reporting in Your php.ini File

As mentioned before, if you run your own server, you can change the error-reporting settings globally (that is, for all sites on the server), from the `php.ini` file, which contains all your PHP settings.

## phpinfo()

If you're not sure where your `php.ini` file is located, simply open a new blank PHP page, and add the following code:

```php
<?php
phpinfo();
?>
```

Save the page, upload to your server, and view the page in your browser. You should see output similar to the following screenshot:

| PHP Version 4.2.2 | php |
|---|---|

| System | Linux ns.buzzinet.co.uk 2.2.16C32_III #1 Fri Nov 9 21:54:54 PST 2001 i586 unknown |
|---|---|
| Build Date | Sep 2 2002 01:19:42 |
| Configure Command | './configure' '--prefix=/etc/httpd/modules/php' '--with-apache=/home/build/apache/apache' '--with-config-file-path=/etc/httpd' '--with-png-dir=/usr' '--with-xml' '--with-jpeg-dir=/usr' '--with-imap' '--with-gd=/home/build/gd-1.8.4' '--with-gettext' '--with-zlib' '--with-system-regex' '--with-ttf' '--with-db' '--with-gdbm' '--with-mbstring' '--with-mbstr-enc-trans' '--with-mysql=/usr' '--with-ming' '--with-swf=/usr/lib/libswf' '--with-dom' '--with-dom-xslt' '--with-dom-exslt' '--with-xslt-sablot=/usr/local' '--with-expat-dir=/usr/local' '--with-xmlrpc' '--enable-xslt' '--enable-sockets' '--enable-exif' '--enable-wddx=shared' '--enable-mm=shared' '--enable-magic-quotes' '--enable-track-vars' '--enable-ftp' '--enable-safe-mode' '--with-curl=shared' '--with-pdflib=shared' '--with-pgsql=shared' |
| Server API | Apache |
| Virtual Directory Support | disabled |
| Configuration File (php.ini) Path | /etc/httpd/php.ini |
| Debug Build | no |
| Thread Safety | disabled |

The third line from the bottom of the first block, shows the *Configuration File Path*, which is where your `php.ini` file is located, which is */etc/httpd/php.ini* in the above example.

The whole page is much longer than the small segment shown in the screenshot, and shows the settings for all of the different aspects of PHP, including the options available and whether they are on or off, as well as information about your server, and can be extremely useful in helping to track down errors.

Whilst you're looking at the *phpinfo* page, check all of the paths mentioned in the information are correct, and that the files that they point to exist on your server.

### Editing php.ini

Once you have found the location of your `php.ini` file, you can open it in a standard text editor, which saves files as plain text.

The `php.ini` is the control center for the whole PHP installation, and controls how all aspects of PHP behave. You can find information on all the settings in the online documentation in the PHP web site, which is located at *http://www.php.net/*.

For the time being, we're just going to look at the settings which apply to error reporting. Scroll down the file until you see the following heading:

```
;;;;;;;;;;;;;;;;;;;;;;;;;;;;;;;
; Error handling and logging ;
;;;;;;;;;;;;;;;;;;;;;;;;;;;;;;;
```

There are four directives that apply to error handling, and these along with their allowed values are:

| Directive | Values | Comments |
|---|---|---|
| error_reporting | Valid expression e.g. E_ALL & ~ E_NOTICE | |
| display_errors | On or Off | display_errors tells PHP whether to display error messages as HTML (On), or as plain text (Off) |
| log_errors | On or Off | log_errors tells PHP whether to log errors to the standard server logs (On), or not to log errors (Off) |
| track_errors | On or Off | track_errors tells PHP whether to keep detailed error information. If this is set to On, information about the last error that occurred will be available to your scripts in the global variable $php_errormsg. |

It's important to note, that changing these settings changes the behavior of PHP for every site on the server. Once you have saved your changes, you need to restart your web server, so that your new changes will be read from the `php.ini` file.

## User-Defined Errors

As well as the standard error types that we have looked at so far, PHP also has three user-definable error types. These types are:

| Constant | Description |
|---|---|
| E_USER_NOTICE | For user defined notices |
| E_USER_WARNING | For user defined warnings |
| E_USER_ERROR | For user defined errors |

By using these error types, we can make PHP, or more importantly, a custom error handler, respond to errors that are generated in our scripts. Why do we want to trigger errors? Although the concept of deliberately creating errors may at first seem strange, it's a very useful facility. PHP is very good at checking that the code and environment is error-free, but there are still areas it can't check. For example, imagine you had an online shopping cart, where a user enters the number they require of a certain product. What would happen if the user entered -1 for the quantity? If the script doesn't check, and just multiplies the quantity and product amount, it will create a negative total. If the user then enters the card details and places the order, as it's a negative amount it could be added to the card as if the user had had a refund! By checking the values are positive, we can make sure the data is acceptable, and if it's not we can trigger a PHP error that will stop the current script from running, and will send a message to the user letting them know they have entered invalid data.

Using error handling we can check for errors that PHP wouldn't normally look for, and create an error if something is wrong, which will stop the script. This allows us to define our own checks on the environment, specific to our script, such as whether a remote server is online or offline, and invoke an error if there is a problem.

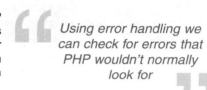

*Using error handling we can check for errors that PHP wouldn't normally look for*

We'll now look at the user-defined types:

- E_USER_NOTICE – This is the same as all other notices, apart from being definable by the user, and is used to display messages to the user that don't affect the running of the script in any way.

- E_USER_WARNING – This is used to inform the user about more serious errors, but not so serious that the script can't recover.

- E_USER_ERROR – This is used when something critical happens in the script, causing the script to stop, this could be caused by attempting to divide a number by 0 for example (which is impossible and causes an error).

## Triggering Errors

You can trigger an error from your script using the `trigger_error()` function, which uses the following format:

```
trigger_error( $message, $errorType )
```

where `$message` is a message that is displayed to the user when the error is triggered, and `$errorType` is one of the three user-defined error constants. Try the following code:

```php
<?php
trigger_error("This creates a User Error", E_USER_ERROR);
?>
```

When this code is viewed in a browser, it displays:

*Fatal error: This creates a User Error in test.php on line 8*

You can see that this is very similar to the default PHP error messages, except that it displays our custom error message. Try the code below, which triggers an error for each of the different user error types.

```php
<?php
trigger_error("This creates a User Notice", E_USER_NOTICE);
trigger_error("This creates a User Warning", E_USER_WARNING);
trigger_error("This creates a User Error", E_USER_ERROR);
echo "This will never be printed to the screen";
?>
```

When viewed in a browser, the following output is seen:

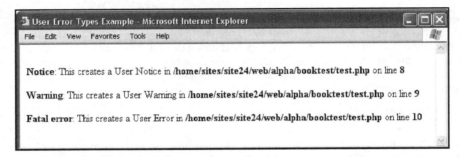

It's important to note, that while the script continued after the User Notice and User Warning, the script stopped at line 10, when the User Error was triggered, and the echo command at the end of the script was not executed.

# Custom Error Handling

We can make error messages more informative and professional looking by creating our own custom error handlers. When a custom error handler is used, the PHP processor calls one of our own functions, passing it all the information about the error that it would normally use itself.

## Setting a Custom Error Handler

First we have to tell PHP to ignore errors itself, and instead call our custom error-handling function. We do this with the PHP function, `set_error_handler()`, the format of which is shown below:

```
set_error_handler(function name)
```

So if our error-handling function was called `errorHandler()`, we would use the following code:

```
<?
set_error_hander("errorHandler");
?>
```

Now our function `errorHandler()` will be invoked in the event of an error. However, before we can try the code above, we first need to make the `errorHandler()` function.

# Creating a Custom Error-Handling Function

When the PHP engine calls our custom error handler, it passes a number of parameters describing the error to our function, which uses them to display information about the problem. There are five parameters passed to our error handler, and these are listed below in the order in which they are sent to the function:

- Error Code: The numerical code representing the error type

- Error Description: The error message

- File Name: The file name of the script in which the error occurred

- Line Number: The line number where PHP discovered the error

- Extra Variables: The array of environment variables present at the time of the error

Our error-handling function needs to be able to accept these five parameters, so when we define the function, we need to create a variable to hold each of the parameters above.

We'll now take a look at a simple example. Create a new PHP page, and enter the following code.

```php
<?php
// Tell PHP to use our function named errorHandler, to handle future errors
set_error_handler("errorHandler");

// This is the error handler function that PHP calls in the event of an error
function errorHandler($errorCode, $errorDescription, $filename, $linenumber,
$extraVars) {
    echo "Error Code: " . $errorCode . "<br>";
    echo "Error Description: " . $errorDescription . "<br>";
    echo "Filename: " . $filename . "<br>";
    echo "Line Number: " . $linenumber . "<br><br>";
    foreach($extraVars as $index=>$data) {
        echo "Extra Variable: " . $index . " : " . $data . "<br>";
        }
    }

// This triggers a test error, so we can see the error handler working
trigger_error("Test Error", E_USER_ERROR);
?>
```

First we use `set_error_handler("errorHandler")` to tell PHP to use our custom function `errorHandler` in the event of an error. Next we define our `errorHandler` function, and add some simple code to print the parameters it receives to the browser. Notice that for the `$extraVars` parameter, we need to use a `foreach` loop to print all of its values because it is an array. Lastly, we trigger an error of type `E_USER_ERROR`, so that we can test our custom error-handling function.

Save the code above, and upload the page to your server, then view it in a browser. You will see results similar to the following screenshot:

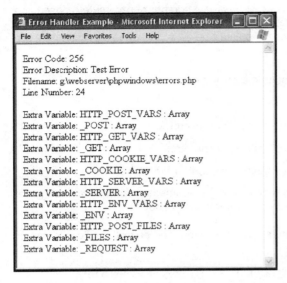

When an error occurs we are provided with a large amount of information in the form of the extra variables array, including, at the bottom, the predefined PHP arrays such as _POST and _COOKIE. If you are using a Linux server with Apache, you'll see many of the variables that can be seen using the phpinfo() function are also present.

So already we have a simple custom error handler, which we've seen working. Now we can start to tidy up the output and show a more informative and nicely formatted error message. The best way to do this is to create the HTML first, using static values to get the look and presentation correct. Once we have the presentation sorted out, we can write the code to swap the static variables for the dynamic ones passed to the function by PHP.

*When you're designing the layout of information like this, which is going to be displayed using some PHP code, it's important not to use HTML font tags and sizes for formatting the text; instead use CSS. If you include the entire HTML formatting commands in your PHP code and later on you decide to change the look for example, you'll need to go back into your code to make the changes. If you've separated the formatting into a CSS stylesheet, you change the way the information looks in the future by simply changing the stylesheet, and the code can stay the same. Another advantage of separating the formatting into a separate CSS stylesheet is that you can reuse your code as it is for any other sites you design, and all you need to do is to change the stylesheet, saving you from having to write all the code again.*

## Creating a Custom Error Page

We're now going to create a custom error page to display the error messages. We start by designing the HTML for the page, and use CSS for the formatting. We use placeholders marked by ##value## to represent the data that were going to replace with the dynamic data. The markers can be anything you choose, ## is easy to see and stands out on the screen. Our example page design is shown in the screenshot overleaf:

This screenshot is taken from Dreamweaver MX, in Code View. The HTML code for this is shown below:

**An Error has Occurred !**

We`re sorry but the following error has occurred :

## Error Message ##

Please try again later, and if you continue having problems email the webmaster at ##email## with details of the error, and we will do our best to resolve the problem.

If you email the webmaster about this error, please copy the following details, and paste them into your email.

Error occurred at ##time## on ##date##

Host Server: ## http_host ##
URL: ## script uri ##
Server IP: ## server_addr ##

Error Type: ## error type ##
Error Message: ##error message ##

Request Method: ## request_method ##
File Name: ## filename ##
Line Number: ## line number ##

```html
<html>
  <head>
    <title>Custom Error Message</title>
    <meta http-equiv="Content-Type" content="text/html; charset=iso-8859-1">
    <link href="errorStyles.css" rel="stylesheet" type="text/css">
  </head>
  <body>
    <p class="errorAlert">An Error has Occurred !</p>
    <p class="plainText">We`re sorry but the following error has occurred :</p>
    <p class="errorMessage">## Error Message ##</p>
    <p class="plainText">
    Please try again later, and if you continue having problems email the
webmaster at <a href="mailto:##email##">##email##</a> with details of the error,<br>
and we will do our best to resolve the problem.
    </p>
    <p class="plainText">
    If you email the webmaster about this error, please copy the following
details, and paste them into your email.
    </p>
    <br>
    <div class="errorDetails">
      <span class="errorHeading">Error occurred at</span>
      <span class="errorData">##time##</span>
      <span class="errorHeading">on</span>
      <span class="errorData">##date##</span>
      <br><br>
```

```
        <span class="errorHeading">Host Server:</span>
        <span class="errorData">## http_host ##</span>
        <br>
        <span class="errorHeading">URL:</span>
        <span class="errorData">## script uri ##</span>
        <br>
        <span class="errorHeading">Server IP:</span>
        <span class="errorData">## server_addr ##</span>
        <br><br>
        <span class="errorHeading">Error Type:</span>
        <span class="errorData">## error type ##</span>
        <br>
        <span class="errorHeading">Error Message:</span>
        <span class="errorData">##error message ##</span>
        <br><br>
        <span class="errorHeading">Request Method:</span>
        <span class="errorData">## request_method ##</span><br>
        <span class="errorHeading">File Name:</span>
        <span class="errorData">## filename ##</span><br>
        <span class="errorHeading">Line Number:</span>
        <span class="errorData">## line number ##</span><br>
      </div>
    </body>
</html>
```

## CSS Stylesheet

As you can see, there is no actual HTML formatting in the error page, it is all formatted using the following CSS stylesheet, which we will call errrorStyles.css.

```
/* Stylesheet for Custom Error Handler */

.errorAlert {
/* Style for Main Error Message Heading */
      font-family: Arial, Helvetica, sans-serif;
      font-size: 16px;
      font-weight: bold;
      color: #006699;
      text-align: center;
}
.plainText {
/* Style for  normal text */
      font-family: Arial, Helvetica, sans-serif;
      font-size: 12px;
      color: #000000;
      text-align: center;
}
.errorMessage {
/* Style for actual error message */
      font-family: Arial, Helvetica, sans-serif;
      font-size: 12px;
      font-weight: bold;
      color: #CC0000;
      text-align: center;
}
```

```
.errorDetails {
/* Style for Box round error details */
      border: thin dashed #000000;
      background-color : #FFFFEE;
      padding: 20px;
      margin-left : 30%;
      margin-right: 30%;
}
.errorHeading {
/* Style for variable headings */
      font-family: Arial, Helvetica, sans-serif;
      font-size: 12px;
      font-weight : normal;
      color: #000000;
}
.errorData {
/* Style for variable data */
      font-family: Arial, Helvetica, sans-serif;
      font-size: 12px;
      color: #000000;
      font-weight: bold;
}
```

Create the stylesheet as a separate file, and then attach it to the HTML page, so the styles are applied to the HTML.

## Adding the Dynamic Error Data

The basic layout is ready. We can now add the dynamic error data that is passed to our error-handling function. We're going to create all the error-handling code in a separate PHP include file which we can add to any future PHP code to make use of our custom error handler functionality.

First create a new PHP page, and delete any HTML code, so the page is completely blank. Save this file as errorhandler.php. We need to tell PHP to use our custom error handler instead of its own, so add the code shown below to the page. We add it in the include file itself, so that on any page we want to use the error handler, all we need is to include the file, we don't have to specifically set the error handler for the page ourselves.

```php
<?php
// Tell PHP to use our function named errorHandler, to handle future errors
set_error_handler("errorHandler");
?>
```

Now we need to add the code for our actual error-handling function. Add the code below to your page:

```php
<?php
// This is the error handler function that PHP calls in the event of an error
function errorHandler($errorCode, $errorDescription, $filename, $linenumber,
$extraVars){
    $email = "webmaster@website.com";
    $date = date("d/m/Y");
    $time = date("H:i");
```

First we set a variable to hold the e-mail address that is given in the message. Next, we set up variables to hold the current date and time, using the PHP `date()` function to retrieve the information. The PHP `date()` function takes a number of parameters, which output various parts of the current system date or time. For example, the command:

```
echo ("d/m/Y");
```

will output the date in the following style:

*26/09/2002*

> *Note that with the `date()` function the parameters are case-sensitive, and `y` means 02, whereas `Y` means 2002. The Time and Date functions are covered in detail in Chapter 7, and are also available in the online manual at http://www.php.net/.*

Next we'll add an array to translate the numerical error type that is sent to our error handler into a more informative message. Add the code below to our error-handling function, just after the variable `$time`.

```
$errorType = array (1=>"Error", 2=>"Warning", 4=>"Parsing Error", 8=>"Notice",
16=>"Core Error", 32=>"Core Warning", 64=>"Compile Error",  128=>"Compile Warning",
256=>"User Error", 512 =>  "User Warning", 1024=>"User Notice");
```

This creates an array, `$errorType`, with all the error types referenced by their error number, which is returned by the PHP processor.

Our last job is to add in the HTML code we designed earlier, so it is printed by the function, and the static values are replaced with the dynamic ones, as shown in the code below:

```
$outputHtml = "
<link href=\"errorStyles.css\" rel=\"stylesheet\" type=\"text/css\">
<p class=\"errorAlert\">An Error has Occurred !</p>
<p class=\"plainText\">We`re sorry but the following error has occurred:</p>
<p class=\"errorMessage\">" . $errorDescription . "</p>
<p class=\"plainText\">
  Please try again later, and if you continue having problems email the webmaster
at <a href=\"" . $email . "\">" . $email . "</a> with details of the error,<br> and
we will do our best to resolve the problem.
</p>
<p class=\"plainText\">
  If you email the webmaster about this error, please copy the following details,
and paste them into your email.
</p>
<br>
<div class=\"errorDetails\">
  <span class=\"errorHeading\">Error occurred at</span>
  <span class=\"errorData\">" . $time . "</span>
  <span class=\"errorHeading\">on</span>
  <span class=\"errorData\">" . $date . "</span>
  <br><br>
```

```
  <span class=\"errorHeading\">Host Server:</span>
  <span class=\"errorData\">" . $_SERVER['HTTP_HOST']  . "</span>
  <br>
  <span class=\"errorHeading\">Error Type:</span>
  <span class=\"errorData\">" . $errorType[$errorCode]  . "</span>
  <br>
  <span class=\"errorHeading\">Error Message:</span>
  <span class=\"errorData\">" . $errorDescription  . "</span>
  <br><br>
  <span class=\"errorHeading\">Request Method:</span>
  <span class=\"errorData\">" . $_SERVER['REQUEST_METHOD']  . "</span><br>
  <span class=\"errorHeading\">File Name:</span>
  <span class=\"errorData\">" . $filename  . "</span><br>
  <span class=\"errorHeading\">Line Number:</span>
  <span class=\"errorData\">" . $linenumber  . "</span><br>
</div>";
```

Here we open a new string, which is stored in a variable $outputHtml. The HTML code is then pasted between the opening and closing quotes. Once that is done, all the quotation marks in the HTML code need to be escaped, by adding a backslash character (\) before each quote mark. This tells PHP to ignore the quotes, and just add them to the string. At each static data marker in the HTML code (for example ## time ##) we close the PHP string, add the appropriate value to the string, and then reopen the quotes. A lot of the data comes from the extraVars array, and the index names to reference certain values, for example, HTTP_HOST, were obtained from the output of our first error handler example earlier in this chapter.

Finally add the following code, which prints to the screen the variable $outputHtml.

```
    echo $outputHtml;
  }
?>
```

This completes our function, and our include file. Save it, and upload it to your server.

## Creating a Test Page

Now that we have our include file ready, we're going to create a simple page to trigger a test error, so that we can see the output from our custom error handler.

```
<?php require_once($DOCUMENT_ROOT . 'errorhandler.php'); ?>
```

Open a new PHP page, and add the following PHP code before the <html> tag at the top of the page: This adds our error handler include file; note that we have used a special PHP variable, $DOCUMENT_ROOT, which contains the path to the root directory of your web site. Then we add the path to the file from the web root directory. Our custom error handler will now be applied to this page instead of the default PHP error handler.

Now we need to trigger an error, so add the PHP code below to the body of the page.

```
<?php
trigger_error("This is a test Error Message",E_USER_ERROR);
?>
```

Finally save this page, and upload to your server. Check that you have also uploaded the include file, `errorhandler.php`, and the CSS stylesheet we created earlier.

Now you can view our test page in your browser, and you should see a nicely formatted output, as shown in the screenshot below:

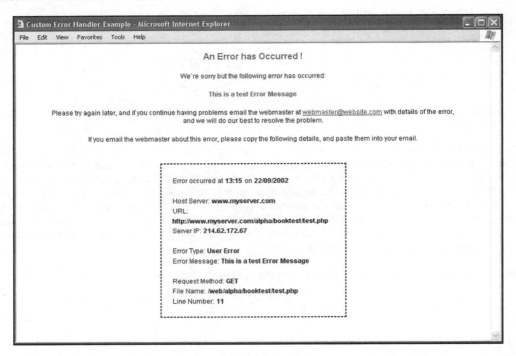

As a quick reminder, temporarily remove the PHP line that includes the `errorhandler.php` code, leave the trigger error code as it is, and upload the page to the server. When you view it in your browser, you will see that exactly the same trigger error command produces the output shown in the screenshot below, using the default PHP error handler:

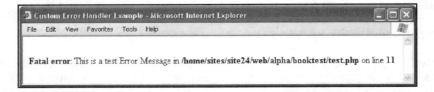

You can see what a difference to the output our custom error handler makes, and how much more professional and user-friendly it is. It's also easy to use, just add the `errorhandler.php` file to any page using an include command, and the page will automatically use the custom error handler, no more coding required. The layout and colors can also be changed quickly and easily, by editing the CSS stylesheet.

## Restoring the Default PHP Error Handler

If at some stage in your script you want to set the error handler back to the PHP default handler, you can use the PHP function, `restore_error_handler()`. This function has no parameters, and is used like this:

```php
<?php
restore_error_handler();
?>
```

Once the function has been processed, any future errors will be passed to the default PHP error handler.

# Special Error Commands and Functions

PHP has some useful functions that can be used to deal with errors. In this section we will look at three functions: the @ directive, the `die()` function, and the `error_log()` function.

## The @ directive

The @ directive tells the PHP processor not to show an error message, and to turn off error reporting for the expression that is used with it. For example, try the following PHP code:

```php
<?php
    $result = 10 / 0;
    echo "test";
?>
```

When the above code is viewed in a browser, the following output is displayed:

*Warning: Division by zero in test2.php on line 9*
*test*

PHP displays a warning, as we are trying to do the impossible: dividing by 0. Now add an @ sign, so that the code reads the same as the code below.

```php
<?php
    @$result = 10 / 0;
    echo "test";
?>
```

Again, view the code in a browser, and this time the browser just outputs the text "*test*" without any warning. It doesn't mean there's no longer an error, it just doesn't tell us about it. This can be useful when we are checking for a particular error ourselves and want PHP to ignore it.

*Use the @ directive with caution, as an error which is suppressed could lead to major problems later on in your script.*

## die()

The `die()` function stops a script, and sends an error message to the browser; its format is simply:

```
die("error message")
```

It's often used for checking a connection to a MySQL database has been made for example, as shown in the following code:

```php
<?php
    $dblink = mysql_connect("localhost", $username, $password);
    if (!$dblink){
        die ("Couldn`t connect to MySQL Server"); }
?>
```

This code attempts to connect to a MySQL database server. `$dblink` contains either `True` or `False`, depending on whether the connection is made or not. If `$dblink` is `False`, then the `die()` function is run, the script stops, and the message "*Couldn`t connect to MySQL Server*" is sent to the browser.

We need to stop the script if a connection to the MySQL server cannot be made, because it means that we can't read or write from the database, and all the rest of the code will fail.

*It's important to realize that when the die() function is called, the script stops dead, and no further code is processed.*

If the script has previously sent an opening `<html>` and `<body>` tag to the browser, the display may become corrupted, leaving an incomplete HTML document, which some browsers may be unable to display.

There's a simple solution to this however, as shown in the following code:

```php
<?php
    $dblink = mysql_connect(_DBHOST, _DBUSER, _DBPASS);
    if (!$dblink){
        $closingTags = "\n\n</body>\n\n\</html>\n\n";
        die ("Couldn`t connect to MySQL Server" . $closingTags); }
?>
```

In the code above, we have included a closing `</body>` and `</html>` tag in the message sent by the `die()` function, which completes the HTML, and ensures the page is a valid HTML document.

## error_log()

The `error_log()` function is used to redirect error messages. `error_log()` uses the following format:

```
error_log($errorMessage, $errorTo, $destinationString)
```

where `$errorMessage` is the error message you want to send somewhere, and `$errorTo` is used to tell `error_log()` what to do with the error message. It has the following four settings:

- 0 – The message is sent to the PHP System Logs

- 1 – The message is sent by e-mail to the address in the $destinationString

- 2 – The message is sent through the PHP Debugging Connection

- 3 – The message is written to the file whose filename is in $destinationString

For example, if we wanted to e-mail an error message we could use the code:

```
error_log("This is a test message",1,"gareth@mysite.com");
```

To save the error to a file we could use:

```
error_log("This is a test message",3,"/web/logs/errors.log")
```

Although error log can be useful, it's pretty basic, and so it's easier to use your own custom e-mail and file-logging functions which can log much more data, and we'll have a look at some example functions to do this now.

# Logging Errors to a File

It can be extremely useful when you're trying to diagnose an ongoing problem, to write error data to a file each time an error occurs. Having a list of the errors and data in front of you can help you find a common pattern for example, which can help get to the source of the error. Take a look at the following code:

```php
<?php
function logError($errorMessage){
    // Filename of file where errors will be logged
    $filename = "error.log";

    // Get current date and time
    $date = date("d/m/Y");
    $time = date("H:i");

    // Check the file exists
    if(!file_exists($filename)){
      // If the file doesn`t exist, create a new file
        touch($filename);
    }
    // Open file for appending, and die if open failed
    $fp = fopen($filename,'a')
        or die("Error: Could not open file " . $filename);

    // Build the line to store in the error log
    $log = "Date: " . $date . " Time: " . $time . " " . $errorMessage . "\n";
```

```
        // Lock File, write the error then Unlock file
        flock($fp,LOCK_EX);
        fwrite($fp,$log);
        flock($fp,LOCK_UN);

        // Close file
        fclose($fp);
}
?>
```

This is the complete code for an error-logging function. First we set the filename of the log, and get the current time and date. Next we check whether or not error.log exists, and if it doesn't, we create it. We then open the file in append mode, lock it, write our error message to it, then we can unlock and close it. We can pass an error message to this function using the code below.

```
<?php
    logError("This is a test Error Message");
?>
```

When the code above is run, the error message "*This is a test Error Message*" will be added to the error.log file. If you then download the error.log file, and open it in a text editor, you will see the error message:

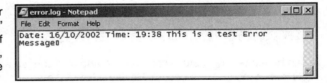

The function can also be expanded, to write more information to the error.log file.

*To find out more about file handling see Chapter 8 of this book.*

You can add the function to our errorhandler.php include file if you wish, and call it from our main errorHandler() function, and then every time an error occurs it gets logged to error.log, as in the code shown below

*Note that permissions on the file error.log need to be set so that it is writable to by everyone, so that PHP can write to the file. In Linux, you would set the permissions for error.log to 777.*

```
<?php
    function errorHandler($errorCode, $errorDescription, $filename, $linenumber,
$extraVars){
        // Previous code here
        logError($errorDescription);
}
?>
```

# Sending Error Details by E-mail

If you're running a web site where any down time is critical, such as an e-commerce site, you need to be notified quickly if an error occurs to minimize lost business. The easiest way to do this is to have the error messages automatically sent to you by e-mail, using the PHP mail() function.

The format for the `mail()` function is:

```
mail($to, $subject, $message)
```

where `$to` is the recipient e-mail address, `$subject` is the subject line of the e-mail, and `$message` is the actual e-mail message.

*We'll be looking at e-mail in much more detail later on in Chapter 9*

Take a look at the code below, which creates a function that sends the error details by e-mail:

```php
<?php
function emailError($errorMessage){
    // Get current date and time
    $date = date("d/m/Y");
    $time = date("H:i");

    // Create subject and email address to send to
    $subject = "An Error has Occurred !";
    $email = "gareth@mysite.co.uk";

    // Build Email Message
    $message = "An error occurred at " . $time . " on " . $date . "\n\n";
    $message .= "Error Message: " . $errorMessage . "\n";

    // Send Email
    mail($email,$subject,$message);
}
?>
```

We capture the current date and time, and set up variables to hold the subject line and the recipient's address. We then build the body of the e-mail, including the error message, and finally we use the `mail()` function to send the e-mail.

When calling the function, you need to pass it an error message, as in the example code below.

```php
<?php
    emailError("This is a test error message");
?>
```

When the code is run, an e-mail will be sent with the subject line *"An error has occurred!"*, and the following in the message body:

*An error occurred at 19:13 on 28/09/2002*

*Error Message: This is a test error message*

*Be careful about which errors you send by e-mail; it's best to limit it to only important error types, otherwise in the event of a major problem, with many people accessing the site, you could well be bombarded with e-mail error messages, causing you further problems and clogging up your mail server. It's a very useful function, but it must be used wisely.*

Again, you can add this `emailError()` function to our `errorHandler.php` include file and call it from our main `errorHandler` function to have the error sent by e-mail.

# MySQL Error Functions

PHP also has two built-in functions, which can give you information if an error occurs when accessing a MySQL database. These functions are:

## mysql_error()

The `mysql_error()` function returns information about the last MySQL error that occurred. You can then log this information, or use it in our custom error handler. The code below shows a short example.

```php
<?php
    $dblink = mysql_connect(_DBHOST, _DBUSER, _DBPASS);
    if (!$dblink){
        die ("Couldn`t connect to mySQL Server: ". mysql_error()); }
?>
```

Here we try and connect to a MySQL server, and if the connection fails we halt the script using `die()`, and write the value of `mysql_error()` to the screen.

## mysql_errno()

The `mysql_errno()` function is almost identical to `mysql_error()` above, except that it returns an error number instead of an error message.

### Debugging SQL Queries

As well as the actual error messages above which can help you track down an error with your database, another useful technique is to temporarily modify your code so that you print the SQL query you are about to execute to the screen, using the `echo` command, for example:.

```php
<?php
    echo $sqlQuery;
?>
```

Often you find that although the SQL query looks right, when you view it "live" on your server you find that the dynamic values aren't filled with the data that should be in them. You can then go back and modify your code accordingly, and when the SQL statement is correct you can remove the line which prints it to the screen.

# Debugging Tips

There are a number of tips that you can use to make debugging easier, adopting these techniques will reduce development time by reducing the likelihood of introducing bugs into the code and making it easier to find an errors and fix them.

# Indent your Code, and Use Comments

The neater you make your code, and the easier it is to read and follow. It makes debugging easier, not just for you, but for anyone else who may need to work on the site in the future. Add comments to your code, you don't need to go over the top and comment every line, but they should be regular enough to be able to quickly get an idea of what is going on. Although it may take a little extra time to code neatly, and add comments, it will saves a great amount of time if you later have to go back and change the code when it's no longer fresh in your mind.

# Build Error Messages into your Code

While you're writing and debugging your code, it's extremely useful to regularly print out the contents of variables, to see what values they store, and how that value changes. Usually these quick tests are deleted from the final code, but it can be more useful to leave them in, and encase them in an `if` structure, as shown in the example code below.

```php
<?php
$showErrors = 0;

if($showErrors == 1){
    "The value assigned to $test is: " . $test;
}
```

Normally, `$showErrors` would be hard coded to 0, and the debugging statements will never show. However, if an error occurs in the future you can just change `$showErrors` to 1, and then all the debugging information will be shown, and you can see the contents of the variables. When the error is fixed, simply set `$showErrors` back to 0.

# Break Your Code into Functions and Classes

It makes life much easier when you're debugging if you're looking at small sections of code, rather than a long complicated section of code. Using functions and classes, which are covered in *Chapter 4* of this book, you can break your code into smaller chunks, and just look at that single function which makes debugging and tracing errors much easier.

Breaking your code into smaller sections that only do certain jobs, also means that you can quickly build yourself a code library, and you can reuse the code in other sites, without having to make major changes.

# Don't Be Afraid to Ask for Help

We list a number of useful sources in the next section. It's more than likely that someone else has had a similar error or problem in the past, and can advise you on how to fix it, saving you a lot of time finding a solution.

It can be extremely useful to find someone else who is at a similar level to you, coding-wise, with whom you can swap code, and help each other solve problems. Often when you're reading your own code, it's hard to think about what the code is actually doing because you already have the idea in your mind of what it *should* be doing, which can be two different things. When someone else reads your code, they can often spot errors quickly, because they are looking at it afresh.

# Sources of Help

As PHP becomes more and more popular, there are a large number of new sites springing up offering support and help with PHP. Here are some reliable web sites and newsgroups you can use for reference.

## Web Sites

### http://www.php.net/

This is the home of PHP, and probably the site you'll visit most. The site has an online copy of the PHP manual, broken into section and functions, and it's often useful to have the manual up in your browser as you develop a site, so you can quickly look up functions. You can also download the latest PHP package here.

### http://www.zend.com/

Zend wrote the PHP engine, and their site contains hundreds of articles, tutorials, tips, and code examples, covering a huge range of subject areas.

### http://www.macromedia.com/

The Macromedia site has a large number of Tech Notes and tutorials for Dreamweaver MX including a recently opened developer center, which is a great resource, and contains a huge amount of information for developers. Macromedia also host their extension exchange, which contains a number of free PHP extensions to make life easier for developers, and is well worth a browse.

### http://php.faqts.com/

This site is a large database of PHP questions and their answers, and is great for quickly getting the answer to a PHP problem.

### http://www.tecnorama.org/phphelp

Tecnorama contains an extremely useful extension from Andres Cayon, which adds a copy of the PHP manual into Dreamweaver MX, so it's instantly available to look up PHP functions and is an invaluable addition for everyone working with PHP in Dreamweaver MX.

### http://www.google.com/, http://groups.google.com/

Although Google is a search engine rather than a PHP site, it's an invaluable resource for finding PHP articles and tutorials. You can also search for a certain error message that your code is creating, as it's likely the solution is already on the Web somewhere.

## Macromedia Newsgroups

The Macromedia Newsgroups should be your first port of call in the event of a problem. Staffed by Tech Support, Team Macromedia, and many thousands of developers, you can often get the answer to a question extremely quickly, as the forums are filled with like-minded developers.

The Macromedia News Server is split into a number of different groups, covering different subject areas, and to get the best chance of a quick answer, you should make sure that you send your question to the appropriate group. Before you post, have a quick scan through the old messages; it's likely that your question has already been answered.

Full details for connecting to the Macromedia news servers can be found on the Macromedia web site at *http://www.macromedia.com/*.

# Summary

In this chapter we first looked at configuring Dreamweaver MX, and at options which are useful for working with code, and some of the functions that can help with debugging your code.

We then looked at the different types of error that can occur with PHP, and how to avoid them. We then looked at the PHP error categories, and learned how to change the error-reporting levels, so that only certain errors are acted on, and the less important notices for example, are ignored.

Next we looked at configuring the error directives in the `php.ini` file, and how to use these settings for a single site only, instead of all the sites on the server. We then looked at the PHP user error type, for creating custom errors, and how to trigger an error from our script.

Custom error handlers can provided a more user-friendly error message, which we can format using CSS, so the look of the error message can quickly be changed, without having to change any of the PHP code. We also looked at error-logging methods, and logging errors to a file, or sending the error in an e-mail message.

Finally we looked at the MySQL error functions, and saw a number of tips to make debugging your PHP code easier, and where to obtain extra help.

Error Handling

# 4

- Object Oriented Programming
- Creating classes
- Inheritance

**Author: Tim Green**

# Object Oriented Programming in PHP

As you work through the chapters of this book, you'll notice that there is a steady shift in programming style, moving away from the typical 'inline' programming methods, to a more modular way of working.

This shift in methodology is entirely intentional. The inline way of working, which Dreamweaver MX does so well, is fine for most simple tasks. However, once you start experimenting with all of the features that PHP has to offer, it can get a little difficult managing your code, when the same routines are repeated on a number of different pages. While this does work well, if for any reason you need to change any of the inserted code, you have to go back over all the pages that you created, ensuring that the same code modifications are made so that everything works.

Working in a more component-based way means that you decrease the amount of repetition in your work, increase your productivity, and enhance your site's manageability. While there are a number of different ways to modularize your work, either by using functions or include files, there is still yet a more efficient method. **OOP (Object Oriented Programming)** has been used for a number of years in a variety of different programming languages.

## What Is OOP?

If you're familiar with other programming languages such as JavaScript, or Visual Basic, then you've probably already made use of OOP. It is a programming technique that was designed specifically to allow greater control, flexibility, and scalability in all your projects, large or small.

The great thing about OOP is that it's easy to learn. Everything that you have learned so far about PHP is applicable here, which means that you don't need to pick up any additional skills. For most people starting out with OOP, the most difficult thing to understand is the concept.

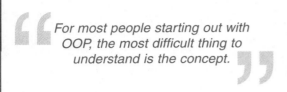

*For most people starting out with OOP, the most difficult thing to understand is the concept.*

**Objects** are like containers, they are used to encapsulate not only data, but also the functionality required to manipulate that data. If you are already familiar with JavaScript, for example, then you will undoubtedly have come across the **Document Object Model**. This object provides a number of facilities, which allow you to directly manipulate and extract all content from your web pages. When using OOP with PHP, you can create similar kinds of facilities that allow you to manipulate the data within your own code.

## The Car

An easy way to understand the concept of OOP is to use the example of a motor car. When you're walking down a street you see lots of them, and though they are different, you know they are cars because they all have specific defining criteria such as wheels, doors, engine, seats, and a tailpipe. Whilst there are many types of car, and they come in all shapes, sizes, and colors, we know what to look for, and so are able to identify them as cars.

In OOP, the car in the above example is an **object**. The elements that define the car, the windows, doors, wheels, fuel consumption, and so on, can all vary from one car to another. Those same elements are used in Object Oriented Programming, and we call them **properties**.

Properties are of little use alone. To be useful, we need some way in which we can manipulate them. Going back to our car example, if we want to use the car then we have to turn the engine on in order to start it. In OOP terms **start** is a **method**, a way of putting the object to use; it sets the engine property to on.

There is one more element of OOP that isn't covered in the above example, a **constructor**. I've purposely left this element to last, as in PHP the constructor is entirely optional. Constructors are a special form of method, which are immediately executed the moment an instance of the object is created, or **instantiated**. This can be very useful if you need to run some code the moment an object is created, so that it functions correctly. If you are familiar with OOP in other languages, it should be noted that PHP does not currently have support for multiple constructors.

### Creating a Classification

Before we can start working with objects, we need to define an **object classification**, or **class**, so that PHP can readily identify the object, and work with it. We do this using wrapping standard PHP code with the `class` keyword.

```
class Car {

   // Properties and Methods are defined here

}
```

The syntax for using the `class` keyword is very simple, as you can see above. In this code sample, we are telling PHP that enclosed by the class definition is an object called `Car`. The next step in defining a class is to determine its properties.

Before we begin defining our class though, we have to look at the object as a whole, and break it down into its characteristic elements. This involves two stages: defining the properties and defining the methods. Taking our car as an example, we might look at various identifying characteristics such as the number of doors, the color, and the size of the engine. These are all properties of a car, and so we can safely use these when defining the classification.

Methods are slightly different to properties, as they are essentially verbs or actions, so we need to think about the different actions that can be achieved with a car. Well, we can start, stop, brake, and accelerate. These are all actions and are valid methods, so we can begin to build up a picture of how we define the car.

This can all get very complex if we want to define every property and method for a car, so it is best to only define the elements that are important to the task at hand. For example, at this level, we don't want to define the spark plug's method **ignite**, though it is still a valid method.

*When we use a property or a method within a* Class *file, we need to use a special syntax to inform PHP that we are using a property or method from the same class. To do this, we prefix the name of the method or property with* $this-> *which tells PHP to use **this** class to obtain the information.*

### Defining Properties

Properties and variables are essentially one and the same. Normally when programming in PHP, there is no requirement to define a variable before use, and the same also applies to objects. However, this is largely considered bad practice with objects, as it is difficult to reuse an object at a later stage if you don't have a section of the class definition that defines its properties.

```
class Car {

    // Property Declarations
    var $engine;
    var $wheels;
    var $doors;
    var $color;
    var $speed;

}
```

Here, we have defined a number of properties for use with the object. To define the property, we use the declaration keyword `var` followed by a standard PHP variable name. When declaring a property in this way, it becomes available to all the methods of the class.

### Defining Methods

Methods are defined by using functions within the class definition.

```
class Car {

    // Property Declarations
    var $engine;
    var $wheels;
    var $doors;
    var $color;
    var $speed;
```

```
  // Constructor Method
  function Car($engine,$wheels,$doors,$color) {
    $this->engine = $engine;
    $this->wheels = $wheels;
    $this->doors = $doors;
    $this->color = $color;
    $this->speed = 0;
  }
  // Methods
  function Start() {
    $this->speed += 10;
  }

}
```

Here we have created a **constructor** called car, and a **method** called start. Both are essentially standard PHP functions, and in fact both of them use the function keyword, but you will notice that there are a lot of lines containing ->. This is a special operator within PHP, which allows you to refer directly to other properties or methods of an object. The PHP interpreter requires this operator so that it can keep properties and methods separate from variables and functions.

When creating the methods for our class, we will often need to refer back to the object's properties, or other methods, so it is essential that you are aware of this operator's syntax:

```
[object]->[property or method]
```

To the left of the operator we state which object is to be used, and to the right we state the property or method that we wish to access:

```
$this->engine = 1600;   // Stores the value 1600 in the engine property.

$this->start();         // Executes the method 'start'.

echo $ferrari->speed;   // Outputs the Ferrari object's speed property.

$jaguar->stop();        // Executes the Jaguar object's 'stop' method.
```

## Instantiating an Object

To instantiate an object, we need to tell PHP that we are creating a new object based on our object classification. We do this using the new keyword. Here we will present three examples, all of which instantiate an object.

When your class definition does not contain a constructor, you would use the following syntax to instantiate an object:

```
$ferrari = new Car;
```

If you do have a constructor within your class definition, then strictly speaking you should use the following syntax:

```
$ferrari = new Car();
```

although note that the first example will also work in this instance.

Finally, if you have a constructor within your class definition that requires one or more parameters to be sent to it, then you must use the following syntax.

```
$ferrari = new Car(5998,4,2,"red");
```

As the constructor of our class definition requires a number of parameters, this is the syntax that we should use for our object.

## Public and Private Lives

In other programming languages, it is possible to define which properties and methods are **Public** (accessible to everyone), and which are **Private** (for internal use only). Unfortunately, this isn't yet possible with PHP, so it has become widely accepted that a naming convention should be used to illustrate that a method or a property is not intended for public use. To mark a property or method as **Private**, you should prefix the name with an underscore character ' '. As this is a naming convention only, it does not stop you from making use of a property or method marked as Private in this way, it is just not a recommended practice.

Public and Private methods do serve a purpose though, even if PHP doesn't really distinguish between the two at the moment. Public methods are defined so that another programmer using your class understands which methods are intended for which use.

The example below illustrates how this convention should be used:

```php
class Car {

  // Property Declarations
  var $engine;
  var $wheels;
  var $doors;
  var $color;
  var $speed;

  var $_fuel;      // a property marked as Private

  // Constructor Method
  function Car($engine,$wheels,$doors,$color) {
    $this->engine = $engine;
    $this->wheels = $wheels;
    $this->doors = $doors;
    $this->color = $color;
    $this->speed = 0;
  }

  // Methods
  function Start() {
    $this->speed += 10;

    $this->_injectFuel();

  }
```

```
    function _injectFuel() {     /     // a method marked as Private
      $this->_fuel += 10;
    }

}
```

# Objects in the Real World

Of course, a PHP class that defines a car in the way that we have done doesn't serve much purpose other than to illustrate the concept. In this section we're going to make a simple PHP Class, which allows us to send e-mail, a subject that is covered in much greater depth in *Chapter 9*.

The great thing about developing PHP classes, is that once the class is complete, to actually use it takes only moments, as you don't need to reinvent the wheel in an attempt to gain the same functionality.

## Turning Code Snippets into Classes

This code snippet will send an e-mail to the named recipient:

```php
<?php

// mail() example
$to = "reader@homepage.com";         // Sets the recipient
$subject = "Your recent purchase";   // Sets the subject

$body = "Order #123456\n\nThank you for your order, which will be dispatched";
$body.= " immediately.\nBest Regards\n\nMyShopping Sales.";

// Now send the email
mail($to,$subject,$body);
?>
```

While it is pretty basic, it is a good starting point for creating a class.

The first place to start is to determine which variables you want to use, as these will become the properties of the class. In our code example we use only 3 variables: $to, $subject, and $body. As we only use one PHP command to manipulate the data, for the moment we can use just one method.

At this point, we need to determine whether this method should be a **constructor** or not. For the purposes of this example, I'm not going to create a constructor with this class. The reasons behind this will become more obvious, as later in this chapter we will be looking at enhancing the functionality of this class.

```php
<?php

// Simple Email Class

class simpleEmail {
```

```php
  // Property Declarations
  var $to;
  var $subject;
  var $body;

  // Methods
  function sendMail() {
    mail($this->to, $this->subject, $this->body);
  }
}
?>
```

The code above replicates exactly the functionality of the original PHP code snippet, and as our first true component we will save it as a separate file `simpleEmail.inc.php`. By saving classes as individual files, we can use a PHP `include_once()` or `require_once()` statement, to use this code on as many pages as we require.

Now that we have this code saved, we need to bring it into our document, and instantiate the class. We can do this by using the code that follows:

```php
<?php

require_once("simpleEmail.inc.php");

// instantiate the class
$myMail = new simpleEmail;

$myMail->to = "reader@homepage.com";          // Sets the recipient
$myMail->subject = "Your recent purchase";    // Sets the subject
$myMail->body = "Order #123456\n\nThank you for your order, which will be ";
$myMail->body.= "dispatched immediately.\nBest Regards\n\nMyShopping Sales.";

// Now send the email
$myMail->sendMail();

?>
```

With the code block above in our page, we can now send an e-mail, in exactly the same way as the original PHP Snippet.

I know what you are thinking now. The original code snippet was 12 lines long. With the PHP class definition, plus the code to instantiate the object and send the e-mail, we've now got 33 lines of code. That's nearly 3 times more code, to do the same task!

While this is true, you should look at this in a different way. This is only a simple example, and isn't entirely illustrative of the power of OOP. Say for example, you wanted to expand on the original PHP snippet, perhaps adding in a system that would parse through a database and send the same e-mail to a number of different recipients, using OOP would now be much more efficient and make your code a lot more flexible and easier to maintain.

Object Oriented Programming in PHP

## Adding Additional Functionality

Let's return to the original PHP code snippet that sent mail without using the class we created. Say we wanted to get e-mail addresses from a database; we could code it like this:

```php
<?php
// parsing a database example

$conn = mysql_pconnect("localhost", "username", "password"); // connect to db
mysql_select_db("myDB",$conn);                               // select database

// Create a query and recordset
$sql = "SELECT email FROM mailingList";
$recordset = mysql_query($sql,$conn);

$row = mysql_fetch_assoc($recordset);

do {

        // Set the information
        $to = $recordset["email"];
        $subject = "Site Updated!";
        $body = "Our website has just been updated.\nFor the latest news and
information ";
        $body.= "please pay us a visit!\n\nBest Regards\n\nWebmaster";

        // Now send the email
        mail($to,$subject,$body);

} while (mysql_fetch_assoc($recordset));

// release the information
mysql_free_result($recordset);

// close the connection
mysql_close($conn);

?>
```

As you can see, adding this kind of functionality adds a significant amount of code to your original snippet; this code block now stands at 33 lines. Now consider if you were using similar code blocks 3 or 4 times within your site with only minor variances, your code would soon become unwieldy and difficult to maintain.

Let's try adding this functionality to the Email class that we've already created. We'll code it so that it retrieves e-mail addresses out of a database and send a mail out to each address in turn. By housing all of this additional code within our class definition, we only need to set the parameters that we require when the object is instantiated, and the additional functionality can be built into the object as methods:

```php
<?php

// Simple Email Class
```

```php
class simpleEmail {

        // Property Declarations
        var $to;
        var $subject;
        var $body;

        // New Properties
        var $host = "localhost";
        var $user = "username";
        var $pass = "password";
        var $db = "myDB";
        var $table = "mailingList";
        var $column = "email";


        // Methods
        function sendMail() {

                mail($this->to, $this->subject, $this->body);

        }
        // New Method
        function sendToList() {


                // connect to db
                $conn = mysql_pconnect($this->host,$this->user,$this->pass);
                mysql_select_db($this->db,$conn);                // select database

                // Create a recordset
                $sql = "SELECT " . $this->column . " FROM " . $this->table;
                $recordset = mysql_query($sql,$conn);

                $row = mysql_fetch_assoc($recordset);

                do {

                        // Set the information
                        $this->to = $recordset["email"];

                        // Now send the email
                        $this->sendMail();

                } while (mysql_fetch_assoc($recordset));

                // release the information
                mysql_free_result($recordset);

                // close the connection
                mysql_close($conn);

        }

}

?>
```

As you can see, the class definition has increased in size. However, there are a number of additional elements in this class, which may not be immediately obvious.

Our class now has two methods: the original sendMail() and a new one called sendToList() which extracts e-mail addresses from a database and sends the message to each address. So, if you want to send an e-mail in exactly the same way as you did previously, you can still do it by using precisely the same code to instantiate the object. However, if you now also want to send an e-mail to your mailing list then you can do so by using the sentToList() method of our simpleEmail object:

```php
<?php

include_once("simpleEmail.inc.php");

// instantiate the class
$myMail = new simpleEmail;

$subject = "Site Updated!";
$myMail->body = "Our website has just been updated.\nFor the latest news and
information ";
$myMail->body.= "please pay us a visit!\n\nBest Regards\n\nWebmaster";

// Now send the e-mail
$myMail->sendToList();

?>
```

You'll also notice that there isn't a single mention of database access in this code snippet. Again, all of this has been built into the class file, and the relevant values have all been assigned to properties.

This of course means that if you wish to use a different table, or retrieve a different column, or even connect to a different database entirely, you can do so by setting the relevant values to the relevant properties.

### Examining the New Class

As this class has evolved over the course of the chapter, it's worth looking more closely at these changes and in more detail.

```php
    // New Properties
    var $host = "localhost";
    var $user = "username";
    var $pass = "password";
    var $db = "myDB";
    var $table = "mailingList";
    var $column = "email";
```

First of all, we looked at the variables that were now being used in the additional code of our original snippet, and have determined the ones that we might at some point in the future need to change, for whatever reason.

These new properties have been given a default value, which happens to be the value that we require at the moment. In the future, you may want to use this class in another project, which uses a different database, or has different authentication information. In that case, you can use the same class definition, and include in the code you use to instantiate the object, your replacement code.

```php
<?php

include_once("simpleEmail.inc.php");

// instantiate the class
$myMail = new simpleEmail;

// new parameter value
$myMail->db = "myNewDB";

$subject = "Site Updated!";
$myMail->body = "Our website has just been updated.\nFor the latest news and
information ";
$myMail->body.= "please pay us a visit!\n\nBest Regards\n\nWebmaster";

// Now send the email
$myMail->sendToList();

?>
```

Here, I've illustrated that point by changing the database name. The code will now send e-mail stored on the MyNewDB instead.

The new method, sendToList(), also illustrates how you can use a combination of parameters and variables to best effect.

```php
// New Method
            function sendToList() {

            // connect to db
            $conn = mysql_pconnect($this->host,$this->user,$this->pass);
            mysql_select_db($this->db,$conn);             // select database

            // Create a recordset
            $sql = "SELECT " . $this->column . " FROM " . $this->table;
            $recordset = mysql_query($sql,$conn);

            $row = mysql_fetch_assoc($recordset);

            do {

                    // Set the information
                    $this->to = $recordset["email"];

                    // Now send the email
                    $this->sendMail();

            } while (mysql_fetch_assoc($recordset));

            // release the information
            mysql_free_result($recordset);

            // close the connection
            mysql_close($conn);

        }
```

As you can see, this function is an amended version of the original code snippet. However, we've made this code more useful by turning some of the variables into parameters as well as some of the standard settings. A good illustration of this is the SQL that is used. Originally the SQL was fixed, in that the name of the column to retrieve, and the name of the table were included directly in the variable:

```
$sql = "SELECT email FROM mailingList";
```

There's nothing at all wrong with this SQL statement, and it works fine with our modified code snippet. However, objects are there to be reused as often as possible, with as little manual editing as possible. If we used this exact SQL statement in the class file itself, we would need to maintain a number of different copies of the same file, if we wanted to use slightly different SQL statements, which defeats the whole purpose of creating an object in the first place.

Instead looking at this code we can see that the email column and the mailingList table could both be different if we're working on a different site. This makes them ideal candidates for properties, so we create a column property, and a table property, and amend the code appropriately.

```
$sql = "SELECT " . $this->column . " FROM " . $this->table;
```

The SQL Statement is now dynamically created, based on the values of the column and table parameters, making this object applicable to more projects.

This feature of OOP is something that can be used time and time again, to expand on your original classes and objects and make them more useful than before.

What happens though, if you're working on a site, using someone else's object class definition, and you need to add some extra functionality, or change the way an existing method already works?

Sometimes changing the original class definition isn't really an option, as you won't necessarily know where else the object is being used. You might feel tempted to copy and paste the whole class definition into another file, but that's just duplicating work, and if anything does get changed in the original class, then you're going to have to amend two files now, instead of one.

Fortunately, there is a feature of OOP that allows you to harness the power of an object through another object. This feature is called **inheritance**, and in essence, it allows you redefine elements of the original object, without making any changes to the original.

## Inheritance

When working with OOP, there will often come a time where you will need to construct an object that is essentially the same as an object you already have, with some very minor differences. However, these differences can be such that you cannot simply extend the original object class definition, to include the additional method.

Thankfully all objects that are created with OOP are able to form the basis of other objects, and pass down to these new objects all the properties and methods that they originally contained. This is called **inheritance**.

```php
<?php

class htmlMail extends simpleMail {

  // New property definitions and methods go here

}
?>
```

The code sample shows how a class definition can inherit the properties and methods of its parent object. In this case, we have created a new class, called `htmlMail`, which **extends**, or **inherits**, all of the properties and methods of the original class `simpleMail`.

If you were to add no more information to this new class definition, when this object is instantiated, it will act and behave exactly like the original object. However, if you add a method to this new class definition that has the same name as a method in the original object, it will override the old method of the same name.

To demonstrate exactly what I mean, we're going to create a new `sendMail()` method, that sends an HTML e-mail instead of a plain text one. This will involve the creation of an additional property, and two new methods, one of which will replace an existing method in the original object.

```php
<?php

class htmlMail extends simpleMail {

  // New Property definitions
  var $headers;

  function sendMail() {

    mail($this->to,$this->subject,$this->body,$this->headers);

  }

  function makeHTML() {

    // To send HTML mail, you can set the Content-type header.
    $this->headers  = "MIME-Version: 1.0\r\n";
    $this->headers .= "Content-type: text/html; charset=iso-8859-1\r\n";

  }
}
?>
```

Here all we have done is added the facility to change the e-mail's content headers, so that it can be identified as HTML e-mail. The new property, `headers`, is used to store the relevant header information. The new `sendMail()` method now takes precedence over the original `sendMail()` method, and the new method `makeHTML()` sets the required values of the header, so that you can send HTML e-mail.

Notice that none of the other properties or methods have been redefined. Thanks to inheritance, we don't need to worry about the rest of the object, and we can focus purely on the elements of this class extension. With this code modification complete, we can add this class definition to the same file as our original class, simpleEmail.inc.php. This is perfectly legitimate when working with classes, and one file can contain multiple class definitions. However, for organization's sake, it is usually best to do this only with related classes.

## Instantiating the Inheritor

Now that we have created our class definitions, we can begin to put this new object to practical use.

```php
<?php

include_once("simpleEmail.inc.php");

// instantiate the class
$myMail = new htmlMail;

// new parameter value
$myMail->db = "myNewDB";

$myMail->subject = "Site Updated!";
$myMail->body = "Our website has just been updated.<br>For the latest news and
information ";
$myMail->body.= "please pay us a visit!<br><br>Best Regards<br><br>Webmaster";

// Send an HTML Mail
$myMail->makeHTML();

// Now send the email
$myMail->sendToList();

?>
```

Here is the code that we use to instantiate this new object. As you can see there is very little difference between this code, and the original code used for our database example, but the differences that do exist are important.

To begin with the name of the object that is instantiated has changed. If you were to write $myMail = new simpleMail; then you would have an instance of the original object, and the new methods and properties would not be available for use. Here, you need to create an instance of the extension object, which then inherits all of the methods and properties of its parent. Most importantly, the constructor is inherited too, and this is automatically instigated, and the object is correctly initialized.

The only other difference, apart from formatting options for the e-mail itself, is the addition of a call to our new method makeHTML(), so that we can ensure that the e-mails that are sent are all sent in HTML format.

## Summary

In this chapter we have looked at how PHP can be made to work in a more modularized form by using OOP. By working in this way, we introduce the obvious benefits of minimizing code rewrites, and centralizing functionality in a single file.

We've also looked at ways in which OOP can be made to grow with the programming tasks at hand, and how we can take a simple object and easily modify it to provide additional functionality without making major changes to the PHP code in your web page.

> *One of the most important things to remember with OOP, is that it is a way of compartmentalizing functionality in an abstract way.*

One of the most important things to remember with OOP, is that it is a way of compartmentalizing functionality in an abstract way. Provided that you have clearly defined properties and methods, you can use the functionality within a class very easily. Once you know how a class is constructed, as we've seen here, the code that provides the functionality becomes essentially transparent. You don't need to know **how** a class works, but rather you need to know the syntax (that is: the properties, methods, and constructor) to make that class work for you. There are a few web sites that allow you to download PHP Classes for use within your own work, and probably the best of these is *www.phpclasses.org.*

# 5

- Strings
- Regular expressions

**Author: Bruno Mairlot**

# Strings and Regular Expressions

This chapter will explore the string and regular expression capabilities of PHP. We will first take an in-depth look at how you can create and declare strings in PHP, and we will be reviewing some of the useful PHP functions that we can use to perform on strings. We will see how we can extract specific sections of a string, and how PHP allows us to perform comparison operations.

For more advanced and complex string manipulation we can use regular expressions. They are very powerful tools for searching for specific characters in a string, and replacing them if required. They are also very useful tool for data validation;in this chapter we will see an example that makes use of PHP's regular expression functionality to test the validity of an e-mail address. We will be looking at PHP functions that work with regular expressions in the second half of this chapter.

## Strings

As a recap, a string refers to a sequence of characters, stored in computer memory, and can be accessed only in its entirety. In PHP a string is represented and accessed with a variable or by an explicit declaration. When a variable contains a string, it is of type `string`.

### Strings Recap

As we discussed in *Chapter 1*, the easiest way to create a string is by using an explicit declaration of the kind:

```php
$newString = "This sequence is a string";
$secondString = 'This sequence is also a string';
```

The second way to create a string is by using other strings and performing an operation that will create a brand-new string. The most used operation to handle strings is **concatenation**. This operation takes two strings and produces a new one that is the first string with the second appended to it. The concatenation of two strings is made with the " . " operator.

The third way to create strings is by using functions that will return them. PHP comes with a huge number of functions that will return strings and you can also define them yourself. The following example shows you the concept of creating a string from a function's returned value:

```
$theString = join("<br>",array(These','strings','will','be','concatenated'));
```

This example uses the `join()` function. It takes two arguments and returns a newly created string. This way, the variable `$theString` contains now a string that is:

*These<br>strings<br>will<br>be<br>concatenated.*

## Using Variables in Strings

String parsing is the concept of constructing a new string from an existing string that contains variables embedded in it. It is one of the features that makes PHP such a powerful and widespread language. This means that when a string is specified with double quotes, variables within the string are replaced by their value. If we specify the string with single quotes, the variables are not parsed.

The general syntax of string parsing is the following: if a $ sign is encountered in the string, the PHP parser will greedily take as many tokens as possible to form a valid variable name. Then the value of this variable is replaced within the string.

To use the complex syntax, you have to use curly braces. If a '{' character is encountered in the string and is immediately followed by a '$' character, the PHP parser will parse your string with the complex syntax, which allows you to use more complex arrays within strings.

# Operation on Strings

We have already seen the two most basic operations on strings: creation and concatenation. We'll now look at different functions that you can use to perform operations on strings. We'll look at a series of common problems, and present popular solutions for them.

## Slicing, Splitting, and Stripping Strings

You will often find yourself handling strings that are either too long, or you only require a particular part of the string, in which case you will need to be able to manipulate it. PHP has several functions that allow you to do this, making it easier for you to design better and more elegant algorithms.

To slice a string into smaller ones, you first need to know which part of the string indicates boundaries between the new ones.

## Slicing with a Substring

As introduced in *Chapter 2*, the easiest way to slice with a substring is to use the `explode()` function. This function takes two arguments: the separator, and the string you want to slice. It returns an array containing all parts of the first one without the separator. A third, optional, argument tells `explode()` to stop slicing after having found a specific number of occurrences in the string. The last element of the returned array is the rest of the string. If the separator string is an empty string, the `explode()` function will return `False`. If the separator string cannot be found in the main string, it will still return an array, but containing only the whole string.

## Slicing String Borders

Sometimes you may want to remove blank characters that surround a string. There are three functions that may help you doing that in PHP: `trim()`, `ltrim()` and `rtrim()`.

The `trim()` function removes the blank characters at the beginning and the end of a string, while `ltrim()` and `rtrim()` remove the blank character at the beginning and the end of the given string respectively. For example:

```
$myVariable=trim("   Some Text Here   ")
```

would set `$myVariable` to `"Some Text Here"`. Each of these functions also takes a second, optional, argument that allows you to specify which characters you want to remove from the surrounding of your string.

If you don't specify any list of characters, PHP will remove any of the following 'blank' characters:

- " " (ASCII 32 (0x20)), an ordinary space.
- "\t" (ASCII 9 (0x09)), a tab.
- "\n" (ASCII 10 (0x0A)), a newline (line feed).
- "\r" (ASCII 13 (0x0D)), a carriage return.
- "\0" (ASCII 0 (0x00)), the Null-byte.
- "\x0B" (ASCII 11 (0x0B)), a vertical tab.

The trim functions are very helpful when storing the input received from a user. Sometimes, the user may have typed a blank character or an extra carriage return which might affect operations where you compare the values entered with something very precise.

## Stream Slicing

Another interesting way of slicing strings is to build a stream of tokens from the natural string. The tokens are defined from a list of characters that you specify. The function that does that is called `strtok()`. This function takes a starting string and a list of characters that will specify the beginning of the new token, and it returns the substring that extends from the first character in the string to the first instance of any character in the delimiter list you specified. Further calls to `strtok()` without a starting string return the next substring from the end of the last token to the beginning of the next.

The function has the following syntax:

```
string strtok(string $completeString, string $charlist);
string strtok(string $charlist);
```

The following example illustrates how strtok() would typically be used. We want to tokenize the $completeString into smaller strings. A token is separated from the following one by either a space character or a newline:

```
$completeString = "/usr/local/apache/htdocs/test.php";

$tok = strtok($completeString,"/");
while ($tok) {
    echo "Path=$tok<br>";
    $tok = strtok("/");
}
```

Execution of this piece of code will produce the following result:

```
Path=usr
Path=local
Path=apache
Path=htdocs
Path=test.php
```

Notice that only the first call to strtok() needs the $completeString variable to be specified. Each subsequent call to strtok() will continue to slice the string in smaller strings.

The interesting thing about this function, is that you can easily and elegantly design your code to parse the content of a very long string. For example, parsing the full content of a mail, with headers and attachment, could be very nicely done by using this function.

## Changing the Case of a String

PHP allows you to manipulate the case of strings; it uses the following functions for this:

- ucfirst(): Sets the first letter of a string to uppercase
- ucwords(): Sets the first letter of all words in a string to uppercase
- strtolower(): Changes all uppercase of a string to lowercase
- strtoupper(): Changes all lowercase of a string to uppercase

In the case of the ucfirst() and ucwords() functions, a word is defined as a group of characters separated by any blank character (space, carriage return, line feed, or tabulation). For example:

```
$str="the words of this string are lowercase";
echo ucfirst($str) . '<BR>';
echo ucwords($str);
```

This will produce:

*The words of this string are lowercase*
*The Words Of This String Are Lowercase*

On the other hand, strtolower() and strtoupper() change the case of the whole string to either lowercase or uppercase. It does not reverse the case of your string. If you want to lower the case of a string that contains both uppercase and lowercase, strtolower() will return the string with all characters being lowercase. strtoupper() does the same but with uppercase. For example:

```
$str="The Words Of This String Are Mixed ";
echo strtolower($str) . '<BR>';
echo strtoupper($str);
```

would give the following output:

*the words of this string are mixed*
*THE WORDS OF THIS STRING ARE MIXED*

When you want to compare two strings, the comparison will normally be case-sensitive. By using these functions on both ends of the comparison you ensure that the comparison is case-*insensitive*. Note that there are functions for comparing two strings that are not case-sensitive, which we will review in the following section.

## Searching and Comparing String

PHP has many functions that provide ways to search, replace, and compare strings.

### Replacing a Character with a String

str_replace() provides basic functionality to replace a specific part of a string with another one. It follows this syntax:

```
mixed str_replace ( mixed search, mixed replace, mixed subject )
```

In the following example, we want to substitute every occurrence of the 'a' character by the string 'XYZ':

```
$str = "Does this string contain the a character?";
echo str_replace("a","XYZ",$str);
```

will produce:

*Does this string contXYZin the XYZ chXYZrXYZcter?*

Later on in this chapter we will be looking at regular expressions that can also be used for this type of operation.

*Note that the mixed type used to describe the str_replace() format is not a specified variable type in PHP. It means that it can be a different type of variable, generally depending upon the arguments that the function receives. If you send arrays to the function, it will return an array. If you use strings only, it will return a string.*

### Replacing Part of a String

`substr_replace()` takes a given string, a replacement string, a start position, and, optionally, an end position. It does not search for an occurrence, all it does is take a string, remove the computed substring with the given position, and insert the replacement string. If the start position is negative, the position of the replaced string is reversed and starts from the end of the given string.

```
string substr_replace ( string completeString, string replacement, int start [, int
length] )
```

Here are some examples of its usage:

```
$str = "Does this string contain the a character?";
echo substr_replace($str,"XYZ",0), '<br>';
echo substr_replace($str,"XYZ",-5), '<br>';
echo substr_replace($str,"XYZ",0,4), '<br>';
echo substr_replace($str,"XYZ",-1,4), '<br>';
```

which will produce:

*XYZ*
*Does this string contain the a charaXYZ*
*XYZ this string contain the a character?*
*Does this string contain the a characterXYZ*

### Comparing Strings

There are six functions that provide a convenient way to compare two strings. They all differ in the way they compare the given strings, but they all return the result in a similar way.

> *You can easily remember the way they compare the string by their name. Here is the convention: if the name contains an 'n' it means that you can specify an amount of characters that you want to compare. If the name contains 'case', it means that the comparison is done case-insensitive. If the function's name contains a 'nat' it means that the natural order is used.*

Here are the functions and the format in which they are used. As you can see, these functions have very similar declarations:

```
int strcmp ( string str1, string str2 )
int strncmp ( string str1, string str2, int len )
int strcasecmp ( string str1, string str2 )
int strncasecmp ( string str1, string str2, int len )
int strnatcmp ( string str1, string str2 )
int strnatcasecmp ( string str1, string str2 )
```

The returned value is an integer that gives information on how the comparison has been done. If the returned value is 0, then the strings are comparatively equal. That doesn't mean they are the same variable, but that the function doesn't see any difference in the two strings. If the result is less than 0, then `str1` is less than `str2`. If the result is greater than 0, then `str1` is greater than `str2`.

What does that mean? A string is said to be less than another one, if on a hypothetical ordered list of these strings, the first string is situated above the second one. In the same way, a string is said to be greater than another one, if on the list it appears below.

For example, if we order the string "bruno" and the string "tim", "bruno" would appear before "tim" on the list, then "bruno" is less than "tim". The following code illustrates this concept:

```
echo strcmp("bruno","tim");
```

will produce:

*-1*

The function strncmp() allows you to test only the *n* first characters of the strings. If the len value is greater than the length of any of the strings, then the len value automatically becomes the size of this string. The following example shows you how you can use the limit in strncmp():

```
$header="Content-Type: image/gif; filename=img0.gif";
$ctype="Content-Type: image/gif";
```

You may now want to compare only the content type of the $header value, without caring about the filename. All you would have to do is:

```
if(!strncmp($header,$ctype,0)){
        echo "The strings have the same value";
}
else{
        echo "The strings are different";
}
```

Executing this code will produce:

*The strings have the same value*

Because you specified 0 as the len value, the matching has been tested against the value of the shorter string, "Content-Type: image/gif", only.

The functions strcasecmp() and strncasecmp() work exactly like strcmp() and strncmp(), with the difference that the comparison is case-insensitive.

The functions strnatcmp() and strnatcasecmp() work a bit differently, but are extremely helpful in some situations. The difference is that the comparison is done using the "natural order" algorithm. The natural order means that it is supposed to represent the way humans would order the list we mentioned above. Let's suppose we have an array of the following value:

```
$arr=array(1,2,3,10,11,12,20,21,22,23,30);
```

This array is naturally ordered in that it is numerically ordered. Now if we want to use the usual `strcmp()` function to order this array we would get:

```
1,10,11,12,2,20,21,22,23,3,30
```

This happens because, when talking about this string, 12 is less than 2! It doesn't sound natural, does it? Now if we use a natural order comparison algorithm, we get the correct array.

To demonstrate the concept, execute the following code:

```
$arr1 = $arr2 =array(1,2,11,12,3,20,21,22,10,23,30);
usort($arr1,"strcmp");
usort($arr2,"strnatcmp");

for($i=0;$i<count($arr1);$i++){
        echo "$arr1[$i] <-> $arr2[$i]<br>";
}
```

The function `usort()` takes a comparison function to execute the ordering of the array. Therefore you can easily see the difference between a computational order and the natural order. The output will be:

```
1 <-> 1
10 <-> 2
11 <-> 3
12 <-> 10
2 <-> 11
20 <-> 12
21 <-> 20
22 <-> 21
23 <-> 22
3 <-> 23
30 <-> 30
```

So, if you have to compare strings and if you care about this peculiarity, don't forget to use the 'nat'ural functions.

### Getting the First or Last Occurrence

`strstr()`, `stristr()`, `strrchr()` provide an elegant way to scan a string and find a particular occurrence in the string: the first or the last one.

This has lots of useful applications, for example often, when handling files, you will be presented with a full path name from which you want to extract the filename only. Here is an example on how to find the name of a file, when given its full path:

```
$path="/usr/local/apache/htdocs/index.html";
echo strrchr($path,"/");
```

will produce:

*/index.html*

The function used was `strrchr()` as this function returns the part of the string that starts at the last occurrence of the forward-slash character.

Here are the prototypes of the functions:

```
string strstr ( string completeString, string subject )
string stristr ( string completeString, string subject )
string strrchr ( string completeString, string subect )
```

The `stristr()` function performs the same operation as `strrchr()` but the search not case-sensitive.

### Finding the Position of a Substring

`strpos()` and `strrpos()` work almost the same way as the previous functions, but instead of returning a part of the given string, they will return its position. They use the following format:

```
int strpos ( string completeString, string subject [, int offset] )
int strrpos ( string completeString, char subject)
```

`strpos()` will return the position of the first occurrence of `subject` in a complete string, while `strrpos()` will return the position of the last occurrence.

There is still a little variation on `strpos()`: you can specify an offset from which the search should begin. The returned position, though, is still relative to the full string. Here's an example:

```
$path="/usr/local/apache/htdocs/index.html";
echo strpos($path,"apache"), '<br>';
echo strpos($path,"apache",5), '<br>';
```

which produces:

*11*
*11*

The returned value is the same even though the second search began at the fifth position, because the position of the 'a' of 'apache' is still at the eleventh position.

### Counting Occurrences of a String

The function `substr_count()` returns the number of times a substring can be found in a string. It has the following form:

```
int substr_count ( string completeString, string subject )
```

Here is an example of usage:

```
$path="/usr/local/apache/htdocs/index.html";
echo substr_count($path,"/");
```

will produce:

*5*

## HTML Specific String Functions

Now that we've looked at the generic string functions, we'll move on to the functions that deal with HTML code and URL parsing. These are particularly useful when turning your strings into pages for the Web.

### Changing Newlines to <br> Tags

This function is probably one of the most frequently used. It is quite simple, but extremely helpful. It inserts `<br>` before all the `\n` characters (whenever a newline is started), in a given string. It is extremely useful for sending long text that comes from a database to an HTML document, or turning user input from a form into HTML.

To illustrate how this function is used, suppose that you want to print the content of a textarea input. When the user will enter his text, he will most likely use the '*enter*' key. When you'll receive this content, your string will have the `\n` character in the places the user has entered the '*return*' key. If you print the text straight to the browser, the `\n` characters will not be printed as a newline. In HTML you have to add `<br>` to create a newline.

Suppose that the textarea is named '`mytext`'. To print it on the browser you can use the following code:

```php
<?php
        echo nl2br($_REQUEST['mytext']);
?>
```

This will output the text with all the newlines converted to <br> tags.

### Dealing with Special Characters

The `htmlspecialchars()` and `htmlentities()` functions are there to help translate an original HTML string into the HTML-encoded format. When you want to output a string to a page that is supposed to be rendered by a browser, you have to be aware that your string may already contain some HTML-specific characters like "<" or "&"; these functions convert these characters into valid HTML.

```
string htmlspecialchars ( string string [, int quote_style [, string charset]] )
string htmlentities ( string string [, int quote_style [, string charset]] )
```

The following table shows how `htmlspecialchars()` translates HTML-specific characters:

| Character | HTML | Encoding |
|-----------|------|----------|
| Ampersand | & | &amp; |
| Double quote | " | &quot; |
| Single quote | ' | &#039; |
| Less than | < | &lt; |
| Greater than | > | &gt; |

The `htmlentities()` function has broader scope than `htmlspecialchars()`; while `htmlspecialchars()` is limited to the above table of characters, `htmlentities()` can translate every character that has an HTML equivalent.

The third argument of each function specifies the character set used in conversion. The default character set is ISO-8859-1, Western European.

The following example illustrates the difference between these two functions:

```php
<?php
$string = "This character é is an accentuated character";
echo "Specialchars :".htmlspecialchars($string)."<br>\n";
echo "Entities :".htmlentities($string);
?>
```

This will produce two lines containing the same string, except for the name of the function. But if you *view source*, you'll see the difference:

```
Specialchars :This character é is an accentuated character<br>
Entities :This character &eacute; is an accentuated character
```

In the first call, `htmlspecialchars()` has not translated the character 'é' but `htmlentities()` has.

You'll notice that there is an optional argument called `quote_style` that tells the function whether to translate the single quote or not. The possible values for this argument are the constants: ENT_NOQUOTES and ENT_QUOTES. Here's an example:

```php
$str="<font color=\"#0000FF\"><b>This text is blue bold</b></font>";
echo htmlentities($str);
```

which will produce:

```
&lt;font color=&quot;#0000FF&quot;&gt;&lt;b&gt;This text is blue
bold&lt;/b&gt;&lt;/font&gt;<br>
```

which will be rendered as an HTML text inside your browser's page, and won't get parsed.

## Url Encoding and Decoding

These functions allow you to turn a string into its URL-encoded counterpart. The difference between the 'raw' function and 'normal' function is that the 'raw' function will use a slightly different encoding, defined in the RFC 1738. They take the following format:

```
string urlencode ( string str )
string urldecode ( string str )
string rawurlencode ( string str )
string rawurldecode ( string str )
```

The `urldecode()` function reverses the encoding to their normal value. Here is an example illustrating how we could encode a string:

```
$arr = array('userID' => '10', 'name' => 'glasshaus & Co', 'company' => 'glasshaus
publishing');
$str="";

foreach($arr as $key=>$value){
        $str.="&$key=".rawurlencode($value);
}

echo $str;
```

will produce:

*&userID=10&name=glasshaus%20%26%20Co&company=glasshaus%20publishing*

where, as you can see, the character & and the spaces have been protected by being replaced with
a percentage sign and its hexadecimal value.

### Splitting a URL

The function `parse_url()` parses a complete URL and returns an array containing information
about the various components of the URL. The associative array returned has the following indexes:

- scheme, or protocol – for example, HTTP

- host

- port

- user

- pass

- path

- query – after the question mark ?

- fragment – after the hashmark #

Note that if a component is not explicitly defined, the index will not be included in the returned array.
Here's an example of how it is used:

```
$url="http://bruno:PASSWORD@www.glasshaus.com:8080/bookInfo.asp?token=180541ZWVtXY32y
XL0YiyWVNhq&bookId=61";
$arr = parse_url($url);
foreach($arr as $key=>$value){
        echo "$key => $value<br>";
}
```

which will produce:

*scheme => http*
*host => www.glasshaus.com*
*port => 8080*
*user => bruno*
*pass => PASSWORD*
*path => /bookInfo.asp*
*query => token=180541ZWVtXY32yXL0YiyWVNhq&bookId=61*

# Regular Expressions

In this section, we will analyze the PERL-compatible regular expression functions of PHP. There is another syntax, which comes from POSIX, but the PERL syntax is also the one used by JavaScript and in the Dreamweaver MX *Find and Replace* tool, and is generally considered faster, so we will only review this one.

**Regular expressions** define a syntax and then perform matching operations on a specified source string to check whether the string conforms to the syntax. Using regular expressions you can also perform replacement operations on part or all of the string. As we will see later, you can use them for data validation such as checking the validity of an e-mail address.

Here is the PHP definition of a regular expression:

More practically, a regular expression is a string that represents a language definition. Which means that it acts as an engine to verify if a given string corresponds to a set of syntactic rules.

*A regular expression is a pattern that is matched against a subject string from left to right.*

Say for example, that we wanted to test a string to see that it conformed to a particular set of rules; we could easily do this with a regular expression. The first step would be to clearly define what rules we want the string to conform to, so let's do this:

- In our example language, all words in the string must contain the letters 'a' and 'b' only

- We will not allow a word to have two 'a's consecutively or two 'b's

- A word should not begin with the letter 'b'

- A word cannot end with the letter 'a'

- Two words are separated by one, and only one, space character

- A sentence is a set of words, and there is no limit to the number of words in a sentence

- The language is made of sentences

The next step now is to define a regular expression that provides a description of the language we have defined above. Then, with this description, we must be able to check if a sentence follows the rules that we defined.

Now, let's have two strings and see if they respect the rules we have defined above:

1 ababab abab ab ab

2 abbaaab bbaab aaba

The second sentence doesn't conform to our rules, because we have two 'b's just after the first 'a', which breaks the second rule of the definition. Now we want a system to describe programmatically the rules we have written to perform a matching process against any given string. In this example we won't be defining all the operations we can do with regular expressions, but it will give you a quick insight into how to define them.

In our example syntax we can only have sets of the sequence 'ab'. Therefore, we have the start of our regular expression:

```
ab
```

When the regular expression analyzer encounters a string that is exactly 'ab', it will match this pattern. We are not limited to the number of sequential occurrences of 'ab', so we will add a meta-character that will tell the computer that the sequence 'ab' can appear multiple times:

```
(ab)+
```

Note that the '+' sign tells that at least one occurrence must match, but there can be more, in other words, the + sign makes what precedes it mandatory. The parentheses make the '+' sign apply to both letters, 'a' and 'b'. Without parentheses, the '+' would have been applied only to the 'b'. Here we have defined a word.

Now, a word must be separated by one and only one space character. We will now include this rule in the regular expression:

```
((ab)+\s)*(ab)+
```

This is now a bit more complicated, but it will become clear in a moment. The meta-character \s describes any space character, except for the newline character ('\n'), and the meta-character '*' tells the analyzer that the sequence immediately preceding the sign can be matched zero or any number of times.

So we have defined the regular expression to look for a word, directly followed by a space (which can be found zero or more times), then at least one word must be found at the end.

The following diagram shows an example of the matching:

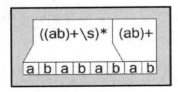

On the diagram you can see that the last section matches the last word.

In the following figures, you can see how the matching is affected by reducing the occurrences of the 'ab' sequence. In the end, when there is only one 'ab' in the string, the sequence ((ab)+\s)* does not match, but that's still fine, because we used the * operator which says it can match *zero or multiple times*, in other words, the * operator makes what precedes it optional:

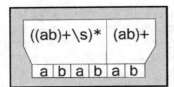
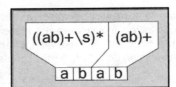
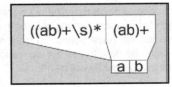

One of our rules says that the language is made of sentences. As we already have the definition for a sentence (a set of words), then it means that we don't want anything else. To complete the regular expression, we will fix the borders:

```
^((ab)+\s)*(ab)+$
```

The ^ sign matches the beginning of the string if placed exactly at the beginning of the regular expression while the $ sign is used at the very end of the regular expression.

In PHP a regular expression is a string delimited by the exact same character. The pattern is considered to be inside these two identical characters. For example, the above regular expression could be defined this way:

```
$regexp="/^((ab)+\s)*(ab)+$/";
```

Now, let's try to test our regular expression against the two sentences given at the start of the section:

```php
<?php
        $str1="ababab abab ab ab";
        $str2="abbaaab bbaab aaba";

        $regexp="/^((ab)+\s)*(ab)+$/";

        if(preg_match($regexp,$str1)){
                echo "$str1 : The string is valid";
        }
        else{
                echo "$str1 : The string is invalid";
        }
        echo "<br>";
        if(preg_match($regexp,$str2)){
                echo "$str2 : The string is valid";
        }
        else{
                echo "$str2 : The string is invalid";
        }
?>
```

will produce:

*ababab abab ab ab :The string is valid*
*abbaaab bbaab aaba :The string is invalid*

So, we have successfully built a pattern that matched correctly our test sentences, but how can we be sure it will match correctly all possible sentences that respect the rules we defined? Well, we can be sure of that, because when we designed the regular expression, we built it by translating exactly those rules into the regular expression. Therefore, if a test sentence matches the rules, it will match the regular expression and vice versa.

*In the real world, it might not always be so straightforward to create the appropriate regular expression to define the syntactic rules you want. Regular expressions can be very powerful, but they should be designed with care and be thoroughly tested before being deployed.*

**Strings and Regular Expressions**

## Syntax and Rules

We will now take a closer look at the syntax and rules we have very briefly introduced above.

## A Character Matches Itself

This is the first rule for constructing a regular expression. Apart from certain special characters, each character matches itself. For example: /a/ will match all strings containing the character 'a'.

The second rule is that the matching begins from the left side of the expression and works its way to the right. This means that, once the analyzer has matched a character or a sub-pattern, it immediately goes to the next character and tries to match it. This means, for example, that the expression /ab/ will match all strings that have the character 'a' with 'b' directly following. But note that it won't match a string that has the character 'a' with the character 'b' somewhere else in the string.

There are also special characters and non-typable characters, represented as follows:

| Character | Meaning |
|-----------|---------|
| \t | The Tab character |
| \n | The newline character |
| \r | The carriage return character |
| \w | Any word character. A word character is any digit, any letter and the underscore character |
| \x*dd* | A character with its hexadecimal code is '*dd*'. |

## Quantifiers

It is possible to specify the number of occurrences of a character or sub-pattern that must or can match.

- *: Means that the preceding sub-pattern can be matched zero or more times

- + : Means that the preceding sub-pattern can be matched one or more times

- ? : Means that the preceding sub-pattern can exist once or not at all, but not more than once

- {n,m} : Means that the preceding sub-pattern must be present at least *n* times but no more than m times

*Note that in the last quantifier, the m value is optional. {0,} is equivalent to *, {1,} is equivalent to +. {0,1} is equivalent to ?. When the ',' is not specified, it is the exact number of the match. For example, if we want to match exactly 3 'a's consecutively, we could either use /aaa/ or /a{3}/.*

## Sub-Patterns and Character Classes

You can define a sub-pattern by surrounding it with parentheses (). In the introductory example, we had `(ab)+`. This pattern means that the sequence 'ab' can be repeated any number of times, but there must be at least one sequence of 'ab'.

The parentheses can be used recursively. We used the following pattern to match a sequence of words:

```
/((ab)+\s)*/
```

This pattern means that words are separated by a space, represented by `\s`. The number of words in this case is 0 or more to match. That's why we added the second word. This way we are sure that there is at least one word. Then why not just use `/((ab)+\s)+/` instead? Because then we would always need a mandatory final space character to match, which is not what we want according to the rules we defined.

> *The term 'sub-pattern' will be widely used in the section about pattern matching; a sub-pattern is a section of the regular expression enclosed in parenthesis.*

It is possible to define a series of characters that can match, independently of their position. This is called a **character class**. The syntax used to define character class is `[list-of-chars]`. For example if we want to match a string that has at least one vowel, no matter which one it is, then we can use the following pattern:

```
/[aeiou]/
```

You can negate the content of the character class by using the syntax `[^list-of-chars]`. If we want to match a string that has at least one character that is not a vowel, then you should use the following pattern:

```
/[^aeiou]/
```

## Pattern Anchors

There are two characters that are very important: the `^` and the `$`. They are **pattern anchors** that attach to the beginning and the end, respectively, of the string. Though, they have this meaning if, and only if, they are positioned at the beginning and ending of the pattern.

> *Previously, we mentioned that the '^' character can be used to negate a character class, this is the case only if it is placed as the first character of the character class. If used anywhere else within the regular expression, it will match itself, and if it is at the beginning of the expression it acts as a pattern anchor.*

## Using a Regular Expression in PHP

Now, it is time to review how to use all that theory we reviewed in the above section.

## Pattern Matching

Pattern matching is the primary purpose of regular expressions. Once you have matched a string or a region of a string, you can perform operations like substitution or splitting. But sometimes all you want to know is if a string matches a pattern. We will see later on how we can use this feature of regular expressions to validate e-mail addresses.

### preg_match()

The function designed to match patterns is called `preg_match()`. We've used this function already in the example above, it follows this format:

```
int preg_match ( string pattern, string subject [, array matches [, int flags]] )
```

The `preg_match()` function takes the regular expression and the subject string as arguments. It returns the number of times the pattern matched the string. If the subject doesn't match, it will return 0. So you can easily design code having the following structure:

```
If(preg_match("/.../",$string)){
        // The string matches at least once
}
else{
        // The string doesn't match
}
```

If there is a sub-pattern in the regular expression, you can capture it in an array. The first optional argument is a reference to an array that will receive the captured sub-pattern, (see *Sub-patterns and Character Classes*). The first value of this array will be the global string that has matched the pattern. Here is an example:

```
$str="<img name='img1' src='/images/img1.gif' border='1'>";

if(preg_match("/<img\s+(.*)\s*>/",$str,$matches)){
        print_r($matches);
}
```

will produce:

```
Array
(
    [0] => <img name='img1' src='/images/img1.gif' border='1'>
    [1] => name='img1' src='/images/img1.gif' border='1'
)
```

in the sourcecode of the page of the browser.

*You don't need to initialize the $matches array, because PHP will do it for you automatically.*

The value of `$matches[0]` is equal to the whole string, because the whole string matches the pattern. The captured sub-pattern, `$matches[1]`, has the value of the attribute of the image in our example string.

### preg_match_all()

The function `preg_match_all()` operates exactly like `preg_match()`, except that instead of stopping after the first matching, it will go on and test the pattern against the whole string, therefore returning all occurrences found in a string.

Here is a example showing the difference between `preg_match()` and `preg_match_all()`:

```
$str="This is a string";
preg_match("/(\w+)/",$str,$matches);
preg_match_all("/(\w+)/",$str,$allmatches);

print "-> preg_match()\n";
print_r($matches);
print "-> preg_match_all()\n";
print_r($allmatches);
```

will produce the following in the source of the browser:

```
-> preg_match()
Array
(
    [0] => This
    [1] => This
)
-> preg_match_all()
Array
(
    [0] => Array
        (
            [0] => This
            [1] => is
            [2] => a
            [3] => string
        )

    [1] => Array
        (
            [0] => This
            [1] => is
            [2] => a
            [3] => string
        )

)
```

In this example, you can clearly see that `preg_match()` has matched the first word, whereas `preg_match_all()` has captured all the words in the string. We now know enough about regular expressions to look at a real-world application of them.

## Validating an E-Mail Address

The basic form of an e-mail is *someone@mailserver.com*, however this is not the only type of valid e-mail address, there are several valid forms which we've listed below:

- someone@mailserver.com

- someone@mailserver.ca

- someone@mailserver.co.uk

- someone@mailserver.org.uk

- someone@mailserver.win.net
- aomeone.something@mailserver.com
- someone@subdomain.mailserver.com
- someone.something@subdomain.mailserver.com

To test an e-mail is valid we can use the following code:

```php
<?php
        $email="bruno@glasshaus.com";
        $regexp = "/^\w(\.?[\w-])*@\w(\.?[-\w])*\.[a-z]{2,4}$/i";
if(preg_match($regexp, $email)) {

            echo "The e-mail is valid";

} else {

    echo "The e-mail is invalid";

}

?>
```

This is the regular expression we used:

```
/^\w(\.?[\w-])*@\w(\.?[-\w])*\.[a-z]{2,4}$/i
```

Let's deal with the first half of the e-mail address, up to the @ symbol. As we mentioned above, the \w class of characters includes all letters, digits, and the underscore character, so we started the expression with this:

```
\w
```

Following this, a valid e-mail address can have a dot followed by any sequence of \w characters, but not two dots in a row. The expression \.?[\w-] matches any \w or dash character, or a dot followed by any \w or a dash character. The dot is a special character so it should be preceded by a \, and the ? indicates that the symbol following it is optional. The * character means that we are adding 0 or more of the section in brackets:

```
\w(\.?[\w-])*
```

Then we have the compulsory @ symbol, followed by a similar pattern describing the mailserver part of the address:

```
\w(\.?[\w-])*@\w(\.?[\w-])*
```

Now we need to validate the final part of the e-mail, which is a dot followed by two to four letters, but which could be followed by another dot and two to four letters. For this we use a character class containing all the letters of the alphabet, and the {} quantifier to specify that the minimum number of characters is two and the maximum is four:

```
\.[a-z]{2,4}
```

So our expression so far is:

```
\w(\.?[\w-])*@\w(\.?[-\w])*\.[a-z]{2,4}
```

This validates the e-mail, however we still need to check that the e-mail address is the only thing in the string; as the expression is now it will validate a string like !!!me@domain.com!!! as a valid e-mail address. We add the pattern anchors: the ^ character which specifies the beginning of the string, and the $ character which specifies the end. We also need forward slashes to delimit the regular expression:

```
/^\w(\.?[\w-])*@\w(\.?[-\w])*\.[a-z]{2,4}$/i
```

Since e-mail addresses are not case-sensitive, we use the i flag which tells it to ignore case.

The rest of the code is fairly straightforward. We use the preg_match() function to check if the e-mail matches the pattern, and if it does we output some text saying so, otherwise we output an invalid e-mail address error message.

## Match and Replace

Matching a string and replacing it on-the-fly is another important application of regular expressions. With a single line of code you can search and replace portions of a string, that match the regular expression. The code generated is generally very readable and maintainable.

### preg_replace()

The basic function to replace a string with pattern matching is called preg_replace().

Before we describe this function, we need to introduce a new idea related to how we reference the captured sub-pattern. When we have a pattern that has a captured sub-pattern, it is possible to get the value of the sub-pattern by using references of the form $n where n is the *n*th captured sub-pattern. n is starting from 1 and can be as high as 99.

If n is 0, it refers to the global matched string, just like in preg_match(), where the third argument was an array, and the first value of this array was the matched string. For example, in the following expression: /<(.*)>/ we can use $1 to get the content of what is between the character '<' and '>'. Preg_replace() follows this format:

```
mixed preg_replace ( mixed pattern, mixed replacement, mixed subject [, int limit] )
```

The prototype of preg_replace() allows us to perform multiple search and replace operations with one call to the function. In the examples below, we will only focus on the function when all arguments are strings. The behavior of the function is the same when provided with arrays.

Suppose we want to change some old HTML code that uses the name attribute instead of the id attribute in an <img> tag. Furthermore, as this code is pretty old, we can't remember if it has the usual quote characters surrounding the name of the image. We want to replace the old string by a correct one with the attribute id instead of name.

Here is the example string:

```
$str="<img name=\"img1\" src=\"/images/img1.gif\" border='0'>";
```

We need to build a regular expression that is able to capture the attribute name, and its surrounding quotes. Here is the example code:

```
$str="<img name=\"img1\" src=\"/images/img1.gif\" border='0'>";
$idstr=preg_replace("/<img name=['\"]?(\w+)['\"]?/","<img id=\"$1\"",$str);
echo htmlspecialchars($idstr);
```

As you can see in the second argument of `preg_replace()`, we have a string containing the sequence $1. The value of $1 is actually replaced by the content of the captured sub-pattern, in this case : "img1".

The example will produce the following output:

*<img id="img1" src="/images/img1.gif" border='0'>*

which was the effective goal of the regular expression.

**preg_replace_callback()**

The function `preg_replace_callback()` provides an advanced and elegant way of providing your own replacement function. It follows this form:

```
mixed preg_replace_callback ( mixed pattern, mixed callback, mixed subject [, int limit] )
```

with the callback function following this form:

```
string callback(array matches)
```

Note that the function doesn't necessarily have to be called `'callback'`. When using the function `preg_replace_callback()`, the second argument is a string containing the name of the callback function. The callback function must return a string containing the replacement.

As an example, we will take the previous one and see how we can develop the same algorithm, but by using the callback function.

```
function callback($matches){
        return "<img id=\"$matches[1]\"";
}

$str="<img name='img1' src=\"/images/img1.gif\" border='0'>";
echo preg_replace_callback("/<img name=['\"]?(\w+)['\"]?/","callback",$str);
```

will produce the following if you *view source*:

```
<img id="img1" src="/images/img1.gif" border='0'>
```

You may wonder why we have to return the whole string `"<img id=\"$matches[1]\""` and not just the `name` attribute and its matched counterpart? Because the string that matched the regular expression is the whole string, beginning with `"<img ...".` And it is *that* string that is going to be replaced.

To understand this, let's try to modify the callback function as follows:

```
function callback($matches){
       return "";
}

$str="<img name='img1' src=\"/images/img1.gif\" border='0'>";
echo preg_replace_callback("/<img name=['\"]?(\w+)['\"]?/","callback",$str);
```

This code will produce:

*src="/images/img1.gif" border='0'>*

## Splitting Strings

`preg_split()` is the last PHP regular expression function we'll look at. It is extremely helpful to split a string using regular expressions. Suppose we have a string, and we want to get an array made of the words of this string, but we don't know how many spaces separate the words. Instead of trimming each substring, we can use the following call:

```
$str="This is    a string with    a        lot    of    space";
$arr = preg_split("/\s+/",$str);
print_r($arr);
```

will produce:

```
Array
(
    [0] => This
    [1] => is
    [2] => a
    [3] => string
    [4] => with
    [5] => a
    [6] => lot
    [7] => of
    [8] => space
)
```

where all elements of the array have been trimmed.

# Summary

In this chapter, we reviewed functionality PHP provides for handling strings. We reviewed the main operations you can perform on strings such as slicing a string from a substring or trimming the spaces that might surround it. We have seen also a way of getting a stream of tokens taken from a string. After that, we looked at different categories of classic string operations: capitalizing strings, searching and comparing strings, as well as HTML–and URL–specific functions.

The regular expression section of this chapter presented a definition of the regular expression. We have seen how they are constructed and explored a few of their applications. Finally we reviewed the different kind of operations possible on strings by using regular expressions: pattern matching, matching and replacing, and splitting a string from a regular expression.

**Strings and Regular Expressions**

# 6

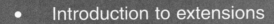

- Introduction to extensions
- Building extensions

**Author: Tim Green**

# Extending Dreamweaver MX

Dreamweaver MX is a very versatile and flexible tool, allowing you to work efficiently, and with very little knowledge about what is actually going on in the background. However, there are limits to what you can achieve with Dreamweaver MX, and these are largely because of the sheer complexity of the different programming languages and technologies that we ask it to cope with.

If you look at all of the web technologies that Dreamweaver MX can recognize: HTML, XHTML, JavaScript, XML, ASP, ASP.NET, Cold Fusion, Java Server Pages, PHP, and more, it soon becomes obvious that what Dreamweaver can do 'out-of-the-box' is really just the tip of the iceberg.

While working through the previous chapters, you will probably have found yourself leaving the confines of the 'nice and friendly' Dreamweaver user interface, and delving into *Code View*. The more that you work on complex projects, the more you will have to do this, as it is impossible for Dreamweaver to encompass all of the functionality that you require of it as standard.

So what's the answer? Do we have to resort to using *Code View* all the time when we're working with something that Dreamweaver doesn't directly support?

The short and simple answer to that question is "No". Dreamweaver MX, like its earlier incarnations, has one further tool up its sleeve, **extensibility**. If you've ever used graphics applications, such as Adobe Photoshop, or Paint Shop Pro, then you will have undoubtedly come across a number of additional extras for these programs, called plugins, that once installed breathe new life, and new functionality, into the software. In Dreamweaver these plugins are called **Extensions**, and they can provide a wide range of additional functionality.

The great thing about Dreamweaver is that you can develop extensions very easily. In fact, there is one major tool that creates extensions for you; all you need to do is to give it the server-side code you want it to use. This tool is called the **Server Behavior Builder**, and we will be taking a closer look at it later in this chapter.

*Throughout this chapter we will mention the configuration folder for Dreamweaver MX. This folder is in the install location of Dreamweaver MX, and is used to store information about Dreamweaver's configuration. On a Windows system with multiple users, you may find some files are stored in* `C:\Documents and Settings\yourusername\Application Data\Macromedia\Dreamweaver MX\`. *On the Mac OS you will find them at* `Macromedia:Dreamweaver MX:Configuration`. *If you are going to alter any files in these folders, it is best to make a backup of them first, just in case anything goes wrong!*

# What Do I Need to Know to Create Extensions?

All extensions for Dreamweaver are built using HTML and JavaScript documents. Yes, that's right. You can extend the capabilities of Dreamweaver by building web pages! You might also need to know a little about XML and Regular Expressions, and as we are going to be focusing on developing extensions for the PHP Server Model, you will also require a rudimentary knowledge of PHP.

The knowledge requirements for building extensions are really dependent on the type and complexity of the extension you want to create. For instance, if you want to build an XML parser in JavaScript that runs within Dreamweaver itself, then you would need an advanced knowledge of JavaScript and a good working knowledge of XML for it to work. On the other hand, if you want to build an object that allows you to insert a predefined anchor tag, then you would only need a rudimentary knowledge of JavaScript and HTML.

## The Dreamweaver MX API

From its earliest beginnings, Dreamweaver has been a versatile tool, and with each new release more and more customization options are made available. These options come via something called the **Dreamweaver API**, or **Application Programming Interface**.

An API is an abstraction interface that allows you to read, store and manipulate information about your environment, without knowing any of the precise mechanics involved in creating this manipulation. If you have already read *Chapter 4*, then this will probably sound very familiar to you. An API is what you create when you define an object class in object oriented programming.

Dreamweaver, from an extensibility point of view, is just another object (albeit a very large and complex one) with pre-defined properties and methods that we can use to create extensions.

Without an API, the only way that we could customize and extend Dreamweaver would be to write programs and utilities in a higher-level programming language like C++. These programs would have to be executed independently, which makes this kind of approach rather clumsy.

Macromedia very cleverly integrated a JavaScript interpreter into Dreamweaver, enabling us to create extensions using languages and technologies that web developers are already familiar with. By following the same syntax rules and the same command set, we can use standard JavaScript code to build on what is already available.

Normally, when working with a web page and using JavaScript there are a few restrictions placed on us for the security and protection of surfers. A typical example is that there is no way to access the hard drive of your visitor's computer. This would ultimately be a huge breach of security, and would be open to abuse from more unsavory characters. However, as Dreamweaver works with files as a part of its core functionality, it was necessary for Macromedia to implement a way to access files from the hard drive.

This is only one example; there are many more examples of this kind of functionality. Essentially, Dreamweaver incorporates a fully featured version of JavaScript that allows us to explore the Dreamweaver Environment to its fullest potential.

Unfortunately, the Dreamweaver API is just far too large to cover fully here. If you want to learn more about the Dreamweaver API, then visit

*http://www.macromedia.com/support/dreamweaver/extend.html*, where the API documentation is available for download.

# Extension Types – A Brief Introduction

Dreamweaver MX is extensible in almost every aspect of its functionality, from menus to objects, from supported tags to server models; it's possible to achieve anything.

In this chapter, we are really going to concentrate on areas of extensibility that will make working with PHP easier and more efficient. However, as there are so many different areas in which Dreamweaver can be extended, it's worthwhile looking at the different types of extensions that are available.

## Behaviors

Behaviors allow you to attach JavaScript code and functions to a particular event, or timeline. They are accessible from the *Behaviors* tab in the *Design Panel*, by clicking on the '+' button you get a context-sensitive menu, where items that cannot be applied are not selectable:

Behaviors are stored in the *Configuration\Behaviors\Actions* folder. Typically they are built using HTML and JavaScript alone.

## Commands

Commands can be accessed via the *Commands* menu in the main Dreamweaver interface. Each menu item typically consists of an HTML file. The entry in the menu takes its name from either the title of the document, or the document's filename. I say 'typically' because commands are a type of extension that are used more widely than you might expect, as they can be executed from any other extension, making them one of the more frequently used and most flexible extensions available.

Another great thing about commands is that there is a command recorder within Dreamweaver that allows you to create your own commands based on your own actions. To use it, open your *Commands* menu, and click on *Start Recording*.

A good example of creating a command extension can be found at:

*http://www.macromedia.com/support/ dreamweaver/extend/creating_simple_cmmd_ext/*

You can also record commands from the *History* Panel.

## Components

Components are new to Dreamweaver MX, and are available in the ASP, ASP.NET, CFML, and JSP Server Models as standard. The default installation of Dreamweaver MX does not provide support for components with PHP.

In the Server Models that support them, they can be accessed via the *Components* tab in the *Application* panel, and generally provide access to web services, or ColdFusion components, and are generally representative of services and code that are hosted on remote servers.

In the previous screenshot, you can see an example of a Shopping Cart component, IntelliCART MX, which is the first custom component especially written for the PHP MySQL Server Model.

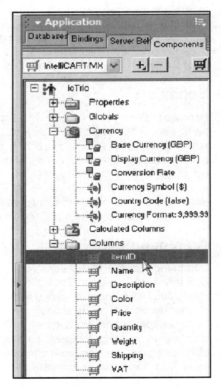

146

## Connections

Connections provide access to different types of databases for different Server Models, and allow you to provide an interface that gathers all of the required information for connecting to that database.

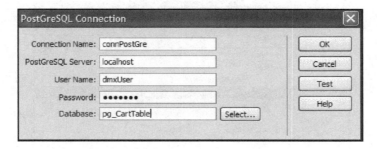

Dreamweaver MX provides the functionality you need to create additional connections. However, whilst connections themselves are fairly easy to develop, in order to be able to use them, you mustalso (under PHP) recreate all of the associated database-related server behaviors that will allow you to put this connection to use.

Creating a new connection is relatively easy and requires a rudimentary knowledge of HTML, JavaScript, XML, and PHP. However, to use a new connection effectively, the additional behaviors needed require a more advanced knowledge of JavaScript and PHP.

## Data Sources or Bindings

Data Sources or Bindings are used to incorporate server-based data into your web pages. A typical example of this is the recordset, which inserts all of the necessary server-side code into your web page, so that you can retrieve information from your database.

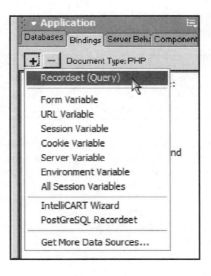

There are different types of data source too, depending on the task that you wish to accomplish. At its simplest level the *Bindings* tab in the *Application* panel allows you to retrieve, display, and keep track of all the cookies, sessions, GET and POST variables used within your site, only adding additional code to your page the moment you want to use them.

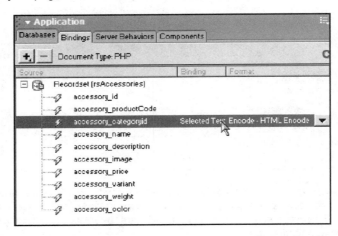

As you can see from the image above, once a data source is created, its various elements are available via a tree-style menu, with additional menus next to each entry that allow you to handle the formatting of the information.

Data sources or bindings are amongst the most difficult of extensions to create, as they usually require additional extensions to work within the Dreamweaver Interface. As a result, to develop new data sources for Dreamweaver MX you need a rudimentary knowledge of HTML, PHP, and XML, and an advanced knowledge of JavaScript.

## Inspectors

Inspectors, or property inspectors to give them their full name, are the context-sensitive panels that you will find at the bottom of the Dreamweaver interface, and the image below shows a typical example of a standard property inspector.

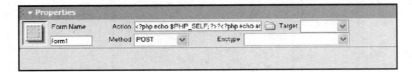

Whilst some of these property inspectors are built directly into Dreamweaver, you can create your own inspectors too, again by using HTML and JavaScript documents. Essentially they are forms, but they do use some special expressions, which are then searched for whenever you highlight an item in the page.

Why would you want to create a new inspector? Well, say there were non-standard properties of a specific object that you wanted to have access to visually, you could create a new inspector which includes these particular properties.

An example of this is the `enctype` attribute of a form that, in earlier versions of Dreamweaver, it was not possible to access visually. You could create a new form inspector that takes precedence over the standard inspector, which includes this attribute.

By and large inspectors are fairly easy to create. As with most of the other extensibility options the more functional you want it to become, the more difficult the creation process is. However, with a rudimentary knowledge of HTML and forms, and a good knowledge of JavaScript, it shouldn't prove too difficult a task.

## Objects

Objects are the elements in the *Insert* Bar, towards the top of the Dreamweaver interface. These typically insert HTML elements directly into your page, which can then be customized later. These elements can range from a single text input field, to a whole login interface.

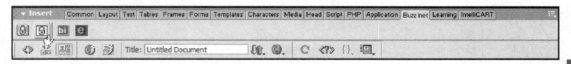

Standard objects tend to only deal with the HTML components that are inserted into your page. As such, they are very easy to create, and require only a rudimentary knowledge of JavaScript and HTML to implement.

Once a new object has been created, it is sufficient to put this object into an existing folder within the `Configuration\Objects` directory for it to become visible within the Dreamweaver interface. If you need to create an additional tab within the *Insert* bar, then you must also edit an XML file called `insertbar.xml`, for that tab to show. This isn't as difficult as it may sound, as this file also defines the other tabs that are used in the *Insert* Bar, and so there are plenty of references within that file to help you on your way. It is advisable to make a backup of `insertbar.xml` before altering it.

For example, you could add a tab called *glasshaus* by adding a directory called `glasshaus` and adding the following code to the `insertbar.xml` file.

```
<category id="DW_Insertbar_Glasshaus" folder="glasshaus">
 </category>
```

If you then wanted to add a button that inserted company-specific copyright information, you would alter the code as follows:

```
<category id="DW_Insertbar_Glasshaus" folder="glasshaus">
<button id="DW_Copy_Info"
        image="glasshaus\info.gif"
        enabled=""
        showIf=""
        file="glasshaus\info.html"/>
</category>
```

You would then place the relevant HTML code in a file called `info.html`, and save it in the folder `glasshaus` along with a GIF image called `info.gif` to act as the button image.

## Floaters or Panels

In earlier versions of Dreamweaver, floaters did exactly that; they floated on your screen, and could be dragged around and placed wherever you wished. Whilst this is still possible in Dreamweaver MX, floaters can now, optionally, be docked to the side. Because of this new functionality they are now more commonly called panels, and if you look at your Dreamweaver interface you have lots of them. The properties panel, application panel, answers panel, insert panel, and code panel to name a few.

As with everything else, Dreamweaver MX even allows you to create your own panels for use. These can be anything from a small window that explores your current document and lists all the form fields found, to a login page for a collaborative environment such as SiteSpring.

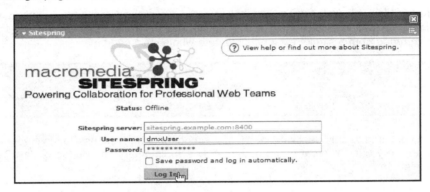

With the release of Dreamweaver MX, it has also become possible to integrate smart Flash applications into a panel that retrieves information from an online database, which can then immediately be inserted into the currently open document.

Panels are generally used for information and reference, though with a little imagination anything is possible! They are not at all difficult to create, and only require a rudimentary knowledge of HTML and JavaScript to get going. What you then decide to do with your new panel is completely up to you.

For example, say we wanted to create a special *glasshaus* panel. First create a file called `glasshausfloat.htm` and save it in the `Configuration\Floaters` folder. Insert the following HTML:

```
<!DOCTYPE HTML SYSTEM "-//Macromedia//DWExtension layout-engine5.0//floater">
<html>
<head>
<title>Glasshaus</title>
<script language="JavaScript">
function isAvailableInCodeView() {
return true;
}
</script>
</head>
<body>
<form name="ghform">
<input type="button" value="Open glasshaus.com"
onClick="dw.browseDocument('http://www.glasshaus.com/')">
</form>
</body>
</html>
```

This creates a floater with a single button, which when clicked opens up *http://www.glasshaus.com* in the default browser. It also tells Dreamweaver that the panel is available in *Code View* as well as *Design View*.

Unfortunately this panel won't appear by default, we need to tell Dreamweaver where to find it. To do this we'll add a button to our *glasshaus* insert bar. Open up `insertbar.xml` again, and add the following code inside our `<category>` tag.

```
<button id="DW_Glasshaus_Panel"
        image="glasshaus\panel.gif"
        enabled=""
        showif=""
        command="dw.toggleFloater('glasshausfloat')" />
```

You will also need to add a GIF image called `panel.gif` to the `Configuration\Objects\glasshaus\` folder you created earlier. This will create a button that toggles the panel on and off.

## Server Behaviors

In the `Configuration\ServerBehaviors` folder you will find a number of subfolders, one for each of the different Server Models, (ASP, PHP, CFML, and so on) that Dreamweaver MX supports.

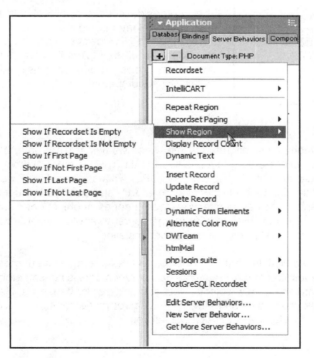

Inside each of these directories you will find any number of HTML, JavaScript, and EDML files.

What are EDML files? EDML (**Extension Definition Markup Language**) is a subset of XML, and is a language that allows Dreamweaver not only to know which server-side code to insert into a page, but it also defines how Dreamweaver can recognize that type of code within a page, and if the behavior is deleted, what elements of the code should be removed from the page. Sounds complicated? Well actually, it isn't. You can create server behaviors using a special tool that comes with Dreamweaver MX, called the **Server Behavior Builder**. This tool handles all of the HTML, JavaScript, and EDML creation for you. It creates the user interface that allows you to change the parameters that are used whenever a behavior is added to the page. Since you can edit these files in Dreamweaver itself, you can create a behavior using the builder and then alter it to your requirements.

Later in this chapter we will take an in-depth look at the server behavior, and show you how you can create your own server behaviors in moments.

## Server Formats

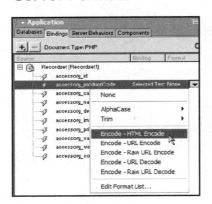

Server formats are a special breed of extension. They are made to combine with any data source and allow you to change the way information from the data source is displayed on the page, by inserting relevant server-side code that transforms the data.

The server-side code element of this is generally not too difficult to implement, and can be done with an intermediate knowledge of PHP. However, server formats themselves can be rather difficult to implement correctly, as they must work with new and existing data sources, and require a high level of JavaScript competency.

## Server Models

The current Server Models implemented within Dreamweaver MX are not the only ones available. There is also another PHP Server Model, called PHAkt (*www.interakt.ro/products/PHAkt*), which is available for free under the Gnu Public License (GPL). This additional PHP Server Model provides additional and slightly different functionality than the standard PHP implementation, as it is database-independent. It uses an abstraction layer, a series of object orientated PHP classes that allow you to easily move your PHP code from one server to another without having to worry about the database system that that particular server has installed.

Dreamweaver MX is so flexible, that it allows you to create additional support for different server-side scripting languages. Of course, creating a new server model is not something to be done lightly; you would need to implement new objects, data sources, server behaviors, inspectors, translators, in fact you would have to create everything for that server model for it to be useful. This is no small task, as Interakt, the developers of PHAkt, will tell you.

## Server Objects

Earlier we talked about objects, and how they typically only inserted the HTML components of a web page. Whilst this is true, server objects are an exception to that rule.

Server objects can be a real boon for the busy web developer, because these objects not only insert the HTML components required on the page, they also add the relevant server behaviors and server-side code necessary to get the most out of these HTML elements.

A good example of this is the **Record Insertion Form** object that inserts all of the fields needed, based on criteria you specify, to insert a record into your database: along with all the PHP code necessary to make that form interact with your database.

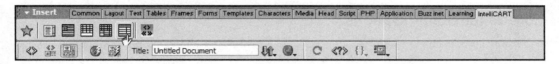

Other server objects allow you to create tables that display all of the data in a recordset, and when working with shopping cart systems, there are also server objects that insert a *view cart* element that allows you to view the contents of a shopping cart, and provide all the necessary functionality to add, amend, or remove items from that cart. All of this available by clicking one icon and completing a simple interface.

## Translators

Translators are a different type of extension. Rather than being accessible in themselves via the Dreamweaver interface, they become a part of the whole Dreamweaver look and feel. Essentially a translator is designed to recognize a specific element of code that is inserted into your web page. Once it finds a piece of code that it recognizes, it can retrieve information about this code, and display it in a more aesthetically pleasing way.

This is highlighted by the image below, taken in the split *Code and Design View*, that shows how a translator immediately recognizes the block of code `<?php echo $row_rsAccessories['accessory_id']; ?>`, and displays this as a highlighted element `{rsAccessories.accessory_id}` in *Design View*:

```
16 <body>
17 <?php echo $row_rsAccessories['accessory_id']; ?><br>
18 <br><br>
19 <?php
20 include_once("simpleEmail.inc.php");
21 // include the class extension
22 // new parameter value
23 $myMail->db = "myContacts";
24 $subject = "Website Update Alert";
25 $myMail->body = "My Site has been updated. Please visit soon!";
26 // Now send the email
27 $myMail->sendToList();
28 ?>
29 </body>
```

{rsAccessories.accessory_id}

The other PHP code in the page does not have a specific translator for it, so instead Dreamweaver places a PHP 'shield', to indicate that at this point in the page there is some PHP code. In fact a translator generates this shield, only this translator is of a more generic nature

There are three ways in which translators can be written: in pure JavaScript, pure EDML, or a combination of both technologies can be used. Typically they can be a little difficult to create, but there are easy ways in which they can be done, using a single EDML file. An example of creating a translator is given in *Chapter 12*.

### More Extensibility Options

In this brief introduction to extension types we've only really covered the more important and better-known ways in which Dreamweaver can be enhanced. You shouldn't at all feel limited by this list, nor should you be put off by the potential complexity of creating an extension. Ultimately, if you are a web developer, you have the skills necessary to easily learn how to extend, enhance, and manipulate the Dreamweaver environment to your own requirements.

There are many more ways in which Dreamweaver MX can be extended. You can create new reference manuals that can be accessed directly via the *Reference* tab in the *Code* panel. You can create your own tag libraries, which recognize specific markup code that you may need to use as a requirement of a particular server-based application. You can even go through all of the menus available within Dreamweaver and add your own options, perhaps creating a *Favorites* menu containing links to your 'must have' web pages. You're limited only by your imagination!

# Extensibility and PHP

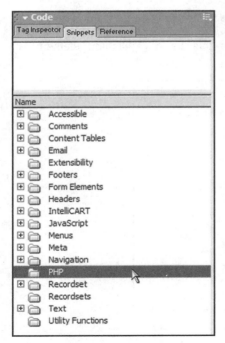

So far in this chapter we've talked about extensibility within Dreamweaver, but we haven't actually gone into any specifics. It's now time to see just how easy some extensions can be implemented. We'll start by looking at the easiest extension type, and probably one of the most useful: snippets.

## Snippets

Snippets can be any combination of server-side code blocks, JavaScript code, or HTML Elements. In fact, anything that can legitimately be put into any type of page within Dreamweaver, can be converted into a snippet. In the majority of cases snippets are created directly from the page itself, as this allows you to work with existing code, or code that you have just typed in. Say for example we have a PHP code block that we wish to convert into a snippet, we could do this quite easily by following a few simple steps.

In the *Snippets* tab of the *Code* panel, select where you want your new snippet to be stored by highlighting an existing folder, or by creating a new folder by right-clicking and selecting the *New Folder* option from the context menu.

Once this has been done, return to the current document. To create a snippet based on an HTML element, select the element in Dreamweaver's window. Alternatively, if you want to create a snippet out of some server-side code or JavaScript, then you will first need to switch to *Code View*, so that the relevant portion of the page is visible. Click and highlight all of the code you wish to be included in the new snippet. Right-click over the highlighted area and in the context menu select *Create New Snippet*.

When the *Snippet* window first opens you will see that the *Snippet Type* is set to *Wrap Selection*, and all of your code is in one of two textarea boxes. The *Wrap Selection* option is useful if you want to make a snippet out of some server-side code that comes before and after an object. To be able to take advantage of this, the original selection must cover the whole area, including the object in the middle. Then, using the *Snippet* editor, you can separate and discard any inappropriate sections of code, and break the code you want to save into its two component parts. These parts can then be placed in the appropriate sections within the *Snippet* editor.

If you are creating a snippet based on a code block, or a single HTML element, click on the radiobutton next to *Insert Block*. This will change the interface, so that all of your highlighted code is inside one large textarea:

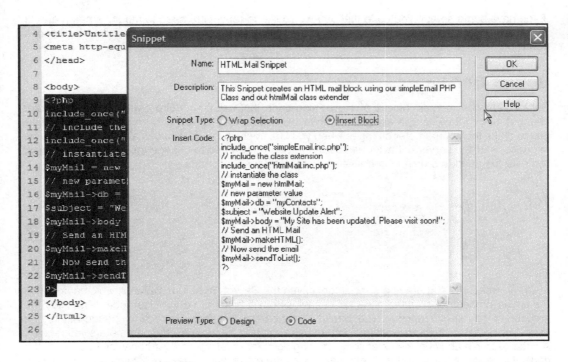

As you can see from the above image, there is space for you to add a name and description for your snippet. It's always a good idea to complete these sections, so that you can more easily identify the snippet at a later date.

The final option in the *Snippet Editor* window is the *Preview Type*. The *Snippets* Panel has an area just above it, where you can preview the currently highlighted snippet. If the snippet is a representation of an HTML element, then you should see the HTML element in its WYSIWYG view. However, this cannot work with server-side code, as it is generally not visible in a web browser. The manner in which a snippet is previewed is controlled by the *Preview Type* setting in each snippet's edit window. The *Preview Type* can be set to either *Design* or *Code*, and this setting should reflect the view that was active in Dreamweaver MX when you created it. However, this setting isn't fixed, and you can change it to whatever you feel is appropriate.

Once you have completed the Snippet Editor interface, all that remains is to click *OK*, and your new snippet is inserted into your pre-selected location. If for any reason the snippet is created in the wrong place within the *Snippets* panel, it can easily be moved by dragging the item to its desired location.

Snippets are a very useful tool, especially if you regularly use specific functions or HTML elements. However, if you need to customize a snippet at any point, then you will need to make these changes by hand, either in code view if it is a piece of scripted code, or by modifying it with the relevant property panels within Dreamweaver if it is a piece of HTML code.

If you have some server-side code that you would like to reuse, but need to modify a parameter or variable name each time you use it, then you have a strong case to turn that code into a server behavior.

## Server Behaviors

Server behaviors contain blocks of server-side code that usually require one or more parameter changes before they can be used. The server behavior presents you with an interface that allows you to make these parameter changes when you first apply the code. You can also access the same interface after the server behavior has been created if you need to change the parameter settings, avoiding the need to switch to *code view* to make the changes manually.

```php
<?php
// Redirect if Recordset Empty
if ($totalRows_rsItem <= 0) {
      header("Location: index.php");
}
?>
```

In Dreamweaver MX, there is a special tool called the **Server Behavior Builder**, which automates the whole process of creating a server behavior from a block of server-side code. It handles the creation of the user interface for you, based on the parameters that you need to change within your code. The first step, then, to creating a server behavior, is to determine what parameters you require. A code example above gives us an ideal starting point for creating a server behavior. Looking at the code, it is relatively easy to identify one parameter, the redirection page. The next parameter is a little more obscure, as it forms part of a variable's name, and is actually the name of a recordset, rsItem. The server behavior builder uses a special syntax to highlight the location of parameters in sourcecode.

## Parameter Syntax

When the server behavior builder is constructing your behavior, it uses the name of each of your parameters as both an internal variable name, and an entry in the user interface. If you have a parameter name that consists of two or more words truncated together, it can appear a little messy when they appear in the user interface. The double underscore is a useful feature, as it tells the server behavior builder to include a space character at that point when creating the user interface.

| Parameter | Displays As |
|---|---|
| @@RecordsetName@@ | *RecordsetName* |
| @@Recordset__Name@@ | *Recordset Name* |

The same parameter can also be used more than once in your code. When you do this, only one entry is created in the user interface for this server behavior, and all of these parameters will be replaced with the same value.

Also, if your code is long, or particularly complex, it is worthwhile marking out all of the parameters that you require before using the server behavior builder, because the builder only provides a limited space, and provides no options to reformat your code. For the purposes of our example, though, we will enter the parameters using tools within the server behavior builder itself.

## The Server Behavior Builder

To access the server behavior builder select the *New Server Behavior* option at the foot of the menu in the *Server Behavior* tab in the *Applications* panel.

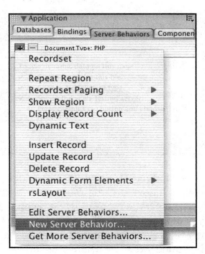

You will then be presented with a window that will ask you to enter a name for your behavior. You are free to call new behaviors whatever you like, as long as the name does not conflict with an existing server behavior, and the name does not exceed 27 characters in length.

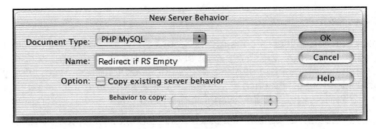

For the purposes of this example, I've given this server behavior an appropriate name. In this same window, there is an additional option *Copy existing server behavior*, which means exactly that. The server behavior builder allows you to create a new server behavior that is based on an existing one. This option allows you to work with the original code of a server behavior and modify it to suit your particular needs, while preserving the code of the original behavior. It should be noted though, that you can only do this with additional server behaviors that have been added to Dreamweaver MX, as the default behaviors are not available to edit in this way.

Once we have decided on a name for our server behavior, we are taken to the main interface of the server behavior builder. Here, our behavior is organized into **code blocks**, which allows us to include portions of code that may be placed in different areas of our web page. We can control the position of these blocks, ensuring that the behavior will work as expected.

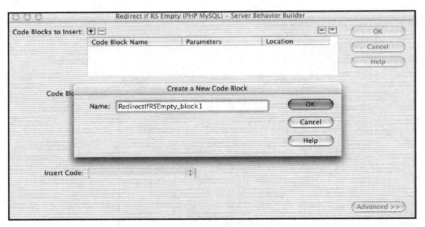

Before we can begin to explore the interface of the server behavior builder, we need to create a new code block. Click once on the + symbol next to *Code Blocks to Insert*, and a pop-up window will ask you for a name for this code block. Each code block must be given a unique name, so it is often best to use some part of your behavior's name in the title. You must also take into account that because of the limitations of the Macintosh filesystem, all names should be less than 27 characters long. This is a restriction that can also be found on PCs when creating server behaviors, allowing cross-platform compatibility for your server behaviors.

Once you have given the code block a new name, click *OK* to return to the server behavior builder.

The main window in the server behavior builder is split into a number of differing sections:

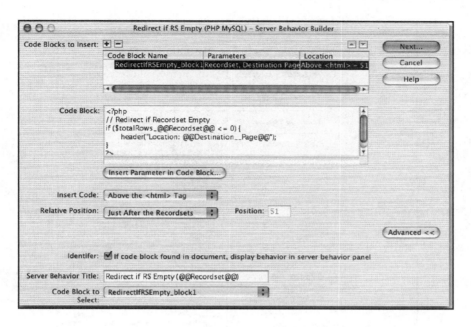

The code block area is at the top of the window, where you can see what code blocks are in your extension, what parameters they contain, and where they will be inserted on the page.

The next section displays a detailed view of the currently selected code block. Here you can type in the code that you wish to use, or if you have the code in another document, you can copy it from there and paste it directly into this window. If you do opt to use this method, any parameters that exist within your code will automatically be recognized by the builder, and will be available for use.

The *Insert Parameter in Code Block...* button, allows us to do exactly that. With our example, if you select the text rsItem, in our original code, and then click this button, you will be asked to enter the name of the parameter you wish to use. When using this method, it is important to know that you do not need to surround the name of your parameter with the @@ markers, as this function will do that for you. Simply enter the name of the parameter: Recordset, and click *OK*, and the selected portion of text is automatically converted into a parameter. You can also see in the code block information, towards the top of the interface, that your code block now has Recordset listed as one of its parameters. Repeat this process now, replacing the text index.php with the parameter name Destination_Page.

Underneath the *Insert Parameter in Code Block...* button, there are two drop-down menus that allow you to control the positioning of the code block on the page. The first menu: *Insert Code*, allows you to decide whether you want the code block to be inserted into the page in a number of different ways. The second menu, *Relative Position*, is a context-sensitive menu, which bases its value on your selection in *Insert Code*.

6

| Insert Code | Relative Position | Code block is inserted ... |
|---|---|---|
| Above the `<html>` tag | The beginning of the file | ... at the very start of the document. |
| | Just before the recordsets | ... just before any recordsets on the page. |
| | Just after the recordsets | ... just after the last recordset on the page. |
| | Just above the `<html>` tag | ... just before the opening `<html>` tag. |
| | Custom position | ... according to a numerical weight. Selecting this option activates a **Position field** where you can give your code block a numerical weight. The higher the number, the closer to the top of the document. Recordsets, for example, have a weight of 50. |
| Below the `</html>` tag | After the `</html>` Tag | ... just after the closing `</html>` tag. |
| | Before the recordset closes | ... just before the closing elements of a recordset. |
| | After the recordset closes | ... just after the closing elements of a recordset. |
| | Before the end of the file | ... at the very end of the document. |
| | Custom position | ... according to a numerical weight. Selecting this option activates a **Position** field where you can give your code block a numerical weight. The higher the number, the closer to the bottom of the document. The closing elements of a recordset, for example, have a weight of 50. |

| Insert Code | Relative Position | Code block is inserted ... |
|---|---|---|
| Relative to a Specific Tag (Selecting this option changes the interface to include a form field called `Tag`. Here you can enter any HTML or XML tag name) | Before the opening tag | ... just before a selected occurrence of the specified opening tag. |
| | After the opening tag | ... just after a selected occurrence of the specified opening tag. |
| | Before the closing tag | ... just before a selected occurrence of the specified closing tag. |
| | After the closing tag | ... just after a selected occurrence of the specified closing tag. |
| | Replace the tag | ... over the selected tag. |
| | As the value of an attribute | ... as the value of an attribute within the selected tag. The interface changes allowing you to specify the attribute that will be given this value. |
| | Inside the opening tag | ... as an additional value within the selected tag, which may not necessarily be an attribute. |
| Relative to the Selection | Before the selection | ... before the selected tag or region. |
| | After the selection | ... after the selected tag or region. |
| | Replace the selection | ... over the selected tag or region, replacing it. |
| | Wrap around the selection | ... before AND after the selected tag or region. This is a special case that requires a complete HTML tag pair in the code block (for example: `<table></table>`) |

In this example, our code will only work once a recordset has been created, so I've chosen the *Just after Recordsets* option of the *Above the <html> tag* insert code for positioning. With this positioning chosen the behavior, when run, will automatically place this code just after the section in the page where the recordsets are generated. If this code were positioned before the recordsets in your document, then the condition would always fail as no recordset has been created, and therefore the total number of rows would be zero.

The server behavior builder interface can be expanded by clicking on the *Advanced* button. This button hides some other settings:

The *Identifier* allows you to specify whether if that code block is found, it will be recognized by Dreamweaver as that server behavior. For the purposes of our example we will leave this checked, but it is important to know that every server behavior requires at least one **Identifier**. The Identifier can be turned off for additional code blocks if necessary, but normally you won't have to do this.

The *Server Behavior Title* can also be modified. Normally it will display the name of your server behavior, followed by brackets that contain a list of all of your parameters. If you have a lot of parameters in your code, then you might need to judiciously edit the contents of these brackets, as the *Server Behaviors* panel cannot display that much information when a behavior is applied. If you have a lot of parameters in your code, many of them may be hidden from view, so it's worth removing them. However, this is purely an aesthetic function.

The *Code Block to Select* menu allows you to determine which code block will be selected when a user clicks on the *Server Behavior* panel entry for this behavior when it is found in a page. This menu is global across the code blocks, so only one selection is permitted here. Generally it doesn't make too much difference which code block you choose to select, but there are general guidelines to follow. First of all, if you are inserting multiple code blocks, you should (under normal circumstances) select the first code block that will be visible in your page. However, if your behavior also incorporates elements that will be visible in *Design View* within Dreamweaver MX, you may decide that these elements will be the best ones to select, as the user can see immediately where the code is located on the page. Again, this is largely an aesthetic option, and it may appear to be only a minor piece of functionality, but it does seem to enhance the user experience. For our purposes, as we have only one code block to insert, it is best to select that code block from this menu.

Once you have completed this interface, you can proceed to the next stage, by clicking *Next*.

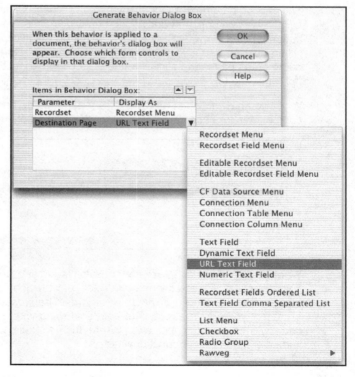

The next stage in creating a server behavior involves the selection of specific user interface elements, that will ultimately save time when applying the behavior. You could of course, just have normal input fields for each behavior you create. However, you would always need to know the names of certain elements from your page, and will have to close the behavior to check what the name of a particular element is. This stage in the process of building a server behavior presents us with a number of choices, so that we can implement a more intuitive server behavior.

First of all, in this window, if you have more than one parameter, you can adjust the position of those parameters in the server dialog that you are creating, using the up and down arrows. When the behavior is created, the positioning of each form element in the new server behavior dialog immediately reflects this order.

You will notice that all parameters default to being displayed as a text field. This can be changed to something a little more intuitive, if required, by selecting the parameter in this window, and then clicking on the down arrow that appears next to *Text Field*. This reveals a menu similar to the previous image, and provides you with a whole list of options. If, for example, your parameter required the name of a recordset on the current page as a value, then you could select the option *Recordset Menu* from the list, and when the finished behavior is opened, you would see a drop-down menu, containing the names of all the recordsets on the page. At the same time, there is a certain amount of validation of data that occurs, for example if you opened this same behavior on a page that didn't contain a recordset, it would tell you that you need a recordset to use the behavior, and then close the window.

It is worth looking through this list of available options, and selecting the most appropriate option for your parameter. In our example, we have two parameters that each require different types of data. The first parameter requires the name of a recordset, so we should use the *Recordset Menu* option. The second parameter requires the name of a page within our current web site, and by selecting the *URL Text Field* option in our server behavior's user interface we will see a text field followed by a button labeled *Browse*. Clicking on this button will allow us to browse through the files and folders within our site and select the page we wish to redirect to. This is great if you don't remember the name of the page, and allows you to select it more intuitively. However, if you do know the name of the page, the text field also allows you to enter the name directly.

When you have finished reordering your parameters, and have selected the relevant user interface components for each parameter, click *OK* and the behavior will be created:

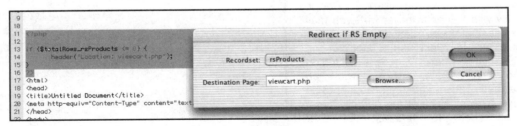

When the *Redirect if RS Empty* behavior is chosen from the *Server Behavior* menu, it will look something like this, and allow you to select any previously created recordset, and allow you to select a page for the redirection. Should no recordset be present on the page, the automatic validation will insist that you create a recordset before allowing you to use the behavior. When you click *OK*, the code will be inserted just after where the recordsets are created on your page, and provide immediate, guaranteed functionality.

## Modifying the Server Behavior

Now that you have built a server behavior you can alter its appearance and functionality by editing the correct files. These files will be stored in Dreamweaver's `Configuration` folder located in `\Configuration\ServerBehaviors\PHP_MySQL\`.

For example, the file `Redirect if RS Empty.htm` contains the user interface of the server behavior we just created. Since it is an HTML file, you can edit it in Dreamweaver, allowing you to customize the interface to your requirements. In order for the changes to take effect you will need to reload extensions by CTRl left clicking on the Menu button to the right of the Insert panel.

## Server Objects

Server objects are much more than just server-side code blocks: they insert all the necessary server-side code and HTML elements to create a fully functional interface within your web pages. This interface can encompass all sorts of functionality, and the standard server objects provide a really good example of this. However, earlier in this chapter I promised to show you an easy way to create server objects, which we will do now, using tools that we already know.

In Dreamweaver UltraDev 4, the forerunner to Dreamweaver MX, there was a Server Behavior Builder, much as is available now. However, it was impossible to combine server-side code elements and HTML page elements in a single code block, as these were considered to be two different elements and areas of the page. However, an undocumented feature of Dreamweaver MX, that has largely been undiscovered, is that this functionality now exists within the Server Behavior Builder. We can now create a single code block containing all the HTML code and server-side code that we need to build a fully functional server object.

To demonstrate this, we're going to take a simple page containing a recordset, a table, and a repeat region behavior, and turn it into a server object. This replicates to some degree functionality already provided by the Dynamic Table Object that is available as a standard Server Object within Dreamweaver MX. However, for this example, we will simplify this object significantly as it provides a good starting point from which you can expand or enhance as required in the future.

## Putting the Page Together

First of all we have to put together a working model of all the functionality that we wish to use within our server object. This involves using Dreamweaver MX and its behaviors to create everything that we are going to use.

To begin with, create a recordset, using an available connection:

Here I have created a recordset that looks at a list of products within a database. It's a simple recordset, as I've opted to retrieve all of the information from the table. In practice you may want to limit the amount of information retrieved based on your own criteria.

Once the recordset has been added to the page, we add an HTML table, and drag some of the columns from the recordset to that table, so that we are directly mixing HTML and PHP elements in a single area:

As you can see from the image above, I have included some basic formatting, though this isn't essential. Normally it is best to keep server objects as simple as possible by not formatting text or other elements. This can all be done once the server object has been inserted into a page, as it is likely that you would want to change elements such as font or background color anyway, to match the site you are designing.

With our table on the page, all that remains is to add our repeat region behavior. We'll add this behavior along the row containing the recordset columns, so that we have a repeating list of items coming from our database. If you wish, you can use a limited recordset so that later, if you needed to, you could add a recordset navigation bar. The navigation bar could be added at this stage, though for the purposes of this example it isn't required. For this example I have chosen to use a repeat region that shows all the rows from the recordset, as a limit repeat region inserts a wealth of other code.

Once you've added the repeat region behavior, it is then time to turn all of this inserted code into a server object. To do this, we start by identifying where the code currently is in our page. If you switch to *Code View*, you will see that there is some code inserted above the `<html>` tab, some has been inserted within the `<body>` tag of the page, and finally, there is a little bit of code after the closing `<html>` tag, at the end of the page.

## Creating the Server Object Code

As we are really only concerned with the main section of code within the `<body>` tags, we will only need one code block for this server object. There is no reason to include the recordset within the server object, because, since the recordset is predefined, it will ultimately limit us. By choosing only the section of code within the `<body>` tag, we can replace all references to recordset names and columns with parameters, which will allow us to reuse this server object with any recordset already inserted onto the page.

The easiest way to turn recordset names and columns into parameters is to change these elements in the page, before we use the server behavior builder. Thankfully, there is a really useful tool, that makes this process very easy for us, the Dreamweaver MX **Find and Replace tool**, which can be accessed via the *Edit* menu:

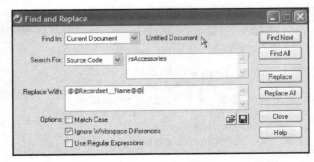

As you can see from the image above, we need to make sure that the *Find and Replace* tool is searching within our sourcecode for the relevant pieces of text. Here, I'm replacing all instances of the recordset name, `rsAccessories`, with the `parameter @@Recordset__Name@@`. All instances of this recordset name will be replaced by the parameter when you click *Replace All*.

All that is left to do is to replace the names of our recordset columns that display information within the table. The columns that I have used in this example are: `accessory_id`, `accessory_name` and `accessory_price`.

```
<!-- Before Change -->
<td align="center"><?php echo $row_rsAccessories['accessory_id']; ?></td>
<td align="center"><?php echo $row_rsAccessories['accessory_name']; ?></td>
<td align="center"><?php echo $row_rsAccessories['accessory_price']; ?></td>

<!-- After Change -->
<td align="center"><?php echo $row_rsAccessories['@@ID@@']; ?></td>
<td align="center"><?php echo $row_rsAccessories['@@Name@@']; ?></td>
<td align="center"><?php echo $row_rsAccessories['@@Price@@']; ?></td>
```

This completes the creation of the parameters. We can now paste this code directly into the server behavior builder. Here is what our sample code looks like:

```
<table border="0">
  <tr>
    <th colspan="3">Accessory Table Browser</th>
  </tr>
  <tr>
    <th>Product ID</th>
    <th>Name</th>
    <th>Price</th>
  </tr>
  <?php do { ?>
  <tr>
    <td align="center"><?php echo $row_@@Recordset__Name@@['@@ID@@']; ?></td>
    <td align="center"><?php echo $row_@@Recordset__Name@@['@@Name@@']; ?></td>
    <td align="center"><?php echo $row_@@Recordset__Name@@['@@Price@@']; ?></td>
  </tr>
  <?php } while ($row_@@Recordset__Name@@ =
mysql_fetch_assoc($@@Recordset__Name@@)); ?>
</table>
```

Start the server behavior builder by clicking on the *New Server Behavior* entry in the *Server Behaviors* menu, and first of all give the behavior a meaningful name. As the heading of the table is *Accessory Table Browser*, this is what I've opted to call the behavior:

6

Extending Dreamweaver MX

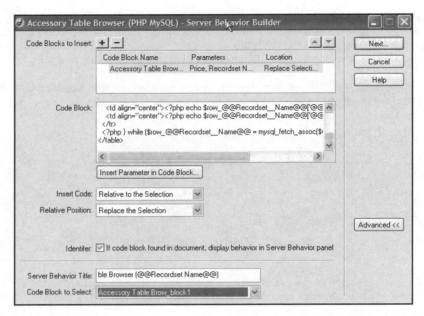

In the server behavior builder, create a new code block, and paste all of the code that we've just created into that block; you will notice how the builder automatically recognizes all of the parameters in the code. Change the *Insert Code* setting to *Relative to the Selection*, and the *Relative Position* setting to *Replace the Selection*. This will ensure that our server object is inserted wherever the current insertion point is.

There is no need to change anything in the *Advanced* section of this behavior, and there's a very good reason for this. By and large, server objects do not display in the *Server Behaviors* panel because they contain other server behaviors themselves, and therefore the original behaviors will show in the *Server Behavior* panel instead. This means that once inserted, the component parts of this object can be edited individually, but cannot be edited as a whole.

Now that we have completed this stage of the server behavior builder, click *Next* to define the user interface elements.

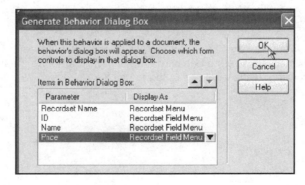

Since we have used a recordset and three recordset columns as parameters, it really makes sense to select the *Recordset Menu*, and *Recordset Field Menu* options from the *Display As* menu. When we use the server object, this ensures that we have a recordset on the page, and also gives us immediate information about all of the recordset columns without having to manually look up what is available.

This also speeds up the process of adding the server object to the page, as this particular server object can be applied to the page in just a handful of clicks, and without using the keyboard at all, making it very efficient and easy to use.

When we click *OK*, the behavior is automatically created, and we can access it directly from the *Server Behaviors* menu.

When you apply this server object to a page, you will reproduce precisely the original element. To create the original part of the page may have taken a few minutes, and investing a little more time into turning this element into a server object means that it can be applied to the page in seconds, with guaranteed results. This process can be repeated time and again for more complex objects that may require multiple code blocks, and multiple user interface components.

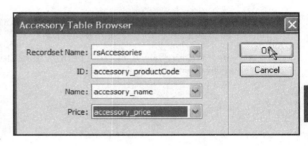

# Summary

In this chapter we've looked at some of the types of extension that can be created in Dreamweaver MX, and how they can be useful to us.

Extensibility is a massively involved subject, which incorporates multiple techniques and technologies, allowing you to customize how Dreamweaver MX works. By exploring the three main categories of extension that are suited to PHP programmers, I hope to have shown that extension development needn't be rocket science, and that there are serious benefits to using these tools to improving your workflow and productivity.

When working with object orientated languages like PHP, combining the power of a PHP object and a server behavior or server object can really bring huge rewards; it is very easy to create user-friendly interfaces for your object's properties and methods, and can really cut down on those programming chores.

There is much more under the hood of Dreamweaver MX for you to explore if this subject has grasped your imagination, and there are a number of sites dedicated to the development of extensions for Dreamweaver MX.

## Resources

- UDZone (http://www.udzone.com): a fantastic resource for extensions, tutorials, and general help with Dreamweaver MX and UltraDev 4.

- DWTeam (http://www.dwteam.com): a group of talented developers dedicated to the development of Dreamweaver products and services.

- Macromedia Exchange (http://www.macromedia.com/exchange): with more than 700 extensions available for Dreamweaver alone, the Macromedia exchange has probably got an extension for every purpose.

- Rawveg.org (http://www.rawveg.org): Home of IntelliCART and IntelliCART MX, shopping cart solutions for Dreamweaver PHP.

- Buzzinet (http://www.dreamweavermxsupport.com/extensions/phploginsuite/): Home of the PHP Login Suite for Dreamweaver MX.

- Yaromat (http://www.yaromat.com): Free extensions for use with most versions of Dreamweaver.

Extending Dreamweaver MX

# 7

- Timestamps
- Formatting timestamps
- Using time functions in Dreamweaver

**Author: Bruno Mairlot**

# Date and Time

Manipulating date and time data is a very common task, and you are likely to face many situations in which you will be writing code using them. Although PHP provides many ways to handle date and time, this profusion of functions can sometimes be very confusing.

In this chapter, we will first take a look at the basic foundation of almost all PHP date and time functions: the timestamp value. A timestamp is a numerical representation of time that is used internally in many systems and it is very important to understand it properly. After looking at the timestamp, we will see how to obtain it from the operating system or by converting a different date representation. Then you will see how to use the timestamp value to fit your needs. Finally, we will see how to integrate these functions into Dreamweaver MX to produce better output when handling date and time.

## The Timestamp

The definition of the timestamp is very easy: it is the number of seconds since the **UNIX Epoch time**. The Unix Epoch Time is the first of January 1970. This figure is used as the basis on which you can perform many operations. For example, to know the date one week from now, all you would have to do is to add the number of seconds a week contains (604800) to the timestamp value for today, and you will have a timestamp whose value represents a week from now.

Almost all date and time functions in PHP operate by either receiving a timestamp or converting a date to a timestamp. To help you understand the remainder of this chapter, never forget this definition:

Note that you can't use a timestamp value to represent a date before the 1st of January 1970. If you want to do computation on a very old date, like which day were we the 4th of march in 1756, you will have to implement an algorithm that will compute this kind of date by knowing the number of days in a month.

*A timestamp value is a numerical representation of the number of seconds elapsed since 1st January, 1970, and is used as the basis of most date and time calculations*

## Obtaining a Timestamp Value

There are many different ways to obtain a timestamp. You can either obtain it from the operating system as the current time, or you can obtain one by converting an existing date.

*Note that we will often refer to the timestamp as the UNIX Timestamp. It is more a naming convention than a real link to the UNIX operating system; all functions based on timestamp also work on the Windows operating system.*

### mktime(), gmmktime()

The functions `mktime()` and `gmmktime()` are almost identical. They return a timestamp value from a given series of arguments. Here is the syntax for using these functions:

```
int mktime( int hour, int minute, int second, int month, int day, int year [, int
is_dst] )
int gmmktime( int hour, int minute, int second, int month, int day, int year [, int
is_dst] )
```

The difference between them is that `gmmktime()` expects its argument to be in GMT (Greenwich Mean Time, often also known as UTC, or Universal Time Constant). It is often useful to know the GMT time as all time zones have their offset from this point.

Here is an example of usage, creating a timestamp for the 28th September 2002:

```
echo mktime(0,0,0,9,28,2002);
```

The very last argument `is_dst` is optional; it tells the function whether it should take **Daylight Saving Time** into account when computing the timestamp. The following table shows the result of the function depending on the `is_dst` value:

| is_dst | Behavior |
|--------|----------|
| 1 | The time is during Daylight Saving |
| 0 | The time is not during Daylight Saving |
| -1 | It is unknown. This is default value of `is_dst`. PHP will try to figure out if the time is within Daylight Saving or not. Note that this can lead to unexpected, but not incorrect result. |

Note that you can omit arguments from right to left. If you don't specify the two last arguments for example, `mktime()` will set the value of these argument from their current local value. If `mktime()` is used without argument whatsoever, it will return the timestamp for the current time, and is therefore completely equivalent to the function `time()`, which we will introduce later in this chapter.

It should be noted that the `mktime()` function will attempt to correct your input if it is an impossible value, rather than throw an error. This can throw some unexpected results if you don't check for valid numbers from the input. Look at the following examples:

```
echo mktime(0,0,0,8,59,2002) . "<BR>";
echo mktime(0,0,0,21,28,2001);
```

Both of these calls to `mktime()` will return the same timestamp. PHP actually corrects your arguments, making them real ones. If you carefully read the value of the first 'wrong' call, it is the 59th day of August. Of course such a day doesn't exist, but PHP has turned it into the 28th of September, since 59-31=28. In the same way, on the second 'wrong' call, there is no 21st month in a year. The 13th month of 2001 is January of 2002 and the 21st month of 2001 is the 9th of the next year.

## time()

The function `time()` is the easiest way to obtain the current timestamp value. It does not require any arguments, and returns a timestamp. It is very widely used when calling other time functions.

Suppose we wanted to set a cookie, and in the expiration argument we want to compute the current time plus one hour (3600 seconds). Here is how we could do that:

```
setCookie('nowCookie','now',time());
setCookie('laterCookie','one hour later',time()+3600);
```

This will produce a result similar to the following in the header section of the HTTP response:

```
Set-Cookie: nowCookie=now; expires=Sat, 28-Sep-02 10:55:28 GMT
Set-Cookie: laterCookie=one+hour+later; expires=Sat, 28-Sep-02 11:55:28 GMT
```

Remember that the function `setCookie()` requires for its expire argument a timestamp and that a timestamp is a measurement in seconds. Therefore, if you want to specify a number of hours or minutes or seconds, you must specify the equivalent value in seconds.

*Here is a little trick to help you get the number of seconds for a different duration. If you remember, the function mktime() will use the current value for its omitted argument. Therefore, if you want to know how many seconds there are in 20 hours, just use the following code:*

```
<?php
        echo "20 hours are ".(mktime(20)-mktime(0))." seconds";
?>
```

*This code will produce:*

*20 hours are 72000 seconds*

## microtime()

The `microtime()` function will return a string containing the timestamp and its value in microseconds. The string follows the format: `"msec sec"`. The `sec` value represents the usual timestamp, while the `msec` value represents the microseconds part. The `microtime()` function returns a string, and not a numerical value; here is a little portion of code to help you manage the content of this string:

```
list($usec,$sec) = explode(" ",microtime());
echo "Microseconds : $usec";
echo "Seconds : $sec";
```

The function `microtime()` gives the precision required when you want to measure time very precisely. Generally, scripts are executed in a few microseconds and so if you want to know precisely how much time your script uses, you can use this code:

```
<?
        function getmicrotime(){
            list($usec, $sec) = explode(" ",microtime());
            return ((float)$usec + (float)$sec);
            }

        $time_start = getmicrotime();

        //Start of your code

        for($count=0; $count<=1000; $count++)

        //End of your code

        $time_end = getmicrotime();
        $time = $time_end - $time_start;

        echo "This script took $time seconds";

?>
```

### strtotime()

The function `strtotime()` is very helpful. It parses English text representing a date and returns its timestamp value. Here is its syntax:

```
int strtotime ( string time [, int now] )
```

The `time` argument is a string representing the textual description of the date. The optional argument, `now`, tells the function which timestamp to calculate the value from. The default value for this argument is the current timestamp. Here are some examples of how it can be used:

```
echo strtotime ("last month"). "<br>";
echo strtotime ("last monday"). "<br>";
echo strtotime ("yesterday"). "<br>";
echo strtotime ("last year"). "<br>";
echo strtotime ("Sat Sep 28 2002 13:30:44 EST"). "<br>";
echo strtotime ("2002-9-28"). "<br>";
```

You'll notice that in the last example we have used a typical MySQL date format, allowing you to easily use the function `strtotime()` to convert a MySQL date value into its timestamp.

To get a complete description of the valid syntax for `strtotime()`, you should refer to: *http://www.gnu.org/manual/tar-1.12/html_chapter/tar_7.html*.

# Formatting and Manipulating a Timestamp

In this section we will review the different tools that will help you work with timestamp values, both in terms of working with dates and converting timestamps to other time formats.

## date(), gmdate()

The `date()` function is very common and very easy to use. It returns a string formatted according to the given string format. Here is its syntax:

```
string date( string format [, int timestamp ] )
```

The `format` argument describes how you want to format your date. The second argument, `timestamp`, is optional. If not specified, the function will work with the current timestamp. There are a variety of different values for the `format` argument. Some of the more common you might wish to use include:

- `a` – "am" or "pm"
- `A` – "AM" or "PM"
- `d` – day of the month, 2 digits with leading zeros; that is, "01" to "31"
- `S` – English ordinal suffix for the day of the month, 2 characters; that is, "st", "nd", "rd"; or "th"
- `j` – day of the month without leading zeros; that is, "1" to "31"
- `D` – day of the week, textual, 3 letters; for example, "Fri"
- `w` – day of the week, numeric, that is, "0" (Sunday) to "6" (Saturday)
- `l` (lowercase 'L') – day of the week, textual, long; for example, "Friday"
- `F` – month, textual, long; for example, "January"
- `m` – month; that is, "01" to "12"
- `M` – month, textual, 3 letters; for example, "Jan"
- `n` – month without leading zeros; that is, "1" to "12"
- `Y` – year, 4 digits; for example, "1999"
- `y` – year, 2 digits; for example, "99"
- `z` – day of the year; that is, "0" to "365"

So, if you wanted to format the date in the manner 25th September 2002, you could use:

```
echo "I wrote this page on: ".date("dS F Y");
```

7

**Date and Time**

To format the date into a more specific time, you could add the following to the format string:

- g – hour, 12-hour format without leading zeros; that is, "1" to "12"
- G – hour, 24-hour format without leading zeros; that is, "0" to "23"
- h – hour, 12-hour format; that is, "01" to "12"
- H – hour, 24-hour format; that is, "00" to "23"
- i – minutes; that is, "00" to "59"
- s – seconds; that is, "00" to "59"
- o – Difference to Greenwich time in hours; for example, "+0200"
- T – Time zone setting of this machine; for example, "EST" or "MDT"
- z – Time zone offset in seconds (that is, "-43200" to "43200"). The offset for time zones west of UTC is always negative, and for those east of UTC is always positive.

So if you wanted to format the date as 25th September 2002 22:49:15 GMT, you would use:

```
echo "I wrote this page on: ".date("dS F Y H:I:s T");
```

Finally, there are a number of other formatting options that you might find useful for formatting the date:

- r – RFC 822 formatted date; for example, "Thu, 21 Dec 2000 16:01:07 +0200"
- U – seconds since the Unix Epoch (January 1 1970 00:00:00 GMT)
- W – ISO-8601 week number of year, weeks starting on Monday (added in PHP 4.1.0)
- B – Swatch Internet time
- I – "1" if Daylight Savings Time, "0" otherwise
- L – Boolean for whether it is a leap year; that is, "0" or "1"
- t – number of days in the given month; that is, "28" to "31"

Note that if the format string contains a letter that is not part of the format specified above, it will be included in the output string.

gmdate() follows the same format, except that the date returned is GMT. So if your machine is in Berlin (GMT +1hr), the gmdate() will give an hour behind your current time.

## getdate()

The function getdate() returns an associative array containing date information about a given timestamp. If you don't specify a timestamp, it will work with the current time. The returned value is an associative array that has the following indexes:

- "seconds" – seconds

- "minutes" – minutes

- "hours" – hours

- "mday" – day of the month

- "wday" – day of the week, numeric : from 0 as Sunday up to 6 as Saturday

- "mon" – month, numeric

- "year" – year, numeric

- "yday" – day of the year, numeric; for example "299"

- "weekday" – day of the week, textual, full; for example "Friday"

- "month" – month, textual, full; for example "January"

This function provides an easy mechanism to get information about a date. The following piece of code illustrates a typical usage of getdate():

```
$arr = getdate();
$year=$arr['year'];
$month=$arr['month'];
$day=$arr['mday'];

echo "$month/$day/$year";
```

will produce a date of the format:

*September/28/2002*

Using the function getdate() in conjunction with mktime() can produce very powerful code. Suppose you want to know the date 60 days later than today.

```
<?
        $arr = getdate();
        $year=$arr['year'];
        $month=$arr['mon'];
        $day=$arr['mday'];

        $later=mktime(0,0,0,$month,$day+60,$year);

        echo "60 days later from now, we will be the " . strftime("%x",$later);

?>
```

As you can see the combination of date() and mktime() gives you a very powerful date computation method. Now, if you have a MySQL date, and want to print the end of the subscription to your user, just turn the date into a timestamp and use it as argument of the function getdate().

**7**

**Date and Time**

## strftime(), gmstrftime()

In the above example we used the function: `strftime()`. The function `strftime()` is handy for formatting a date. It is easy to use and the code written using `strftime()` is very elegant. Here is its syntax:

```
string strftime ( string format [, int timestamp ] )
```

If you don't specify the last argument, `strftime()` will use the current time. `gmstrftime()` is the equivalent function for GMT and follows the same format. The syntax for both these functions is very similar to that of the `date()` function, and indeed, it works almost the same way. The real difference resides in the `format` argument.

The `format` string uses the following characters for formatting the date:

- `%a` – abbreviated weekday name according to the current locale

- `%A` – full weekday name according to the current locale

- `%b` – abbreviated month name according to the current locale

- `%B` – full month name according to the current locale

- `%c` – preferred date and time representation for the current locale

- `%C` – century number (the year divided by 100 and truncated to an integer, range 00 to 99)

- `%d` – day of the month as a decimal number (range 01 to 31)

- `%D` – same as %m/%d/%y

- `%e` – day of the month as a decimal number, a single digit is preceded by a space (range ' 1' to '31')

- `%G` – The 4-digit year corresponding to the ISO week number (see %V). This has the same format and value as %Y below, except that if the ISO week number belongs to the previous or next year, that year is used instead

- `%g` – like %G, but without the century

- `%h` – same as %b

- `%j` – day of the year as a decimal number (range 001 to 366)

- `%m` – month as a decimal number (range 01 to 12)

- `%u` – weekday as a decimal number [1,7], with 1 representing Monday

- `%U` – week number of the current year as a decimal number, starting with the first Sunday as the first day of the first week

- `%V` – The ISO 8601:1988 week number of the current year as a decimal number, range 01 to 53, where week 1 is the first week that has at least 4 days in the current year, and with Monday as the first day of the week. (Use %G or %g for the year component that corresponds to the week number for the specified timestamp.)

- %W – week number of the current year as a decimal number, starting with the first Monday as the first day of the first week

- %w – day of the week as a decimal, Sunday being 0

- %x – preferred date representation for the current locale without the time

- %y – year as a decimal number without a century (range 00 to 99)

- %Y – year as a decimal number including the century

And the following for the time information:

- %H – hour as a decimal number using a 24-hour clock (range 00 to 23)

- %I – hour as a decimal number using a 12-hour clock (range 01 to 12)

- %M – minute as a decimal number

- %S – second as a decimal number

- %p – either `am' or `pm' according to the given time value, or the corresponding strings for the current locale

- %r – time in am and pm notation

- %R – time in 24-hour notation

- %T – current time, equal to %H:%M:%S

- %X – preferred time representation for the current locale without the date

- %Z – time zone or name or abbreviation

And the following for useful formatting information:

- %t – tab character

- %% – a literal `%' character

- %n – newline character

The strftime() function is very powerful when combined with the strtotime() function that we saw in the previous section:

```
echo strftime("%x",strtotime("last month")), "<br>";
echo strftime("%x",strtotime("last monday")),  "<br>";
```

This would give us the dates of last month and last Monday, formatted according to the server's locale setting.

# File Date Functions

There are times when we need to obtain date and time information from a file, such as when it was created, or when it was last accessed. PHP provides special functions for this, which we will review in this section.

## fileatime(), filectime(), filemtime(), stat()

These four functions provide the time related to a file. The three available times are: last accessed, created, and last modified time. The `stat()` function returns a structure that provides all these times and some additional information, like the size of the file, the owner, and the group.

They follow this syntax:

```
int fileatime ( string filename )
int filectime ( string filename )
int filemtime ( string filename )
array stat ( string filename )
```

For example, if you want to know the creation date of the file you are writing in, just use the following code:

```
$filename=$_SERVER['PATH_TRANSLATED'];
echo "The current file was created on ".strftime("%x",filectime($filename));
```

This will produce a result similar to the following:

*The current file was created on 07/10/02*

The function `stat()` will return an associative array, containing the following indexes:

- `mtime` – When the file was last modified
- `ctime` – When the file was created
- `atime` – When the file was last accessed

The values of the indexed array are timestamps. These timestamps are exactly the same given by the individual file time functions discussed above.

## getlastmod()

The function `getlastmod()` is actually a shortcut to get the last modified time of the current page. In the above example we wanted to know when the current file had been created. This function will return a timestamp representing the last modified time of the current file. For example:

```
echo "Last modified on: ".strftime("%x",getlastmod());
```

might produce the following output:

*Last modified on: 09/28/02*

# Using Date and Time in Dreamweaver MX

Now that we have had an extensive review of PHP date and time functionality, it is time to see how to integrate these functions within your page development.

## Hand Coding Time and Date Functions

Even though Dreamweaver MX comes with many server behaviors for the PHP Server Model, it doesn't allow you to design exactly what you want with drag-and-drop features. We must sometimes resort to hand code ourself the specific portion of code we want to integrate in our development page. This section shows you how to use the built-in functionality of Dreamweaver and use the so-called hand-coding technique.

### Formatting Date and Time

Suppose we have a classic table showing an element from a recordset. The recordset contains a field of type date named `'bon_date'`. A typical Dreamweaver screen would look like this:

If we leave the usual code as is, without changing anything, the result will contain values like "2002-1-1" in the bon_date column, which is the MySQL date format. Now, say we want to format this date with a bit more user-friendly information like the name of the month and the day.

While designing our example page, we have named the recordset rsList. So you will find in the code the recordset variable '$rsList'. Now, if you switch to the dual view in Dreamweaver, and select the dynamic element in the page, you should see something like this:

```
22    </tr>
23    <?php do { ?>
24    <tr>
25      <td><?php echo $row_rsList['ID']; ?></td>
26      <td><?php echo $row_rsList['bon_date']; ?></td>
27      <td><?php echo $row_rsList['client_ID']; ?></td>
28      <td><?php echo $row_rsList['fourn_ID']; ?></td>
29    </tr>
30    <?php } while ($row_rsList = mysql_fetch_assoc($rsList)); ?>
31  </table>
32
33  </body>
```

The code Dreamweaver uses for printing the bon_date column is:

```php
<?php echo $row_rsList['bon_date']; ?>
```

We know this code will just output the value of the array `$row_rsList` at index `bon_date`. We also know that this value is a MySQL date. We have seen that the `strtotime()` function can turn the MySQL date string into a timestamp, and we know many functions that will turn a timestamp into whatever we may want. Therefore, we will edit the code to become:

```php
<?php echo strftime("%A %e %B %Y",strtotime($row_rsList['bon_date'])); ?>
```

In Dreamweaver, that should look like this:

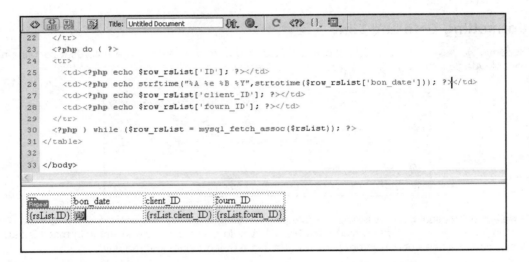

You'll notice that the blue region in the Design View of Dreamweaver has been turned into a PHP icon. It does this because Dreamweaver cannot recognize your code and it doesn't know how to show it in the Design View.

Now if you look at the page in your browser, you should see the date being formatted in the form "*Friday 22 October 1999*".

# Summary

The foundation of all date and time functionality in PHP is the timestamp value. A timestamp is the numerical value that represents the number of seconds elapsed since the first of January 1970. All time functions either receive a timestamp as argument, produce a timestamp, or will use a timestamp for their internal computation.

In this chapter we reviewed several functions that output a timestamp, the simplest is of which is the time() function which returns a timestamp representing the current time. For more advanced date and time manipulation you should consider using strtotime(), a very powerful function that transforms strings into timestamps. PHP also has many functions that you can use to turn timestamps back into dates and times. The most flexible function for this is strftime().

PHP also has special functions that return timestamps related to files, such as when the file was created or last modified. This can be useful when maintaining a cache of pre-generated pages, which need to be updated when older than a certain date.

Finally we have seen how to integrate these functionalities in Dreamweaver by slightly changing the code generated.

7

Date and Time

# 8

- Reading and writing to files
- The directory system
- File uploads

**Author: Bruno Mairlot**

# File Handling

In this chapter we will review all the mechanisms and functions that PHP provides to let you manipulate files and directories, and upload data via HTTP. We'll look at creating and deleting files on our server via a browser, navigating our web server's directory tree, and eventually we will see how we can integrate all this knowledge into extending and customizing Dreamweaver MX with our own Server Behavior to manage file Uploads.

First, let's discuss the different ways of creating, opening, reading from, and writing to files that are stored on the web server's hard drive.

## Reading from and Writing to Files

In this section, we'll discuss the different mechanisms that will let you work with file content. First, we will present the concept of opening, reading, writing to, and closing a file. This is the standard way of accessing file content. But PHP provides many other functions to perform other well-known tasks.

### General Mechanism

The following figure shows you the two usual mechanisms to read from, and write to, a file:

The reading process is as follows: open the file, specifying that you want to read it. As long as you haven't reached the end of the file, keep reading it. When the end of the file is reached, close it. The writing process is much simpler: open the file, specifying you want to write to it, write the content to the file, then close it.

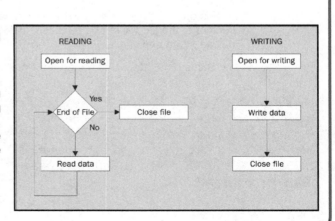

Filenames and paths will be reviewed in the next section, where we talk about directories, but in the examples that follow, my convention is to use the `$filename` variable to contain the complete path to the file.

## Opening and Closing a File

A file is opened by obtaining a **resource identifier**, which is an integer value, provided by the system. It is simply a number that identifies your file, and is also sometimes called a **file pointer**. When you use this value in different functions, PHP will know which file you are referencing and will communicate your operations to the underlying system.

The function required to open a file is `fopen()`. Its prototype is shown below:

```
int fopen ( string filename, string mode [, int use_include_path [, resource
zcontext]] )
```

`fopen()` returns an integer value if the operation succeeds. If not, it will return `False`. The following code shows the basic syntax we can use to test whether a file has been correctly opened:

```
if($fh = fopen("myfile.txt","r")){
        // Successful
}
else{
        // Failure
} )
```

The first argument, `filename`, contains the full path of the file, the `mode` tells `fopen()` what kind of operation you want to do on this file. Here are the different possible values for the `mode` argument:

- r: This opens the file for reading.

- r+: This opens the file for reading and writing.

- w: This opens the file for writing. If the file exists, its contents will be erased.

- w+: This open the file writing and reading. As for the w value, if the file exists, its content will be removed.

- a: This open the file for appending. This means that you are in the writing mode, but the content of the file will not be removed. Instead every character you write in the file will be placed at the end.

- a+: Same as a, but you can read the file.

*Note that on a Windows system, you may need to add the "b" character to the mode argument if you want to open a binary file. The mode argument then becomes "ab". UNIX systems do not differentiate between binary and text files, so on UNIX systems this argument is not used.*

The argument `use_include_path` tells the function whether or not to use the PHP constant `include_path`, which is pre-defined in the `php.ini` file. Just use the value `True` if you want it to be activated.

The corollary to `fopen()` is `fclose()`. This simply tells PHP to close the file and free up the file pointer it is using to reference it. In fact, when the script finishes, PHP will automatically clean up all resources allocated during execution. However, for code cleanliness and readability, it is a good idea to close files explicitly.

*The zcontext argument is beyond the scope of this book. We include it only for the sake of completeness.*

`fclose()` takes one argument which is an integer representing the file pointer of the file you want to close. The returned value indicates if the close operation was successful. It returns `True` on success, and `False` on failure. Here is its syntax:

```
fclose( int filepointer );
```

In the above prototype, `filepointer` is simply the integer value of the file pointer assigned previously by the `fopen()` function. For a call to `fclose()` to succeed, the value of `filepointer` must be a valid file pointer.

Here is a sample of code that shows both these functions in action. Save this file in the **root web directory** of your web server and open it in a browser.

```php
<?php
        $filepath=realpath(".").$_SERVER['PHP_SELF'];

        if(!$ri = @fopen($filename,"r")){
                echo "File could not be opened";
        }else{
                echo "File has been opened, look:<br />";
                echo $ri;
                fclose($ri);
                }
?>
```

In this example, we set the variable `$filename` to the complete path of the current file we are executing.

> *Note that if this file is not saved in your web server's root directory, $filename will not be assembled correctly, and this example will not work. Users of Apache systems can substitute $_SERVER['$DOCUMENT_ROOT'] in place of realpath(".") in order to run this script from any web directory, however. Because of the way IIS reads the $_SERVER['$DOCUMENT_ROOT'] variable this will not work for IIS users. For the sake of platform agnosticism, we will not be doing this here, but it may be worth bearing in mind when reading the other examples in this chapter.*

This PHP script reads itself. The variable `$ri` stores the resource identifier of the opened file. If you run the code, you'll probably get the output:

*File has been opened, look:*
*Resource id #1*

For the further examples, we will use a file called `sample.txt` located in the same directory as your script. Don't worry about creating the file yourself: the script will do that for us the first time it tries to open it.

**File Handling**

```php
<?php
        $ri = fopen("sample.txt","w");
        fclose($ri);
?>
```

*The .txt file extension is only needed on Windows systems, but its inclusion will not cause any problems for UNIX users.*

Save this script as a PHP file and execute it. The file sample.txt should appear in the same directory as your PHP file. If you open it, you will see that it is empty.

## Writing to the file

Now that we have opened the file, we may as well write something into it. The function that PHP provides for doing this is called fwrite(). PHP also provides the function fputs(), but this is just an alias for fwrite(), and behaves identically to it. Let's look at fwrite() now.

### fwrite()

Here is the prototype for fwrite():

```
int fwrite ( int fp, string string [, int length] )
```

fwrite() takes the file pointer, fp, as an argument, and the string, string, you want to write to your file. Optionally, it can also take the value we've shown here as length, which is equal to the number of bytes to be written. When called, fwrite() returns the number of bytes successfully written in the file, or -1 if an error occurred. To check if your write operation has been a total success, you may want to compare the returned value of the fwrite() call with the length argument you gave to it. Here is some of code to do that:

```php
$len=strlen($str);
if($len == fwrite($fp,$str,$len)){
        echo "Write has been successful";
}
else{
        echo "An error occurred";
}
```

To continue our example using the file sample.txt, here is how we could write something to the file:

```php
<?php
        $fh = fopen("sample.txt","w");
        if($fh){
                fwrite($fh,"Hello, this is text in a file\nThis is the second
line.");
                echo "File written to successfully.";
                fclose($fh);
        }else{
                echo "Could not open file sample.txt for writing.";
        }
        fclose($fh);
?>
```

Run this script. If successful, you will get the output *File written to successfully* in your browser. Open `sample.txt` and you will see two lines of text as its contents: *Hello, this is text in a file*, and *This is the second line*. We used the `\n` escape sequence to insert a newline into our text and write our input on two lines.

## Reading the File

Now that we have a file containing some text, we also want to be able to read it from within our scripts. Interestingly enough, PHP provides multiple functions for retrieving data from files, depending on how you want to use that data. We will cover these functions now.

### fread()

Later in this section you will be presented with functions that read the whole file in one call, but under some circumstances it might be more useful to read it chunk by chunk and operate some action upon it. The function `fread()` reads a specified number of bytes from a file, and returns the content as a string. Here is the syntax for using `fread()`:

```
string fread ( int fp, int length )
```

For example, if you wanted to search for some very specific content that is somewhere in the file, and you don't want to read the entire file into memory, all you would do is search the file until you find the required content, then close the file. If the file is very large this could save lots of memory.

If `fread()` detects the end of the file before it has read `length` number of bytes, it will stop and return a string containing the number that it *did* read. Otherwise it will return a string containing `length` bytes of text.

To illustrate the usage of the `fread()` function, we will continue our earlier example. This time, we want to print the content of the `sample.txt` file on screen. Here is how we could do that (note the comments regarding the value you give to `$filename`):

```php
?php
    /* Comment one of these lines out, depending on whether
    you are running on Windows, or a UNIX, such as Mac OS X */
    $filename="/sample.txt";      //On UNIX
    $filename="\\sample.txt";     //On Windows

    $fullfilename=realpath(".").$filename;

    if(!$fp = @fopen($fullfilename,"r")){
        echo "File could not be opened";
    }else{
        while(!feof($fp)){
            echo fread($fp,128);
        }
        fclose($fp);
    }
?>
```

In this example we've used the function `feof()`, which checks for the end of the file. We get the output *Hello, this is text in a file This is the second line.* The file is read faithfully, and the file is output including the newline we inserted in our earlier example (select *View Source* in your browser if you want to check this). The browser, of course, treats this simply as whitespace and inserts a single space in its place.

### fgetc()

The function `fgetc()` reads the file character by character. This is generally only useful in very specific cases. It returns a string that contains only one character. If there are no more bytes to read in the file, `fgetc()` will return `False`. In the next example, we've changed our code to make use of `fgetc()` (again, take care to comment out the irrelevant assignment for `$filename`):

```php
<?php
        /* Comment one of these lines out, depending on whether
        you are running on Windows, or a UNIX, such as Mac OS X */
        $filename="/sample.txt";        //On UNIX
        $filename="\\sample.txt";       //On Windows

        $fullfilename=realpath(".").$filename;

        if(!$fp = @fopen($fullfilename,"r")){
                echo "File could not be opened";
        }
        else{
                while(!feof($fp)){
                        echo fgetc($fp);
                }
                fclose($fp);
        }
?>
```

This code produces identical output to that of the previous example.

### fgets()

The function `fgets()` is a little more interesting than `fgetc()` and `fread()` in that it reads the file for a specified amount of bytes, but stops when one of the three following circumstances is met:

- the specified length has been reached

- a newline character is found

- the end of file is reached

*The real attraction of fgets() is that it enables you to read a file one line at a time.*

Here is its prototype:

```
string fgets ( int fp [, int length] )
```

The second argument, length, became optional with PHP version 4.2.0 and later. If not specified, fgets() tries to read 1024 bytes at once. As of PHP 4.3, however, omitting length will cause fgets() to keep reading from the stream until it reaches the end of the line. A very important difference between this function and fread() is that, instead of returning a string containing length bytes, it returns length-1 bytes.

Now let's change the example to make use of fgets(). This time, though, we will introduce a little element that will show exactly the content of the read operation on a file. We will store the content of fgets() in a variable, $str, and output something slightly different:

```php
<?php
    /* Comment one of these lines out, depending on whether
    you are running on Windows, or on a UNIX system, such as Mac OS X */
    $filename="/sample.txt";        //On UNIX
    $filename="\\sample.txt";       //On Windows

    $fullfilename=realpath(".").$filename;

    if(!$fp = @fopen($fullfilename,"r")){
            echo "File could not be opened";
    }
    else{
            while(!feof($fp)){
                    $str=fgets($fp,5);
                    echo " |(".strlen($str).")".$str."|";
            fclose($fp);
    }
?>
```

As you can see, we've set up this code so it encloses each string returned by fgets() with the pipe symbol "|", and pre-pends the length of the string in brackets. This makes it possible to see exactly what is being output from the fgets() calls:

*|(4)Hell| |(4)o, t| |(4)his | |(4)is t| |(4)ext | |(4)in a| |(4) fill |(2)e | |(4)This| |(4) is | |(4)the | |(4)seco| |(4)nd |I| |(4)ine.| |(0)|*

We set the length argument of fgets() to 5. The first string results returned are four characters long and this continues to be the case until we reach the end of the first line, where we get only two characters. Two? Well, yes; the newline is treated as a character. As you can see, fgets() stopped reading when it reached a newline. It then proceeded to iterate through the second line, ending only when it reached the end of the file.

## PHP Shortcuts to File Reading

The previous section introduced standard file manipulation methods. However, PHP provides many functions to greatly accelerate the job of reading a file. There are two different categories of shortcut. The first set of functions reads a file and outputs it to the browser. The second reads the entire file and returns a string variable containing its contents.

## Outputting Files to Browsers

The first category of the shortcut functions provides a mechanism to output the content of a file to the browser. There are two functions in this category:

- `fpassthru`: This reads an opened file using its file pointer, and prints the output
- `readfile`: This reads a file using its name, and prints the output

Basically the difference between those two functions is that `fpassthru()` uses a file pointer while `readfile()` needs a filename.

Here is an example that outputs our `sample.txt` file to the browser using the `fpassthru()` function:

```php
<?php
        $filename="sample.txt";

        if(!$fp = @fopen($filename,"r")){
                echo "File could not be opened";
        }
        else{
                fpassthru($fp);
        }
?>
```

Now, let's do the same thing using `readfile()`:

```php
<?php
        $filename="sample.txt";
        readfile($filename);
?>
```

## Storing File Content in Variables

Now let's look at those functions that store the contents of a file in a variable. The two functions that fall into this category are:

- `file_get_content()`: This reads a file and returns the content as a string
- `file()`: This reads a file and returns an array with each line of the file stored as a separate element

Both of these functions take the filename as a string. Neither requires file pointers.

The `file()` function will return `False` if it can't open the file. If the operation is successful, each element in the array will still contain the newline character used to split the file. Note that, at time of this writing, the function `file_get_contents()` is still in development, but will almost certainly prove very useful. It should appear in PHP version 4.3.0.

# Files As a Whole

Now that we have a good understanding of manipulating file content, it is time to see how to handle files as a whole. In this section, we will review most of the tools PHP provides to handle, move, check, and delete files. Don't forget that the operations performed by these functions are done under the hood of the web server process. Therefore, the PHP script will only be able to execute them if correct file permissions are set for this process on the server.

## Basic Functions

The functions reviewed in this section will present the basic tools you will need:

- `copy` : This copies a file from one place to another
- `delete, unlink` : This removes a file from the system
- `rename` : This renames a file
- `filesize` : This gets the size of a file

### copy()

The `copy()` function works exactly like the DOS `copy` or UNIX `cp` command. It duplicates the given file to another location on the system. Here is its prototype:

```
int copy ( string source, string dest )
```

You can either specify the full path of the file you want to copy, or use a relative file path. Note that if you use a relative file path, it will be relative to the script that is making the call to the `copy()` function, and not to the file being copied, or its destination.

The following example would create a backup file of the current script:

```
$filename=$_SERVER['DOCUMENT_ROOT'].$_SERVER['PHP_SELF'];
copy($filename,$filename.".bak");
```

The function `copy()` will return `True` if successful, `False` otherwise.

### unlink()

`unlink()` is the function you should use if you want to delete a file. `delete()` can be used as an alias for `unlink()`, but in future versions of PHP, `delete` will become a keyword and this won't be available anymore, so it is highly recommended that you don't use this alias.

`unlink()` takes the filename as a string. Again, like `copy()`, if you want to specify the filename relatively, it must be relative to your script. It will return a value of `True` if successful, `False` otherwise.

### rename()

`rename()` will change the name of a file. It acts like the DOS command `ren` or the `mv` UNIX shell command. Here is how it is used:

```
rename ( string oldname, string newname )
```

The remarks about `copy()` and `unlink()` also apply to `rename()`. If you use a relative filename, it must be relative to your script. It will return the value `True` if successful, `False` otherwise.

### filesize()

The function `filesize()` will return the size, in bytes, of the specified file. It takes the filename as a string. Here is an example:

```
function file_get_contents($filename){
    if($fp = fopen($filename,"r")){
        return fread($fp,filesize($filename));
    }
    else{
        return false;
    }
}
```

## Checks and Validity

This section looks at the functions you can use to perform validity tests and checks on file properties. Here is a list of these functions:

- `file_exists`: This tells you about the existence of a file
- `stat`: This returns the statistics about a file
- `is_dir`: This tells you if the file is a directory
- `is_file`: This tells you if the file is a file and not a directory or a device file
- `is_link`: This tells you if the file is a symbolic link
- `is_readable`: This tells you if the file is readable
- `is_writable`: This tells you if the file is writable
- `is_executable`: This tells you if the file is executable

These functions can be very useful (if you wanted to develop a web-based file manager, for example, for manipulating files on your machine's hard drive). All except `stat` return simple Boolean values. Once again, if you specify a relative filename, it must be relative to your script.

### file_exists()

The `file_exists()` function takes the filename as a string and will return `True` if the specified file exists, `False` otherwise. You can also use this function to check the existence of a directory.

## stat()

The `stat()` function will return an associative array containing statistics about a file. The array returned may appear somewhat confusing because the information contained in it is duplicated: the values are returned as both an associative and an index-based array. The array has the following keys:

- `0` or `dev`: device.
- `1` or `ino`: inode.
- `2` or `mode`: protection mode.
- `3` or `nlink`: number of links.
- `4` or `uid`: user ID of owner.
- `5` or `gid`: group ID owner. Which group the owner of the file belongs to.
- `6` or `rdev`: device type if inode device.
- `7` or `size`: size in bytes.
- `8` or `atime`: time of last access.
- `9` or `mtime`: time of last modification.
- `10` or `ctime`: time of last change. Similar to `mtime`, except `ctime` also logs changes to privileges, and other factors external to the actual data stored in the file itself.
- `11` or `blksize`: blocksize for filesystem I/O (will return -1 on Windows system).
- `12` or `blocks`: number of blocks allocated (will return -1 on Windows system).

Here is an example showing how you could use `stat()`, illustrating the information returned:

```php
<?php
        /* Comment one of these lines out, depending on whether
        you are running on Windows, or a UNIX, such as Mac OS X */
        $filename="/sample.txt";        //On UNIX
        $filename="\\sample.txt";       //On Windows

        $fullfilename=realpath(".").$filename;
        $arr = stat($fullfilename);
        header("Content-Type: text/plain");
        print_r($arr);
?>
```

This will produce in your browser:

**is_dir(), is_file(), is_link(), is_readable(),
is_writable(), is_executable()**

These functions check the properties of the file. They return
`True` if the file exists and the property is verified, or `False`
otherwise. Here are their prototypes:

```
bool is_dir ( string filename )
bool is_file ( string filename )
bool is_link ( string filename )
bool is_readable ( string filename )
bool is_writable ( string filename )
bool is_executable ( string filename )
```

# Directories and Paths

Having reviewed files as containers for data and the
operations we can perform on them as individual objects,
we will now look at operations on files as elements of the
filesystem. To do that, we will discuss the functions that help
us find information about a file: its real name and its real
position in the filesystem structure. Then, we will look at
how to navigate, create, and delete directories.

```
Array
(
    [0] => 2
    [1] => 0
    [2] => 33206
    [3] => 1
    [4] => 0
    [5] => 0
    [6] => 2
    [7] => 150
    [8] => 1036427935
    [9] => 1036427935
    [10] => 1036427761
    [11] => -1
    [12] => -1
    [dev] => 2
    [ino] => 0
    [mode] => 33206
    [nlink] => 1
    [uid] => 0
    [gid] => 0
    [rdev] => 2
    [size] => 150
    [atime] => 1036427935
    [mtime] => 1036427935
    [ctime] => 1036427761
    [blksize] => -1
    [blocks] => -1
)
```

## File Path

Before going into the intricacies of file path and filename, it is important to note that, on a Windows
machine, PHP will automatically turn the forward slash character to the backward slash (which only
Windows uses as a directory separator). It is useful that you train yourself in using the forward slash
as a directory separator, since even if you develop on Windows, you will almost certainly *deploy* on an
industrial-strength UNIX operating system.

## Canonical Filenames

The canonical name of a file is its name relative to the root directory, without any symbolic link or
directory element like "." or ".." or even "../../../".

The following are canonical filenames:

- `/usr/local/apache/htdocs/mysite/index.php`

- `/var/log/maillog`

- `C:\Program Files\Apache Group\Apache\bin\httpd`

... while these ones are not:

- `../images/img2.gif`
- `./images/../products/images/images2.png`
- `C:\Program Files\Apache\php\..\Apache Group\Apache\bin\httpd`
- `/var/log/../spool/mail/../../maillog`

### realpath()

The function `realpath()` will transform a filename into its canonical version. Here is its prototype:

```
string realpath ( string path )
```

Here is an example that will give you the canonical name of your script:

*Note that on some earlier versions of PHP, realpath() returned False when the file did not exist. This is not the case anymore.*

```
echo realpath("./".$_SERVER['PHP_SELF']);
```

This will output the physical path of the script.

### basename()

`basename()` returns the filename as a string without the directory associated. If you specify an extension on the file you are searching, it will return the name without its extension.

*Note, this needs to be run in your web server's root web directory – for example, c:\program files\apache group\apache\htdocs\nn.php for Apache/Windows, /Library/WebServer/Documents on OS X, or /usr/local/httpd/htdocs/ on SuSE Linux.*

Here is its prototype:

```
string basename ( string path [, string suffix] )
```

To illustrate the usage of `basename()`, suppose the following script is called `test.php`, and is run from the web server's root web directory:

```
$filename=realpath(".").$_SERVER['PHP_SELF'];
echo basename($filename)."<br />";
echo basename($filename,"php");
```

This would produce the following output:

*test*
*test.php*

### dirname()

The `dirname()` function is the opposite of `basename()`: it returns the directory part of a filename as a string. Here is its prototype:

```
string dirname ( string path )
```

This example will use the same file as in the previous case:

```
$filename= realpath(".").$_SERVER['PHP_SELF'];
echo dirname($filename);
```

This will output the location of the web server's root web directory, for example:

*c:/program files/apache group/apache/htdocs*

### pathinfo()

The `pathinfo()` function returns an associative array containing the information returned by `basename()`, `dirname()` and the extension of the file as well; you can use this function if you need all this information. For instance the following code, when run from the web server's root web directory:

```
$filename=realpath(".").$_SERVER['PHP_SELF'];
header("Content-Type: text/plain");
$arr = pathinfo($filename);
print_r($arr);
```

…will produce this output on a machine running Apache on OS X:

*Array*
*(*
 *[dirname] => /Library/WebServer/Documents*
 *[basename] => test.php*
 *[extension] => php*
*)*

Note that this function will not return a canonical directory name in the `dirname` index. Instead, it slices your filename into its different parts. The following example illustrates this difference:

```
header("Content-Type: text/plain");
$arr = pathinfo("../../exec/test.php");
print_r($arr);
```

This produces the following output on all platforms:

*Array*
*(*
 *[dirname] => ../../exec*
 *[basename] => test.php*
 *[extension] => php*
*)*

# Reading and Handling Directories

In this section we will discuss how to manage your directories.

## Manipulation of Directories

PHP provides a set of functions to create, delete, and rename directories. Here is the list of functions that provide these tools:

- `mkdir()` for creating directories
- `rmdir()` for deleting directories
- `rename()` although we have seen this in use in the earlier section on files, since directories are a type of file, this function can be used to change the name of a directory in exactly the same way

### mkdir()

`mkdir()` creates a directory in the place specified. The argument specified must be a directory, and your web server process must have write permission on this directory. Here is its prototype:

```
int mkdir ( string pathname,[ int mode ] )
```

The `pathname` argument can be a relative path or an absolute path. The optional `mode` argument tells the function the permissions that you want to set on the directory. This argument must be an octal number such as `0755` – the same permissions when presented as an integer (`755`) or a string (`u+w`) will not work. An octal number is represented as a normal number, but has a leading 0. Note that this will work only under UNIX systems. Using a mode argument under windows will not produce an error but will not have any effect.

This function returns the value `True` if successful, `False` otherwise.

### rmdir()

`rmdir()` deletes an empty directory. The web server process must have the permission to do so. Here is its prototype:

```
bool rmdir ( string dirname )
```

As with `mkdir()`, the `dirname` argument can be a relative or absolute path. This function returns `True` if successful, `False` otherwise.

## Reading Directories

It might sometimes be useful to be able to know exactly which files are present in a directory. PHP provides a set of functions to let you scan a directory for files. Here is the list:

- `opendir()`: For allocating a directory pointer, allowing you read its content
- `readdir()`: For reading the directory's content file by file
- `rewinddir()`: For resetting the directory's pointer position to the start of the directory
- `closedir()`: For closing the directory pointer returned by `opendir()`

**opendir(),readdir(),rewinddir(),closedir()**

All these functions are closely related, so we will review them together. Here are their prototypes:

```
resource opendir ( string path )
string readdir ( resource dir_handle )
void closedir ( resource dir_handle )
void rewinddir ( resource dir_handle )
```

The following example will show you how to scan the current directory to know what files are present:

```
<?php
        $dirpointer=opendir(".");
        while($file=readdir($dirpointer)){
                echo "$file<br />";
        }
        closedir($dirpointer);
?>
```

In my case, the script was in the default /htdocs/ directory of a typical Windows/Apache installation. Here is a portion of what was output:

# File Upload

Now we have enough background knowledge of file management to dive into a really neat feature: **HTTP Upload**. PHP can handle the uploading of both text and binary files via the POST method of any RFC-1867-compliant web browser (this includes all current versions of Opera, Netscape, and Internet Explorer).

## HTML Section

This section will present you with the steps required to design a page with a file upload form, and the file input tag. Feel free to skip this section if you already know how to set up an HTML file for file uploading.

## Prerequisite to File Upload: the Form Encoding

When designing a web page that lets a user send a file by posting a form, there is an important point that you must be aware of: the encoding attribute of the form tags must be set to "multipart/form-data". You should see the following in Dreamweaver MX:

```
8  <form action="" method="post" enctype="multipart/form-data" name="form1">
9  </form>
```

To set the encoding attribute in Dreamweaver MX, select the `<form>` tag by clicking on the *<form>* element in the bottom bar of the Dreamweaver MX *Design View* window (see the accompanying image):

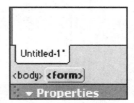

Now, select the `enctype` attribute menu, and set the encoding type to "multipart/form-data":

## The Form Design

Now that we have a form that can accept file upload, all we have to do is to add the file `<input>` tag. Place the cursor inside your form in Dreamweaver MX and click on the button named *File Field* in the *Form Insert* toolbar, as shown in the following picture:

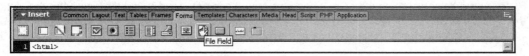

In *Design View*, this looks like a combination of a textfield and a button. The HTML simply reads: Let's rename this input to `myfile`.

```
<input type="file" name="file" id="file">
```

## The Form Action

In this example, we will use two different web pages to handle the upload: an HTML input form, and a PHP page, upload.php, containing the script that receives the file and places it into the correct directory. So, now we need to set the `action` of our HTML form to `upload.php`. The HTML code for our form now becomes:

```
<form name="form1" enctype="multipart/form-data" method="post" action="upload.php">
```

**8**

File Handling

Now we just need to add a *submit* button. Your file should look like this in Dreamweaver MX:

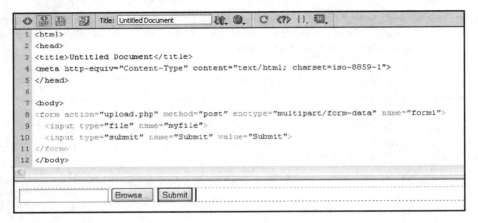

Save this as `input.html` in one of your active web directories. When using this page, you would use the *Browse...* button, to navigate the filesystem of your client machine and select a file to upload to the server. The path to the file on the client machine would then be displayed in the textfield – indeed it could be entered manually using this textfield to obtain the same result.

# PHP Code

This section describes the PHP script that will handle the uploaded file. The page is called `upload.php` and is located in the same web directory as `input.html`.

## The $_FILES Array

We will be using the predefined array $_FILES. This is a global array that is created as soon as a PHP page receives an uploaded file. It contains everything you need to get the uploaded data into the right place on your server's filesystem. Here is the structure of this array as it would appear in a PHP script which has been posted to by the HTML input form we just created:

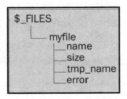

The myfile element is taken from the field name in the form. This way, if you are uploading more than one file in your HTML page, you can easily retrieve the information for each file by referencing its name. $_FILES['myfile'] has the following structure:

| Variable | Comments |
|---|---|
| name | The original name of the file on the client machine |
| size | The size in bytes of the original file |
| tmp_name | The name of the file on your server |
| error | The error code of the upload procedure. Here are the possible values, and their meanings:<br>UPLOAD_ERR_OK (0): There is no error, the upload has been completed successfully.<br>UPLOAD_ERR_INI_SIZE (1): The uploaded file size exceeded the maximum file size allowed by the server<br>UPLOAD_ERR_FORM_SIZE (2): The uploaded file size exceeded the maximum file size specified in the form code.<br>UPLOAD_ERR_PARTIAL (3): The file has been partially uploaded.<br>UPLOAD_ERR_NO_FILE (4): There was no uploaded file |

## Verification

The first step in making our upload.php page, is to verify that everything in the HTML form is correct. The following code provides a way of doing this, and gives an overview of the $_FILES array structure:

```php
<?php
        header("Content-Type: text/plain");
        print_r($_FILES);
?>
```

Save this file as upload.php in the same web directory as input.html, and submit to it using input.html (simply browse to a suitable file on the machine your browser is running on and submit that file). If everything has been correctly set up in your page, you should get something similar to this:

```
Array
(
    [myfile] => Array
        (
            [name] => 3.gif
            [type] => image/gif
            [tmp_name] => C:\WINDOWS\TEMP\php8AD.tmp
            [error] => 0
            [size] => 3518
        )
)
```

As you can see from the output, the $_FILES array contains a *myfile* array, which in turn, contains all elements concerning the file. You can see that the file we used to test the upload was called 3.gif. The type of this file is "image/gif". PHP automatically stores it in a temporary location: C:\WINDOWS\TEMP\php8AD.tmp. The error code was 0, which means that the upload was successful, and the size was 3518 bytes.

File Handling

## The Function getUploaded()

All through the rest of this section we will build, step by step, a function called `getUploaded()`. This function will take care of whole uploading processes, and you will be able to reuse it later.

### Arguments of getUploaded()

The function `getUploaded()` will take the following arguments:

- `$fileref`: The name of the field type. This argument will be used to access the data in the `$_FILES` array.

- `$destination`: The directory where you want to put the uploaded file. This directory should be relative to the root of your web site. For example: `/images/uploaded`, where `images` and `uploaded` are directories.

- `$mode`: The `mode` argument will tell the function what to do if the file already exists, whether to overwrite it or create a new file.

Here is the code for the call of the `getUploaded()` function:

```
$myfile = getUploaded("myfile","/images/upload","new");
```

The function `getUploaded()` will return the name of the file, relative to the root of your web site. If `getUploaded()` cannot retrieve it, it will return `False`.

### getUploaded Body

Now, we can start writing the `getUploaded()` function. The first thing we need to do, is make sure there is no error in the upload. To this end, we need to check the value of the error code given in `$_FILES`. Here's the start of the function:

```
function getUploaded($fileref,$destination,$mode){
        if(!$_FILES[$fileref]["error"]){
                // The file has been correctly uploaded.
        }else{
                echo "File was not correctly uploaded.<br />";
                return false;
        }
}
```

This test works because "no error" returns 0, which is also a Boolean value for `False`. Now we need to get the destination filename.

### The Destination Filename

The value of `$_FILES[$fileref][name]` is that of the original filename, as it was submitted. We will use it as the destination basename of the file on our server. We must make sure that by concatenating the variable `$_SERVER['DOCUMENT_ROOT']` and the variable `$destination`, we obtain a writable directory.

The code to validate this could be done like this:

```
// Checking the destination directory
$destdir = $_SERVER['DOCUMENT_ROOT'].$destination;
if(is_dir($destdir) && is_writable($destdir)){
        // We can write in this directory.
}else{
        echo "Directory $destdir does not exist or is not writable.<br />";
        return false;
}
```

You may recall that we looked at the is_dir() and is_writable() functions earlier. Now we can determine the canonical destination filename using the following code:

```
$destfilename=realpath($destdir."/".$_FILES[$fileref]["name"]);
```

## Checking the Existence of the File

To check if a file of that name already exists, we use the file_exists() function. Here is the code that checks for the existence of the destination file:

```
if(file_exists($destfilename)){
        // The file exists
}else{
        // The file doesn't exist
}
```

If the file does not exist, all we have to do is copy the temporary file in the destination directory. If it does exist, then the value of the $mode argument decides what we need do next. If $mode is set to overwrite, we can copy the file over the old one. If the mode is set to new, we will have to get another name for this file.

## Generating a Unique Name for a New File

To generate a new unique name for a file we will use a little algorithm that will browse the directory and stop when it has found a name that is not present. We'll check for the existence of a file using a numerical convention. For example, if we have a directory containing the files "0.gif" and "1.gif", the next unique name for a .gif file would be "2.gif". Here is the function we'll design to do that:

```
function getUniqueName($dir,$ext){
        $i=strftime("%Y%m%d");
        while(file_exists($dir."/$i.$ext")){
                $i++;
        }
        return "$i.$ext";
}
```

We use the date we transferred the file, if the filename already exists, and proceed to increment that until we arrive at a unique filename. We can modify our code now to get the final destination name of the file:

```
if(file_exists($destfilename) && $mode=="new"){
        $pInfo = pathinfo($destfilename);

$destfilename=realpath($destdir."/".getUniqueName($destdir,$pInfo["extension"]));
}
```

### Copying the File

Now we are ready to copy the file. The variable `$_FILES[$fileref]["tmp_name"]` will give us the source filename and the variable. `$destfilename` will give us the destination filename. We need to call the function `copy()`. Here is some code for copying a file:

```php
if(@copy($_FILES[$fileref]["tmp_name"],$destfilename)){
      // The copy is successful
}else{
      echo "The copy failed.<br />";
      return false;
}
```

### Final Step:Returning the Filename

The final step is to return the filename relative to the `$destination` argument. Here is the code required to do that:

```php
// The copy is successful
return $destination."/".basename($destfilename);
```

### The Complete Code

Now we have everything in place, here is the complete code for the two functions, `getUploaded()` and `getUniqueName()`:

```php
<?php
function getUniqueName($dir,$ext){
  $i=strftime("%Y%m%d");
  while(file_exists($dir."/$i.$ext")){
    $i++;
  }
  return "$i.$ext";
}

function getUploaded($fileref,$destination,$mode){
  if(!$_FILES[$fileref]["error"]){ // The file has been correctly uploaded.
    // Checking the destination directory
    $destdir = $_SERVER['DOCUMENT_ROOT'].$destination;
    if(is_dir($destdir) && is_writable($destdir)){
      // We can write in this directory.
      $destfilename=realpath($destdir."/".$_FILES[$fileref]["name"]);
      if(file_exists($destfilename) && $mode=="new"){
        $pInfo = pathinfo($destfilename);

$destfilename=realpath($destdir."/".getUniqueName($destdir,$pInfo["extension"]));
      }
      // Here we copy
      if(@copy($_FILES[$fileref]["tmp_name"],$destfilename)){
        // The copy is successful
        return $destination."/".basename($destfilename);
      }else{
        echo "The copy failed.<br />";
        return false;
      }
    }else{
```

```
        echo "Directory $destdir does not exist or is not writable.<br />";
        return false;
    }
  }else{
    echo "File was not correctly uploaded.<br />";
    return false;
  }
}

if($myfile = getUploaded("myfile","/images/upload","new")){
        echo "File written to directory $myfile";
}else{
        echo "An error occurred";
}
?>
```

Create an `/images/uploaded` directory on your web server, and try submitting a few files for upload using `upload.html`; you should see them start appearing in the directory.

## Extending Dreamweaver MX with a File Upload Server Behavior

### Include File

It would be interesting to create a separate file dedicated to these two functions so that you could just use an `include()` statement to access them. To do this, create a new file containing only the code for these two functions, and save it as `upload.inc.php`.

Now in your PHP pages you could access these functions like this:

```
<?php
include("upload.inc.php");

if($myfile = getUploaded("myfile","/images/upload","new")){
        echo "File written to directory $myfile";
}
else{
        echo "An error occurred";
}
?>
```

As you can see, this is much more readable. We can go one stage further, though. We could create a **Dreamweaver Extension**.

### Creating an Extension for Uploading Files

As the piece of code in your main file is pretty small, we could build an extension with the Dreamweaver Server Behavior Builder. The goal of this extension would be to change the value of the input file to represent the correct path to your images, so that you can easily use it with a "*SQL insert*" Server Behavior.

To create a new server behavior, click on *New Server Behavior* in the *Server Behavior* tab of the *Application* panel as shown in the following picture:

File Handling

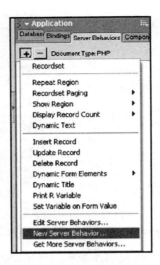

In the dialog that opens, click on the + button next to *Code Blocks to Insert*. Name the new Server Behavior *Get Uploaded File*, and, in the code block section, enter the following code:

```php
<?php
  include_once("@@Upload File Location@@");
  if(!$myfile = getUploaded("@@File Name@@","@@Destination@@","@@mode@@")){
    $myfile="";
  }
?>
```

This code will define the three arguments we want to give to `getUploaded` and the location of the include file. The *Insert Code* menu should be selected as *Above the <html> tag*. The *Relative Position* should be set to *Just before the Recordset,* because if you want to use the value of the variable in a insert or update SQL statement, all you would have to do isuse the value of the variable `$myfile`.

Click on *Advanced>>* and set the *Server Behavior Title* to *Get Uploaded File (@ @File Name@ @, @ @mode@ @)*. Set the *Code Block to Select* as the first code block: *Get Uploaded File_block1*.

Your Server Behavior Builder window should now look like this:

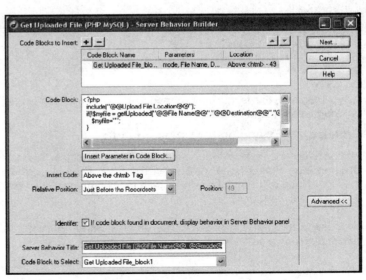

208

Click the *'Next...'* button to define the parameters. Select the following parameter types:

- *Mode : Radio Group*
- *File Name : Text Field*
- *Destination : Text Field*
- *Upload File Location : URL Text Field*

Your *Parameter Type* dialog box should look like this:

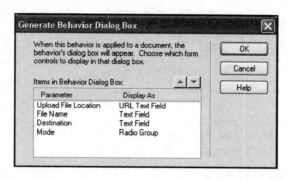

Click *OK* to close the dialog. Now we have to set the labels of the *Radio Group* for the *Mode* parameter. Open the HTML document that has been made by the Server Behavior Builder, it is stored in your *Application Data Directory* on Windows. The complete path of your document might look something like this:

*C:\Documents and Settings\Bruno\Application Data\Macromedia\Dreamweaver MX\Configuration\ServerBehaviors\PHP_MySQL\Get Uploaded File.htm*

Your Dreamweaver *Design View* window should now look something like this (the order of the form controls may vary slightly, depending on your system):

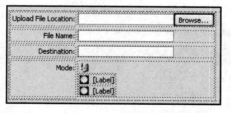

Change the *[Label]* text for the radiobuttons of the *Mode* parameter to *New* and *Overwrite*, respectively. You should also set the value of each radiobutton. The following picture shows you the Dreamweaver interface when setting the default value of the radiobutton to *New*:

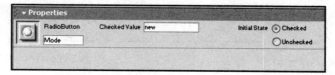

You can play around with this interface quite a bit, since it is just an HTML form. Here is an example of what you can achieve:

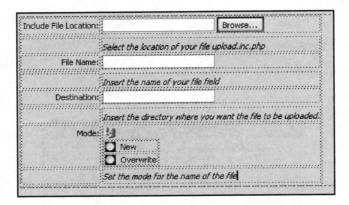

Now, save your document and close it. You'll need to reload your extensions for Dreamweaver to recognize your changes. To do that, Press the *Ctrl* key of your keyboard and left-click on the menu button of the *Insert Panel*, as shown in the following picture:

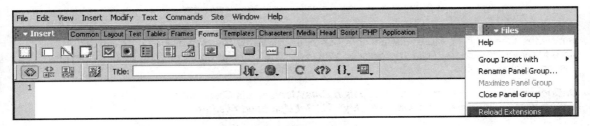

Now, open a new Dynamic PHP file. Click on the + button to insert a new Server Behavior in the *Server Behavior* tab of the *Database Panel*. You'll see that there is a menu item named *Get Uploaded File*. Click on this item.

The new interface of your Server Behavior should look like this:

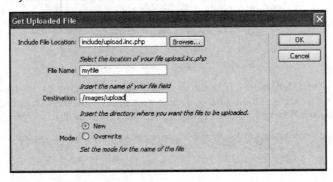

And you have your extension!

# Summary

In this chapter, we have reviewed the tools PHP provides to handle files. We have analyzed files at different levels, starting from a low level, where files were seen as a container for data. We've seen how to open files, then read from or write to them, and then close them.

PHP provides two kinds of shortcut: one that outputs the content of a file to the browser, the other that reads the content of a file into a variable.

Next, we saw how to handle files as a whole. PHP provides basic manipulation functions as well as functions that allow you to perform different types of checking and validity operations. We've used some of these functions in the section on uploading.

On a higher level, we've seen how to handle directories and paths: PHP has some very interesting functions for path checking. We have had a look at the notion of canonical filenames. PHP lets you scan a directory in the same manner as you would do for a file, just by opening it, reading, and closing it.

Finally, we used all this information to design a piece of code that will let you manage a file received from a browser. We've seen what is required to get the file back into its normal directory.

The final section of this chapter showed you how to package the upload PHP code into a nice Dreamweaver MX Server Behavior.

**8**

**File Handling**

# 9

- Configuring PHP for e-mail

- Sending e-mail

- HTML, attachments, and other mime e-mails

**Author: Bruno Mairlot**

# Using PHP E-mail

Over the last few years e-mail has become a vital communications tool for businesses, so it is important to be familiar with PHP's functionality for mail handling. E-mails are sent between mail servers via SMTP (Simple Mail Transfer Protocol). An SMTP server handles the outgoing mail and a POP3 server (Post Office Protocol) handles incoming mail. PHP will let you send basic plain-text e-mail quite easily, but if you want to do something more complicated, like send attachments or HTML-rendered mail, then you will have to tell it exactly what to do.

In this chapter we will learn how the PHP mail function works on UNIX and Windows systems. We will also look at how to design MIME (Multipurpose Internet Mail Extensions) and HTML e-mails, with attachments, and build a mail with multiple types of content. But before we can do any of that we need to configure PHP so it knows how to handle our mail.

## Configuring PHP Mail

Although the `mail()` function is used in exactly the same way on both UNIX and Windows systems, you need to configure PHP slightly differently, depending which platform you are running it on. If you are using PHP on Windows, you will need to have an Internet connection to a remote SMTP server.

For the `mail()` function to work, you need to have specified a working local mail server in the `php.ini` file. There are three configuration variables in your `php.ini` file that you need to set up:

- SMTP : For Win32 only, set the SMTP server.
- Sendmail_from : For Win32 only, to set the From: header, which identifies the sender of the mail.
- Sendmail_path : For UNIX only, to set the path to the sendmail executable.

Here is what your `php.ini` might look like when opening:

```
[mail function]
; For Win32 only.
SMTP = localhost

; For Win32 only.
sendmail_from = me@localhost.com

; For Unix only.  You may supply arguments as well (default: 'sendmail -t -i').
;sendmail_path =
```

If you are using Windows and you specify a remote SMTP server to relay your messages, the server must be configured to allow relays otherwise your e-mail messages will get bounced, you should be aware that many ISPs will not have their SMTP servers set to allow relays.

On UNIX systems PHP relies on sendmail: a program which is installed by default on almost any UNIX system and which handles the details of actually sending the mail to the recipient's e-mail server.

## UNIX Configuration

On UNIX the `mail()` function works by calling the sendmail executable on your server and feeding it the information it needs, such as headers, subject, and content. Therefore, all you have to do when configuring PHP for mail on UNIX, is make sure the configuration variable `sendmail_path` is correct.

By default this variable has the value `sendmail -t -i`. If the `php.ini` file has no value for this variable, PHP will automatically use this default value. This means two things:

- You must have a mail transfer agent (MTA) on your server that is called sendmail
- This executable must accept the parameters –t and -i

Normally, you won't have to worry about this, but if your system doesn't have sendmail installed, you must set up the variable `sendmail_path` to point to your mail transfer agent. You need to ensure that the executable you are pointing at can be fed with raw mail data because this is the way PHP works with this executable.

The `phpinfo()` function will give you information on the actual value of your `sendmail_path` variable. The following picture illustrates the default configuration. This `phpinfo()` result has been obtained on a Linux system with sendmail installed as the mail transfer agent.

| standard | |
| --- | --- |
| Regex Library | Bundled library enabled |
| Dynamic Library Support | enabled |
| Path to sendmail | /usr/sbin/sendmail -t -i |

# Windows Configuration

On Windows, configuring PHP e-mail is a little simpler. All you have to tell PHP is where your SMTP server is.

Configuring the SMTP server is done by setting the value of the `SMTP` variable in the `php.ini` file. Your SMTP server must be configured to accept mail from your web server, of course. If your Windows server has an SMTP server running, it will normally be configured to relay mail from the localhost. If your mail server is another server in your network, you need to make sure that it will relay mail from your server's IP address. The `SMTP` variable normally requires a hostname, but an IP address will work too.

Next to the `SMTP` variable, there is a second configuration variable for Windows systems that can be set up: the `sendmail_from` variable. This variable just sets the *From:* header when PHP connects to your mail server. We will see in the next section why it is important to set this variable correctly.

*If you don't have a running SMTP server on your network, you can use your ISP's. If you don't remember what your ISP's SMTP server is, all you have to do is use the same SMTP server that you use with you e-mail Client like MS Outlook, Eudora, Netscape, or whatever. Just search for the SMTP configuration, and use the same.*

The following picture shows you part of what the `phpinfo()` function returns under a Windows system about mail:

| standard | |
| --- | --- |
| Regex Library | Bundled library enabled |
| Dynamic Library Support | enabled |
| Internal Sendmail Support for Windows | enabled |

# The mail() Function

The `mail()` function is the PHP function used to send e-mail. Of course, it is always possible for you to open a network connection to a mail server, but in that case you would have to re-implement an SMTP client.

Here is the `mail()` function prototype:

```
bool mail ( string to, string subject, string message [, string additional_headers
[, string additional_parameters]] )
```

The `mail()` function will return a value of `True` if the mail has been accepted for delivery, and `False` otherwise. Note that a `True` value doesn't mean the mail has been sent, it just means that your mail server has accepted the job of sending the mail. Sending a mail is an asynchronous process. Once your mail server has received your mail, it will put it into a queue for processing. This may happen instantaneously or it may be processed after the existing queue and any other tasks have cleared.

The mail() function takes three essential arguments: the recipient's e-mail address, the subject of the e-mail, and the body of the e-mail. You can also specify two more arguments, a string containing any additional headers and another string containing additional parameters:

- **to**: As its name indicates, the to argument will specify the primary recipient of the e-mail. Multiple recipients can be specified at once by separating them with a comma (',') character. All these recipients will appear in the To: header. You should not use this if you want to use the Cc or the Bcc header.

- **subject**: The subject argument will set the subject of your mail. There is one thing to bear in mind however, if you are trying to send a complex e-mail containing HTML or attachments, you will have to place all specific header information in the additional_headers argument, but PHP will still tell sendmail the subject of the mail by using the value of the subject argument. We will look at the additional_headers argument shortly.

- **message**: The message argument contains the basic content of your mail. Again, if you are building a complex e-mail it is recommended that you leave this argument empty and use the additional_headers argument instead.

- **additional_headers**: This argument is the first of the two optional arguments of the mail() function. When you send a basic plain-text e-mail, you probably won't need it, but if you are sending a MIME e-mail, you should place all of your mail content in this argument. When the mail() function sends data to the sendmail process or to the mail server, it will first build a set of two headers containing to and subject. Then, if specified, the function will send the value of this argument, and finally the content of the message argument. So if the value of the additional_headers argument contains the content of your mail, you can safely leave the message argument empty.

- **additional_parameters**: This argument is only used on UNIX systems, and is used to send additional parameters to the sendmail executable. You remember that the default configuration value of the sendmail_path variable is sendmail –t –i. Using this argument you can add other parameters such as -fSenderAdress that will tell sendmail the sender's address. Note that since version 4.2.3, this has been disabled by default and cannot be used in safe mode.

*Note that you must use the character sequence '\r\n' to separate your headers. Some UNIX mailers will accept '\n' only, but it is safer to use the full sequence.*

## Sending Mail

In its basic form, the mail() function requires a value for the first three arguments only. In this example we want to send an e-mail with the following information:

```
The recipient is 'support@glasshaus.com'
The subject is 'There is an error on page 798'
The message is:
'Hello,

There is an error in your Dreamweaver MX: Advanced PHP Development book at page
798.'
```

The code that would send such a mail would look like this:

```php
<?php
        $subject="There is an error on page 798";
        $message= "Hello,\n";
        $message.="There is an error in your Dreamweaver MX: Advanced PHP";
        $message.="Development book at page 798.\n";

        mail('support@glasshaus.com',$subject,$message);
?>
```

## An Example with Additional Headers

That last example shows us the simplest uses of the `mail()` function: send a plain-text message to a single address. We supposed that the configuration variables were set correctly and we did not specify any headers. In the following example, we will set different headers and we will check that the mail has been correctly sent.

Here is the list of headers we will set and their meanings:

- From: Sets the from value in the header segment
- Reply-To: Optional, sets the value of the reply address.
- X-Mailer: Sets the name of the mailer. Usually it is PHP and the current version.
- X-Priority: Sets the priority of the mail.

The above example's code would now look like this:

```php
<?php
        $subject="There is an error in your book at page 798";
        $header="From: mail@server.com\r\n";
        $header.="Reply-To: mail@server.com\r\n";
        $header.="X-Mailer: PHP ".phpversion()."\r\n";
        $header.="X-Priority: 1\r\n"; // Urgent Message
        $message= "Hello,\n";
        $message.="There is an error in your Dreamweaver MX : Advanced PHP";
        $message.="Development book at page 798.\n";

        if(!mail('support@glasshaus.com',$subject,$message,$header)){
                echo "Mail could not be sent.";
        }
?>
```

You will also notice that we now test to see whether the call to the `mail()` function succeeded, and react by printing a message if it did not.

9

Using PHP E-mail

# MIME E-mails

Previously, we looked at how to send basic plain-text e-mail. This section will show you how to build more complex e-mails, with HTML and text content as well as attached files.

To design such e-mails, we will need to use the **MIME format**; the **Multipurpose Internet Mail Extension**.

## The MIME format

MIME format is a specification for enhancing the capabilities of standard e-mail. It is somewhat similar to a directory structure, in that it is made of a list of MIME blocks, with some of these blocks encapsulated into other blocks of a higher level.

Each of these blocks has a set of headers that tells the mail client what this block's purpose is. Here is an example of a MIME block:

```
Content-Type: text/html; charset="us-ascii"

<html>
<i>Hello,<br><br>
this is a MIME html mail</i></html>
```

In this example, the headers just tell the mail client that this block represents the HTML content of the mail.

### The MIME syntax

Here is the list of syntax rules for defining MIME e-mails:

A MIME mail always has the `MIME-Version: 1.0` header in its main headers section. A MIME mail consists of a list of MIME blocks. A list of MIME blocks can either be one single block or a series of blocks, all listed one after the other.

A MIME block is made of two segments: the header segment and the content segment. The sequence '\r\n\r\n' sets the end of the header segment and the start of the content segment. Actually this sequence shows as an empty line, just after the last header.

A MIME block's content can be either another MIME block list or plain content, such as text, HTML code, or a file. The following figure shows a typical mail, containing the HTML content, the text-only alternative, and an attached file.

If we analyze the structure of this e-mail, we'll see that the main block is the *mixed* block. This mixed block's content is a list of two blocks: the *alternative* block and the *attached* file. The alternative block's content is also a list of two blocks: the plain-text block and the HTML code block.

Now, the following schema shows you a mail with only plain-text content and three attached files:

In this diagram, we have two levels of MIME block: The *mixed* block, which has a list of sub-blocks, each consisting of plain text or attached files. Now there is one last rule in the MIME format. It is not exactly a syntax rule, but a grammatical rule. There is a hierarchical order in the block structure: if you only send an HTML mail, you are not going to use a mixed type block. In the same way, if you want to send plain text plus attached file you cannot use the alternative block type.

Let's now look at the definitions of the MIME list and the five main types of MIME block.

**General Definition of a MIME Block : the Content-Type Header**

As defined earlier, a MIME block is made of two segments: the header segment and the content. In the header segment you **must** have the `Content-Type` header which is used to set the character set and the data format. It is the only header section that is not optional. The following code shows a function that could be used to design a MIME block:

```
function getMIMECode($header,$content){
        if(preg_match("/\r\n$/m",$header)){
                return "$header\r\n$content";
        }
        else{
                return "$header\r\n\r\n$content";
        }
}
```

This function simply checks if your `$header` argument terminates with the sequence `\r\n`. If it does, then it will just add a single `\r\n` to separate the header from the content; if it doesn't, it will add the complete '`\r\n\r\n`' sequence. You can pass it the two arguments, `$header` and `$content`, formatted correctly, and they will be assembled to form the full definition.

Now, suppose we want to send an HTML e-mail only. This mail will be made of only one block. The content-type of this block is "`text/html`". Here is the code we could use to make an HTML MIME block:

9

Using PHP E-mail

```php
<?php

    function getMIMECode($header,$content){
        if(preg_match("/\r\n$/m",$header)){
            return "$header\r\n$content";
        }
        else{
            return "$header\r\n\r\n$content";
        }
    }

    $htmlHeader="Content-Type: text/html";
    $htmlContent="<html><b>Hello</b>, this is HTML</html>";

    $htmlMIME = getMIMECode($htmlHeader,$htmlContent);

    mail("youraddress@yourdomain.com","MIME Test","","MIME-Version:
1.0\r\n$htmlMIME");
?>
```

By using this code, you already have enough information to build HTML-mail. All you would have to do is to set the variable `$htmlContent` to your desired value. But we can build much more interesting e-mail…

### The MIME boundary

As said previously, MIME consists of either a series of blocks or just one block. If you are building a list with only one block, there is no specific code to add, but if you are building a list of blocks, you must use **MIME boundaries**. A MIME boundary is used to separate two or more blocks in the list. It is a sequence of characters that is unique in your mail. You can use any sequence, as long as it is unique.

As a list of blocks is, itself, a MIME block, it has a header segment and a content segment. In the header segment, you can specify the boundary definition. In the content segment, each block in the list will be separated by the sequence "–" and the boundary itself. After the last block in your list, the boundary will appear again, but with the sequence "–" at the end of it, to signify that it terminates the list.

The following figure shows the same mail as before, but adds the boundaries to it:

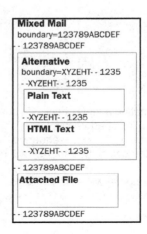

220

In this structure, there are two lists containing more than one block: the mixed block, containing the alternative block and the attached file. The second list is the alternative block. Therefore, in this structure you see that we have two different boundaries. The boundary for the mixed block is `123789ABCDEF`, while the boundary for the alternative is `XYZEHT-1235`.

Don't forget that you can use any boundary sequence you want, but it has to be unique. Here is a suggestion for automatically building a unique boundary:

```
function computeMIMEBoundary(){
        return substr(md5(time().rand()),0,38);
}
```

This function will return a random boundary for your mail based on the `time()` and `rand()` functions using PHP's `md5()` function. Now, let's see exactly how to code the different types of MIME block.

### The Mixed Block Type

We previously mentioned that a MIME block is a list. We will therefore have to use the boundary definition for the mixed block type. The `Content-Type` header value for a mixed type block is `multipart/mixed`. The boundary definition must be placed in the header segment, but it is not exactly a header in itself. It must be attached to the `Content-Type` header.

Suppose we have a mixed block with the following boundary: **123789ABCDEF**. Here is how it should be coded:

```
Content-Type: multipart/mixed; boundary="123789ABCDEF"
```

*Note the semicolon character. It is there to separate the different attributes of the header `Content-Type`. You will see it again in the file block type section.*

The mixed type block is mainly used when you have an attached file. For example, suppose we have an e-mail where we have HTML content and one file attachment. We will suppose we have the code of these blocks in two variables: `$htmlMIME` and `$fileMIME`.

First we will see the code required to build the mixed list:

```
function getMixedCode($mimeArr){
        // $mimeArr is an array of MIME block code.
        $boundary = computeMIMEBoundary();
        $mixedHeader="Content-Type: multipart/mixed; boundary=\"$boundary\"";
        $mixedContent="";
        foreach($mimeArr as $block){
                $mixedContent.="-$boundary\r\n";
                $mixedContent.="$block\r\n";
        }
        $mixedContent.="-$boundary-\r\n";

        return getMIMECode($mixedHeader,$mixedContent);

}
```

The function `getMixedCode()` will take as argument an array of MIME block code and will build the list. Each block is separated by the `$boundary` value. At the end of the list, we add the boundary one last time, but with a "–" sequence at the end.

Here is the code we could use to create a mixed block with HTML and an attached file. Don't worry about the file headers, we will discuss them soon:

```php
<?php

    function getMIMECode($header,$content){
        if(preg_match("/\r\n$/m",$header)){
            return "$header\r\n$content";
        }
        else{
            return "$header\r\n\r\n$content";
        }
    }

    function computeMIMEBoundary(){
        return substr(md5(time().rand()),0,38);
    }

    function getMixedCode($mimeArr){
        // $mimeArr is an array of MIME block code.
        $boundary = computeMIMEBoundary();
        $mixedHeader="Content-Type: multipart/mixed; boundary=\"$boundary\"";
        $mixedContent="";
        foreach($mimeArr as $block){
            $mixedContent.="–$boundary\r\n";
            $mixedContent.="$block\r\n";
        }
        $mixedContent.="–$boundary–\r\n";

        return getMIMECode($mixedHeader,$mixedContent);

    }

    $htmlHeader="Content-Type: text/html";
    $htmlContent="<html><b>Hello</b>, this is HTML</html>";
    $htmlMIME = getMIMECode($htmlHeader,$htmlContent);

    $fileHeader="Content-Type: text/plain\r\n";
    $fileHeader.="Content-Transfer-Encoding: base64\r\n";
    $fileHeader.="Content-Disposition: attachment; filename=\"test.php\"\r\n";

$rawFileContent=join('',file($_SERVER['DOCUMENT_ROOT'].$_SERVER['PHP_SELF']));
    $fileContent=chunk_split(base64_encode($rawFileContent));
    $fileMIME = getMIMECode($fileHeader,$fileContent);
    $mixedMIME = getMixedCode(array($htmlMIME,$fileMIME));

    echo $mixedMIME;

    mail("youraddress@yourdomain.com","MIME Test","","MIME-Version:
1.0\r\n$mixedMIME");
?>
```

Executing this code will produce the following output in your browser, thanks to the `echo $mixedMIME` line:

```
Content-Type: multipart/mixed; boundary="58ec91fe69f5b650298b3fae0bc1cff8"

—58ec91fe69f5b650298b3fae0bc1cff8
Content-Type: text/html

<html><b>Hello</b>, this is HTML</html>

—58ec91fe69f5b650298b3fae0bc1cff8
Content-Type: text/plainContent-Transfer-Encoding: base64
Content-Disposition: attachment; filename="test.php"
```

```
PD9waHAKCQoJZnVuY3Rpb24gZ2V0TUlNRUNvZGUoJGhlYWRlciwkY29udGVudC17CgkJaWYocHJl
1
Z19tYXRjaCgiL1xyXG4kL20iLCRoZWFkZXIpKXsKCQkJcmV0dXJuICIkaGVhZGVyXHJcbiRjb25
0
ZW50IjsKCQl9CgkJZWxzZXsKCQkJcmV0dXJuICIkaGVhZGVyXHJcblxyXG4kY29udGVudCI7Cgk
J
fQoJfQoJCglmdW5jdGlvbiBjb21wdXRlTUlNRUJvdW5kYXJ5KCl7DQoJCXJldHVybiBzdWJzdHI
o....
```

## The Alternative Block Type

The alternative block type is used when you want to send both HTML content and plain text. The content of the plain text and the HTML is supposed to be the same, because generally mail clients are configured to show either one or the other.

The alternative block type is built almost the same way as the mixed block type. The `Content-Type` header looks like this:

```
Content-Type: multipart/alternative
```

Here is a function that we can use to build the code of an alternative block type:

```php
function getAlternativeCode($plainMIME,$htmlMIME){

        $boundary = computeMIMEBoundary();
        $altHeader="Content-Type: multipart/alternative; boundary=\"$boundary\"";

        $altContent="—$boundary\r\n";
        $altContent.="$plainMIME\r\n";
        $altContent.="—$boundary\r\n";
        $altContent.="$htmlMIME\r\n";
        $altContent.="—$boundary—\r\n";

        return getMIMECode($altHeader,$altContent);
}
```

Now, here is the code you could use to build an alternative e-mail:

```
$htmlHeader="Content-Type: text/html";
$htmlContent="<html><b>Hello</b>, this is HTML</html>";
$htmlMIME = getMIMECode($htmlHeader,$htmlContent);

$plainHeader="Content-Type: text/plain";
$plainContent="Hello,\r\n this is Plain text";
$plainMIME=getMIMECode($plainHeader,$plainContent);

$altMIME = getAlternativeCode($htmlMIME,$plainMIME);
echo $altMIME;

mail("bruno@local.maehdros.com","MIME Test","","MIME-Version: 1.0\r\n$altMIME");
```

This code would output the following:

```
Content-Type: multipart/alternative; boundary="407aee880e1ce93bce6c01900eab7255"

—407aee880e1ce93bce6c01900eab7255
Content-Type: text/html

<html><b>Hello</b>, this is HTML</html>
—407aee880e1ce93bce6c01900eab7255
Content-Type: text/plain

Hello,
 this is Plain text
—407aee880e1ce93bce6c01900eab7255—
```

### The HTML and Plain Text Block Type

The HTML and plain text code block are the easiest to design. All you have to specify, again, is the `Content-Type` header. As you probably have already seen in the previous example, the type for HTML code is `text/html` while it is `text/plain` for plain text.

### The File Block Type

The file block type is the most complex, because very often the value of the headers is quite different and depends heavily on the file itself.

Here is a list of headers you should use when sending a file in an e-mail:

- Content-Type: The usual and required header. This header can also have the filename attribute.

- Content-Transfer-Encoding: This header will tell the mail client how to decode the file.

- Content-Disposition: This optional header will tell the mail client how to render the file in the mail window. Note that this header is optional. By default, most mail clients will render them as attached files.

The `Content-Type` of a file may not be so easy to find. You will have to do some research about MIME types to find the correct one.

Here is a short list of file extensions and their possible MIME types. You will find a complete list of MIME types in the code dowload section of *http://www.glasshaus.com*.

| Variable | Comments |
|---|---|
| name | The original name of the file on the client machine |
| size | The size in bytes of the original file |
| tmp_name | The name of the file on your server |
| error | The error code of the upload procedure. Here are the possible values, and their meanings:<br>UPLOAD_ERR_OK (0): There is no error, the upload has been completed successfully<br>UPLOAD_ERR_INI_SIZE (1): The uploaded file size exceeded the maximum file size allowed by the server<br>UPLOAD_ERR_FORM_SIZE (2): The uploaded file size exceeded the maximum file siz specified in the form code.<br>UPLOAD_ERR_PARTIAL (3): The file has been partially uploaded. |

Many content types that can be transmitted by e-mail are represented as 8-bit characters or binary data. This data cannot be transported over certain protocols, among them STMP which restricts e-mail messages to 7-bit US ASCII data with lines containing less than 1000 characters. You can use the Content-Transfer-Encoding header field to overcome this limitation. Content-Transfer-Encoding specifies an encoding transformation that converts the format of the e-mail to one compatible with SMTP. If you don't set it correctly you can ruin all your mail. In the example with the attached file, I used the encoding base64. My advice is to always use base64 encoding when attaching a file, and any non-textual data.

To encode a file in base64 encoding, you can use the function base64_encode() and chunk_split() consecutively. The first one will encode your content into a base64 string and the chunk_split() function will insert a '\r\n' every 76 characters, which is the correct formatting for a MIME mail.

Here is an example of code to encode a string in base64:

```
$encodedString = chunk_split(base64_encode($rawString));
```

The Content-Disposition tells the mail client how to render the file in its window. It is mainly used with images and HTML files, when the HTML is not HTML content, but instead an attached HTML file.

You can have two different values for this header:

- attachment : The file appears in the list of attached files
- inline : The file will be rendered directly in the client's window.

The header Content-Disposition can accept a second attribute: filename. Multiple attributes for the header value are separated with the semicolon (;) character. We have already seen a case where it is needed: the mixed and alternative block types require boundary definitions.

9

Using PHP E-mail

In the following example, we have a file named "`image.gif`". We want this image to be base64 encoded, and we want it to appear in the client's window. Here is the code you can use for headers:

```
Content-Type: image/gif; filename="image.gif"
Content-Transfer-Encoding: base64
Content-Disposition: inline; filename="image.gif"
```

# Summary

In this chapter, we have seen how to send e-mail with PHP. The first thing you should remember when you want to send e-mail is to make sure your PHP mail functionality works correctly. There are three configuration variables required to set up PHP mail. Two are dedicated for Windows, one is dedicated to UNIX systems.

The basic function that sends mail with PHP is `mail()`. We have reviewed its arguments, and noted that this function can be used to send basic, plain-text e-mail, or more complex e-mail using the MIME standard.

The MIME standard describes a format for your e-mail content. It is basically made up of different blocks, each with its own header. We have reviewed MIME syntax and seen that the format for a MIME block consists of two segments, the header and the content, separated by a blank line.

If your MIME block is actually a list of other MIME blocks, you must use a boundary definition, and separate each block by this boundary.

To create a mail with one or more attachments, you have to use the mixed block type, while if you want to send a mail with HTML and plain text content you must use the alternative block type. The content of this block will be a list containing two other MIME blocks: the HTML block and plain text. HTML plain text, and file blocks are assembled using the correct `Content-Type` header in the block definition.

Using PHP E-mail

# 10

- XML Technologies

- Processing XML in PHP

**Author: Gareth Downes-Powell**

# XML

XML (Extensible Markup Language) is a powerful, platform-independent technology that enables data exchange, and separation of content from presentation. In this chapter we look at XML itself, and demonstrate how it can be used to make your web site much more efficient and easier to maintain. We look at the three XML technologies in this chapter, namely the Simple API for XML (SAX), the Document Object Model (DOM), and the eXtensible Stylesheet Language Transformation (XSLT). We look at some of the advantages and disadvantages of each of these technologies and explore how they can be used.

We will also take a look at the XML capabilities of Dreamweaver MX, and how Dreamweaver MX can be used as a development environment for working with XML. We then look at XHTML (Extensible Hypertext Markup Language), and explain what it is and how it differs from HTML. We see how we can create XHTML documents automatically in Dreamweaver MX, and have it enforce all the XHTML rules for us.

In this chapter we will be looking at a real-life example of using XML to process the Macromedia Developers XML feed, which is a live XML feed from the Macromedia web site. It contains details of the current resources in the Macromedia Developer Center. We will demonstrate how to process this XML feed using SAX, then DOM, and finally XSLT.

## Installing XML with PHP

Generally, the default installation of PHP doesn't have XML options enabled, so you'll need to install the XML components yourself. Installation is different, depending on whether you're running PHP on Windows or Linux.

### Windows Installation

You should already have the software you need for XML processing because it's included in the bundled PHP package, although the XML options may not be enabled. For information about installing PHP on Windows, and which libraries are bundled in the PHP package, take a look at: *http://www.php.net/manual/en/install.windows.php*

To activate the XML extensions, you need to edit your `php.ini` file. The following extensions need to be activated, by removing the semicolon (;) from in front of the line:

- `php_domxml.dll`
- `php_xslt.dll`
- `php_sockets.dll`

The DLLs should be copied from your PHP DLL directory, into a directory in the Windows path; suitable directories are:

- `c:\windows\system` for Windows 98/ME
- `c:\WINNT\system32` for Windows NT/2000/XP

You will also need to copy the files called `sablot.dll` and also `expat.dll` there (they come in the PHP zip download, and should also be in your PHP DLL directory).

Once you have activated the extensions in the `php.ini` file, you need to restart your Web Server, so that it uses the new settings. We're now going to look at what the above DLLs provide, and if necessary, any extra software you need installed.

# Linux Installation

To enable basic XML options, you will need to recompile PHP with the following option:

```
--with-xml
```

If you're using PHP as a dynamic Apache Module, you just need to recompile PHP, and then copy the new PHP module into your Apache modules directory.

If you are using PHP with a static Apache build, you will need to recompile both PHP and Apache to use the XML commands.

XML needs a version of the Expat parser installed on your system to run. You should be running Apache v 1.3.20 or greater, and this has a cut-down version of Expat built in, which is suitable for the XML extension. Alternatively, you can install the full version of Expat on your system, but if you do this you need to recompile Apache to exclude the built-in cut down Expat version, as you cannot run the two together.

You also need to install the Gnome XML library on your system, which is described below.

## Installing the Gnome XML Libraries, libxml

The Gnome XML libraries, also known as libxml, are available from *http://xmlsoft.org/,* the current version at the time of writing is version 2.4.2x. The files can either be compiled from the downloadable source, or alternatively you can find an RPM library for your particular Linux distribution, which makes installation easy.

To install libxml from source use:

```
tar -zxpf libxml2-4.2.tar.gzip
cd libxml2-4.2
./configure -prefix = install location
make
make install
```

## Installing Expat

Although Apache has a cut-down version of Expat included, if you want to use Sablotron and other XML extensions, you will need to install the full version of Expat. This is available from: *http://sourceforge.net/projects/expat*.

You can either install Expat by compiling the sourcecode as described shortly, or you can download and install the RPM file, which is the easiest option.

Once you have the full Expat Library installed, you need to add the following option when you compile PHP, which tells PHP where you installed the Expat library:

```
—with-expat-dir = install location
```

Note: If you install the full version of Expat, you MUST rebuild Apache with the option:

```
—disable-rule=EXPAT
```

This tells Apache not to install its cut-down Expat version, and instead to use the full version now installed on the system.

### Installing Expat from Source

First download the Expat file, in this example we used `expat-1.9.5.4.tar.gz`. Connect to your server, and enter the following commands in a shell:

```
tar -zxpf expat-1.95.4.tar.gz
cd expat-1.95.4
./configure -prefix = install location
make
make install
/sbin/ldconfig
```

Make sure that the generated files `xmlparse.h` and `xmltok.h` are in a directory in your system path, such as `/usr/include`. You will need root privileges to use the `make   install` and `ldconfig` commands.

## Installing zlib

The zlib library is needed for the DOM XML functions to install. It is a compression library, and can be downloaded from *http://www.gzip.org/zlib/*. The current version at the time of writing is v 1.1.4. When you have installed zlib you need to recompile PHP with the following option:

```
—with-zlib
```

10

XML

### Installing zlib from Source

You will need to connect to your server, and execute the following commands:

```
tar -zxpf zlib-1.1.4.tar.gz
cd zlib-1.1.4
./configure -prefix = install location
make
make install
```

## Installing DOM XML

To use the DOM XML parser, which parses complete documents in one go, you need to compile PHP with the following option:

```
-with-dom
```

You can find the complete reference to DOM XML in the PHP manual at: *http://www.php.net/manual/en/ref.domxml.php.* You must have the zlib library detailed above to be installed, before you compile PHP with the `-with-dom` option.

You can also use the following two options to enable DOM XSLT and DOM EXSLT:

```
-with-dom-xslt
-with-dom-exslt
```

## Installing Sablotron

Sablotron is an XML extension from Ginger Alliance, which enables XML and XSLT to be processed from PHP. The original PHP XSLT extension to interface with the Sablotron was developed by Sterling Hughes, and is now maintained by an independent group of PHP Developers. You can download both RPMs and source files from the Ginger Alliance at: *http://www.gingerall.com/.*

If you install the Sablotron, you need to first install the full Expat as described above, and remove the default cut-down Expat from your Apache web server. The current version of the Sablotron at the time of writing is 0.96.

### Installing Sablotron from Source

To install Sablotron from source, log into your server, and execute the following commands:

```
tar -zxpf sablot-0.96.tar.gz
cd sablot-0.96
configure -prefix = install location
make
make install
```

## Installing XSLT

To enable XSLT support in PHP, once you have the Sablotron installed, you need to recompile PHP with the following options:

```
—enable-xslt
—with-xslt-sablot = install location
```

## Compiling PHP

It's important to note that the options above to include certain extensions need to be present every time you compile PHP. So for example, if you wanted to include all the options above, you would need to compile PHP using a configure line similar to:

```
./configure –with-xml   —with-expat-dir=install location –with-zlib –with-dom —
enable-xslt -with-xslt-sablot=install location –with-dom-xslt –with-dom-exslt
```

as well as any other options that you wish to include.

# Checking XML Is Correctly Installed

Once you have compiled PHP with the relevant options, you need to check that the options have been correctly installed. Create a new blank PHP page, and add the following:

```
<?php
phpinfo();
?>
```

Save the page and upload it to your server, then view it in your browser. As we've seen in earlier chapters, the phpinfo() command displays the current PHP installation settings. The relevant parts are show in the following screenshots:

Right, we can see that XML has been installed correctly, and that we're using a full version of Expat 1.95.4.

| xml | |
|---|---|
| XML Support | active |
| XML Namespace Support | active |
| EXPAT Version | expat_1.95.4 |

In the screenshot opposite we can see the DOM XML options that are installed:

| domxml | |
|---|---|
| DOM/XML | enabled |
| libxml Version | 2.4.23 |
| HTML Support | enabled |
| XPath Support | enabled |
| XPointer Support | enabled |
| DOM/XSLT | enabled |
| libxslt Version | 1.0.15 |
| DOM/EXSLT | enabled |
| libexslt Version | 1.0.15 |

The screenshot below shows XSLT is enabled:

**xslt**

| XSLT support | enabled |
|---|---|

You can quickly see which options PHP has been configured with, by looking at the configure section, which is at the top of the `phpinfo()` generated page. An example is shown in the screenshot below.

| Configure Command | './configure' '--prefix=/etc/httpd/modules/php' '--with-apache=/home/build/apache/apache' '--with-config-file-path=/etc/httpd' '--with-png-dir=/usr' '--with-xml' '--with-jpeg-dir=/usr' '--with-imap' '--with-gd=/home/build/gd-1.8.4' '--with-gettext' '--with-zlib' '--with-system-regex' '--with-ttf' '--with-db' '--with-gdbm' '--with-mbstring' '--with-mbstr-enc-trans' '--with-mysql=/usr' '--with-ming' '--with-swf=/usr/lib/libswf' '--with-dom' '--with-dom-xslt' '--with-dom-exslt' '--with-xslt-sablot=/usr/local' '--with-expat-dir=/usr/local' '--with-xmlrpc' '--enable-xslt' '--enable-sockets' '--enable-exif' '--enable-wddx=shared' '--enable-mm=shared' '--enable-magic-quotes' '--enable-track-vars' '--enable-ftp' '--enable-safe-mode' '--with-curl=shared' '--with-pdflib=shared' '--with-pgsql=shared' |
|---|---|

# XML

XML is a huge subject in itself, and could easily fill a book on its own. In this chapter, rather than just being an XML reference, we're going to look at how to process XML with PHP. And rather than dwelling on the technical details, we're going to show how XML can be used on a web site in real life, and how you can benefit from using XML.

If you'd like to study XML in-depth take a look at *Practical XML for the Web* (Dave Addey et al., glasshaus, ISBN 1904151086).

# What Is XML?

XML stands for **Extensible Markup Language**, and is what is known as a **meta language**. Meta languages are languages used to describe other languages. In fact, XML is a data-modeling standard designed to allow data to flow between systems, but also to be easy for a human to read, as XML is self-describing and describes the type of data that it contains.

The XML 1.0 specification can be found on the W3C web site: *http://www.w3.org/TR/REC-xml*.

You're already familiar with one markup language, HTML. HTML documents contain a number of pre-defined tags that tell the browser how the web page should be displayed. XML, on the other hand, allows you to create your own tags to describe what the information in the document actually means.

# XML Document Format

XML is similar to HTML, except that it is much more structured, with stricter rules as to whether a document is valid or not. We can see a valid XML document below, which describes the first four chapters of this book.

```xml
<?xml version="1.0" encoding="iso-8859-1"?>
    <booklist>
        <book name="Dreamweaver MX: Advanced PHP Web Development">
            <chapter number="1">
                <title>PHP Syntax</title>
                <author>Allan Kent</author>
            </chapter>
            <chapter number="2">
                <title>Control Structures</title>
                <author>Gareth Downes-Powell</author>
            </chapter>
            <chapter number="3">
                <title>Error Handling</title>
                <author>Gareth Downes-Powell</author>
            </chapter>
            <chapter number="4">
                <title>Object Orientated Programming in PHP</title>
                <author>Tim Green</author>
            </chapter>
        </book>
    </booklist>
```

There are a few simple rules that every document MUST obey; it must be **valid** and **well-formed**:

- The first line of the document should be the **XML declaration**

- Every document must have a root element, in this case it is `<booklist>`

- Tag names and attributes are case-sensitive, that is, `<chapter>` is a different tag from `<Chapter>`

- Every opening tag must have a closing tag, unless it's an empty element

- Attribute values must be contained in quotation marks

- A nested tag pair cannot overlap another tag pair

The first line of the document is the XML declaration, `<?xml version="1.0" encoding="iso-8859-1"?>`, which tells the XML parser that is processing the page what type of XML document it's dealing with. This line should be at the top of every XML document. Notice that the tag starts with `<?xml`; this is known as a **processing instruction**, as it's not part of the data, but information for the XML parser. You'll notice that the `<?xml` tag is very similar to the PHP tag, `<?php`, which is also a processing instruction.

**10**

**XML**

Next, we have what is called the **root element**, which in this case is `<booklist>`. This is the outermost tag, and marks the start of the data. We then have a `<book>` tag to define the following data as applying to a certain book, which is the book given by the `name` attribute. In XML attribute values must always be enclosed by quotation marks. An **element** is made up of an opening tag, a closing tag, and all the information in between.

You'll notice that none of the tags overlap, for example the following XML is **invalid**:

```
<chapter number = "1">
    <title>PHP Syntax</title>
    <author>Allan Kent </chapter>
</author>
```

The above XML would cause an error if you tried to process it, because the `<chapter>` tag is closed before the `<author>` tag. With XML you must close all the tags in the same order that they were opened.

In HTML we have a number of single tags such as `<br>` or `<hr>`, which don't require a closing tag. However XML requires that every opening tag have a closing tag. We can have what's called an **empty element**. An empty element has no data, and is a closing tag merged in with the opening tag. So the tag `<br>` would become `<br />`, and `<hr>` would become `<hr />` in XML. Note that there is a space in the middle between the tag name, and the closing part of the tag.

We can also specify a DTD (Document Type Definition) file for the XML document, for example:

```
<?xml version="1.0" encoding="iso-8859-1"?>
<!DOCTYPE booklist SYSTEM "booklist.dtd" >
```

This tells the XML processor to validate the data held by the root element `<booklist>`, against a DTD file called `booklist.dtd`.

So what is a DTD file? A DTD file describes your markup language, and describes rules for the type of data the tags can contain. For example you could decide that a `<total>` tag should only hold numerical data, and not allow characters. Using the DTD file, the XML processor can check that all the tags are valid, and contain data of the correct type, so if the file is corrupted, or someone has entered the wrong data, XML will know there is a problem with the data. We don't have to include a DTD file, and we won't for the simple examples in this chapter, but without it the XML processor cannot validate and find errors in your data. XML documents without a DTD are known as well-formed, and all that is required is that the rules of XML are upheld. Documents that reference a DTD are known as valid documents, as the data contained in the document can be validated against the DTD.

## Creating an XML File in Dreamweaver MX

You can create an XML document from within Dreamweaver MX. Open a new page, and select type XML, from the *Basic Page* menu. Dreamweaver opens up a blank page, and automatically inserts the XML declaration:

```
<?xml version="1.0" encoding="iso-8859-1"?>
```

We can now start entering some XML. Try entering the following XML:

```
<?xml version="1.0" encoding="iso-8859-1"?>
<chapter>
    <number pages=30>10</number>
    <author>Gareth Downes-Powell</author>
</chapter>
```

Dreamweaver will color all the tags in blue, and any data between tags is black. If you enter this into Dreamweaver, you will also see that the number 30 is red, which indicates an error caused by omitting quotation marks round the attribute value. Add quotation marks round the 30 to make the tag: you will then see the 30 turn green, indicating the attribute and value are using the correct syntax. This syntax coloring means you can quickly see if there are any errors in the format of your document.

## Adding Custom Tags to Dreamweaver MX

We can make Dreamweaver even more useful by defining our own custom tags. As an example we are going to add a `<chapter>` tag, a `<number>` tag, and an `<author>` tag.

From the main Dreamweaver MX menu, select *Edit > Tag Libraries*. A new dialog box will appear that lists all the categories of tags that are used in Dreamweaver MX. Click the + button, and select *New Tag Library*, and type in "*PHP Book Tags*" for the tag library name. This creates a new PHP *Book Tags* folder, which will store our tags. This is shown in the screenshot below:

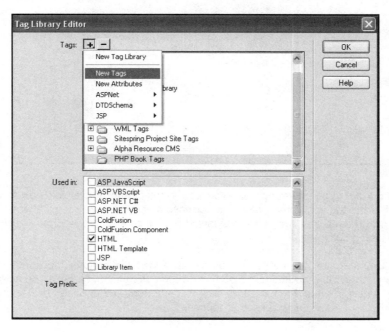

Next, click the + button and select *New Tags*; a dialog box similar to the one below will appear:

Enter "*chapter*" for the tag name, and make sure *Have Matching End Tags* is selected, then click *OK* to add our new chapter tag. We then go back to the previous dialog box, where we can see the new `<chapter>` tag, along with some new options, as shown in the screenshot below:

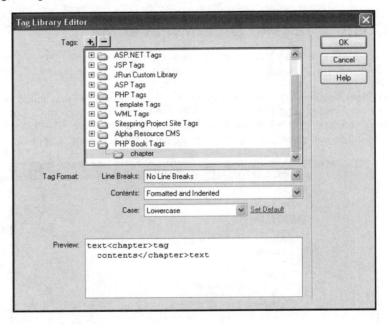

The new *Tag Format* options that appear allow you to tell Dreamweaver MX how to treat the tag, such as whether the tag is automatically indented, has a line break before or after it, or is used as lowercase or mixed case. You can see a preview of your chosen settings in the *Preview* box at the bottom of the dialog box.

Next add an `<author>` tag, in the same way as we added the chapter tag above, and also the `<number>` tag. However, the number tag also has an attribute, `pages`, so once you have created the `<number>` tag, select it in the *Tag List*, then click the + button, and choose *New Attributes*. Add an attribute called `pages`, as in the screenshot opposite:

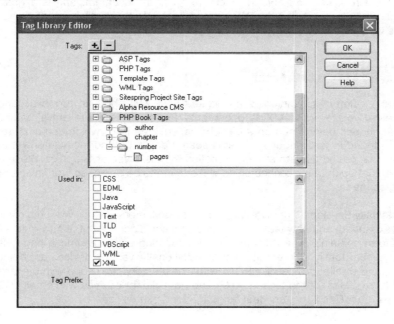

This adds the `pages` attribute to our `<number>` tag. The last job is to click on the *PHP Book Tags* folder, and the following will be displayed:

In the above screenshot you can see our new *PHP Book Tags*, along with the `pages` attribute for the`<number>` tag. When you click on the actual *PHP Book Tags* folder, the middle panel changes, and gives a list of languages, and you can select the ones you want your new tags to be used in. HTML is selected by default, so unselect this, and check XML at the end of the list.

Now create a new XML page, and again type the following:

```
<?xml version="1.0" encoding="iso-8859-1"?>
<chapter>
    <number pages="30">10</number>
    <author>Gareth Downes-Powell</author>
</chapter>
```

10

XML

You will notice that this time, when you typed the `<chapter>` tag, Dreamweaver MX also automatically added the closing `</chapter>` tag for you. Also when you type the `<number>` tag, a code hint box appears listing the attributes for the number tag, as shown below:

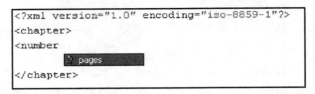

This makes it much easier and quicker to create an XML document, and is a great help when showing which attributes each tag has. You can go back into the Tag Library at any time, and add new attributes or tags, or delete tags from the library.

# XML Technologies

There are many different technologies associated with XML, both in terms of languages, and parsers that allow you to process XML documents. For example, there are already a number of XML-based languages being used on a daily basis, such as RDF, which contains descriptions of the information found in web pages and helps search engines to correctly interpret the data, and SVG, which is a language used to store information to create Vector Graphics. We're now going to take a quick look at each of the technologies we're going to be using, so you have an idea of what the technologies mean.

HTML was originally developed for displaying scientific documents, which were mainly text. Over the years, HTML expanded, and new tags were added so it could cope with the new media types. HTML in its current form contains over 100 tags and is becoming unwieldy, and a page viewed in one browser, may appear totally different in another. Additionally, various devices are being hooked up to the Internet, and smaller devices like PDAs with less memory can't cope with the large number of tags that HTML has. Most of the tags in HTML are not valid for devices with small LCD screens or other limitations, so HTML is not an ideal language for these devices.

## XHTML

A lot of HTML on the Web is not true HTML in that it doesn't conform to the original HTML specification. However modern browsers are sophisticated enough to render this sloppy HTML reasonably well, which has led to an acceptance of poor markup. The problem with this is that smaller devices that are now accessing the Internet, do not normally have the processing power to decipher this bad markup and cannot render it. Also several browsers developed their own propriety tags such as the infamous `<marquee>` tag, that are not part of the standard.

The current XHTML version used by Dreamweaver MX is version 1 which was initially published in January 2000 and revised in August 2002. The details of this specification can be found at:

*http://www.w3.org/TR/xhtml1/*

There are three different types of XHTML version 1, which vary in their support of HTML 4.0 features.

- **Strict** – The strict version means that no presentation elements can be used.

- **Transitional** – This is the standard that Dreamweaver MX uses by default, and allows HTML elements to be used for formatting.

- **Frameset** – The frameset standard is also used by Dreamweaver MX, but only if you are using framesets within your page, and allows extra tags for the use of frames.

XHTML became an official W3C recommendation in January 2000; it is in fact a reformulation of the three HTML 4 document types as applications of XML 1.0. XHTML can be read by any browser or device that can process XML, and is also backward-compatible with older browsers and so provides a bridge to the future, while maintaining compatibility with the older browser versions, as it's based on HTML 4.0.

*It's a good idea to start using XHTML now, as your site will still be compatible with the older browsers, but also compatible with any future browsers, and it's a good way to ease yourself into XML.*

Dreamweaver MX is fully XHTML-compatible, when creating a new HTML document simply select the "*Make document XHTML compliant*" option. It's useful to note that Dreamweaver MX can automatically convert existing HTML to XHTML, using the *CONVERT* option in the main file menu.

## XSL and XSLT

One thing to bear in mind with XML is that it does not describe the presentational aspects of the document. Data is captured in XML in the backend and is then **transformed** into another format for display. This could be HTML for a browser, or WML (Wireless Markup Language) for a WAP-enabled device for example.

XSL stands for **Extensible Stylesheet Language**. Because XML allows you to define your own tags, a browser has no idea what the tags themselves mean. A `<table>` tag could be an instruction to format the data into a table, or it could be an element containing data about a pine dinner table. We can use XSL to change data from one format to another, so it would take the data in the `<table>` element, and send it to the browser or device in a format it can understand.

XSL consists of three parts:

- XSLT (XSL Transformations): the language used for transforming XML documents into other forms, such as HTML, or WML for a WAP-enabled phone for example.

- XPath – a language to query structure and content in an XML document.

- XSL Formatting Objects – A vocabulary for formatting XML Documents.

XSL is much more than just a stylesheet however, it can actually process the XML data, and while it's formatting the XML data for output, it can also sort the data, and perform operations depending on the value of certain pieces of data.

**10**

**XML**

# Parsers

Now that we've looked at some of the different XML-related languages, we're going to look at the PHP software modules that you use to process these different languages. The software that processes a language is called a **parser**, and it reads the language and allows you to perform operations based on the data and tags in the document. Different parsers work in different ways, and with different languages, and we're now going to look at the main types.

## SAX

SAX stands for **Simple API for XML**, and it basically interprets XML documents. It's an open standard, and is created by a group of independent developers. SAX reads through an XML document, a tag at a time, and calls an event handler each time it comes across an open tag, or a closed tag, or the data in between two tags.

Because it processes only a small part of a document at any one time, it can deal with huge documents, as it only has to store part of the document in the server's memory at once, rather than the whole document. It can work with most standards because it's an open standard, and is not developed by any independent organization. The only downside is that it has limited capabilities for manipulating the actual XML content because it reads only equal-length sections of the document at a time. This methodology is known as **Event-Driven** processing; SAX signals an event has occurred as it encounters each tag, attribute etc., and then calls the appropriate handler function for that event.

Because of the low overhead however, it's probably the type of parser you'll end up using most, and we look at SAX processing later in this chapter. You can also find more about SAX at the official site: *http://www.saxproject.org/*.

## DOM

The DOM, or **Document Object Model**, is a standard API to allow programs to access and manipulate markup documents. Instead of reading an XML document in small segments, it reads the whole document in one go, and creates a tree structure representing the entire document in memory.

Because the whole XML document is read, or created, at once, you can move up and down through the tree, and read different data elements, without just moving from start to finish. You can also create new XML documents, and change values in existing documents, something you can't do with the SAX model.

The downside to DOM is that because the whole XML document is loaded into memory, it uses a lot more resources than the SAX model. If the XML documents are small, this shouldn't prove a major problem, but if you have large documents the server's memory can quickly be used up.

## Sablotron

Sablotron, created by Ginger Alliance, is an XML toolkit that contains support for XSLT, XPath, and DOM. It's free of charge, for both Linux and Windows, and can be downloaded from *http://www.gingerall.com/*.

Sablotron isn't actually related to PHP, it can be used with many different languages, or run as a standalone application. PHP provides an XSLT extension so you can use Sablotron from within your PHP scripts.

Because XML processing isn't turned on, or even installed by default, you may have to install several PHP extensions before using the code provided in this chapter. Installation details can be found in the Code Download section of *http://www.glasshaus.com.*

# Processing XML – A Real-Life Example

Now that we've looked at the basics of XML, we're going to look at a real-life example, using the Macromedia Developers XML Feed. We're then going to process this feed to produce nicely formatted output, using the three different methods mentioned earlier: SAX, DOM, and XSLT.

## The Macromedia Developer Feed

The Macromedia Developers Feed is a live XML feed from the Macromedia Developers Center, which contains details on the latest articles on the site, etc. This allows developers to process the feed and format the contents, to add their own custom view of the Macromedia Developer Center articles, etc.

More details about the feed can be found at:
*http://www.macromedia.com/desdev/articles/xml_resource_feed.html*

And the actual feed itself comes from the following URL:
*http://www.macromedia.com/desdev/resources/macromedia_resources.xml*

## The Feed Contents

Open the URL of the feed in Internet Explorer 5.5 or Netscape 6.2 or later (these can display the XML properly), and look at the structure of the XML. A cut-down version of the XML is shown below:

```xml
<?xml version="1.0" ?>
<macromedia_resources
xmlns:macromedia_resources="http://www.macromedia.com/desdev/resources/macromedia_res
ources.dtd">
<resource type="Article">
    <title>Sneak Preview Tips from DevCon 2002</title>
    <author>Macromedia</author>
    <url>http://www.macromedia.com/desdev/articles/sp_frontdoor.html</url>
    <product name="ColdFusion" />
    <product name="Dreamweaver" />
    <product name="Fireworks" />
</resource>
</macromedia_resources>
```

First is the standard XML declaration that appears at the top of every XML file. Next comes a `<macromedia_resources>` tag, which is the root node for the document, and indicates the start of the data. It also tells the XML processor to validate the document against an online DTD file.

Next are the actual articles themselves, each contained in a `<resource>` tag. The `<resource>` element has the following structure:

```
<resource type="">
  <title></title>
  <author></author>
  <url></url>
  <product name="" />
</resource>3
```

The resource type may be an article, or a White Paper and so on, and is defined in the `type` attribute of the `<resource>` tag. Next we have the `<title>`, `<author>`, and `<url>` tags. The last tag is an empty tag, and contains the applicable product name in the name attribute of the `<product>` tag. There can be more than one `<product>` tag per resource.

Full details of the feed can be found at the following URL, which lists all the possible values that can appear for the resource type, and the product field at: *http://www.macromedia.com/desdev/ articles/xml_resource_feed.html*

## Creating a Style Sheet to Format the XML Feed

Before we start on the actual code, we're first going to create a CSS stylesheet to format the output from our XML parser. We have the following information that needs formatting:

- Title (which is a link obtained from the URL)
- Author
- Resource Type
- Product1, Product2,etc

Add the following code to a blank page, and save the file as `mmStyles.css`:

```
/* Stylesheet for Macromedia Developers Feed */

/* Style for Resource Title, which is also a link */
.title {
      font-family: Arial, Helvetica, sans-serif;
      font-size: 16px;
      font-weight: bold;
      color: #0033CC;
}
a.title:link {
      color: #0033CC;
      text-decoration : none;
}
a.title:visited {
      color: #999999;
      text-decoration : none;
}
a.title:hover {
```

```css
        color: #999999;
}
a.title:active {
}

/* Style for Author */
.author {
        font-family: Arial, Helvetica, sans-serif;
        font-size: 12px;
        color: #000000;
        width: 280px;
}

/* Style for Resource Type */
.resourcetype {
        font-family: Arial, Helvetica, sans-serif;
        font-size: 12px;
        color: #000000;
}

/* Style for Product Names */
.product {
        font-family: Arial, Helvetica, sans-serif;
        font-size: 14px;
        color: #003366;
}
/* Style for Product Header text */
.productHeader{
        font-family: Arial, Helvetica, sans-serif;
        font-size: 14px;
        color: #000000;
}

/* Create Box with border and fill color to hold Resource*/
.article {
        border: thin dashed #000000;
        background-color : #EAF5FF;
        padding: 20px;
        margin-left : 20%;
        margin-right: 20%;
}
.White_Paper {
        border: thin dashed #000000;
        background-color : #FFFFFF;
        padding: 20px;
        margin-left : 20%;
        margin-right: 20%;
}
.Tutorial {
        border: thin dashed #000000;
        background-color : #DDFFBB;
        padding: 20px;
        margin-left : 20%;
        margin-right: 20%;
}
```

10

XML

245

```
.Column {
        border: thin dashed #000000;
        background-color : #FFFFCC;
        padding: 20px;
        margin-left : 20%;
        margin-right: 20%;
}
```

This creates some of the styles shown below:

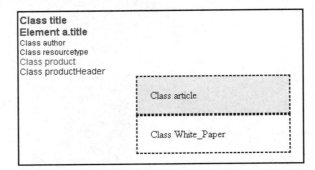

We'll apply the styles to the data using PHP to output HTML. It is worth noting that we have only created styles for the following feed types: White Paper, Article, Tutorial, and Column, in order to conserve space and to keep the example clear. In a real application you would need to create CSS styles for every type that can appear, for example component, extension, sample_application, etc.

## Creating an XML Helper Class

We're going to create this example using classes; as we saw in *Chapter 4*, there are many advantages to this approach. When we're parsing an XML document, there are a number of similar tasks we have to do, whichever method of parsing the document we use. The basic flow is:

● Read in the Macromedia feed XML file

● Process the XML data

● Output the data to the browser in HTML format

The only operation which will differ, depending on what method of parsing we're using, is the second step, which is to process the XML data. To avoid creating classes that contain the same blocks of code, we're going to create a helper class first, which contains the processes that each of the three parsing methods have in common. This class will not actually do anything on its own, but will contain code to read the Macromedia XML feed into a variable, and then to process the output to display in HTML format. We can then use this class as a base for each of the actual XML processing classes, as they will be extensions of this class.

Create a new blank PHP page, and add the following code:

```php
<?php
################################################################
# PHP XML Parser Example                                      #
#                                                          #
# Parses Macromedia Developers Feed at                        #
# http://www.macromedia.com/desdev/resources/macromedia_resources.xml #
################################################################
class xmlClass{

        var $xml;
        var $html;

        function xmlClass(){
            // No constructor functions needed
        }

}
?>
```

This creates a basic class container; to which we're going to add functions to read in the XML Developers feed, and then output the data. No constructor function is needed for this class, as the classes that extend it will control it, as we'll see later. Save this file as `xmlClass.php`.

## Reading in the XML Developers Feed

Add the following function to the empty class container:

```php
function readXML(){
    // Connect to the Macromedia Developers Feed
    $feed = "http://www.macromedia.com/desdev/resources/macromedia_resources.xml";
    $xfp = @fopen($feed, "r")
            or die("Cannot retrieve Macromedia XML Feed");
    // Read in the XML in blocks of 1024 Bytes (1Kb)
    while(!feof($xfp)){
        $this->xml .= fread($xfp,1024);
    }
    // Now that the data is in $this->xml, close the feed
    fclose($xfp);
}
```

First we use the PHP `fopen()` function to connect to the Macromedia Developer XML Feed URL. Note that we use an @ sign before the `fopen()` function, to suppress any error messages if we can't connect to the URL for some reason. We can do this safely, because we next check that a valid file pointer is present, and if it's not we display our own error message, using the `die()` function, which also terminates the script.

Next we read the file into the object variable `xml`, in blocks of 1Kb. We use a `while` loop to keep reading the feed until we reach the end. We then close the file pointer.

So we now have the whole XML document, which can be referenced from anywhere in the class by using the variable `$this->xml`.

**10**

**XML**

## Writing the Output in HTML Format

We're going to write the format in exactly the same way to the screen, no matter which method of XML processor we're using. The data is formatted using the mmStyles.css stylesheet we have already created. Add the following function to the xmlClass.php file:

```php
function outputResource(){
    // Create the HTML to be output, containing the formatted feed
    // Expects array in $this->resource, containing the indexes
    // [resourcetype], [author], [url], [title], [products] = array

    $newline = "\n";

    // Add HTML for current resource, styled using CSS stylesheet
    // mmStyles.css

    $this->html .= "<div class=\"{$this->resource['resourcetype']}\">\n";
    $this->html .= "<a href=\"{$this->resource['url']}\" class=\"title\">\n";
    $this->html .= $this->resource['title'] . "</a>\n";
    $this->html .= "<br />\n";
    $this->html .= "<span class=\"author\">Author: {$this->resource['author']}
                    </span>\n";
    $this->html .= "<span class=\"resourcetype\">Resource Type: \n";
    $this->html .= str_replace("_"," ",$this->resource['resourcetype']) .
                    "</span>\n";
    $this->html .= "<br /><br />\n";
    $this->html .= "<span class=\"productHeader\">Applicable Products:
                    </span>\n";
    $this->html .= "<span class=\"product\">\n";
    $count = 0;

    // Read products array, and output each product separated by a comma

    foreach($this->resource['products'] as $product){
        if($count == 0){
            $this->html .= $product;
            $count++;
        } else {
            $this->html .= ", " . $product;
            $count++;
        }
    }
    $this->html .= "</span>\n";
    $this->html .= "</div>\n";
    $this->html .= "<br />\n";
}
```

This function works on an array in $this->resource, which is populated by the XML processor classes we're going to create next. The resource array needs to have the following indexes: resourcetype, author, url, title, and another index product which contains an array of product names. It then writes the data along with the HTML to the $this->html variable. The function formats the data, along with the mmStyles.css stylesheet, so that it looks like the screenshot opposite:

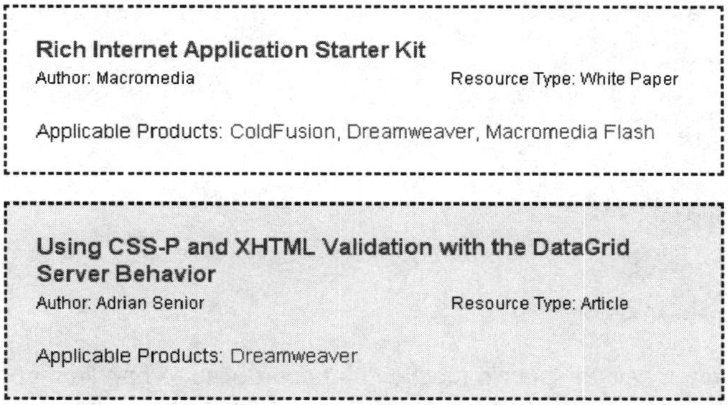

The above screenshot shows the two types of data in the Macromedia XML Developers Feed at the time of writing, and to keep our code short, we've only created styles for these resource types, `White_Paper` and `Article`, but the class can easily by extended to deal with all the different resource types as they appear.

This completes our XML helper class, `xmlClass.php`, so save the file and upload it to your server.

# Processing the XML Feed Using SAX

SAX is what is called an **event-based parser**. This means that it works through the document a tag at a time, and triggers an event depending on the current tag. As an example of how SAX parses XML, take a look at the following snippet from the XML feed.

```
<resource type="Article">
    <title>Macromedia Flash for ColdFusion Users</title>
    <author>Matt Boles</author>
    <url>http://www.macromedia.com/desdev/articles/sp_mboles.html</url>
    <product name="ColdFusion" />
    <product name="Macromedia_Flash" />
</resource>
```

The SAX parser will work through the XML and trigger the following events:

- **Open Tag** `<resource>`

- **Open Tag** `<title>`

- **Character Data** "`Macromedia Flash for ColdFusion Users`"

- **Close Tag** `</title>`

- **Open Tag** `<author>`

- **Character Data** "`Matt Boles`"

- **Close Tag** `</author>`

- **Open Tag** `<url>`

**10**

**XML**

- **Character Data** `"http://www.macromedia.com/desdev/articles/sp_mboles.html"`

- **Close Tag** `</url>`

- **Open Tag** `<product>`

- **Close Tag** `</product>`

- **Open Tag** `<product>`

- **Close Tag** `</product>`

- **Close Tag** `</resource>`

When it fires an event, it calls a specific function that you define to handle that data, and passes it the current tag information. So we need a function that handles opening tags, a function that handles character data, which is text between an opening and closing tag and CDATA statements, and finally a function to process closing tags.

## Creating the SAXParser Class

We're now going to create our SAX parser class, and explain what each part does as we go along. Start with a blank PHP page, and add the following code to contain our class.

```php
<?php
######################################################################
# PHP SAX Parser Example                                          #
#                                                                    #
# Parses Macromedia Developers Feed at                            #
# http://www.macromedia.com/desdev/resources/macromedia_resources.xml #
######################################################################

// Requires xmlClass
require_once("xmlClass.php");

class SAXParser extends xmlClass{

    var $parser;
    var $currentTag;
    var $resource;

    function SAXParser(){
        $this->createParser();
        $this->readXML();
        $this->processXML();
        $this->freeParser();
    }

}
?>
```

First we add the code from our XML helper class, `xmlClass.php` using a PHP `require_once()` function.

Next we create a new class, called `SAXParser`, which extends `xmlClass`. This means that all the functions and variables in `xmlClass` are now also available to our new `SAXParser` class, saving us having to rewrite those functions.

Next we set up a global variable, `$parser`, which will contain a pointer to the SAX parser that we create later in the code. The variable, `$currentTag`, will hold the current XML tag being parsed, and finally we have the `$resource` variable, which will hold the array of data from the XML file for the `outputResource()` function in our XML helper class.

In the constructor function `SAXParser`, which is run when the class is created, we have the functions that process the XML data that we are going to create. The `readXML()` function comes from `xmlClass`.

This creates the basic container for the `SAXParser` class. Save the class as `SAXParserClass.php` in the same directory as the XML helper class, `xmlClass.php` and the `mmStyles.css` stylesheet.

## Creating a New Sax Parser

Next add the following function to the `SAXParser` class:

```
function createParser(){
        // Create new SAX Parser
        $this->parser = xml_parser_create();
    }
```

This function creates a new instance of the SAX Parser, and puts a pointer to it in the variable `$this->parser`. Every time we need to send a command to the SAX Parser, we refer to it by this pointer.

## Creating the processXML() Function

Again add the following code to the `SAXParser` class:

```
function processXML(){
    // Set Callback functions
    xml_set_object($this->parser, $this);
    xml_set_element_handler($this->parser, "startElementTag",
                                           "endElementTag");
    xml_set_character_data_handler($this->parser, "characterData");
    // Parse XML, return detailed error if problem
    if (!xml_parse($this->parser, $this->xml)){
        die(sprintf("XML error: %s at line %d",
        xml_error_string(xml_get_error_code($this->parser)),
        xml_get_current_line_number($this->parser)));
    }
}
```

As we're using the parser in a class, we first need to set the XML parser to the current class using:

```
xml_set_object($this->parser, $this)
```

Next, we tell the parser that we want to use the function `startElementTag()` to handle opening tags, and the function `endElementTag()` to handle closing tags, using the `xml_set_element_hander()` function, which has the following format:

```
bool xml_set_element_handler (resource parser, string start_element_handler,
                              string end_element_handler)
```

These custom functions are sent parameters indicating the current tag etc.,,, and we create these in the next section. We then define the function that will handle any character data the parser finds, that is text between an opening and closing tag. We use the command `xml_set_character_data_handler()` which uses the following format:

```
bool xml_set_character_data_handler (resource parser, string handler)
```

For the XML Developers feed, we only need handlers for opening and closing tags, and for character data. We then use the `xml_parse()` function, to start the parser to work on our XML which is held in the global variable `xml`, referred to as `$this->xml`. The format for the `xml_parse()` function is:

```
bool xml_parse ( resource parser, string data [, bool is_final])
```

If the XML parser fails, then we use the `die()` function to terminate the script, and print an error message using the following XML error functions:

- `xml_get_error_code($parser)`: this function returns a number from the SAX Parser, representing the type of error that has occurred.

- `xml_error_string(xml error code)`: this function takes the numerical XML error code, and converts it into a more user-friendly string describing the error.

- `xml_get_current_line_number($parser)`: this function tells you which is the line number in the XML that the error occurred on.

*There are more processing commands available to process extra XML types, and these are listed at: http://www.php.net/manual/en/ref.xml.php.*

## Creating the startElementTag() Function

Next we create the `startElementTag()` function, which is called by the SAX parser whenever it encounters an opening tag. It passes the following parameters to our `startElementTag()` function:

- `$parser`: a pointer to the SAX parser

- `$tag`: the current opening tag

- `$attributes`: any attributes the opening tag may have in an array

Add the following function code to the `SAXParser` class:

```
function startElementTag($parser, $tag, $attributes){
// Process all opening tags
    switch($tag){
        case "RESOURCE":
            // Save the resource tags type attribute
            $this->resource['resourcetype'] = $attributes['TYPE'];
            break;
        case "PRODUCT":
            // Replace _ in a Product Name with a space, add to product
            // array
            $temp = $attributes['NAME'];
            $temp = str_replace("_"," ",$temp);
            $this->products[] = $temp;
            break;
        default:
            // Keep track of current tag being processed
            $this->currentTag = $tag;
            break;
    }
}
```

First we use a `switch` statement to choose some code based on the opening tag passed by the SAX parser. If it's an opening `<resource type="">` tag, then we place its type attribute in our global resource array which is used by the output function.

If the opening tag is a `<product name=""  />` tag, then we remove the underscore character that is in the product name, and replace it with a space, so for example, Macromedia_Flash would become Macromedia Flash. We then place it in the `products` array, which in turn is part of our `resource` array.

For any other opening tags, we don't have to do anything to them, as no other opening tags in the XML feed have attributes. Instead we just store the tag name in the `$this->currentTag` variable, where it will stay until the parser comes to a closing tag

*It's important to note that the SAX Parser converts the tags to uppercase, so you need to use uppercase for your tags in the `switch` statement, otherwise the tags won't be matched.*

## Creating the characterData() Function

The `characterData()` function is called whenever the SAX parser encounters some text between an opening and a closing tag. It passes the following parameters to the `characterData()` function:

● `$parser`: pointer to the SAX Parser

● `$characterData`: the actual text

Add the following function to the `SAXParser` class:

```
function characterData($parser,$characterData){
    // Process all Character Data
    $currentTag = strtolower($this->currentTag);
    $this->resource[$currentTag] .= $characterData;
}
```

This code first reads the variable $this->currentTag, which was set by the startElementTag()
function, and converts the tag to lowercase. Next we add the text in $characterData which is sent
by the SAX Parser, and add it to the resource array, using the current tag as the array index.

It's important to realize that character data may not be read all at once; instead it could be read in
bits and pieces, so you need to add all the character data together in one variable, to get the whole
line, or block, of text. For example, imagine that we had an XML tag containing the following data:

```
<product>Macromedia MX</product>
```

The character data between the tags may not be processed in one block, that is, "Macromedia MX",
but could be processed in smaller sections, for example "Macromedia" , "MX". To create the text in
its original form, we need to "glue" all the parts back together again, by adding each section of
character data to any previous data sent for the section using the PHP concentration operator.

## Creating the endElementTag() Function

Our last XML handler function is endElementTag(), which is passed the following two attributes by
the SAX Parser:

- $parser: pointer to SAX Parser

- $tag: current closing tag

Add the function endElementTag(), shown below, to class SAXParser.

```
function endElementTag($parser, $tag){
    // Process Closing Tag
    switch($tag){
        case "RESOURCE":
            // Clear Product and resource Arrays
            $this->resource['products'] = $this->products;
            $this->outputResource();
            $this->currentTag = "";
            $this->resource = "";
            $this->products = "";
            break;
        default:
            // Clear current tag reference
            $this->currentTag = "";
            break;
    }
}
```

Here again we use a switch command, to run certain code for certain tags. For a closing
</resource> tag, we put the product array into the global $this->resource array, using the index
products. We then clear all the current variables, so they can be set again by the
openElementTag() function.

## Freeing the SAX Parser

Add the code shown below to the SAXParser class:

```
    function freeParser(){
        // Free XML parser
        xml_parser_free($this->parser);
    }
```

This function simply closes the SAX Parser, as we no longer need it, and frees the memory used by any associated SAX objects.

## Creating the PHP Page That Calls SAXParser

We now need to create the PHP page that opens the SAXParser class, and then displays the resulting HTML. Create a new PHP page, and add the code shown below.

```
<?php require_once("saxParserClass.php"); ?>
<html>
<head>
<title>SAX Parser Example</title>
<link href="mmStyles.css" rel="stylesheet" type="text/css" />
<meta http-equiv="Content-Type" content="text/html; charset=iso-8859-1">
</head>
<body>
<?
    $saxParse = new SAXParser();
    echo $saxParse->html;
?>
</body>
</html>
```

First we use a PHP require_once() command to load in our saxParserClass.php file. Next, we create a new instance of the SAXParser class in the page body, and read the resulting HTML from the class, and display it on the screen. Save this page as sax.php, and upload the page to your server.

## Viewing the End Result

When you view sax.php in your browser, you will see a result similar to the screenshot below, showing the resources currently in the Macromedia Developer XML feed.

The screenshot opposite only shows a couple of resources, your sax.php page will display many more than thisscreenshot. At the time of writing there are currently 15 resource entries.

In this example we've only used a small part of the SAX Parser's capabilities. To find out more, consult the XML section of the PHP online manual at *http://www.php.net/manual/en/ref.xml.php*.

**Logged In: Certification**
Author: Tiffany Beltis                              Resource Type: Article

Applicable Products: ColdFusion, Dreamweaver, Macromedia Flash

**Rich Internet Application Starter Kit**
Author: Macromedia                              Resource Type: White Paper

Applicable Products: ColdFusion, Dreamweaver, Macromedia Flash

**Using CSS-P and XHTML Validation with the DataGrid Server Behavior**
Author: Adrian Senior                              Resource Type: Article

Applicable Products: Dreamweaver

# Processing the XML Feed Using DOM

As we mentioned earlier, the DOM is different from the SAX Parser in that it keeps the whole XML document in memory at once, and represents it as a tree. The DOM parser allows us to manipulate the XML data, rather than just reading it, and it also allows us to move up and down the tree, rather than just working through in one direction like the SAX Parser. The downside is that because DOM keeps the whole document in memory at once, rather than just a small section, it uses a lot more memory than SAX.

With DOM you work through the tree by first looking at the root element `<macromedia_resources>`, and then looking at its children which are the `<resource>` elements, and then looking at the children of the `<resource>` element, for example `<title>` or `<author>` and so on.

The advantages of the DOM method is that new XML documents can be created, and then populated with data, and you can also modify the nodes and attributes of the DOM tree, unlike SAX, which only allows you to read the XML document.

The disadvantages are the fact that the whole document is stored in memory at once, which leaves less memory for the other applications running on the server. The code is also more complicated than SAX, and isn't broken so easily into smaller segments, so can be harder to follow.

It should be noted that the DOM functions in PHP are subject to change, due to being experimental. If you have problems with this example, it may be that the function names have been changed since this book's publication. Refer to *http://www.php.net/manual/en/ref.domxml.php* for the latest information.

## Creating the DOMParse Class

First create a new blank PHP page, and add the following code:

```php
<?php
#####################################################################
# PHP DOM Parser Example                                            #
#                                                                   #
# Parses Macromedia Developers Feed at                              #
# http://www.macromedia.com/desdev/resources/macromedia_resources.xml #
#####################################################################

// Requires xmlClass
require_once("xmlClass.php");
class DOMParse extends xmlClass{

        var $resource;

        function DOMParse(){
                $this->readXML();
                $this->processXML();
        }
}
?>
```

This creates the basic container for the DOMParse class. Again we include the xmlClass.php code, as the DOMParse class extends xmlClass. We also create a constructor function DOMParse() which runs when a new instance of the class is created. This calls readXML() from xmlClass, and we will create the processXML() function in the next section. Save this page as domParserClass.php.

## Creating the processXML() Function

Add the following function to the DOMParse class:

```
function processXML(){
    // Process XML in $this->XML
    $doc = xmldoc($this->xml);
    // get <macromedia_resources> root element
    $root = $doc->document_element();
    // get child nodes of <macromedia_resources> that is, <resource>
    $resources = $root->child_nodes();
    // Parse each <resource>
    foreach ($resources as $resourceNode){
        $this->parseResourceNode($resourceNode);
    }
}
```

First we create the XML tree using the xmldoc() function. The xmldoc() function allows us to create the DOM XML tree using XML stored in a variable. If we wanted to use XML from a file instead, we can use the xmldocfile() function, which takes a filename as its only argument.

The XML tree is created as various objects, containing an element and all its child elements. To get the root element, which in this case is the <macromedia_resources> tag, we use the code:

```
$root = $doc->document_element()
```

The variable $root now holds an object containing the root element <macromedia_resources> and all of its child elements, and their child elements etc.

Next we use the command:

```
$resources = $root->child_nodes()
```

to put the child nodes of <macromedia_resources>, that is, the <resource> tags and their child element into an object in variable $resources.

Next we use a foreach loop to cycle through each <resource> node, and call a function parseResourceNode() which we create in the next section, to which we pass the current <resource> node.

## Creating the parseResourceNode() Function

We are now going to create the parseResourceNode() function. This function processes each <resource> node, and extracts the data from its attributes and child tags. Add the following code to the DOMParse class:

```
function parseResourceNode($resourceNode){
  // Check current Node is a <resource> tag, not whitespace
  if($resourceNode->tagname != ""){
    // Get type attribute from <resource>
    $mmResource['resourcetype'] = $resourceNode->get_attribute('type');
    // Get Child Nodes of <resource> that is, <title>, <author>, <url>, <product>
    $resourceChildren = $resourceNode->child_nodes();
    // Process each Child node of <resource>
    foreach($resourceChildren as $childNode){
      // Check each child node is a valid tag, and not whitespace
      if($childNode->tagname != ""){
        // Choose appropriate action for each child tag
        switch($childNode->tagname){
          case "product":
            // Get attribute name from a <product> tag and put in array
            $resourceProducts[] = $childNode->get_attribute('name');
            break;
          default:
            // If not a product tag, read text between open and close
            // tag
            $resourceDetailNodes = $childNode->child_nodes();
            foreach($resourceDetailNodes as $detail){
              // Check that current node is a text node
              if($detail->node_type() == XML_TEXT_NODE){
                // Add text to mmResource array, indexed by tagname
                $mmResource[$childNode->tagname] = $detail-
>get_content();
              }
            }
        }
      }
    }
    // Put Product array into $mmResource array
    $mmResource['products'] = $resourceProducts;
    // Put current $mmResource array in $this->resource
    $this->resource = $mmResource;
    // Output current resource
    $this->outputResource();
  }
}
```

This is the longest function so far, so it will take a bit of explaining. When the function is called, it's passed a resource element, which contains the <resource> tag and all its child elements such as <title> and <url>. An example of a resource node and its child elements is shown below.

```
<resource type="">
  <title></title>
  <author></author>
  <url></url>
  <product name="" />
</resource>
```

First we check that the tagname is actually a <resource> tag and not whitespace, using the code:

```
if($resourceNode->tagname != "")
```

If the passed parameter `$resourceNode` is a proper resource tag, `$resourceNode->tagname` will contain "resource". To retrieve the tag name we are using the tag name function of the `domElement` class, which is created for each element as the document is read, and which uses the format.

```
$element->tagname();
```

We then extract the type attribute from the `<resource>` tag, and place it in `$mmResource['resourcetype']`, so that we can use it later. To do that we use the following code:

```
$mmResource['resourcetype'] = $resourceNode -> get_attribute('type');
```

We use `get_attribute('type')` to extract the type attribute from the `<resource>` tag, which again is part of the DOM Element class and uses the format:

```
$element->get_attribute('attribute name');
```

We now move on and process the child nodes belonging to the `<resource>` tag using the following command:

```
$resourceChildren = $resourceNode->child_nodes()
```

This refers to the `child_nodes()` function in the DOM Node class which contains details about the node passed to the `parseResourceNode()` function.

```
$node->child_nodes();
```

This returns an array of child nodes of the node passed.

We now use a `foreach` loop, to work through each of the child nodes, using the following command:

```
foreach($resourceChildren as $childNode)
```

`$childNode` now contains the current tag being worked on. We need to check that this tag is actually a proper tag, and not just whitespace, using the following `if` statement:

```
if($childNode->tagname != "")
```

Again, each child node will have an instance of the element class, and we can use the `tagname()` function of the element class to get the tag name of the current element. We can now be sure that we have a proper tag. We then use a `switch` structure to execute code depending on the contents of the tag.

If the tag is a `<product>` tag, then we extract the `name` attribute from it, and place it in the `$resourceProducts` array, using the code:

```
$resourceProducts[] = $childNode->get_attribute('name')
```

Again here we use the `get_attribute()` function of the element class created for the current element, to get the name attribute of the current element. So we build up an array of applicable products for the current resource in `$resourceProducts`.

We cover all the other tags using the default statement in the `switch` structure because there are no attributes for the other tags, so we only need the text between the tags. We use the following code to read the text between the tags, and to descend to the next level of the tree:

```
$resourceDetailNodes = $childNode->child_nodes()
```

We then use a `foreach` loop to cycle through the child nodes, using the following code:

```
foreach($resourceDetailNodes as $detail)
```

Text between tags is of the type `XML_TEXT_NODE`, and so we check that the current node in `$detail` is of that type, using the `node_type()` function of the DOM Node class, created for the current node in `$detail`, using the code:

```
if($detail->node_type() == XML_TEXT_NODE)
```

`XML_TEXT_NODE` is a constant built into the PHP XML module. A full list can be found in the online PHP Manual. Once we know that the current node is an `XML_TEXT_NODE`, we put the text into the `$mmResource` array, referenced by its parent tag name, using the code:

```
$mmResource[$childNode->tagname] = $detail->get_content();
```

Here we use the `get_content()` function of the DOM Node class created for the current node in detail. The format of this command is:

```
$character date = $node->get_content();
```

To finish off we put the `$resourceProducts` array into the `$mmResource` array indexed by the name products, as shown in the code below:

```
$mmResource['products'] = $resourceProducts
```

We put the `$mmResource` array in the global array `$this->resource`, and call the function `outputResource()`, which is in the XML helper class, to create the HTML to display the data.

This completes the `DOMParse` class.

## Creating the PHP Page That Calls DOMParse

Create a new PHP page, and add the code shown below so it looks like the following:

```php
<?php require_once("domParserClass.php"); ?>
<html>
<head>
<title>DOM Parser Example</title>
<link href="mmStyles.css" rel="stylesheet" type="text/css" />
<meta http-equiv="Content-Type" content="text/html; charset=iso-8859-1">
</head>
<body>
<?
```

```
    $domParse = new DOMParse();
    echo $domParse->html;
?>
</body>
</html>
```

First we include our `domParserClass.php` file. Then the code creates a new instance of the `DOMParse` class, and sends the HTML created by the class to the browser. Save your page as `dom.php`.

## Viewing the End Result

Upload the `dom.php` page we just created to your server, and view it in your browser. You should see the same output as with the previous SAX example, except that we have processed the XML in a different way. A screenshot of a section of the output is shown below:

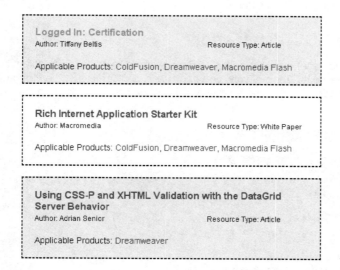

# Processing the XML Feed Using XSLT

The last method of processing XML files we're going to look at in the chapter is XSLT. XSLT stands for eXtensible Stylesheet Language Transformations, and is used to transform an XML document into another form, for example HTML or WML, rather than actually parsing it like SAX or DOM.

Parsers like SAX or DOM can be overly complex for simple operations, and XSLT is ideal for transforming XML documents into XHTML for example. XSLT is a language in itself, and requires an XSLT parser to process it. It has decision-making abilities using `if` conditions, and full sorting facilities, as well as regular expression-based searches.

To process a document using XSLT, you create an XSLT stylesheet, in a similar way that a CSS stylesheet formats an HTML document, except that you have extra commands, so that you can work and perform operations on the data, for example you can sort all character data into alphabetical order. You then apply the XSLT stylesheet to the XML document, and the XLST processor creates the new output.

XSLT works by dealing with all the elements, attributes, character data, etc., as nodes, in a similar way to the DOM method. In our XSLT stylesheet, we create a series of rules that tell the XSLT processor what to do when it comes across a particular node. The rules are created using a language called XPath, which is part of XSLT.

The XSLT processor scans through the document and at each node it checks a set of rules, and picks the best rule that matches the current node. Once a rule is matched the XSLT processor then deals with any instructions for the rule.

## Creating the XSLT Stylesheet

Create the XSLT stylesheet in a text editor as Dreamweaver MX currently doesn't recognize XSLT pages, and alters the code. Alternatively, you can use a dedicated XSLT editor, such as XML Spy. Enter the following code, which is the entire stylesheet, we'll then go through the stylesheet section by section:

```
<?xml version="1.0" encoding="iso-8859-1"?>

<!- Macromedia Developer Feed Transform->

<xsl:stylesheet version="1.0" xmlns:xsl="http://www.w3.org/1999/XSL/Transform">
<xsl:template match="/">

<!- Process Root Node macromedia_resources ->
<xsl:for-each select="macromedia_resources">

    <!- Process each resource node->
    <xsl:for-each select="resource">

        <!- Add opening div for <resource> ->
        <xsl:text disable-output-escaping="yes">&lt;div class="</xsl:text>
        <xsl:apply-templates select="@type" />
        <xsl:text disable-output-escaping="yes">"&gt;</xsl:text>

        <!- Print url, title and author from templates ->
        <xsl:apply-templates select="url" />
        <xsl:apply-templates select="title" />
        <xsl:apply-templates select="author" />

        <!- Resource Type ->
        <xsl:text disable-output-escaping="yes">&lt;span
            class="resourcetype"&gt;</xsl:text>
        <xsl:text disable-output-escaping="yes">Resource Type: </xsl:text>
        <xsl:apply-templates select="@type" />
```

```
            <xsl:text disable-output-escaping="yes">&lt;/span&gt;</xsl:text>
            <xsl:text disable-output-escaping="yes">&lt;br /&gt;&lt;br
                /&gt;</xsl:text>

            <!-- Print Product List Header -->
            <xsl:text disable-output-escaping="yes">&lt;span
                class="productHeader"&gt;</xsl:text>
            <xsl:text disable-output-escaping="yes">Applicable Products:
                </xsl:text>
            <xsl:text disable-output-escaping="yes">&lt;/span&gt;</xsl:text>
            <xsl:text disable-output-escaping="yes">&lt;span
                class="product"&gt;</xsl:text>

            <!-- Work through each <product> -->
            <xsl:for-each select="product">

                <!-- Sort Products into Alphabetical Order -->
                <xsl:sort select="@name" data-type="text"/>

                <!-- Print <product> name attribute -->
                <xsl:apply-templates select="@name" />

            </xsl:for-each>

            <!-- Print closing HTML for </resource> -->
            <xsl:text disable-output-escaping="yes">&lt;/span&gt;</xsl:text>
            <xsl:text disable-output-escaping="yes">&lt;/div&gt;&lt;br
                /&gt;</xsl:text>

        </xsl:for-each>
    </xsl:for-each>
</xsl:template>

    <!--Templates-->

    <!-- Match <resource> name attribute -->
    <xsl:template match="@type" >
        <xsl:value-of select="." />
    </xsl:template>

    <!-- Match <url> tag  -->
    <xsl:template match="url" >
        <xsl:text disable-output-escaping="yes">&lt;a href="</xsl:text>
        <xsl:value-of select="." />
        <xsl:text disable-output-escaping="yes">" class="title" &gt;</xsl:text>
    </xsl:template>

    <!-- Match <title> tag -->
    <xsl:template match="title">
        <xsl:value-of select="." />
        <xsl:text disable-output-escaping="yes">&lt;/a&gt;</xsl:text>
        <xsl:text disable-output-escaping="yes">&lt;br /&gt;</xsl:text>
    </xsl:template>

    <!-- Match <author> tag -->
    <xsl:template match="author">
```

```
<xsl:text disable-output-escaping="yes">&lt;span class="author"&gt;Author:
</xsl:text>
      <xsl:value-of select="." />
      <xsl:text disable-output-escaping="yes">&lt;/span&gt;</xsl:text>
  </xsl:template>

  <!— Match <product> tag name attribute —>
  <xsl:template match="@name">
      <xsl:if test=".='ColdFusion'">
          <xsl:text disable-output-escaping="yes"> ColdFusion</xsl:text>
      </xsl:if>
      <xsl:if test=".='Dreamweaver'">
          <xsl:text disable-output-escaping="yes"> Dreamweaver</xsl:text>
      </xsl:if>
      <xsl:if test=".='JRun'">
          <xsl:text disable-output-escaping="yes"> JRun</xsl:text>
      </xsl:if>
      <xsl:if test=".='Macromedia_Flash'">
          <xsl:text disable-output-escaping="yes"> Macromedia Flash</xsl:text>
      </xsl:if>
      <xsl:if test=".='Fireworks'">
          <xsl:text disable-output-escaping="yes"> Fireworks</xsl:text>
      </xsl:if>
      <xsl:if test=".='Freehand'">
          <xsl:text disable-output-escaping="yes"> Freehand</xsl:text>
      </xsl:if>
      <xsl:if test=".='Homesite'">
          <xsl:text disable-output-escaping="yes"> Homesite</xsl:text>
      </xsl:if>
      <xsl:if test=".='Director'">
          <xsl:text disable-output-escaping="yes"> Director</xsl:text>
      </xsl:if>
  </xsl:template>

</xsl:stylesheet>
```

Save this file as `mmFeed.xslt` in the same directory as our other example files. We'll now look each part of the stylesheet and explain how it works.

## The XSLT Stylesheet Step by Step

Because an XSLT stylesheet is an XML document, we start off with the standard code to declare the document as an XML Document, with the declaration shown below, as well as the XSL declaration:

```
<?xml version="1.0" encoding="iso-8859-1"?>
<xsl:stylesheet version="1.0" xmlns:xsl="http://www.w3.org/1999/XSL/Transform">
```

XSLT works by matching nodes against a series of user-defined templates. The first node that we match is the root node, which is the `<macromedia_resources>` tag. We match the root element using the following code:

```
<xsl:template match="/">
```

We process the root node, `<macromedia_resources>`, using the following code:

```
<xsl:for-each select="macromedia_resources">
    ...
</xsl:for-each>
```

This creates an XSL `for-each` loop, within the XSLT Processor. The code in the `for-each` structure will be run for every instance of the `<macromedia_resources>` tag. As the `<macromedia_resources>` tag is the root element, the loop will only be run once.

So now we are at the `<macromedia_resources>` tag in the XML tree. Next, we now process each `<resource>` node, using the following code:

```
<xsl:for-each select="resource">
    ...
</xsl:for-each>
```

Again this sets up a `for-each` loop, and the code in the loop structure will be run for each instance of the `<resource>` tag that is found.

## Displaying Each Resource

In the previous examples, we have used the `outputResource()` function in `xmlClass` to create the HTML to display. In this example the XSLT creates the HTML itself. To start off a new resource, we use the following HTML:

```
<div class="Article">
```

where the class is the value of the `type` attribute in the `<resource>` tag. To output this from the XSLT stylesheet, we use the following XSL commands:

```
<!— Add opening <div> for <resource> —>
<xsl:text disable-output-escaping="yes">&lt;div class="</xsl:text>
<xsl:apply-templates select="@type" />
<xsl:text disable-output-escaping="yes">&gt;</xsl:text>
```

The `<xsl:text>` command outputs first :

```
<div class="
```

Next we use the command:

```
<xsl:apply-templates select="@type" />
```

which outputs the value of the `<resource>` tag `type` attribute. We then output the rest of the HTML:

```
">
```

*Note that we have to change the opening brackets to their HTML symbols, for example, `&lt;` for < and `&gt;` for >. This is so that they are not recognized as tags by the XSLT processor, which would cause an error, and also why we can't create the document in Dreamweaver MX, as it turns the bracket symbols for example, `&lt;` and `&gt;` back into the actual brackets which messes up the code.*

to make the complete line of HTML shown below:

```
<div class="Article">
```

Next we use the following commands to tell the XSLT processor to apply templates when it comes across the `<url>`, `<title>`, and `<author>` tags. We define the actual template code that is to be applied later on in the template section of the stylesheet:

```
<!— Print url, title and author from templates —>
<xsl:apply-templates select="url" />
<xsl:apply-templates select="title" />
<xsl:apply-templates select="author" />
```

Next we use the following commands to output the resource type:

```
<!— Resource Type —>
<xsl:text disable-output-escaping="yes">&lt;span
class='resourcetype'&gt;</xsl:text>
<xsl:text disable-output-escaping="yes">Resource Type: </xsl:text>
<xsl:apply-templates select="@type" />
<xsl:text disable-output-escaping="yes">&lt;/span&gt;</xsl:text>
<xsl:text disable-output-escaping="yes">&lt;br /&gt;&lt;br /&gt;</xsl:text>
```

This creates the following HTML:

```
<span class="resourcetype">Resource Type: @type </span>
<br /><br />
```

where `@type` is replaced with the `type` attribute from the `<resource>` tag. Next we use the following commands to output the `Applicable Products` label:

```
<!— Print Product List Header —>
<xsl:text disable-output-escaping="yes">&lt;span
class="productHeader"&gt;</xsl:text>
<xsl:text disable-output-escaping="yes">Applicable Products: </xsl:text>
<xsl:text disable-output-escaping="yes">&lt;/span&gt;</xsl:text>
<xsl:text disable-output-escaping="yes">&lt;span class='product'&gt;</xsl:text>
```

which creates the following HTML:

```
<span class="productHeader"> Applicable Products: </span>
<span class="product">
```

### Displaying the Products

Next we need to show all the applicable products for the current resource, which we do with the following code:

```
<!— Work through each <product> —>
<xsl:for-each select="product">
```

```
<!- Sort Products into Alphabetical Order ->
<xsl:sort select="@name" data-type="text"/>

<!- Print <product> name attribute ->
<xsl:apply-templates select="@name" />

    </xsl:for-each>
```

We use an XSL `for-each` loop to process each product. We then use the XSL command:

```
<xsl:sort select="@name" data-type="text"/>
```

This command sorts the products, so that they are sorted in alphabetical order, by the `name` attribute of the `<product>` tag. We then tell the XSLT processor to apply a template each time it comes across the name attribute of the `<product>` tag.

## Closing the Resource

Now we have all the data output for the resource, we need to add the closing HTML to close the `<div>` tag that we opened at the start of the resource and create a space between the resources. We use the following code:

```
<!- Print closing HTML for </resource> ->
    <xsl:text disable-output-escaping="yes">&lt;/span&gt;</xsl:text>
    <xsl:text disable-output-escaping="yes">&lt;/div&gt;&lt;br
/&gt;</xsl:text>
```

which outputs the following HTML:

```
</span>
</div>
<br />
```

We then need to close the open XSL tags with the following commands:

```
        </xsl:for-each>
    </xsl:for-each>
</xsl:template>
```

We close the open XSL `for-each` loops, and then have a closing `</xsl:template>` tag to close the `<xsl:template match="/">` we opened for the root node.

We have now worked from the `<macromedia_resources>` root node, through each of its `<resource>` nodes, and output the data which is extracted from the `<resource>` child tags such as `<author>`, `<title>`, `<url>`, and `<product>`.

## Creating the Templates

A template contains output that is generated if certain pattern-matching criteria is met. It can be applied to a single node, or a group of nodes, and used to transform certain parts of the XML tree. The template element can contain an optional attribute **match**, which is used to match certain parts of the XML tree.

**10**

**XML**

267

You can also apply an optional priority value to the template rule. If part of the XML tree matches more than one template rule then the template with the highest priority is run. XSLT stylesheets can also import other XSLT stylesheets. If part of the XML tree matches templates in the original and the imported stylesheet, the original stylesheet template will take precedence over the template in the imported stylesheet. If part of the XML tree does not match any of the templates, then the XSLT parser will continue deeper into the tree until it can find a match.

Earlier we saw that we could apply a template each time a certain node was processed, such as the command below, which applies a template every time the `type` attribute of the `<resource>` tag is processed:

```
<xsl:apply-templates select="@type" />
```

The first template we define matches the `type` attribute above, and the code is shown below:

```
<!- Match <resource> name attribute ->
<xsl:template match="@type" >
    <xsl:value-of select="." />
</xsl:template>
```

This tells the XSLT processor to insert the current value of the `<resource>` type attribute wherever the template is called.

Next we have a template that is applied every time the `<url>` tag is encountered, which is defined with the code below:

```
<!- Match <url> tag  ->
<xsl:template match="url">
    <xsl:text disable-output-escaping="yes">&lt;a href="</xsl:text>
    <xsl:value-of select="." />
    <xsl:text disable-output-escaping="yes">" class="title" &gt;</xsl:text>
</xsl:template>
```

When a `<url>` tag is found, it outputs the following HTML:

```
<a href="<url>" class="title" >
```

where `<url>` is the text between the opening and closing `<url>` tags.

Below is the code for the template that matches the `<title>` tag:

```
<!- Match <title> tag ->
<xsl:template match="title">
    <xsl:value-of select="." />
    <xsl:text disable-output-escaping="yes">&lt;/a&gt;</xsl:text>
    <xsl:text disable-output-escaping="yes">&lt;br /&gt;</xsl:text>
</xsl:template>
```

This outputs the following HTML for each instance of the `<title>` tag:

```
<title></a>
<br />
```

where the `<title>` tag is replaced by its current value.

Next we define a template to match the `<author>` tag using the following code:

```
    <!— Match <author> tag —>
    <xsl:template match="author">
        <xsl:text disable-output-escaping="yes">&lt;span
class="author"&gt;Author: </xsl:text>
        <xsl:value-of select="." />
        <xsl:text disable-output-escaping="yes">&lt;/span&gt;</xsl:text>
    </xsl:template>
```

For each instance of the `<author>` tag, the following HTML code is output:

```
<span class="author">Author: <author> </span>
```

where the `<author>` tag is replaced by the current value of the `<author>` tag.

The last template is a long one, and matches the name attribute of the `<product>` tag. You'll notice that in the Macromedia XML feed, the product names consisting of two words, for example Macromedia Flash, are actually written as `Macromedia_Flash` and both words are joined by an underscore.

In the template below, we match the `name` attribute using its XML form, that is, `Macromedia_Flash`, and instead we print out the tag name without the underscore. We have a template section for each product, so that we can output different HTML depending on the product name:

```
    <!— Match <product> tag name attribute —>
    <xsl:template match="@name">
        <xsl:if test=".='ColdFusion'">
            <xsl:text disable-output-escaping="yes"> ColdFusion</xsl:text>
        </xsl:if>
        <xsl:if test=".='Dreamweaver'">
            <xsl:text disable-output-escaping="yes"> Dreamweaver</xsl:text>
        </xsl:if>
        <xsl:if test=".='JRun'">
            <xsl:text disable-output-escaping="yes"> JRun</xsl:text>
        </xsl:if>
        <xsl:if test=".='Macromedia_Flash'">
            <xsl:text disable-output-escaping="yes"> Macromedia Flash</xsl:text>
        </xsl:if>
        <xsl:if test=".='Fireworks'">
            <xsl:text disable-output-escaping="yes"> Fireworks</xsl:text>
        </xsl:if>
        <xsl:if test=".='Freehand'">
            <xsl:text disable-output-escaping="yes"> Freehand</xsl:text>
        </xsl:if>
        <xsl:if test=".='Homesite'">
```

**10**

**XML**

```
                <xsl:text disable-output-escaping="yes"> Homesite</xsl:text>
        </xsl:if>
        <xsl:if test=".='Director'">
                <xsl:text disable-output-escaping="yes"> Director</xsl:text>
        </xsl:if>
    </xsl:template>
```

Lastly we use the following tag to close the stylesheet:

```
</xsl:stylesheet>
```

This finishes our look at the XSLT stylesheet. Although the code is fairly long, it's fairly easy to get used to, and it is the quickest way to develop code to transform an XML document

## HTML Code Generated for Each Resource

When the stylesheet is used with the XML file, it generates the HTML shown below for each `<resource>` element:

```
<div class='@type'>
    <a href="<url>" class="title" >
    <title></a>
    <br />
    <span class="author">Author: <author></span>
    <span class="resourcetype">Resource Type: @type</span>
    <br /><br />
    <span class="productHeader">Applicable Products: </span>
    <span class="product"> @name @name</span>
</div>
<br />
```

where the tags `<url>`, `<title>`, `<author>` are replaced by the contents of those tags, `@type` is replaced by the `type` attribute of the `<resource>` tag, and `@name` is replaced by the `name` attribute of the `<product>` tag. This block of HTML is repeated for each `<resource>` element.

# Creating the PHP Code to Process the XSLT Transformation

When the `mmFeed.xslt` stylesheet is finished, the next step is to create the PHP code that actually initiates the XSLT transform. Create a new PHP page, and add the code below. As there is so little code needed, we'll look at the whole page at once.

```php
<?php
###################################################################
# PHP XSLT Parser Example                                         #
#                                                                 #
# Parses Macromedia Developers Feed at                            #
# http://www.macromedia.com/desdev/resources/macromedia_resources.xml #
###################################################################

// Requires xmlClass
```

```
require_once("xmlClass.php");

class xsltClass extends xmlClass{

        var $parser;

        function xsltClass(){
            $this->readXML();
            $this->processTransformation();
        }

    function processTransformation(){
        // Create XSLT Processor
        $xparse = xslt_create()
            or die("Can't create XSLT handle!");
        // Open mmFeed.xslt XLST Stylesheet
            $sh = fopen("mmFeed.xslt", "r") or die("Can't open XSL file");
        // Read in the XSL Stylesheet
        $xslContent = fread($sh, filesize("mmFeed.xslt"));
        // Close File
        fclose($sh);
        // Get XML Feed Data
        $xmlContent = $this->xml;
        $arguments = array('/_xml' => $xmlContent, '/_xsl' => $xslContent);
        // Perform the XSL transformation
        $this->html = xslt_process($xparse, 'arg:/_xml', 'arg:/_xsl', NULL,
                    $arguments);
        // Free up the resources
        xslt_free($xparse);
    }

}
?>
```

Save this page as `xsltClass.php` in the same directory as the `mmFeed.xslt` stylesheet and our other examples.

First we create a new class, `xsltClass`, which extends `xmlClass`. This time the function we need to read from this class is `readXML()`. In the `xsltClass` constructor statement, which is run when a new instance of the class is created, we first use the `readXML()` function to read in the XML feed as normal. We then apply the `processTransformation()` function, which we look at next.

## The processTransformation() Function

The first job of this function is to create a new XSLT parser, using the function `xslt_create()`. We use the following code:

```
$xparse = xslt_create()
  or die("Can't create XSLT handle!");
```

This creates a pointer to our XSLT parser in `$xparse`. If there is an error and the parser couldn't be created, we exit the script and print out an error message using the PHP `die()` function.

Next we use the PHP `fopen()` function to open the `mmFeed.xslt` stylesheet, and create a pointer to the file. Then we use the `fread()` function to read in the content of the stylesheet. When the whole file has been read, we close the file using the `fclose()` function.

**10**

**XML**

The next block of code is shown below:

```
// Get XML Feed Data
$xmlContent = $this->xml;
$arguments = array('/_xml' => $xmlContent, '/_xsl' => $xslContent);
```

This reads the XML feed from the global variable $this->xml which is obtained from the readXML() function which is located in the xmlClass object. We then create an array of arguments for the XSLT processor, using our two variables $xmlContent and $xslContent. We pass this array of arguments to the XSLT processor using the code:

```
$this->html = xslt_process($xparse, 'arg:/_xml', 'arg:/_xsl', NULL, $arguments);
```

This performs the XSLT transformation, and puts the HTML output by the transformation into the global variable $this->html.

Finally we free up the XSLT processor with the following command:

```
// Free up the resources
xslt_free($xparse);
```

This completes the xsltClass.php page, and is all the code needed to perform the XSLT transformation.

## Creating the PHP Page That Calls xsltClass

Create a new PHP page, and add the code shown below so that it looks like the following:

```
<?php require_once("xsltClass.php"); ?>
<html>
<head>
<title>XSLT Transform Example</title>
<link href="mmStyles.css" rel="stylesheet" type="text/css" />
<meta http-equiv="Content-Type" content="text/html; charset=iso-8859-1">
</head>
<body>
<?php
    $xslt = new xsltClass();
    echo $xslt->html;
?>
</html>
```

First we add the xsltClass.php file, and then we create a new instance of xsltClass(). The XSLT transformation is run automatically by the xsltClass.php constructor function, so all we need to do is to display the resulting HTML which is stored in the global variable $xslt->html. Save this file as xslt.php, and upload it to your server.

# Viewing the End Result

Open the `xslt.php` page in your browser, and you should see the same output as for the last two examples, a small section of which is shown below.

*Note that we have left the underscore in resource type `White_Paper`, in order to keep the code shorter so the example is easier to follow. It can be removed in exactly the same way as we removed the underscore from the product names.*

# Overview of XSLT Processing

XSLT doesn't provide the high level of processing that the SAX or DOM Parsers offer, but it's ideal for smaller simpler transformations, especially with its built-in sorting and processing abilities. It's usually faster and simpler to create an XSLT stylesheet than to create a custom DOM or SAX parser, so it's ideal when you need fast development times.

XSLT stylesheets are extremely useful for converting an XML file into a different format. So you can create a single XML file which holds the data for a web page, and then you can transform that XML file using XSLT into HTML that's compatible with the older browsers, XHTML for normal browsers, WML for a WAP device, HTML for a printable version of a web page without the site's header graphics, the possibilities are endless. You can then send the appropriate code for the device that's requesting it, without having to manually create a page for each different browser or device.

The full details of the XSLT syntax are listed on the following page of the online PHP manual: *http://uk.php.net/manual/en/ref.xslt.php*.

An Online Reference for XSLT can be found at: *http://www.w3schools.com/xsl/xsl_w3celementref.asp*.

10

XML

# XML in the Future

There are many XML-based languages now, and the number will keep increasing as more and more people realize the benefits of using XML, but they're all processed in the same way, so once you have learned the principles of XML, you can work with any XML-based language.

It's likely that one of the main applications of XML will be syndicating content, that is, sharing data between web sites. The Macromedia Developer XML feed, as well as being a useful resource likely to be used on a lot of sites, is also great advertising for their site because everyone who clicks on one of the links in the feed ends up on their site. The XML feed, however, should be useful in and of itself, and not just publicity for your site, or no one will want to use your feed.

Using XML it's easy to create your own feed, either by manually creating an XML document, or by creating a dynamic XML file using DOM to create the XML from data in your database.

XML is becoming more and more common, so it makes sense to become an early adopter. Hopefully we've shown in this chapter that XML isn't as complex as it sounds, and encouraged you to want to know more. There are a huge number of XML resources around, with hundreds of books available, as well as the many tutorials in magazines and on the Internet.

# Summary

In this chapter we started off looking at the SAX, DOM, and XSLT XML technologies, and what each type did, as well as some of the advantages and disadvantages of each type. We then moved on and looked at how to create XML documents in Dreamweaver MX, and how to add our own custom XML tags which are used in code view. Next we looked at XHTML, and explained the differences between HTML and XHTML. We then saw how to create XHTML documents using Dreamweaver MX, so that it automatically enforces the rules of XHTML.

Finally we looked at a real-life use of XML, by using the Macromedia Developers XML field to create our own styled guide to the latest resources on the Macromedia Developers Site, by processing the XML feed using SAX, DOM, and XSLT. We created the output in the same format each time, but for each example we used a different method of processing the XML.

# 11

- Maintaining state

- Sessions

- Cookies

Author: George McLachlan

# Sessions and Cookies

The web is a **stateless environment**. This means that the web server cannot identify the user that requests a page. What's more, it doesn't care. Requests come and go: as far as your web server is concerned once it has served up a page that was requested, that job is done and the request is forgotten about. By using sessions or cookies, we are able to store information about users as they navigate around a site. Generally, in computing, this is known as **maintaining state**.

However, there is a big difference between sessions and cookies. Cookies are small pieces of data that are stored on the client's machine. If the client's browser accepts cookies then the cookie will be sent along with the HTTP response. A cookie can be set to last as long as we wish, and as long as this cookie exists it is sent back to the server as part of the HTTP request.

Sessions allow you to relate a series of page requests together. PHP stores session information as temporary files on the server's hard drive. These files can be manipulated to contain the information you wish to keep about a user. A PHP session will expire when the browser is closed or if we use the `session_unregister()` or `unset()` functions.

Sessions and cookies are important for building applications like forums or shopping carts. In fact, they will be used in almost all applications which require the ability to track user details across multiple pages.

In this chapter we will look at:

- An introduction to sessions and cookies.
- Common problems when using sessions and cookies.
- How to build a simple session application.
- How to build a more complex application using cookies.

# Introduction to Sessions

Native session support was first introduced in PHP4. Before that, in PHP3, session support was achieved by using a class library called PHPLib (*https://sourceforge.net/projects/phplib/*). This meant you had to include these classes within every page that required you to use sessions. However, you will be pleased to know that the PHP developers have done a good job in PHP4 by making it as easy as possible for us to use sessions.

So how do sessions work? Anyone accessing our web site will be assigned a unique ID, called the **session ID** or **SID**. This is either stored in a cookie in the browser, or is passed through the URL (this is an ideal solution when a user has disabled cookies in their browser). When a user sends a request for a page, the SID is also sent; this tells PHP which user session to associate with the request.

In order to check that session support has been enabled, and to view our default session settings, we use `phpinfo.php` as we did in *Chapter 3*. Scroll down until you see the section headed **session.**

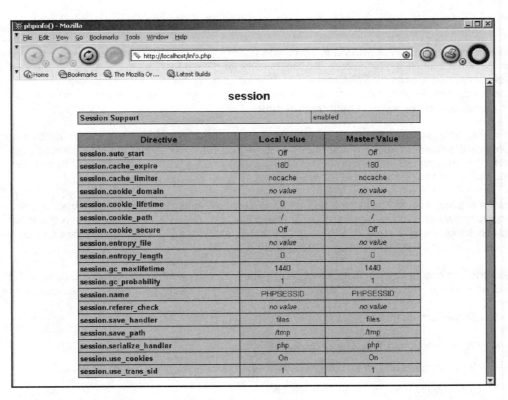

Nearly all of the default settings can be left unchanged. However, if you are using Windows, there is one important change we must make in order to make our sessions work. We must tell PHP where to store the session files on our server.

Looking at the screenshot above we can see the ***session.save_path*** is set (by default) to the `/tmp` directory. This directory does not exist in Windows. If you installed PHP with a package like **PHPDev** or **PHPTriad**, then this setting may have already been changed for you. If it hasn't, we will need to make the changes ourselves. This is easy to do and can be broken down into 3 simple steps.

1   Create a folder on your hard drive. In my case, I created a folder in my C drive called phpsessions.

2   Open up the php.ini file and change the session.save_path, so that it points to the folder you just created. So in my case I change  /tmp to c:\phpsessions.

3   Finally, if PHP is running as a module, we need to restart the web server in order for the changes to take effect.

One other setting to take note of is the `session.use_trans_sid`. This option will be used if cookies cannot be used to hold the session ID. PHP will instead add the session ID to local URLs in the page after it has been processed.

## Creating Our First Session

In *Chapter 1* we looked briefly at the `$_SESSION` array. How do we register a session? Again, the PHP developers have made it nice and easy for us, as you can see from the example below.

```
$_SESSION['nickname'] = "Bob";
```

This will register a session variable with the name of *nickname* and a value of "*Bob*".

As a quick exercise, create a new PHP page in Dreamweaver MX and add the following code at the top of it:

```
<?php
    session_start();
    $_SESSION['nickname'] = "Bob";
?>
```

Then somewhere in between the `<body>` tags enter:

```
<?php echo "Hello " . $_SESSION["nickname"] ."!"; ?>
```

If you press *F12* you should see something like this:

## Using Sessions

This example will show how a session can remember information. To do this, we shall write a script that counts the number of times a user has visited a page.

When working with sessions, the first thing we have to do is begin with the `session_start()` function, which tells PHP to find the existing session ID for this user, or create a new one. We will create a session variable called **views** and increment it by 1 each time the session is called. Create the following new PHP file in Dreamweaver MX:

```php
<?php
  session_start();
  if (!isset($_SESSION['views'])) {
    $_SESSION['views'] = 1;
} else {
    $_SESSION['views']++;
}

?>
<html>
<head>
<title>Session Example</title>
<meta http-equiv="Content-Type" content="text/html; charset=iso-8859-1">
</head>

<body>
<?php
echo "You have viewed this page " .$_SESSION["views"]. " time(s)<BR />";
?>
</body>
</html>
```

First the code checks to see if `views` has been registered using the `isset()` function. If it doesn't exist, it creates it with the value 1. If the session already exists, then the value of `views` is increased by 1.

Save this file as `session_count.php` and press *F12* to preview the page, and you should see the following message:

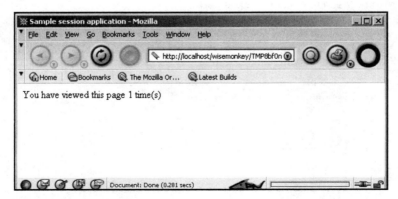

Refresh the page a few times, and you will see the count increase. Close the browser and return to MX, then reopen the file in a browser. You may be surprised to see that the value is back at 1. This is because the session is destroyed when the browser is closed.

## Using unset() to Destroy a Session

In our last example we showed that closing the browser destroyed the session. However, there will be times when we build applications that we may need to destroy a session from within the script. For example, a user may wish to empty all the items from their shopping cart, or perhaps log out. We do this using the `unset()` function.

We will modify the `session_count.php` page we used earlier. This time, however, we are going to destroy the session when the value of `$_SESSION["views"]` reaches 10. We do this by adding a conditional block after our `session _start()` statement.

```php
<?php
  session_start();
  $_SESSION["views"]++;
  if($_SESSION["views"]==10){
    unset($_SESSION["views"]);
  $_SESSION["views"]++;


  }
?>
<html>
<head>
```

Press *F12* to preview the page. As you refresh the browser, the number will still increment by one each time. However this time when the value reaches 10 the session is destroyed and the value returns to 1.

## Sessions and Security

A developer can never be sure that only one user has access to any one session, since a session is either sent in the header or embedded in the URL. It is possible that more than one person will use a PC, or a user may cut and paste a URL. It is important to keep this in mind when storing data in a session, as there is always the possibility of somebody hijacking the session ID, it is therefore always best to avoid storing sensitive information within a session.

# Introduction to Cookies

Before we start the next section, let's take a more detailed look at cookies. Cookies have had a bad press recently with many users viewing them with suspicion (and as such may choose to reject them in their browser options). However, a cookie is no more than a text file which contains a series of `name=value` pairs. For instance, a cookie may contain the text `foo=bar`, which means the cookie is named `foo` and the value of `foo` is `bar`. Cookies were originally created by Netscape for version 1 of Navigator, and followed the following specification:

- In total, you can have no more than 300 cookies on your machine at any given time.

- The maximum limit per domain is 20, if a domain should exceed this limit then the browser may delete the least used.

- A site can only access a cookie that has been set from its own domain.

- A cookie can be no bigger than 4k.

# PHP and Cookies

You can set a cookie in PHP using the `setcookie()` function. This is simply a specialized header function; however cookie information must be sent before any other headers. Let's look at the general format of a call to the `setcookie()` function:

```
Boolean setcookie(string name[, string value[, int expire[, string path[, string domain[, int secure]]]]])
```

Notice that it takes a sequence of arguments. All arguments apart from `name` are optional, but they must be in order, so if you wish to skip an argument then you can replace it with an empty string (`""`).

## Name

```
setcookie("my_first_cookie");
```

This will set a cookie called `my_first_cookie`, however it won't have a value

## Value

```
setcookie("my_first_cookie", "Yummy");
```

This sets a cookie called `my_first_cookie` with a value of `Yummy`. You can access the value of this cookie by using `$_COOKIE["my_first_cookie"]`. Note that the cookie doesn't exist until the page with the cookie is retrieved. If you set and test the cookie in the same page it will not be there.

As we haven't entered a expiry time for the cookie, it will expire when the browser is closed, a cookie that does not contain a expiry value, or whose value has been set to "0" is called a session cookie. We can change this by using the third argument `expire`.

## Expire

```
setcookie ("my_first_cookie","Yummy",time()+3600);
```

The `time()` function gets the current system time and returns it. So in the example above, the cookie is set to expire 3600 seconds (1 hour) after it is set. Of course many web sites rely on setting a cookie with an almost unreachable expiry date. We can do this by using the `mktime()` function.

```
setcookie ("my_first_cookie","Yummy",mktime(21,00,0,12,31,2014));
```

The `mktime()` function returns a UNIX timestamp for a date. In our example the cookie is set to expire at 9pm on the 31st of December 2014.

## Path

What happens if we want to prevent the cookie being accessed from other directories? For this, we can use the `path` argument.

```
setcookie ("my_first_cookie","Yummy",mktime(21,00,0,12,31,2014),"/glasshaus/");
```

The value of the cookie set above can only be accessed in the `/glasshaus/` directory. Of course we could also limit the cookie to a single page.

```
setcookie
("my_first_cookie","Yummy",mktime(21,00,0,12,31,2014),"/glasshaus/index.php");
```

If you want to allow it to be accessible from all directories of your web site you would use "/".

```
setcookie ("my_first_cookie","Yummy",mktime(21,00,0,12,31,2014),"/");
```

## Domain

This sets the domain from which a cookie is accessible.

```
setcookie ("my_first_cookie","Yummy",mktime(21,00,0,12,31,2014),"/",
".my_domain.com");
```

You will notice from the above example the domain value is `.my_domain.com`. It's important that you include the "." at the start of the domain name. We shall look at why we have to do this later on in this chapter. In general you should be as restrictive as possible when setting the cookie domain, this will help prevent other sites accessing the cookie.

## Secure

This argument sets whether the cookie is only accessible from within HTTPS requests. The default value for this is `0`, meaning the cookie will be accessible from any regular HTTP request.

```
setcookie ("my_first_cookie","Yummy",mktime(21,00,0,12,31,2014),"/",
"www.my_domain.com", 0);
```

If we wanted to use a cookie in a secure HTTPS request then we must replace the 0 with 1:

```
setcookie                    ("my_first_cookie","Yummy",mktime(21,00,0,12,31,2014),"/",
"www.my_domain.com", 1);
```

The cookie detailed above would be accessible from any folder within *https://www.my_domain.com*.

## Deleting a Cookie

There can sometimes be some confusion about how to delete a cookie, but it couldn't be easier. To delete a cookie, simply use the `setcookie()` function with the name of the cookie that you wish to delete.

```
setcookie ("my_first_cookie");
```

You could also delete the cookie using the `time()` function:

```
setcookie ("my_first_cookie","Yummy",time()-3600);
```

Using `time()-3600` sets the expiration date of the cookie an hour in the past, forcing the browser to remove it.

## Common Problems When Using Cookies

Most people encounter the same problem when using cookies for the first time: the dreaded *Cannot add header information* error. The `setcookie()` function is similar to the `header()` function in this way. If you output whitespace, hard returns, or any HTML to the browser before either of these functions, it will result in an error message.

Let's look at a piece of code that will trigger this error as we send text to the browser using the echo statement before we send the **setcookie()** information.

```
<?php
  echo "hello\n <br />";
  setcookie("my_first_cookie","Yummy");
?>
```

If you run this, you will see the resulting output in your browser.

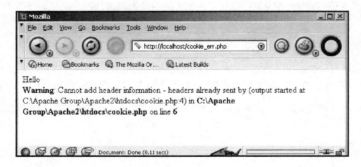

Another common problem is setting the domain with only one dot (.). This is to prevent people setting a cookie that might be sent to a, for instance, .net domain. This means that the `setcookie()` example detailed below will not work.

```
setcookie ("my_first_cookie","Yummy",mktime(21,00,0,12,31,2014),"/",
"my_domain.com");
```

Further, setting the domain to *www.my_domain.com* can also cause problems:

```
setcookie ("my_first_cookie","Yummy",mktime(21,00,0,12,31,2014),"/",
"www.my_domain.com");
```

This means the cookie will only be sent if the domain name is *http://www.my_domain.com*. This creates a problem as people often access the same site using *http://my_domain.com*. Anyone using this URL will not receive the cookie. A solution would be to redirect all users accessing your site at *domain.com* to *www.domain.com* using the `header()` function.

Finally, Internet Explorer 4 and some versions of IE5 require you to supply both expire and path values or neither. We shall look at this in the next section when we build our simple cookie application.

## A Simple Cookie Example

Now that we have learned more about setting cookies with PHP, let's put this to the test. In the previous section, when we dealt with sessions, we looked at how to build a simple application, `Session_count.php`, which counted the number of times a page had been viewed. We shall build the same application again but this time we will use a cookie instead of a session to store our information.

Create a new PHP page in Dreamweaver and add the following code above the opening `<html>` tag:

```
<?php
if(isset($_COOKIE['views']))
   $_COOKIE['views']=1;
else
   $_COOKIE['views']++;
   setcookie('views',$_COOKIE['views']);
?>
```

Next we will print out the value of the cookie to the browser by placing the code below within the `<body>` tags.

```
<?php echo "You have viewed this page " .$_COOKIE["views"]. " time(s)"; ?>
```

Save this file as `cookie_test.php` and open it up in your browser. Like the counter we made using sessions, earlier in this chapter, every time the browser is refreshed the number increments by *1*.

Close your browser, and then reopen it. Browse back to `cookie_test.php`; the value will have returned to *1*. This is because in the cookie example above we didn't set a value for the expire value of the cookie, which means that when the browser is closed the cookie is destroyed.

Of course, the main use of cookies is to remember user information *between* visits to a web site. To do this, we will supply a value for the cookie's expiration. Earlier in the chapter, we dealt with some of the common problems involving cookies. We will look at how some versions of IE4 and IE5 will not set the cookie unless we supply a value for both the expire and path arguments, so remember to keep this in mind.

If we go back to `cookie_test.php` we can add the expire and path values to our `setcookie()` function. We will set the cookie to expire in one hour and set the path to "/" which means it's accessible from all directories and sub-directories on our site.

```php
<?php
  $_COOKIE["views"]++;
  setcookie("views",$_COOKIE["views"],time()+3600,"/");
?>
```

Save the changes to `cookie_test.php`. Now open the page in your browser, refresh the page several times, and then take a note of the value. Once you have done this, close your browser. The next time when we visit the page, we will see that the value hasn't reverted back to *1*. The cookie has stored the previous value and increments it, as before.

## A Cookie Application

Now that we have a better understanding of cookies, we can build a more complex application. Web users can be a fickle bunch, and often will have no loyalty to a particular site. To combat this, many web sites come up with ideas to help keep their users loyal and one of the more popular methods is to allow a user to customize how the site looks when they visit it. After all, isn't it great to go to a web site when it appears as though it was designed just for you? With this in mind, we are going to write an application that allows users to personalize our site.

Let's take some time to look at the scope of our project. The object of our application is to:

- Allow a user to set a custom color scheme on our web site.
- Allow a user to enter their first name, which will be displayed along with the style selection.
- Every time the user re-visits the page we shall remember their selections and display the appropriate information.
- A user is able to change the style any time they wish.

Now that we have detailed the objectives, how do we put them into practice?

- We will use a mixture of CSS and cookies to allow a user to select a style.
- The user will be able to select from three different styles contained in a drop-down menu and enter their name in a textfield. These are contained in a form on our index page.

- We shall process this form via the GET method to a separate PHP page, which is called change_style.php. This will, in turn, process the information and direct the user back to our index page using the header() function.

- We must always check any information a user enters to ensure that it does not contain any malicious code. We do this with the help of the strip_tags() function.

It is assumed that anyone reading this chapter will have a good understanding of HTML and CSS, so we will not cover any of these topics here. You can, however, download the files for this example. They are available in the code download for the book at *www.glasshaus.com*.

So let me introduce you to our web site, it's a site dedicated to cookies and coffee; *The PHP Cookie Company*.

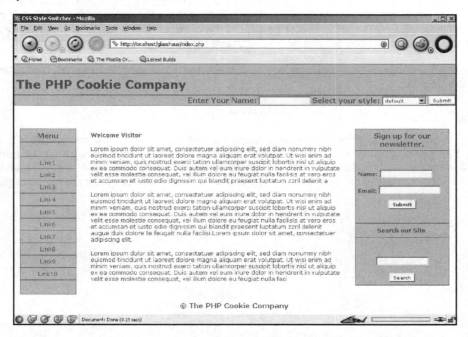

As you can see from above, our index page contains a textfield, which is called first_name, and a drop-down menu which is called style_selection. The drop-down menu contains three different options, one for each of our three stylesheets. These field elements are held within a form that submits to change_style.php using the GET method.

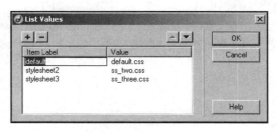

Let's begin by adding the PHP code to our index page.

```php
<?php
if(isset($_COOKIE["style_selection"])) {
        $style= $_COOKIE["style_selection"];
} else {
 $style="default.css";
}
?>
```

We looked at the `isset()` function earlier in this chapter. We are using it to check if the cookie has been set with a value; if so, we assign the value of that cookie to the variable $style. However, if the cookie hasn't been set, we will assign a default value to $style. Which, in this case, is the name of our default stylesheet. We do this to ensure that first-time visitors to our site, those that haven't chosen their style, will at least be assigned the default stylesheet. As we described earlier in this chapter, the `setcookie()` function must be sent to the browser before any other information. This means the code detailed below must be placed above the opening <html> tag.

Now that our variable $style has a value, we will use this to provide the name of our stylesheet within the CSS tag.

```html
<link rel="stylesheet" type="text/css" href="<?php echo $style;?>">
```

In the last piece of PHP code in our index page, we use the `isset()` function to check that the cookie that contains the first name has been set. If it does contain a value, then we print the information out to the browser. If it doesn't then we shall print out the message "*Welcome Visitor*". Place this piece of code in the body of the page where you wish the user's first name to be displayed.

```php
<?php

 if(isset($_COOKIE["first_name"])) {

  echo "Welcome back ". $_COOKIE["first_name"];

 } else {

  echo "Welcome Visitor";

}
?>
```

## Processing the Information

Now we have to create the PHP page that processes our information, and then sets the cookies. Create a new PHP page in MX and save it as `change_style.php`. Let's look at the code for this page.

```php
<?php
  $style_selection=strip_tags($_GET["style_selection"]);

  $first_name=strip_tags($_GET["first_name"]);

  if($style_selection == "" || $first_name == "") {
   header("Location: $_SERVER[HTTP_REFERER]");
   }

  setcookie("first_name", $first_name, mktime(21,00,0,12,31,2014),"/",
".my_domain.com", 0);

  setcookie("style_selection", style_selection, mktime(21,00,0,12,31,2014),"/",
".my_domain.com", 0);

  header("Location: $_SERVER[HTTP_REFERER]");
?>
```

Again, there is nothing that complicated in the code, but so you have a clear understanding of it, let's break it down.

```php
<?php
  $style_selection=strip_tags($_GET["style_selection"]);
  $first_name=strip_tags($_GET["first_name"]);
```

At the start of this section, we briefly touched on the `strip_tags()` function. One of the most important things that you need to do, when allowing a user to enter information, is to ensure that they don't pass any malicious code. By using this function, PHP will strip out all HTML tags from the user input. What the code above does, is assign the variables `$style_selection` the value of `$_GET["style_selection"]` once it has been passed through the `strip_tags()` function. We also do the same for the variable `$first_name`.

Next we look at:

```php
  if($style_selection == "" || $first_name== "") {
   header("Location: $_SERVER[HTTP_REFERER]");
   }
```

This piece of code checks that both variables that we passed to this script, `$style_selection` and `$first_name`, have a value. If either or both are empty then the user is sent back to the main page. This is done by using the `header()` function and `$_SERVER[HTTP_REFERER]`.

Let's move on to the `setcookie()` function:

```php
setcookie("first_name", $first_name, mktime(21,00,0,12,31,2014),"/",
".my_domain.com", 0);
```

Looking at what we learned earlier in this chapter, we can see that we are setting a cookie, named `first_name`. Its value is the value of the variable `$first_name`. We have set this cookie to expire at 9pm on the 31st of December 2014. The path has been set to "/" which means the cookie can be accessed from any folder or page in your domain. We have set the domain, but obviously you will need to change this to suit. We have set the final argument to `0`, so that the cookie can be accessed from any normal HTTP request.

```
setcookie("style_selection", $style_selection, mktime(21,00,0,12,31,2014),"/",
".my_domain.com", 0);
```

The only difference between this and the first cookie is the name and value. All the other arguments are the same. In this case, the name of the cookie is style_selection and its value is the value of the variable $style_selection.

The final bit of code uses the header() function again.

```
eader("Location: $_SERVER[HTTP_REFERER]");
?>
```

This code redirects the user back to the page where they entered the information. In our case it redirects them back to the index page. The finished code should look like this in Dreamweaver:

```
1  <?php
2    $style_selection=strip_tags($_GET["style_selection"]);
3    $first_name=strip_tags($_GET["first_name"]);
4
5    if($style_selection == "" || $first_name == "") {
6       header("Location: $_SERVER[HTTP_REFERER]");
7    }
8    setcookie("first_name", $_GET["first_name"], mktime(21,00,0,12,31,2004),"/", ".my_domain.com", 0);
9    setcookie("style_selection", $_GET["style_selection"], mktime(21,00,0,12,31,2004),"/", ".my_domain.com", 0);
10   header("Location: $_SERVER[HTTP_REFERER]");
11 ?>
```

## Testing Our Application

Open up your web browser and go to the index page of our *Cookie and Coffee* site.

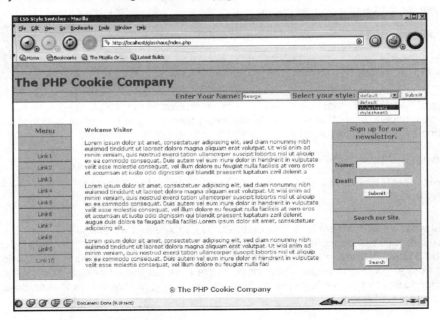

Enter your name into the textfield and select *stylesheet2* from the drop-down menu. Then click *submit.* Once you have done this, the cookies will be set and you will be redirected back to the index page. The changes will have taken effect:

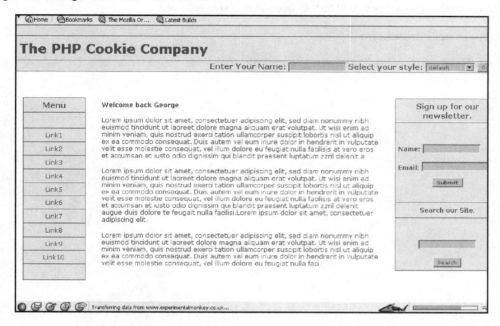

If you close down your browser, then reopen it and browse back to the index page. You will see that all information has been remembered.

Finally, if you wish, you can go back at any point and change your choice of style or first name. The value of the old cookies will be overwritten with the value of the new ones.

# Summary

We started this chapter by looking at native session support within PHP. We went on to build a simple session application, which counted the number of times a user had viewed our page. We also looked at how to delete a session without the user closing their browser.

Next we had an introduction to cookies, and looked at a few facts and misconceptions regarding them. We covered the setcookie() function and the various arguments this function accepts. We also took some time to look at common issues and problems when using cookies. We rebuilt our session application using cookies, and then we went on to show how a cookie could store information between visits. Finally, we built a more complex cookie application.

Hopefully, after reading this chapter, you will have a sound understanding of how sessions and cookies work. With this you can go on to build applications that require sessions and cookies. Common applications that use cookies or sessions include: login/registration applications, shopping carts, and message boards.

# Useful Resources

There is an abundance of information and resources on the Web that deals with cookies. Hopefully the URLs below will help with any further questions you may have.

*http://www.cookiecentral.com*

*http://www.w3.org/Security/Faq/wwwsf2.html#CLT-Q10*

**Sessions and Cookies**

# 12

- Creating server side graphics in PHP
- Using dynamic graphics

**Author: Dan Radigan**

# Server-Side Graphics

At this point I'm sure you're convinced that PHP is a very powerful language to generate all sorts of text content on a web page. In this chapter, we are going to look at how PHP can create non-textual dynamic content: graphics.

We'll start off with a short discussion of image formats and their relative merits. We'll also look at the basic constructs of HTML and how they are used in conjunction with static images. Next we'll take a short look at the way images are transferred over HTTP and the different methods that we can output graphical content from PHP.

*The function library for image manipulation in PHP is quite extensive. We'll take a short tour of the most important tools for server-side graphics creation rather than an exhaustive look at each of the functions in detail.*

We'll then take that core set of functions to create some practical examples seen in many web pages. First we start off with building a dynamic button, one that we can use in a navigational toolbar. We then move on to two implementations of a counter, one using a dynamic image and another using a collection of static ones, comparing and contrasting the approaches. We finish with creating a chart bound to data from a MySQL database. We'll turn that functionality into a Server Behavior for reusability in other applications.

Much of the content in this chapter relies on concepts previously explained in earlier chapters. Beyond a basic mastery of PHP, we'll be using several concepts from other chapters, mainly from *Chapter 4*, and *Chapter 6.* While by no means required, having read and mastered the other material will make the concepts in this chapter clearer.

# Graphics Basics

Let's begin with a basic understanding of what an image is and how images are represented in a computer. An image is no more than a collection of pixels, or dots with a certain color. All images are rectangular, in that they have a certain width and height, creating a matrix of pixels. A 300 by 100 image has 30,000 pixels. In PHP, images are represented with a coordinate system. Let's have x equal to 300 and y equal to 100.

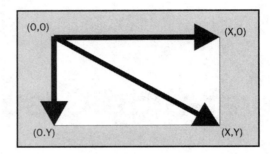

The upper-left corner of the canvas is always (0,0). The x values increase moving to the right along the canvas, as the y values increase moving down the canvas. When placing content onto the canvas, it is always relative to the upper-left corner. In the example above, the coordinates (180, 50) places us close to the right side of the canvas, halfway down.

Let's take a real-world example of how images are represented in a computer. Imagine you've got 100 yellow pegs in a grid 10 long by 10 high, basically a yellow square. Replace some of those yellow pegs with green pegs so that you have a green H inside of the yellow square. Congratulations, you've just made your first dynamic image.

One other point worth noting is **transparency**. Transparency is the ability to include "clear" pixels. If you make all the yellow pegs invisible, in essence making the color yellow transparent, you can see the grid where pegs are placed along with the H that is left.

## Image Formats

The construct that HTML gives to display images on the web page has remained relatively static. Image formats have changed slightly over the years. The three main formats on the web today are GIF, JPEG, and PNG.

GIF is short for **Graphics Interchange Format**. A few years ago the GIF format was widely used on the web primarily because of image transparency. The GIF format is restricted to 8-bit color, which means you can only have 256 colors in a single image. Because of limited color capacity, GIF images are good for large flat areas of color. However in recent years Unisys Corporation, the owner of LZW compression which the GIF format uses, has been enforcing that patent. Thus the use of the GIF Format has declined. This patent is due to expire in June of 2003.

JPEG, **Joint Photographic Experts Group**, is a format suited for photographic-type images. JPEG files have no provisions for transparency thus they are not suitable for toolbars or shapes that are not rectangular.

The PNG, **Portable Network Graphics**, format is a newer format that is now fully supported in all the major browsers. PNG has all the advantages of GIF, including transparency. One thing of note however, is that the transparency property is not supported in Netscape 4, which renders a white background instead. This bug seems to have been fixed in Netscape 6 and the Mozilla browsers. Some early versions of IE exhibit this behavior as well. If using the PNG format, test the graphic in all browsers with which your web site needs to be compatible.

# Graphics Manipulation with PHP

GD is an ANSI C library for the dynamic creation of images. Much like PHP, GD is an open source library that is maintained by Boutell.com; the official home page of GD is *http://www.boutell.com/gd*. As of this writing the current version of GD is 2.0.3 for the stable version. GD was once able to output both the GIF format and the JPG formats, however because of the Unisys patent, version 1.6 was the last with GIF support. The GD developers moved in favor of PNG, which we'll be using here.

## Installing GD from Source

Installing GD is pretty straightforward on both Windows and Linux. On the Macintosh I'd recommend a precompiled binary. An excellent source for Mac users is from Marc Liyanage at *http://www.entropy.ch.* GD is going to be standard in the next upcoming release of PHP 4.3. Once this version becomes available, GD will be there by default. Many precompiled versions of PHP come with GD support.

### Windows

Getting GD enabled on the Windows platform is very easy. The GD module is included in the PHP distribution, but is not enabled by default. You will need to modify your `php.ini` file and uncomment the line:

```
;extension=php_gd2.dll
```

Then make sure the `php_gd2.dll` library is in the correct directory. You will have to restart your web server if PHP is running as a module. No restart is needed if PHP is running as a CGI.

If your ISP does not have the GD library compiled in to PHP, you can use the `dl()` function. Although it's slower, you can also choose to load the GD module on demand.

```php
<?php
  dl('php_gd2.dll');
?>
```

### Linux

Binding GD to PHP under Linux is more challenging, but only required if running a PHP version earlier than 4.3. You'll need to download GD as well as FreeType if you plan to do TrueType font manipulation You can get GD from the Boutell homepage at *http://www.boutell.com/gd/*. You can get FreeType at *http://www.freetype.org/*.

Unpack the GD and FreeType distributions, and run the following commands in each.

**12**

```
make
make install
```

Once GD is built you need to bind it to PHP. In the directory that contains the PHP source, type:

```
./configure --with-gd --with-freetype-dir
make
make install
```

If you have any additional parameters to configure PHP, you'll need to add them to the configure statement.

For RedHat and other RPM users, binary installs for the i386 platform are available at: *http://rpms.arvin.dk/php/*.

A simple call to phpinfo() reports whether the GD library is bound to your install of PHP.

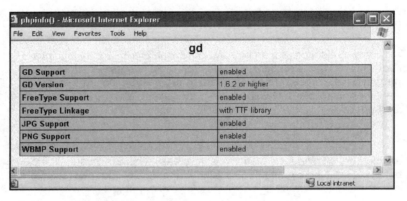

This version of PHP is correctly bound to GD as the output of phpinfo() has an entry for the GD extension. This version has JPG and PNG support.

# The GD API

The GD API is a set of functions that allow you to create and modify graphical content from within PHP. The entire API is beyond the scope of this text. We'll focus on four main areas: the basic functions, color manipulation, drawing primitive shapes, and working with text. These will give you a firm foundation from which to explore the GD yourself.

## The Basic Functions

Let's begin with the core set of functions that you'll use in any server-generated graphic. These functions load images from disk, modify them in memory, and write the image to disk or stream it to the browser.

### Creating Images

To create a new image resource for modification we can call the imagecreate() function:

```
resource imagecreate (int x_size, int y_size)
```

The function `imagecreate()` returns a resource representing an image in memory, much like `mysql_connect()` returns a resource to a recordset. You cannot access this variable directly, but will pass it to the image manipulation functions. The resulting image has a size of `x_size` pixels by `y_size` pixels.

## Using Existing Images

In addition to creating blank images, we can also read an existing image from disk.

```
resource imagecreatefrompng (string filename)
resource imagecreatefromjpeg (string filename)
```

Much like `imagecreate()`, on success these functions return an image resource that is equivalent to the pixel size of filename on disk. On failure both functions return an empty string. If you have `fopen_wrappers` enabled (you can do this by editing the appropriate line of `php.ini`), you can use a URL as the filename. Look out for performance issues when retrieving content over HTTP. Each time the function is called with a URL reference rather than afile on disk, the script must retrieve the file over the network. Since network access is much slower than disk access, performance can be a major factor here. `fopen_wrappers` currently work on UNIX-based versions of PHP. They will be fixed in the Win 32 PHP with version 4.3.

## Finding an Image's Size

Many times in a web application it is useful to know the size of an image. We can use this information for example to properly size a pop-up window in a photo album or fill in the `height` and `width` attributes of an `<img>` tag.

```
array getimagesize (string filename [, array imageinfo])
```

The `getimagesize()` function returns a four element array:

- Element 0: Width of the image referenced by filename in pixels
- Element 1: Height of the image referenced by filename in pixels
- Element 2: Integer corresponding to the file type of the image. (1 = GIF, 2 = JPG, 3 = PNG)
- Element 3: String that can be added to the <img> tag to represent its dimensions, for example, "height=100 width 200"

The optional parameter `imageinfo`, is an array passed by reference to get some extended information from the image file. At writing, this will return the different JPG APP markers as an associative array.

## Retrieving the Width and Height

If we just need one dimension of the image or do not need to mess with the complexity of an array, we can use the scalar functions `imagesx()` and `imagesy()`.

```
int imagesx (resource image)
int imagesy (resource image)
```

**12**

As expected, `imagesx()` returns the width of the image and `imagesy()` returns the height of the image. It should be noted though that unlike the `getimagesize` function above, `imagesx()` and `imagesy()` functions take an image resource, not a file path. You'll have to create the image resource by calling `imagecreate()` then use it as an argument for `imagesx()` and `imagesy()`.

## Copying and Resizing an Image

We can both copy images and resize them. This function is very useful in making thumbnails for a photo album.

```
int imagecopyresized (resource dst_im, resource src_im, int dstX, int dstY, int
srcX, int srcY, int dstW, int dstH, int srcW, int srcH)
```

This function copies a rectangular portion of the source image to the destination image.

- dst_im, src_im – the destination and source image resources
- int dstX, int dstY – the upper-left corner of the replaced content in the destination image
- int srcX, int srcY – the upper-left corner of the source content in the source image
- int dstW, int dstH – the width and height of the rectangular area to replace in the destination image
- int srcW, int srcH – the width and height of the rectangular area to copy in the source image

If the rectangular areas are not of the same dimensions between the source and destinations images, the function performs the appropriate scaling. This function can be used to copy regions within the same image (if `dst_im` is the same as `src_im`), but if the regions overlap the results will be unpredictable.

## Outputting to the Browser

Once we're done modifying the images we need a way to return the content to the browser. For this use we have the `imagepng()` and `imagejpeg()` functions.

```
int imagepng (resource image [, string filename])
int imagejpeg (resource image [, string filename])
```

This function outputs the raw image data to the browser. If a filename is provided then it writes the image data to the file specified. The filename must be valid on the destination drive and PHP must have appropriate permission to write to that location. When outputting directly to the browser, an HTTP header needs to be sent to the browser using the `header()` function to alert it to the content. This practice will be explained in more detail in the *Examples* section.

## Reclaiming Used Memory

Once we're done with the image we need to free the resources that the image used:

```
int imagedestroy (resource image)
```

The `imagedestory()` function frees the resources of image. Images can require a lot of memory, so it's important to free any resources once you're done.

## An Example Using Basic Functions

Using these functions we can create a simple thumbnail creator that loads an image, shrinks it to 1/8 its original size, and writes it out to disk.

```php
<?php

  //load the image into memory and get its properties
  $img = imagecreatefrompng("goldengate.png");
  $imgsz = getimagesize("goldengate.png");

  //create new image for thumbnail 1/8 the size of the original
  $thumb = imagecreate($imgsz[0]/8, $imgsz[1]/8);

  //shrink the original image to 1/8th its size
  imagecopyresized($thumb, $img, 0, 0, 0, 0,
$imgsz[0]/8, $imgsz[1]/8, $imgsz[0], $imgsz[1]);

  //write the thumbnail to disk
  imagepng($thumb, "goldengate_thumb.png");

  //get the image size of the thumbnail for use in the HTML below
  $thumbsz = getimagesize("goldengate_thumb.png");

  //free resources occupied by the images
  imagedestroy($img);
  imagedestroy($thumb);
?>
<html>
  <body>
    <img src="goldengate.png" <?php echo $imgsz[3] ?>>
    <img src="goldengate_thumb.png" <?php echo $thumbsz[3] ?>>
  </body>
</html>
```

The above returns 2 images, the second one eighth the size of the first.

## Working with Color

Once you've imported existing graphics with the above functions, you'll want to make changes to them other than resizing. To perform this task, you'll probably have to work with some type of color. As with HTML constructs, the GD library sees any color as a mixture of red, green, and blue. We can take the hexadecimal value of any color and translate it into its core colors. In any HTML color, the first two digits are red, followed by two for green, and the final two are blue. The table below lists the equivalencies for several common colors.

| Color | HTML Hexadecimal Representation | GD Triplet Representation |
|-------|-------------------------------|--------------------------|
| Black | #000000 | (0,0,0) |
| White | #FFFFFF | (255,255,255) |
| Red | #FF0000 | (255, 0, 0) |
| Yellow | #00FFFF | (0, 255, 255) |
| Purple | #FF00FF | (255, 0, 255) |

We'll be using these functions in examples in the next two sections: *Creating Primitive Shapes* and *Working with Text*. The most straightforward use of these functions is in conjunction with a drawn element.

### Adding a Color to the Palette

To use a color in an image, you must allocate it to the palette in the image. The function `imagecolorallocate()` puts a specific color in the current palette.

```
int imagecolorallocate (resource image, int red, int green, int blue)
```

The `imagecolorallocate()` function allocates the color specified by the triplet (red, green, blue) into the graphic resource specified by `image`. The graphic resource specified by `image` must come from one of the `imagecreate()` or `imagecreatefrom()` functions. The values of red, green, and blue must be integers between 0 and 255. The function returns -1 if the allocation failed. It is good practice to use a variable that has some resemblance to the color allocated. The first color allocated becomes the background color.

```
$darkred = imagecolorallocate($myImage, 186, 0, 0);
```

### Retrieving a Color from an Existing Image

To retrieve the color at a specific point in the image a combination of functions is required.

```
int imagecolorat (resource image, int x, int y)
array imagecolorsforindex (resource image, int index)
```

`imagecolorat()` returns the index in the palette of the color specified at point ($x$, $y$) in the graphic resource image. It does not return the actual color. A palette is no more than an array of color resources. For 8-bit images, the color information is stored in an array, or palette of 256 colors. The function `imagecolorsforindex()` returns an associative array of the red, green, and blue values.

```
$colorIndex = imagecolorat($myImage, $x, $y);
$colorArray = imagecolorsforindex($myImage, $colorIndex);
printf('Red: %d Green: %d Blue: %d', $colorArray['red'],
  $colorArray['green'], $colorArray['blue']);
```

## Getting the Closest Match for a Color

When working in a confined palette, it is sometimes useful to use an existing approximate color rather than allocate a new one, either because allocating colors to images increases file size, or because there is no more space in the palette.

```
int imagecolorclosest (resource image, int red, int green, int blue)
```

imagecolorclosest() returns the closest color in the palette in the image to the color specified by the RGB triplet (red, green, blue).

## Removing a Color from the Palette

When a color is no longer needed in the palette, it can be de-allocated.

```
int imagecolordeallocate (resource image, int color)
```

The function de-allocates the color in the image with the index specified by color making it available for reuse. A subsequent call to imagecolorallocate() would change the color of the pixels assigned to that index in the palette.

## Altering a Color

To change a color throughout an image, we can directly alter the palette.

```
bool imagecolorset (resource image, int index, int red, int green, int blue)
```

This changes the color in the palette at index to the RGB triplet (red, green, blue). This function is useful to change large sections of color without the expense of a flood fill.

## Counting How Many Colors Are Used

To calculate the number of colors in an image we can use this function.

```
int imagecolorstotal (resource image)
```

This function returns the number of colors in the image's palette.

## Making a Transparent Color

To make certain areas of an image transparent, we can apply this function to a color in the palette:

```
int imagecolortransparent (resource image [, int index])
```

**12**

Server-Side Graphics

This function takes the color in the palette specified by `index` and renders it transparent. Transparency is a property of the image palette, not the pixel. Once a color is made transparent any prior or future instance of that color in the image will be transparent. It is helpful to use a very different color, such as magenta in a green image, as the transparent color because it is easier to spot when the operation fails. If you set transparent properties, you'll need to export to a format that supports transparency, namely PNG or GIF. Transparency is lost if the image is exported to JPEG.

## Creating Primitive Shapes

Now that we have a color allocated in our image, we can use that color to create shapes in an image. GD has functions for drawing lines and polygons as well as circles. We can use the coordinate system to specify the points where we want GD to draw the shapes. We can either draw images from scratch, or modify an existing one.

### Lines

The most basic shape we can draw is a line.

```
int imageline (resource image, int x1, int y1, int x2, int y2, int col)
```

This function draws a line in a graphic resource image from point (x1, y1) to (x2, y2) in color `col`. To draw a dark red line on an image that is 200x200 from the upper left to lower right we can call:

```
$darkred = imagecolorallocate($myImage, 186, 0, 0);
imageline($myImage, 0, 0, 199, 199, $darkred);
```

### Rectangles

Building on the example above we can easily draw rectangles as well.

```
int imagerectangle(resource image, int x1, int y1, int x2, int y2, int col)
int imagefilledrectangle(resource image, int x1, int y1, int x2, int y2, int col)
```

These functions draw outlined and filled rectangles respectively. The top-left corner of the rectangle is (x1, y1) and the bottom right is (x2, y2). In this case x2 > x1 (it's further to the right) and y2 > y1 (it's further down). Specifying your rectangles in this fashion will help the readability of your code and prevent errors.

### Polygons

GD provides these functions to draw more general polygons such as triangles and hexagons:

```
int imagepolygon (resource image, array points, int num_points, int col)
int imagefilledpolygon (resource image, array points, int num_points, int col)
```

These functions draw outlined and filled objects respectively. You specify a polygon as a series of points. When GD applies the polygon it connects them linearly and connects the first point to the last point. Num_points must be less than or equal to the number of vertices of the polygon. If num_points is greater than the number of vertices, the function throws an error because the function does not have enough information on how to draw the polygon. If num_points is less than the number of vertices, the polygon renders with num_points vertices and the first and last points are not connected. The array is a vector of points alternating between x coordinates and y coordinates. To draw a triangle we can use the following code:

```
darkgreen = imagecolorallocate($myImage, 0, 67, 0);
$myPoints = Array(10, 10, 10, 60, 60, 60);
imagepolygon($myImage, $myPoints, 3, $darkgreen);$
```

In the above snippet we're drawing a simple right triangle in a dark green color. The points in the triangle are (10, 10), (10, 60), and (60, 60).

### Ellipses

We're not just limited to straight lines. We can also draw curved shapes.

```
int imageellipse (resource image, int cx, int cy, int w, int h, int col)
int imagefilledellipse (resource image, int cx, int cy, int w, int h, int col)
```

These functions draw an ellipse centered at the point (cx, cy) of width w and height h. PHP has no imagecircle() function because that would be a special case of this function. If the width equals the height, the ellipse becomes a circle. This function is only available in PHP 4.0.6 and later and requires GD 2.0.1.

### Arcs

The arc functions are derivatives of the ellipse functions. They draw partial ellipses.

```
int imagearc (resource image, int cx, int cy, int w, int h, int s, int e, int col)
int imagefilledarc (resource image, int cx, int cy, int w, int h, int s, int e, int col, int style)
```

These functions draw an arc centered at the point (cx, cy) of width w and height h. The start and end points, s and e respectively, represent the starting and ending points of the arc in degrees. Zero degrees is equivalent to the three o'clock position. PHP draws arcs clockwise, thus 90 degrees would be six o'clock, 180 degrees would be nine o'clock, and so on. These functions are only available in PHP 4.0.6 and later, and requires GD 2.0.1.

imagefilledarc() has an additional parameter, style, that specifies how the arc should be drawn. It takes the following options:

- IMG_ARC_PIE – Produces a rounded edge and fills in the arc like that of a pie graph.

- IMG_ARC_CHORD – Connects the starting and ending points with a straight line and fills in the resulting triangle.

- IMG_ARC_NOFILL – Suspends the filling of the arc.

- IMG_ARC_EDGED – Paints the edge of the arc. Used in conjunction with IMG_ARC_NOFILL to make an outlined pie slice.

### Fills

We can fill oddly shaped areas of our images with color by a technique known as flood filling.

```
int imagefill (resource image, int x, int y, int col)
int imagefilltoborder (resource image, int x, int y, int border, int col)
```

Server-Side Graphics

12

This function changes the color of all the pixels in a bounded region to the color `col`. `imagefilltoborder()` only flood fills to the color specified by border.

## An Example Using Primitive Shapes

Now that we have the basics for working with primitives, let's look at a small example that uses each of the functions in a real example:

```php
<?php
  header('Content-Type: image/png');
```

Create an image resource that is 300 by 300 pixels:

```php
$myImage = imagecreate(300, 300);
```

Allocate black and white as colors in the image. Black is the background color since it was declared first.

```php
$black = imagecolorallocate($myImage, 0, 0, 0);
$white = imagecolorallocate($myImage, 255, 255, 255);
```

Place a white rectangle in the center of the image to give the illusion of a black border.

```php
imagefilledrectangle($myImage, 25, 25, 275, 275, $white);
```

Draw a straight line down the middle of the rectangle. We know it's a vertical line because x1 = x2.

```php
imageline($myImage, 150, 30, 150, 270, $black);
```

Set up the array of points for the right triangle. The triangle will cover the area spanned by the points (50, 50), (50, 100), (100, 100). We then pass that array to the `imagepolygon()` function and tell it that the triangle has three vertices. We draw a rectangle in the same fashion as before.

```php
$myTriangle = array (50, 50, 50, 100, 100, 100);
imagepolygon($myImage, $myTriangle, 3, $black);
imagerectangle($myImage, 50, 150, 100, 250, $black);
```

We now draw a filled, vertically stretched ellipse. We know that the ellipse is stretched vertically because h > w. In this example the height is 100 and the width is 50.

```php
imagefilledellipse($myImage, 225, 200, 50, 100, $black);
```

Lastly, we draw a "Pac-Man"-style ellipse with the `imagefilled()` arc function.

```php
imagefilledarc($myImage, 225, 75, 50, 50, 45, 315, $black, IMG_ARC_PIE);
```

We then send the image to the browser and free used resources.

```
    imagepng($myImage);
    imagedestroy($myImage);
?>
```

Running the above code generates the following graphic:

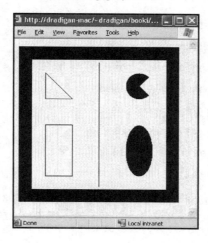

You'll notice that we can draw anywhere on the canvas at any time. There is no flow or order which needs to be followed as in HTML where things must go left to right and top to bottom. I'd recommend finding a convention and sticking with it, as it will make the debugging of your graphics easier.

## Working with Text

Text is the final area that we'll explore in server-generated graphics. All the examples we'll discuss further in the chapter pull from these four areas. Adding text is one of the most common uses of server-generated graphics. Tedious operations such as button creation turn from chores into easily automated tasks. Automating button creation has two benefits: global changes can be made once and applied everywhere, and the graphic is generated in one place, which means less error in the process.

We'll focus on working with TrueType fonts as the implementation is the most straightforward and the concepts apply across other font types. TrueType fonts are standard outline fonts first developed by Apple Computer, and later advocated by Microsoft in Windows 3.1. TrueType fonts on Windows systems are available in the *c:\windows\fonts* or *c:\winnt\fonts* directories. They use the extension of TTF. For users of other platforms, TrueType fonts are available on the Web as well. To use TrueType fonts you'll need FreeType, available at *http://www.freetype.org*.The Windows binary install of PHP has FreeType compiled into the GD library.

### Textboxes

This function returns the bounding rectangle (box) of the area encompassed by the font. When calculating the size of the background or an area to place text, use this function:

```
array imagettfbbox (int size, int angle, string fontfile, string text)
```

It takes four parameters: the size of the text in points, the angle the text is to be drawn at relative to the horizontal, the absolute path to the TrueType font file, and the text to draw. The path on UNIX-based systems must be the full path, while on Windows systems it seems to take either the full or relative path. The manual specifies to use full paths; however, on some configurations relative paths work. The function returns an array of eight values:

- returnArray[0] – lower-left corner, X position
- returnArray[1] – lower-left corner, Y position
- returnArray[2] – lower-right corner, X position
- returnArray[3] – lower-right corner, Y position
- returnArray[4] – upper-right corner, X position
- returnArray[5] – upper-right corner, Y position
- returnArray[6] – upper-left corner, X position
- returnArray[7] – upper-left corner, Y position

All positions in this array are relative to the lower-left corner. Positive values are to the right and down. Conversely, negative values are to the left and up from the original point. If (x,y) is the lower-left corner, then (x+$returnArray[6], y+$returnArray[7]) is the upper-left corner.

### Text

To render the text onto an image in memory we call the `imagettftext()` function.

```
array imagettftext (resource image, int size, int angle, int x, int y, int col,
string fontfile, string text)
```

Unlike other functions, the coordinates (x,y) refer to the bottom left, or the basepoint of the first character. Angle is the angle in degrees with 0 referring to horizontal text and higher values representing a counter-clockwise representation. For example, an angle of 270 degrees would render text top to bottom. `fontfile` is the path to the TrueType font you wish to use. `Text` is the string to render. You may include UTF-8 characters by using the numeric sequence of the form &#123;. The return value is the same as `imagettfbbox()`.

### An Example Using Text

Let's look at a short example to show the relationship between `imagettftext()` and `imagettfbbox()`.

```
<?php
```

As in prior examples, we send the HTTP header since we are outputting binary, graphical content directly to the browser. Next create an image resource that is 300 by 300 pixels. We then allocate black and white as the two colors in the image.

```
header ('Content-Type: image/png');
$myImage = imagecreate(200, 200);
$black = imagecolorallocate($myImage, 0, 0, 0);
$white = imagecolorallocate($myImage, 255, 255, 255);
```

First we calculate the area that the text will use by calling `imagettfbbox`. Make sure the path to the font is valid on your system.

```
$boundingbox = imagettfbbox(25, 0, '/usr/local/fonts/arial.ttf', 'Hello Greg');
```

Next we apply the text, "`Hello Greg`" to the page. We've specified a size of 25, that the text is horizontal (angle = 0), in white, using the font `arial.ttf` in the local directory.

```
imagettftext($myImage, 25, 0, 10, 50, $white, 'arial.ttf', 'Hello Greg');
```

We then draw a rectangle to show the bounding box returned by `imagettfbbox()`. Since `imagerectangle()` works with upper-left and lower-right coordinates, we can use the returned array to calculate those points.

```
imagerectangle($myImage, 10+$boundingbox[6], 50+$boundingbox[7],
   10+$boundingbox[2], 50+$boundingbox[3], $white);
```

We then repeat the following three steps for angled text:

```
$boundingbox = imagettfbbox(25, 45, 'arial.ttf', 'Hello Greg');
imagettftext($myImage, 25, 45, 30, 175, $white, 'arial.ttf', 'Hello Greg');
imagerectangle($myImage, 30+$boundingbox[6], 175+$boundingbox[7],
   30+$boundingbox[2], 175+$boundingbox[3], $white);
```

Finally, send the image to the browser and free resources.

```
imagepng($myImage);
imagedestroy($myImage);
?>
```

Running this code we get the following image:

The functions to get the bounding box information have some bugs in them, so proceed with caution and test thoroughly. Sometimes the bounding box does not encompass all of the text, especially where letters extend below the horizontal like with g and y or when text is at an angle as above.

**12**

# Using GD in Applications

Now that we have a basic understanding of the services provided to PHP from GD, we can begin to see how we can use this functionality in our applications. Generating graphics on the fly can be very processor-intensive, so they should be used sparingly in real-time. GD can also be used in the design-time stage of building of a web application.

## Creating a Dynamic Button

One of the most time-consuming tasks in the development of a web site can be the creation of the buttons on the toolbar. With PHP, GD, and a little ingenuity, we can create a script to output all of the needed buttons to link into an HTML page. This technique allows us to make sure the button will fit all the text we need, that the font looks good, and when we do need to make a change, we can see it on all instances of the button with one change.

I've got a site that has a toolbar with a set of images that are buttons. When the user moves their mouse over the button, I'd like to change the text on the button from white to gray by using the onMouseOver event, and change the text to yellow using the onClick event. The button should remain the same in all other respects. I've first created a file button.png that has the background of the button on it. I can then load this image into GD and apply the white and gray texts onto it and save the new instance of the button.

```
<html>
<body>
<?php
```

We create a separate function for each class of button so that it's easily identifiable from the other image types. In this case it's a toolbar button. The function will output all three image types to disk. We supply the text to place on the button and the filename to output as parameters into the function. For this example we'll need a buttons folder at the same level of the script. The script will place all the created images in the buttons folder.

```
function generateToolbarButton($text, $filename) {
```

Initialize the variables that are common across the different outputted buttons. The source image, the font size, and the offset from center are common on all three buttons. Make sure the variable $font points to the correct location on disk of the font file.

```
$srcimage = "button.png";
$font = "arial.ttf";
$textsize = 20;
$offsetx = 0;
$offsety = 0;
```

Load one instance of the button for each of the button states, normal, over, and down. Since the size of the button is common for all three buttons we only need to load that information once.

```
$button = imagecreatefrompng($srcimage);
$buttonover = imagecreatefrompng($srcimage);
$buttonclick = imagecreatefrompng($srcimage);
$buttonsz = getimagesize($srcimage);
```

Set the color of the text in each image to its specific resource. The normal image is white, the over image is gray, and the clicked image is yellow.

```
$white = imagecolorallocate($button, 255, 255, 255);
$black = imagecolorallocate($buttonover, 180, 180, 180);
$yellow = imagecolorallocate($buttonclick, 255, 255, 0);
```

imagettftext() places text in the image relative to the lower-left corner of the rendered text. Since we want the text to be centered on the button, we need to calculate the position of the lower-left corner of the rendered text. We call imagettfbox() to get the dimensions of the rendered text.

```
$textsz = imagettfbbox($textsize, 0, $font, $text);
```

The x coordinate of the placed text is the middle of the image minus half the distance of the text size. We add an offset in case we need to tweak the placement of the text.

```
$startingx = $buttonsz[0]/2 - ($textsz[2] - $textsz[0])/2 + $offsetx;
```

Likewise, the y coordinate of the placed text is the middle of the image plus half the distance of the text size. Again, we add an offset in case we need to tweak the placement of the text.

```
$startingy = $buttonsz[1]/2 + ($textsz[1] - $textsz[5])/2 + $offsety;
```

We then apply the text with the appropriate color to each image.

```
imagettftext($button, $textsize, 0, $startingx, $startingy,
  $white, $font, $text);
imagettftext($buttonover, $textsize, 0, $startingx, $startingy,
  $black, $font, $text);
imagettftext($buttonclick, $textsize, 0, $startingx, $startingy,
  $yellow, $font, $text);
```

We call imagepng() to write the file to disk. By programmatically assigning the filename to each of the button states, we're assured of a consistent naming scheme.

```
imagepng($button, $filename . ".png");
imagepng($buttonover, $filename . "_over.png");
imagepng($buttonclick, $filename . "_click.png");
```

We then free the resources used.

```
imagedestroy($button);
imagedestroy($buttonover);
imagedestroy($buttonclick);
```

This section is not required, but we'd like to return some HTML to call the image up in the browser so that we can verify that the buttons are generated correctly.

```
return "<img src=\"" . $filename . ".png\" $buttonsz[3] >
    <img src=\"" . $filename . "_over.png\" $buttonsz[3] >
    <img src=\"" . $filename . "_click.png\" $buttonsz[3] ><P>";
}
```

We finally call the function to create our instances of the buttons.

```
echo generateToolbarButton("Home", "buttons/home");
echo generateToolbarButton("E-mail", "buttons/email");
?>
</body>
</html>
```

When we run this page, we can see the different instances of the button:

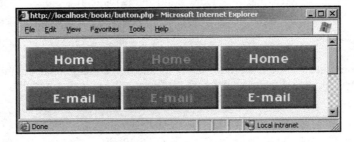

I find it useful to store all my buttons and other generated images in a common place and my image-generation script in a different directory. In the above example we could have our buttons in /buttons and the generation script in /adminutils. While the script will overwrite existing files, if you change the buttons you're generating, you may have orphaned files. When we need to rerun the button generation we can delete /buttons and execute the script to clean up any orphaned files..

## A GD-Based Page Counter

One of the ways to display traffic that a page accumulates is with a page counter. Everyone has seen the text "*this page has been viewed*" so many number of times. Most counters are graphical and have some flair to them. Let's take a look at the simplest implementation of a server-side counter, white text on a black background.

```
<?php
```

Since we want this PHP file to be the equivalent of a PNG file, we have to send the HTTP header to the browser so it knows that the arriving content is not text, but an image. If you see garbage in the browser when calling a server-side graphic, the header is most likely missing. Likewise, if you get a broken image, most likely an error has been thrown.

```
header('Content-Type: image/png');
```

Set the counter variable to the contents of `$_GET['count']`, otherwise use the string `'Error'`.

```
$text = (isset($_GET['count']) ? $_GET['count'] : 'Error');
```

Set a few preferences on what we want the counter to look like, in this case Arial text at size 15. Abstracting this content makes maintaining the images easier.

```
$font = "arial.ttf";
$textsize = 15;
```

Calculate the size of the text. Since the text is horizontal, the values returned from `imagettfbox` are reliable.

```
$textsz = imagettfbbox($textsize, 0, $font, $text);
```

Create the image. We only want an image as big as the page count so we must size the image dynamically. We take the absolute values of the x and y offsets of the upper-right corner in the bounding box. We need the absolute values because these values are negative. We pad each side by 3 pixels so the text is not right on the border of the image.

```
$counter = imagecreate($textsz[4]+6, abs($textsz[5])+6);
```

We then allocate colors for black and white.

```
$black = imagecolorallocate($counter, 0, 0, 0);
$white = imagecolorallocate($counter, 255, 255, 255);
```

We render the text on the image. Since `imagettftext()` works from the `lowerleft()`, we have to calculate that point from the bounding box.

```
imagettftext($counter, $textsize, 0, 2, abs($textsz[5])+2, $white, $font, $text);
```

We finally send the image to the browser and free used resources.

```
imagepng($counter);
imagedestroy($counter);
?>
```

Now let's link our script into an HTML page to display the page count. We can create a simple page that starts a session and counts how many times the user visits that page in a session.

```
<?php
```

If the variable count is not currently in the session, initialize it at one, otherwise we know the user has been to this page and has a session. In that case we increment the session variable count.

```
session_start();
if (!session_is_registered('count')) {
    session_register('count');
    $_SESSION['count'] = 1;
}
else {
    $_SESSION['count']++;
}
?>
<html>
<head>
<title>GD Page Counter</title>
<meta http-equiv="Content-Type" content="text/html; charset=iso-8859-1">
</head>
<body>
Hey, you've been to this page
```

Notice the `src` attribute on the image tag. We've got a PHP file in a field that is meant for a graphic. The PHP page is behaving just like a graphic. The content returned will be that of an image. We pass the page count to the image generator via a `GET` variable. The image is then server-generated and returned to the browser.

```
<img src="counterimg.php?count=<?php echo $_SESSION['count'] ?>" alt="<?php echo
$_SESSION['count'] ?>"> times.
```

We then provide a link to let the user load the page again.

```
Want to see it <a href="<?php echo $_SERVER['PHP_SELF']; ?>">again?</a>
</body>
</html>
```

We can see the final representation here:

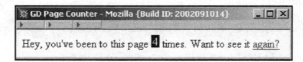

There are no orphaned image files left on the server as the content is sent right to the browser.

## Graphical Page Counter – Without GD

Just because we can do a server-side graphic doesn't mean we should. As we mentioned at the beginning of the chapter, server CPU time is much cheaper than it was a few years ago, but it's still not free. We need to be looking for more efficient ways of designing our applications. Let us look at the page counter example implemented differently. We've seen a GD-based example where the graphic is created on the fly. Now we'll take an approach using static graphics.

```
<?php
```

We start off with the same session-handling code and HTML as we saw before.

```
session_start();
if (!session_is_registered('count')) {
    session_register('count');
    $_SESSION['count'] = 1;
}
else {
    $_SESSION['count']++;
}
?>
<html>
<head>
<title>Non GD Page Counter</title>
<meta http-equiv="Content-Type" content="text/html; charset=iso-8859-1">
</head>
<body>
Hey, you've been to this page
<?php
```

We need to convert the page count into a string. To accomplish this we cast it directly to the string data type. Casting is forcing a conversion of one data type to another. The count is a number, but to access its digits we need to convert it to a string to see it as a collection of digits rather than a number. For more information on string handling, see *Chapter 5, Strings and Regular Expressions*. Once it is a string we can apply the appropriate graphic for each of the digits.

```
$text = (string)$_SESSION['count'];
```

We run a loop from the beginning of the string to the end taking each numeric character and associating it with the PNG file on disk that it represents. We send an `<img>` tag back to the browser for each digit.

```
for ($i=0; $i < strlen($text); $i++) {
    echo('<img src="numbers/' . $text{$i} . '.png" alt="' . $text{$i} . '">');
} ?>
times.
Want to see it <a href="<?php echo $_SERVER['PHP_SELF']; ?>">again?</a>
</body>
</html>
```

This approach has one main advantage, it's faster. For the number 53, the script will output:

```
<img src="numbers/5.png" alt="5"><img src="numbers/3.png" alt="3">
```

The server only has to serve up two static images rather than generating one itself. So we have to ask, are there any drawbacks to this method? Having the graphic generated on the server means that the browser only gets one image, so for pages that are visited heavily, you'll see the counter load fully. The static approach can have digits further to the right appear before the ones to the left show. You've also got to create 10 static images on your server and have one hit for each digit. Performance concerns usually are resolved by a bit of trial and error. While this example would probably work well in either implementation, performance testing is always a good idea when doing server-side graphics.

**Server-Side Graphics**

**12**

# Creating Dynamic Charts

For applications that display statistical data, creating charts is usually a requirement. Several libraries are available for creating dynamic charts, but **JpGraph** is one of the best available today. JpGraph is not open source and is only free for some uses. A GPL chart library, PHPLOT, is available at *http://www.phplot.com/examples/*. JpGraph was started and is maintained by Johan Persson and is available from *http://www.aditus.nu/jpgraph/*. This section relies heavily on the principles of object oriented programming. For more information on this topic, see *Chapter 4*.

Installing JpGraph is very straightforward.

- Download the latest version from http://www.aditus.nu/jpgraph/. As of this writing it is 1.8.1.

- Extract the source to any directory in your web root. The only files that you need are the ones in the src directory. To make including required files easier, I recommend copying these files to /jpgraph in your web root.

- Edit the file jpgraph.php to make sure all the constants marked with DEFINE represent what is on your system. Pay close attention to USE_LIBRARY_GD2.

- Make sure you have write permission to the cache directory if you use that feature, or to a place in your web root if you write out files rather than streaming them to the browser.

- To confirm that your installation is working, many examples are in the examples directory. Make sure the include/require statements in the example files reflect the correct paths.

Now that we have JpGraph installed, we can use this library on top of GD to create dynamic charts. For brevity, I am assuming that JpGraph resides at */jpgraph*. You'll need to modify your scripts accordingly if the library is installed in a different location.

Let's start with a simple bar chart with JpGraph. We'll create a recordset and base the chart on that recordset. The database comes from Trio Motors, the sample database that Macromedia ships with Dreamweaver MX. Alternatively, you can create two arrays if you do not want to connect to a database. We start off by including the necessary includes and create a recordset with Dreamweaver.

```
require_once("jpgraph/jpgraph.php");
require_once("jpgraph/jpgraph_bar.php");
require_once('Connections/mainConn.php');

mysql_select_db($database_mainConn, $mainConn);
$query_ChartRS = "SELECT regions.name, count(dealer.id) as totalcount FROM
regions,dealer WHERE regions.id=dealer.region GROUP BY regions.name";
$ChartRS = mysql_query($query_ChartRS, $mainConn) or die(mysql_error());
$row_ChartRS = mysql_fetch_assoc($ChartRS);
$totalRows_ChartRS = mysql_num_rows($ChartRS);
```

We need to pass the information from the recordset to the JpGraph library in two arrays, one for the labels on the bottom and the values of each entry. We use a do-while loop and the array_push() function to push the values from the recordset onto the array:

```
$datay=array();
$labelx=array();
do {
  array_push($datay, $row_ChartRS['totalcount']);
  array_push($labelx, $row_ChartRS['name']);
} while ($row_ChartRS = mysql_fetch_assoc($ChartRS));
```

We're going to create a chart of size 600x300 pixels. We create an instance of the `Graph` class from the JpGraph library. For more information on the classes and methods of JpGraph, a download is available from *http://jpgraph.techuk.com/jpgraph/downloads/jpgraph_docs.tar.gz*. Since it's a bar chart, we want the $y$ axis to be linear and the $x$ axis to be text. A text axis is one of the user-supplied labels.

```
$graph = new Graph(600,300, 'auto');
$graph->SetScale("textlin");
```

We set a 7 percent grace on the $y$ axis to give some buffer at the top of the bars so they are not all the way to the top of the chart. We then set margins around the image's border. A call to the `SetShadow()` method places a drop shadow around the image edge.

```
$graph->yaxis->scale->SetGrace(7);
$graph->img->SetMargin(50,30,40,60);
$graph->SetShadow();
```

We then call the appropriate methods to set the titles of the axes, along with font information.

```
$graph->title->Set("Trio Dealers Worldwide");
$graph->yaxis->title->Set("Number of Dealers");
$graph->xaxis->title->Set("Region");
$graph->title->SetFont(FF_FONT2, FS_BOLD, 14);
$graph->yaxis->title->SetFont(FF_FONT1, FS_NORMAL,12);
$graph->xaxis->title->SetFont(FF_FONT1, FS_NORMAL, 12);
```

After we have set up the graph, we need to declare the bar chart. We then bind the labels and the values to the appropriate axes.

```
$bplot = new BarPlot($datay);
$graph->xaxis->SetTickLabels($labelx);
$graph->Add($bplot);
```

We then set the bars to be orange, set a shadow behind each bar to give a 3D look, and place the value on top of the bar.

```
$bplot->SetFillColor("orange");
$bplot->SetShadow();
$bplot->value->Show();
```

We then stream the image to the browser and free resources for the recordset.

```
$graph->Stroke();
mysql_free_result($ChartRS);
```

**Server-Side Graphics**

**12**

The following chart is rendered in the browser:

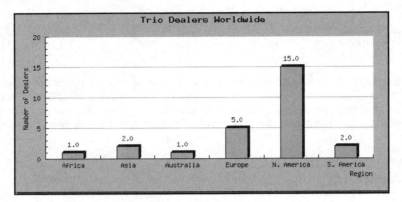

One of the benefits of an object oriented system is that you can quickly change parameters without having to worry about the details of how the objects work. To make the above chart into a line chart, we just have to change three lines of code: `require_once("jpgraph/jpgraph_bar.php")` is changed to:

```
require_once("jpgraph/jpgraph_line.php")
```

`$bplot = new BarPlot($datay)` is altered to:

```
$bplot = new LinePlot($datay)
```

And the line `$bplot->SetShadow()` is removed.

# Integration with Dreamweaver

Now that we've been able to generate server-side graphics, how can we use them to our benefit in design view? Through the extensibility layer, we can create server behaviors that have associated translators. For more information on extensibility, please see *Chapter 6, Dreamweaver Extensibility*. Translators are search patterns that render a portion of code between the body tags in the design view as an alternative form of HTML.

We can begin our server behavior with two participants (code blocks): one for the includes that is to sit on the top of the page and the other to be the chart code that is to be inserted after the cursor (after the selection in the server behavior builder).

Participant 1 (*Relative to <HTML> tag, top of file*):

```
<?php
require_once("@@includePath@@jpgraph.php");
require_once("@@includePath@@jpgraph_bar.php");
?>
```

Participant 2 (*Relative to selection*, *after selection*):

```php
<?php
$datay=array();
$labelx=array();
do {
  array_push($datay, $row_@@RecordsetName@@['@@yValues@@']);
  array_push($labelx, $row_@@RecordsetName@@['@@xLabels@@']);
} while ($row_@@RecordsetName@@ = mysql_fetch_assoc($@@RecordsetName@@));
$graph = new Graph(@@chartWidth@@,@@chartHeight@@, 'auto');
$graph->SetScale("textlin");
$graph->yaxis->scale->SetGrace(7);
$graph->img->SetMargin(50,30,40,60);
$graph->title->Set("@@chartTitle@@");
$graph->yaxis->title->Set("@@yAxisTitle@@");
$graph->xaxis->title->Set("@@xAxisTitle@@");
$bplot = new BarPlot($datay);
$graph->xaxis->SetTickLabels($labelx);
$graph->Add($bplot);
$bplot->SetFillColor("@@fillColor@@");
$graph->Stroke(GenImgName());
echo("<img src=\"" . GenImgName()."?" . microtime() . "\" border=0>");
?>
```

We then have the server behavior builder loaded with the two participants:

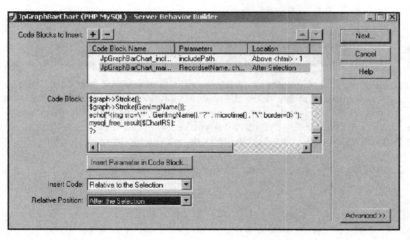

We can then bind the `RecordsetName`, `yValues`, and `xLabels` parameters to a recordset and its columns.

12

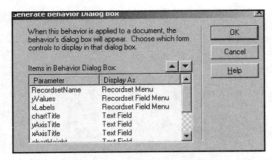

Once we commit the behavior we can use it as a reusable element in Dreamweaver. When we apply the behavior however, we get the PHP shield.

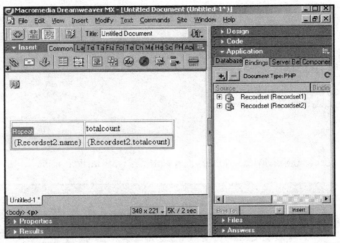

At this point we can use a translator to translate participant two (the part containing the image code) into an image placeholder. If we open the server behavior, we can add a translator. The server behavior will be located in your server behaviors directory. Open the `JpGraphBarChart_mainBlock.edml` (or what you've named the code participant in the document body) file for participant two, since that is the code we wish to translate.

We need to add this translation code to the `<participant>` node.

```
<translator priority="500">
  <searchPatterns>
    <searchPattern paramNames="*someval*" isOptional="false"
limitSearch="all"><![CDATA*someRegEx*/i]]></searchPattern>
  </searchPatterns>
  <translations>
    <translation whereToSearch="directive" translationType="as is">
      <display><![CDATA[<img src="" alt="" name="@@chartTitle@@"
width="@@chartWidth@@" height="@@chartHeight@@" style="background-color:
@@fillColor@@">]]></display>
    </translation>
  </translations>
</translator>
```

The two parts of note are the `<searchpattern>` and `<display>` nodes. The `<searchpattern>` node tells the translator what to translate. You'll see a search pattern in the file that was generated by the server behavior builder. It's the long string encased in a CDATA structure. Replace `someval` and `someRegEx` with the parameter names and the regular expression from the original server behavior. The display node tells the translator what to render. In this case we are using an image placeholder. We capture the size of the image, the color of the bars, and the title of the chart. Once saved into the server behavior and after a restart of Dreamweaver, we see the placeholder in design view.

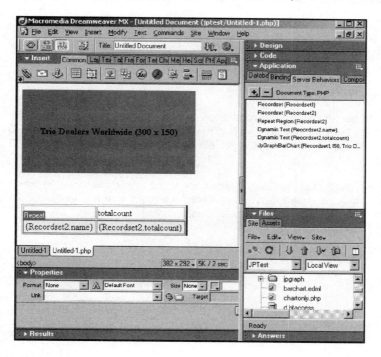

We can use translators in all kinds of server-side graphics. Using an image placeholder allows us to render more effectively in the design view what our actual page will look like when displayed.

> As with the counter example, the generation of server-side graphics is expensive in terms of CPU requirements. One area where we can speed up our application is the caching of the chart. In most applications the server-side chart does not need to be real time. We could add in some logic to only generate the chart once a day. We could alternatively have an update button on the web site to force the regeneration of the chart. In all other cases we'd show the one on disk. Each application will have its own specific requirements.

The other area that affects performance is the size of the chart. A 300x150 chart uses much less memory than a 600x300 chart. Use the smallest size you can while preserving the clarity and integrity of the chart.

# Summary

In this chapter we've explored the basics of graphics. We've seen different types of image formats, in particular GIF, JPG, and PNG. We've also seen how PHP interprets images in memory with a coordinate system. We've covered transparency, an important benefit in Internet graphics.

We took a short look at the GD API and focused on four main areas:

- The Basic Functions
- Working with Color
- Creating Primitive Shapes
- Working with Text

We then used those functions in several applications. We looked at a design time use of GD in generating buttons for a toolbar on a web site. We compared and contrasted a GD- and non GD-based approach to implementing a counter. We concluded with a server-generated graph with the JpGraph library.

We then explored how to translate server-side code into a renderable entity in design view. We used a translator to extract the relevant data and placed it into an image placeholder. Then design view rendered a box to fill the space of the actual graphic.

# 13

- Interacting with Flash

- Creating Flash movies with PHP

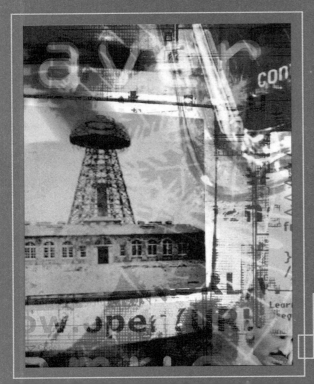

**Author: Allan Kent**

# Using Flash with PHP and Dreamweaver MX

Very few people who use or work with the Web are unfamiliar with Macromedia Flash. You'll find it used in all sorts of applications, in every situation from providing really useful functionality to wowing the person browsing the site. Full-screen introductions for web sites, interactive banners, or even simple navigation buttons are all examples of what people are using Flash for. In this chapter we are going to look at how we can leverage the power of PHP with Flash, and how the two can interact.

We will cover:

- Traditional use of Flash and Flash interaction
- Generating Flash content dynamically from PHP
- Integrating our PHP code into Dreamweaver MX

## Installing Ming

In order to use the Ming library we will have to make sure that it is installed on our system as well as enabled in PHP.

### Windows

Getting Ming up and running on your Windows machine is straightforward. The Ming module is included in the PHP distribution, but is not enabled by default. You will need to edit your `php.ini` file and uncomment the line:

```
extension=php_ming.dll
```

You will have to restart your web server before any change in your `php.ini` takes effect (if you are running PHP as a module). You can also choose to load the Ming module dynamically in any script that requires it using the `dl()` function:

```
<?php
  dl('php_ming.dll');
?>
```

### Linux

Installing Ming under Linux requires a little bit more work. The first thing you will need to do is grab the latest source distribution of Ming. You can get it from the Ming homepage at *http://ming.sourceforge.net*. Unpack the Ming distribution, go to the Ming directory, and run:

```
make
make install
```

This will build and install Ming. Once this is done you will have to configure and compile Ming into PHP. In the directory that contains your PHP source distribution type:

```
./configure –with-ming
make
make install
```

If you have any additional parameters that you normally include in your configure you will have to include them as well.

Whichever platform you are using, you can verify that Ming is installed correctly by using the `phpinfo()` function. It should show in the results like this:

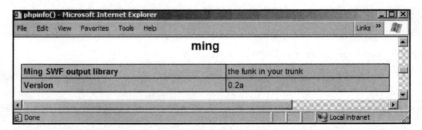

# Plugging in a Flash Movie

We're all familiar with the traditional uses of Flash, so I'm not going to list them here. What we will do however is take a look at what the code looks like for plugging a Flash movie into our web page. We'll need to know this later in the chapter when we start building our own SWF files, as we'll want to display them in a page.

Macromedia publishes both Flash MX and Dreamweaver MX, so it would be surprising if they did not provide some sort of collaboration with one another. You'll find it in Dreamweaver MX under the *Media* tab of the *Insert* toolbar. There are also a number of Flash templates for creating your own custom SWF buttons, and a button for inserting an SWF file into the page.

I created a simple Flash movie in Flash MX, `dwmx.swf`, and used the *Flash* button on the *Media* tab of the *Insert* toolbar to insert it into a blank HTML page. The *Properties* palette picked up the width and height of the SWF movie and automatically set it for me:

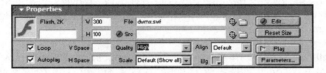

Previewing the file I can see that my page is all in order:

Let's take a look at the code that Dreamweaver has created:

```
<object classid="clsid:D27CDB6E-AE6D-11cf-96B8-444553540000" codebase=
"http://download.macromedia.com/pub/shockwave/cabs/flash/swflash.cab#version=6,0,29,0
" width="300" height="100">
  <param name="movie" value="dwmx.swf">
  <param name="quality" value="high">
  <embed src="dwmx.swf" quality="high"
pluginspage="http://www.macromedia.com/go/getflashplayer" type="application/x-
shockwave-flash" width="300" height="100"></embed>
</object>
```

The first set of tags to look at are the `<object>` and `</object>` tags. Any browser that supports the ActiveX control will use these tags. These tags define the `classid` of the ActiveX component (the Flash movie player), the `codebase` (where to download the Flash player), and the version of Flash. These attributes will always be the same for Flash MX content. The `width` and `height` parameters of the tag are important to us, as this will change, depending on the SWF movie dimensions.

The next important tag is `<param>` which contains the `name` movie. This specifies the path to the SWF movie for this Flash player.

Netscape uses the `<embed>` tag and not the `<object>` tag, so in order to ensure consistent playback across all browsers, you also need to include the `<embed>` tag. This tag includes similar information to the `<object>` tag, but all of the information is included in its attributes. The `<embed>` tag also has to appear just before the closing `</object>` tag.

A little bit more complex than a standard HTML tag, but there are only 3 things that will change from SWF to SWF: the `src` of the SWF movie (including the value passed in the `<param>` tag), its `width` and its `height`. Later in the chapter we will point the `src` tag at a PHP script that will generate the Flash file.

# Flash Interaction

Before we take a look at how we can generate our own SWF movies, we need to understand the ways in which Flash can interact with its environment. The most common way for this to happen is for Flash to call a remote page itself.

We can use this method to get information from a PHP script into our Flash movie; the Flash movie uses an ActionScript function to call a PHP script on the server. The PHP script then returns its output in a MIME URL-encoded format, which Flash can then interpret. Let's take a look at this process in more detail.

> **What is ActionScript?**
> ActionScript is the scripting language that you can use within Flash to control a movie's behavior. ActionScript, like JavaScript, is based on the ECMA-26 specification, so the languages are virtually indistinguishable. All of the language constructs and syntax that you know from JavaScript are the same in ActionScript.

To begin with I'm going to create a Flash movie in Flash MX:

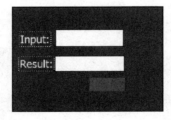

The movie is straightforward – we have 2 labeled textboxes and a button. The first textbox, `Input`, we make an input text type, the second, `Result`, we make a dynamic text type.

The important part for both of these textboxes is to give them a variable name. In the *Var:* box for the properties of the first textbox, I've entered `strInputText` – this is the name of the variable within the Flash movie that will refer to the contents of that textbox.

We also give a variable name `strScriptResult` to the second textbox. We will use these variables to pass information from Flash to PHP and then back again.

The code that does the actual information exchange is a Flash ActionScript function called `loadVariables`. The `loadVariables` function loads data from an external URL. The syntax for the function is:

```
loadVariables(url, level, [variables]);
```

The `url` parameter is a string specifying the URL to load the variables from. The `level` parameter specifies the level within the Flash movie at which to load the variables. We will discuss levels within a Flash movie a bit later in the chapter. The `variables` parameter is optional, but if you wish to send variables from within Flash you must specify the string, either `GET` or `POST`. This determines the method by which variables within the Flash movie are sent to the specified URL.

The code for the button is as follows:

```
on (release) {
        loadVariables('results.php','_root','POST');
}
```

What we are saying is that when the user releases the mouse button, we load the variables from the script `results.php` into the topmost level of the Flash movie. We are also going to send the variables that exist in our Flash movie to the `results.php` script using the `POST` method.

The script, `results.php`, looks like this:

```
<?php
 print ('strScriptResult='.strrev($_POST['strInputText']));
?>
```

All the script is doing is printing out a string that is `strScriptResult=` and then whatever the person typed in the input textbox in Flash, but reversed. Remember we set the variable name of the input box to `strInputText`, and this value has been `POST`ed through to the script. We will therefore have to access it using the `$_POST` array.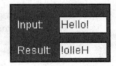

You will notice that the result from the script immediately appears in the result textbox. This is because our script is setting the variable `strScriptResult`, and this is the variable name that we have assigned to the result textbox. The moment we set the value of that variable in Flash, the textbox is immediately updated.

You could use this technique to create a Flash-based login screen, or dynamically populate a listbox in Flash with the results from a database.

*Although it is beyond the scope of this book, while we are talking about interacting with Flash, we should also mention that it is possible to initiate actions in the Flash movie from outside the movie by using client-side JavaScript or VBScript. Not only can you call certain ActionScript functions, but you can also control the timeline of the Flash movie. Since this is not related to PHP we cannot spend any time on the specifics here, but if you are interested in being able to do this, there is some information in the Flash Help as well as on the Macromedia web site.*

# Generating Flash Movies

While being able to dynamically pull information into your Flash movie is certainly a useful tool, you could grab that information from a Perl script or an XML file. The focus for this chapter is going to be a PHP library called Ming.

## Ming

**Ming** is used for generating Flash movies on the fly. Within PHP we have a number of functions that use the Ming library, and with these functions we can build an SWF file from scratch. These functions provide us with tools for creating basic Flash objects, and by building these Flash objects into the hierarchy of a Flash movie we can create advanced Flash applications.

If you are familiar with Flash you will find that Ming will allow you to build Flash movies that are as complex as any you are used to creating. Textboxes, sprites (what Flash calls Movie Clips), shape tweens, and even ActionScript are all supported. The only thing that you will find missing is support for sound events.

## Ming Limitations

Before you start thinking that Ming is a viable alternative to using the Macromedia Flash package, there are a few drawbacks that you should be aware of:

1   The Ming extension in PHP is considered experimental. This means that the way that the extension currently works, the functions that you use to perform certain tasks in Ming and indeed anything else about the extension, could change in a future version of PHP. This is not to say that it will change, but you should be aware that it could. In any case, it is a good idea to regularly check with http://ming.sourceforge.net to keep up with any new developments

2   While the extension does support streaming of MP3 files, there is no sound event support. You cannot, in the current version of Ming, write code that will make your Flash movie play certain sounds in response to mouse or keyboard events.

3   Handling of text on the Windows platform is not entirely stable. Under Linux you will be able to use any font face that you have a Font Definition Block for. Under Windows you will only be able to make use of the system font faces that are included in the Flash player. Using a non-system font under Windows will cause your web server to hang.

# Anatomy of a Flash movie

Before we start creating Flash movies, we need to understand the basic structure of a Flash movie. The most basic property of a Flash movie is its dimension. In order for us to see something on our screen it has to have a height and width – this area of the Flash movie is referred to as the **stage** and is the visible area onto which we will add our animations and objects.

All Flash movies have a **timeline** – a sequence of frames that the Flash player will show one after the other to create the illusion of movement – this is your standard technique for creating any animation. As with any animation, we need to be able to control the speed at which the animation plays, and therefore one of the things that we can set in a Flash movie is the number of frames that are played per second (fps). By combining the number of frames in our Flash movie and the rate at which they are played (fps) we will know exactly how long our movie will take to play – a 36 frame movie at 12 frames per second will take 3 seconds to play.

Not all Flash movies will be animations. If you recall the example I created earlier to demonstrate pulling data into the Flash movie, we had no animation. The entire movie was on a single frame, but the functionality or interest in the movie was because of objects we had placed on the movie.

We can place Flash objects anywhere on our stage, or even off it. Only objects that are placed within the visible portion of our stage will be visible when published to the browser. The coordinate system of the stage, and the one we will use for placing objects on it, starts at 0,0 in the top left-hand corner and radiates to the right and down. This is the same coordinate system that you will have come across when using the GD functions. Note that in the introduction to Ming in the PHP manual it says that all values are measured in TWIPS (20 units per pixel) but this is no longer true – all values are measured in pixels.

Besides objects like shapes, buttons, and textboxes, we can also place other movies on our main timeline and stage. Flash allows us to nest movie clips within each other. The ability to nest movies within one another allows us to compartmentalize pieces of our Flash application which makes it easier to maintain in the long term. Once we start nesting movie clips within one another, we start creating additional **levels** to our movie. We mentioned this in passing earlier, when we looked at the `loadVariables` function.

Each movie clip or sprite can be given a name, and we can then use that name in ActionScript to reference it. The main movie timeline is known as `_root` and we then use dot notation to move through the nested levels of movie clips.

If we created a movie clip on the main timeline of my movie and gave it the name of 'chapter', we would refer to it in ActionScript as `_root.chapter`. Similarly if we then placed a textbox inside the chapter movie clip and gave it the name of `title`, we would refer to that textbox as `_root.chapter.title`.

We can attach ActionScript to any frame or button object. In the case of a frame, the ActionScript is executed when the Flash player reaches that frame, or in the case of a button, we can define on what events the code is executed. In the example we looked at previously, the code was executed when the user released the mouse button.

Now that we have an idea as to what sorts of things we can put on a Flash movie, let's take a look at how we can go about doing this with Ming.

**13**

# Ming Tools

In this section we will take a look at how we can use the Ming tools to create a Flash movie. Rather than detail each Ming function and how it is used, we will work our way through creating some Flash movies and cover each of the Ming functions as they arise. Once you have a basic idea of how to go about creating a Flash movie, you will be able to look up the functions in the PHP manual.

## Creating a Basic Flash Movie

To begin with we will create a basic Flash movie. For the moment we won't include anything, we'll just look at what is needed to create the framework for a Flash movie.

If you remember in *Chapter 1*, we mentioned that there were certain variables in PHP that had the type of resource. In the following pages of this chapter we will encounter many PHP functions that return resource type information. In fact, most of the Ming functions will return a resource of some kind.

The first resource that we will always create will be an `SWFMovie`. We create this object with the `SWFMovie()` function:

```php
<?php
  $movie = new SWFMovie();
```

`$movie` will now contain an instance of the `SWFMovie()` class. Once we have created our movie object, we can then use its member functions to set the initial information about the movie. As we mentioned earlier, a movie needs to have dimensions and a frame rate:

```php
$movie->setDimension(300, 200);
$movie->setRate(12);
```

The `setDimension()` function sets the dimensions of the movie to 300 pixels wide by 200 pixels height, while the `setRate()` function sets the frame rate for our movie in fps (frames per second).

Additionally we can set the background color for the movie, using the `setBackground()` function. This function takes as its three arguments, the red, green, and blue values of the color that you want the background to be. We will set it to blue:

```php
$movie->setBackground(0,0,255);
```

Now that we have set the initial values for our movie we can output it to the browser. Before we output the actual SWF content, we need to tell the browser what it's about to get. Normally a web browser would use the filename to determine what it was getting. Since our SWF file is being generated by a PHP script it would have the file extension of `.php` and not `.swf` – therefore we use the `header()` function to first send the MIME type of the file to the browser:

```php
header('Content-type:application/x-shockwave-flash');
$movie->output();
?>
```

Save the file as `movie.php` inside your *Site* folder. We could browse directly to the SWF file but if we did that it would stretch to fill the entire browser window and any content in it would be stretched out of proportion, which is not the behavior we want. Instead, we will embed our movie in an HTML page.

If you recall at the beginning of the chapter we looked at how to embed a Flash file in our HTML page. We can use the Dreamweaver MX *Insert* toolbar to include the SWF file, but as it physically does not exist until the PHP script runs, we will have to manually edit the width and height of the SWF movie ourselves.

Create a new HTML file and save it as `movie.html` in your *Site*. Then from the *Media* tab of the *Insert* toolbar, choose the *Flash* button and select the `movie.php` script. The code that Dreamweaver will include for you is:

```
<object classid="clsid:D27CDB6E-AE6D-11cf-96B8-444553540000"
codebase="http://download.macromedia.com/pub/shockwave/cabs/flash/swflash.cab#vers
ion=6,0,29,0" width="32" height="32">
  <param name="movie" value="movie.php">
  <param name="quality" value="high">
  <embed src="movie.php" quality="high"
pluginspage="http://www.macromedia.com/go/getflashplayer" type="application/x-
shockwave-flash" width="32" height="32"></embed></object>
```

If you preview that now, you will get:

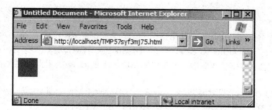

We wanted our movie to be 300 pixels high by 200 pixels wide, so we need to go and edit the width and height parameters in the object and embed tags:

```
<object classid="clsid:D27CDB6E-AE6D-11cf-96B8-444553540000"
codebase="http://download.macromedia.com/pub/shockwave/cabs/flash/swflash.cab#version
=6,0,29,0" width="300" height="200">
  <param name="movie" value="movie.php">
  <param name="quality" value="high">
  <embed src="movie.php" quality="high"
pluginspage="http://www.macromedia.com/go/getflashplayer" type="application/x-
shockwave-flash" width="300" height="200"></embed></object>
```

You could do this either by hand, or right-clicking both the `<object>` and `<embed>` tags and choosing *Edit Tag* and then editing the *Width* and *Height* values in the dialog. The result of saving that file and previewing the changes is:

**13**

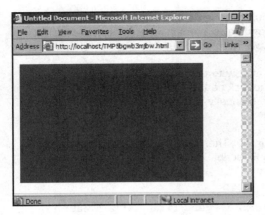

Pretty straightforward, but it's not doing anything useful yet. Let's extend the example further by adding some additional frames, a shape, and animating it across the movie stage.

In order to create animation, we're going to need additional frames and something to animate the movie. We begin our new script in the standard way, by creating a new `SWFMovie()` object and setting the properties for it:

```php
<?php
$movie = new SWFMovie();
$movie->setDimension(300,200);
$movie->setRate(12);
$movie->setBackground(0,0,255);
```

Before we add something to the stage, we need to create it first. To do this we first create an `SWFShape()` object:

```php
$shpSquare = new SWFShape();
```

The `SWFShape()` object is the resource that will hold the shape that we create. Once we have finished creating it, we will be able to add it to our stage. The way that we create shapes in Ming is the same as we would on paper. We have a virtual pen and with this we describe our shape.

The first thing we have to do is tell the `SWFShape()` the size and color of the pen that we will be using to draw with. We'll use a single pixel-wide pen and draw in white:

```php
$shpSquare->setLine(1,255,255,255);
```

The `setLine()` member function of `SWFShape()` takes four arguments: the size of the pen in pixels, and then the red, green, and blue values of the color we want to draw in.

If you wish to fill the shape with color, you'll need to create an `SWFFill` object and then set this as the fill for the shape. This sounds complicated, but it's not really that difficult. There are two functions that we will need to use, both of them member functions of the `SWFShape()` object.

The first function is the `addFill()` function, which simply takes the RGB values of the color for the fill as its arguments. The `addFill()` function creates an `SWFFill()` object, which we can then set as the fill for our shape with the `setRightFill()` member function. The function takes a single argument which is the `SWFFill()` object. We'll want to fill our shape with white as well, so the code to do this is as follows:

```php
$shpSquare->setRightFill($shpSquare->addFill(255,255,255));
```

Now that we have set up the shape, we can begin drawing. The first thing to do is to move the pen to its starting position:

```
$shpSquare->movePenTo(0,0);
```

Now we can use the `drawLineTo()` member function to draw the outline of the square. The arguments for the `movePenTo()` and `drawLineTo()` functions are the X and Y co-ordinates on the stage that we want:

```
$shpSquare->drawLineTo(10,0);
$shpSquare->drawLineTo(10,10);
$shpSquare->drawLineTo(0,10);
$shpSquare->drawLineTo(0,0);
```

The four lines draw the four sides of the square. Because we have set a fill for the shape, it will automatically be filled with the color that we set for the `SWFFill()` object. It's worth noting that you do not have to fill a shape with a solid color. Ming also has `SWFGradient` and `SWFBitmap` objects for creating gradient fills or loading images, and you can also use these objects as fills for shapes.

At this point in the code we have created our base `SWFMovie()` and created the `SWFShape()` that we will be animating across the stage. Our next step is to add the shape to our movie:

```
$resSquare = $movie->add($shpSquare);
```

The `add()` member function of the `SWFMovie()` object adds the shape to our movie and returns a resource handle to the shape within the movie. This resource handle is what is known in Ming as an `SWFDisplayItem` object, which has its own member functions. With these member functions we will be able to scale, rotate, move, and transform the object on the stage. We will be using the `move()` member function to animate the square across the stage.

We'll animate the square from the top left to the bottom right-hand side of the stage, and we'll do it in 10 pixel increments down and 15 pixel increments to the right. This means that we will have 20 steps to get to the bottom right-hand corner. Each of the steps will involve:

- Adding a new frame to the main timeline
- Moving the shape 10 pixels down and 15 pixels across

This is best achieved using a `for` loop:

```
for ($i=0;$i<20;$i++) {
$movie->nextFrame();
$resSquare->move(15,10); }
```

`$movie->nextFrame()` adds a new frame to the timeline. `$resSquare->move(15,10)` moves the object identified by the `$resSquare` resource 15 pixels to the right and 10 pixels down.

This loop will have the effect of adding 20 frames to our movie. We set the frame rate to 12 frames per second, so it should take just under 2 seconds to play the animation. Unless we specifically tell the Flash player to stop playing the movie at the end, it will go back to the beginning of the movie and keep looping through it.

Using Flash with PHP and Dreamweaver MX

13

We can then output the movie as we normally do:

```
header('Content-type: application/x-shockwave-flash');
$movie->output();
?>
```

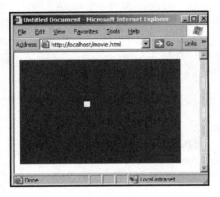

Since we've edited `movie.php`, we can simply browse to `movie.html` and see the updated SWF file that it generates (if the movie hasn't changed it may be that your browser is caching the file):

## Adding ActionScript

Now that we have seen how to create a basic movie and some basic animation, we need to look at how we can add interactivity to the movie. We'll do this in 2 ways:

- Adding button objects to the movie
- Adding ActionScript to our movie

As I mentioned earlier in the chapter we can attach ActionScript to a button or just have it attached to a frame. If it is attached to a frame, then the ActionScript will only execute when the Flash player reaches that frame. We will look at attaching ActionScript to a button, as well as at how we can add text and text objects to our movie. To do this we will rebuild the example we initially created with Macromedia Flash, but this time we will create it dynamically using Ming.

We'll use a file called `scriptresult.html` file, containing the following code:

```
<OBJECT classid="clsid:D27CDB6E-AE6D-11cf-96B8-444553540000"
codebase="http://download.macromedia.com/pub/shockwave/cabs/flash/swflash.cab#version
=6,0,0,0"
 WIDTH="300" HEIGHT="200" id="scriptresult" ALIGN="">
 <PARAM NAME=movie VALUE="scriptresult.php">
 <PARAM NAME=quality VALUE=high>
 <PARAM NAME=bgcolor VALUE=#0000FF>
 <EMBED src="scriptresult.php" quality=high bgcolor=#003399  WIDTH="300"
HEIGHT="200" NAME="scriptresult" ALIGN=""
 TYPE="application/x-shockwave-flash"
PLUGINSPAGE="http://www.macromedia.com/go/getflashplayer">
</EMBED>
</OBJECT>
```

Now let's take a look at `scriptresult.php` – the PHP script that is going to build our SWF:

```php
<?php
$movie = new SWFMovie();
$movie->setDimension(300,200);
$movie->setRate(12);
$movie->setBackground(0,0,255);
```

As we have seen in all our examples, we start off by creating the `SWFMovie()` object. We will keep the dimensions the same as those specified initially in our HTML file.

Just as we did when we created our animation, we first have to create our objects that we will be placing on the stage. It's useful to create everything that we will need for the movie at the beginning of the script. That way when we start adding them to the stage, we won't have object creation code mixed up with the code for adding them to the movie. This also makes it easier to locate code: to find code that creates specific objects, we look at the top of the script, and to find code that builds the layout of the stage and timeline, we look towards the bottom of the script.

The first set of objects that we will be creating are the text labels and textboxes. Ming has two objects that we can use to create text elements, an `SWFText()` object and `SWFTextField()`. As you would imagine, `SWFText()` is static text, the kind of thing you would use as a label, while `SWFTextField()` creates an editable text element, like a text input form element in HTML.

The first thing that you need to do when creating a text object in Ming is create a font for it to use. As I mentioned earlier, we'll stick to using the Flash system fonts – these are fonts that are embedded in the Flash player and will be available to anyone viewing your movie. The three system fonts are `_serif`, `_sans` and `_typewriter`.

*The problem that you will have here if you are working on a Windows machine, is that the `SWFText()` object will generate an error with your web server. This is not a huge problem as the `SWFTextField()` easily doubles up as a label, so to maintain compatibility for Windows users, we'll use the `SWFTextField()` object in place of `SWFText()`.*

If you are using UNIX and you want to use your own fonts, you will have to first create a Font Definition Block. You can create an FDB file with the `makefdb` utility included with Ming.

Once you have your FDB file, or decided to use a system font, you can go ahead and create an `SWFFont()` object which defines the font face that will be used for the text object:

```php
$font = new SWFFont("_sans");
```

We'll use the same font for all of our text elements, so we only have to create the one. Now we can go ahead and create the individual text elements themselves. When we create these elements, we are going to have to set certain properties for the object so that it displays correctly.

```php
$labelInput = new SWFTextField(SWFTEXTFIELD_NOEDIT | SWFTEXTFIELD_NOSELECT);
$labelInput->setBounds(50,15);
$labelInput->setFont($font);
$labelInput->setColor(255,255,255);
$labelInput->addString('Input:');
```

When we create the `SWFTextField()` object, we pass some flags to the constructor function to make it behave like a label, and not a text input box. The `SWFTEXTFIELD_NOEDIT` flag makes the textbox non-editable, and the `SWFTEXTFIELD_NOSELECT` flag stops the user from selecting the text in the label. Once the object is created and we have the resource handle, we can use the member functions of the object to set:

- The size of the textfield: setBounds() takes two arguments, the width and height of the textfield in pixels
- The font: setFont() takes a single argument of the font resource handle we created earlier
- The color of the text: setColor() requires the red, green, and blue values of the color
- The text to put in the textbox: addString() adds the text passed as the argument to the function to the textbox

Since we'll need two labels, we can create a second label in exactly the same way:

```
$labelResult = new SWFTextField(SWFTEXTFIELD_NOEDIT | SWFTEXTFIELD_NOSELECT);
$labelResult->setBounds(50,15);
$labelResult->setFont($font);
$labelResult->setColor(255,255,255);
$labelResult->addString('Result:');
```

Now that we have the two labels, we need to create the two textboxes themselves. This time when we create the `SWFTextField()`, we will actually want the user to be able to fill something in, so we pass the flag of `SWFTEXTFIELD_DRAWBOX` – this will draw the text ield with a border around it, so that the user can actually see where it is on the screen.

```
$textInput = new SWFTextField(SWFTEXTFIELD_DRAWBOX);
$textInput->setBounds(50,15);
$textInput->setFont($font);
$textInput->setColor(0,0,255);
$textInput->setName("strInputText");
```

As before, we set the size of the textfield and the color of the text, but since the user will be inputting data here, we don't want to set it to anything to begin with. What we will do though, is use the `setName()` member function to set the internal name of the textbox within the Flash movie. The contents of the textbox will be available within the Flash movie as a variable with the name specified in the `setName()` function. In this case, the variable will be `strInputText`.

We can then create the second textbox that will hold the results:

```
$textResult = new SWFTextField(SWFTEXTFIELD_DRAWBOX);
$textResult->setBounds(50,15);
$textResult->setFont($font);
$textResult->setColor(0,0,255);
$textResult->setName("strScriptResult");
```

The one problem with using `SWFTextField()` objects is that you can't position them on the screen. The `SWFText()` object has a member function `moveTo()` which allows you to move the textbox to any position on the stage, but `SWFTextField()` does not have this. We get around this problem by placing the textfield inside a sprite (symbol), and then position it on the stage.

We will therefore have to create a holder sprite for each of the text fields that we have created. The way that we do this is create a new `SWFSprite` object, add the text object to it, and advance it a frame:

```
$hldLabelInput = new SWFSprite();
$hldLabelInput->add($labelInput);
$hldLabelInput->nextFrame();

$hldLabelResult = new SWFSprite();
$hldLabelResult->add($labelResult);
$hldLabelResult->nextFrame();

$hldTextInput = new SWFSprite();
$hldTextInput->add($textInput);
$hldTextInput->nextFrame();

$hldTextResult = new SWFSprite();
$hldTextResult->add($textResult);
$hldTextResult->nextFrame();
```

The member functions of the `SWFSprite` object are similar to those of the `SWFMovie` object.

All our text elements have been defined and are ready to be placed on the stage, all we need is a button. A button is created in Ming with an `SWFButton` object. The shape and area of the button is defined by an `SWFShape` object, so we'll create that first:

```
$button_shape = new SWFShape();
$button_shape->setRightFill($button_shape->addFill(255,255,255));
$button_shape->movePenTo(0,0);
$button_shape->drawLineTo(50,0);
$button_shape->drawLineTo(50,15);
$button_shape->drawLineTo(0,15);
$button_shape->drawLineTo(0,0);
```

So now we have a white square, 50 pixels wide by 15 pixels high. We can now use this shape to define the button.

The first thing to do is create the button object:

```
$button = new SWFButton();
```

Then, using the `addShape()` member function, we specify the shape of the button. The `addShape()` function takes two arguments, the first is the shape resource to use, the second is a flag that specifies the state of the button that this shape is for. A button has three visible states and one invisible state. The three visible states are `SWFBUTTON_UP`, `SWFBUTTON_OVER` and `SWFBUTTON_DOWN`, which correspond to the up, over, and down states of the button respectively.

If you want a button that changes color when the user passes a mouse over it, you could create a second shape of the same size but with a different color fill, and add that as the SWFBUTTON_OVER state. Whenever the mouse cursor passes over the button the second shape will be displayed.

The invisible shape is used to define the area of the button that is active. The shape defined as the SWFBUTTON_HIT state of the button is never displayed, but describes the area of the button that is 'clickable'.

In our example we'll use the same shape for all the states:

```
$button->addShape($button_shape, SWFBUTTON_UP | SWFBUTTON_HIT | SWFBUTTON_OVER |
SWFBUTTON_DOWN);
```

In order to load the results from our PHP script, we're going to have to add some ActionScript to the button. In Macromedia Flash, we added the following code to the button:

```
on (release) {
        loadVariables('results.php','_root','POST');
}
```

The way that we add actions in Ming, is to first create an SWFAction() object. Then we add the action to the button, specifying which mouse event to trigger the action for. Since we'll be using a flag to specify the mouse event, we don't need to include the on (release) structure of the ActionScript, only the loadVariables line.

In the last example we used POST to send all the variables within the movie to the script, so let's alter it to only send the single variable we're interested in. To do that we'll build the query to append to our URL, made up of the name of the variable and its contents.

The variable name is strInputText, and so the URL and query that we will want to build is:

*results.php?strInputText=value_of_textbox*

Remember when we created SWFSprite objects as holders for our text elements earlier in the script? Well when we add the sprite to the stage, one of the things we can do to it is give it a name. In the case of the *Input* textbox, we're going to call the holder sprite input. We also mentioned earlier that we could nest movies on our stage, and this is exactly what we are doing. The way that we will refer to the contents of the input textbox will therefore be:

```
_root.input.strInputText
```

The results box is also inside a holder sprite, which we will name result, so when we load the variables into the movie, we need to specify that the variables must be loaded at the _root.result level.

In ActionScript you concatenate strings with the + operator, so if we were building the loadVariables function arguments in Macromedia Flash, we would say:

```
loadVariables('results.php?strInputText='+_root.input.strInputText,'_root.result');
```

To create the SWFAction object with this line of ActionScript, we just pass it as a string the constructor function:

```
$buttonAction = new
SWFAction("loadVariables('results.php?strInputText='+_root.input.strInputText,'_root.
result');");
```

We can then add the action to the button, and pass it a flag to say that it must execute this code on the mouseup event:

```
$button->addAction($buttonAction, SWFBUTTON_MOUSEUP);
```

That's all the setup work we need to do to get the ball rolling. We can now move into the next phase: creating the movie and start add our elements to the stage:

```
$handle = $movie->add($hldLabelInput);
$handle->moveTo(10,20);
```

$handle is going to be an SWFDisplayItem resource and we can use it to position the movie clip on the stage. Once the movie clip has been positioned, we won't need access to that resource again, so we use the same variable name for all of our resource handles:

```
$handle = $movie->add($hldTextInput);
$handle->setName('input');
$handle->moveTo(60,20);
```

In the case of the movie clips that contain the text-input elements, we need to give them a name as we mentioned earlier. The setName() member function does this for us.

```
$handle = $movie->add($hldLabelResult);
$handle->moveTo(10,50);
$handle = $movie->add($hldTextResult);
$handle->setName('result');
$handle->moveTo(60,50);
$handle = $movie->add($button);
$handle->moveTo(60,75);
```

Once all the elements are added we can output the movie to the browser:

```
header('Content-type: application/x-shockwave-flash');
$movie->output();
?>
```

One thing we will need to change in our results.php script, is the fact that we were sending the variables as POST and now we're sending them using GET.

results.php:

```
<?php
print ('strScriptResult='. strrev($_GET['strInputText']));
?>
```

**13**

We can now test the movie by browsing to `scriptresult.html` in a browser:

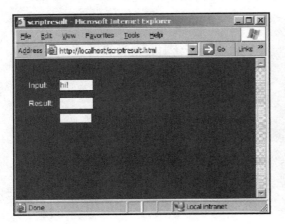 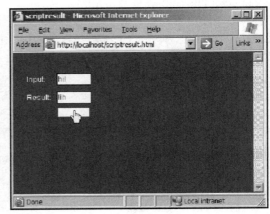

# flashbutton Class

We can use the tools we've learned in this chapter to create a class that we can use to create generic Flash buttons. There is an option within Dreamweaver MX to create Flash buttons, but by creating a class to generate them from within Ming, we can create our buttons on the fly from a database or user input.

In order to be able to output the SWF, we're going to need two scripts. The one will be the class itself; the second will be the script that actually builds the SWF.

To begin with let's take a look at the class script.

```php
<?php
class FlashButton
{
    var $button;
```

## class_flashbutton.php

The only variable that we will need in the class is the one that will hold all the button settings: width, height, label, that sort of thing. `$button` is an associative array of all the information. The reason that we are using an array for the information and not a whole lot of individual variables, is because later on we will have to pass all of this information to the script that will be building the movie itself. If we had all the information as individual variables it would be quite a mess sending it all across. By keeping it all in one associative array, we can just encode the information and send it as one chunk. I'll explain this in more detail when we get there.

The first method in our class is the constructor function, and here we will provide default values for all of the arguments. By providing default values, the person using the class can choose to pass all the values through with the constructor, or use the methods provided later to set the values manually.

The values that we will need to be able to build a Flash button are:

- width

- height

- text color

- button color when first loaded

- button color when mouse passes over

- the actual text for the button

- the URL to link to

- and the target window of the URL

```
function FlashButton($width = 50, $height = 15, $fgColor = '#000000', $bgColorN
= '#FFFFFF', $bgColorR = '#C0C0C0', $label = 'A button', $url = 'http://localhost',
$target = '_blank')
   {
     $this->button['buttonWidth'] = $width;
       $this->button['buttonHeight'] = $height;
     $this->button['buttonTextCol'] = $fgColor;
       $this->button['buttonButtonColNormal'] = $bgColorN;
       $this->button['buttonButtonColRollover'] = $bgColorR;
     $this->button['buttonLabel'] = $label;
       $this->button['buttonURL'] = $url;
       $this->button['buttonTarget'] = $url;
   }
```

In the function, all we do is take the values for each of the button properties and assign them to the `$button` associative array.

If you decide not to pass all the information through with the constructor function, it sets some default values for the button to begin with. You can then set the properties manually, with the following methods:

```
function setDimensions ($width, $height)
 {
   $this->button['buttonWidth'] = $width;
     $this->button['buttonHeight'] = $height;
 }
```

`setDimensions()` sets the width and height of the button.

```
function setButtonColors ($normal, $over)
 {
   $this->button['buttonButtonColNormal'] = $normal;
     $this->button['buttonButtonColRollover'] = $over;    }
```

**13**

`setButtonColors()` sets the background colors of the button, for its normal and rollover states.

```
function setLabel ($label, $fgColor)
{
   $this->button['buttonLabel'] = $label;
   $this->button['buttonTextCol'] = $fgColor;
}
```

`setLabel()` sets the properties that concern the text label on the button – in this case the text itself and the color of the text.

```
function setLink ($url, $target = '')
{
    $this->button['buttonURL'] = $url;
    $this->button['buttonTarget'] = $target;
}
```

`setLink()` sets the target URL and window that we are linking to.

All colors are passed through as their HTML hexadecimal values. Rather than using RGB values here and having to pass 3 values for each color, it is neater and more efficient to use the hexadecimal values and then convert them to RGB as we need them.

Now we get to the `output()` function. This is the function that takes the information that has been passed to the class and builds the HTML tags for the SWF from it. When we get to outputting the `src` of the SWF movie, we are going to have to pass all of the information stored in the `$button` array to the script that will build the SWF. In order to do this we will use two PHP functions, `serialize()` and `unserialize()`. `serialize()` takes a variable, array, or object, and returns a string that represents that object. If I had an array of two items:

```
$fruit = array('Apple','Banana');
```

and I serialized it:

```
$serialFruit = serialize($fruit);
```

`$serialFruit` would be a string that looked like:

```
a:2:{i:0;s:5:"Apple";i:1;s:6:"Banana";}
```

PHP also has another function called `unserialize()`, which will take that string and convert it back into the `$fruit` array.

What we will do then is use `serialize()` to convert the `$button` array into a string, and pass that as an argument to the script that is building the SWF. The script building the SWF will then `unserialize()` the data to recreate the `$button` array. The only problem is that there are inverted commas in the string, and we don't want to pass them as part of the argument, so we use the function `urlencode()` on the string to encode it into a format that is the same as data that is POSTed from a form. This format is valid and correct to pass as the query part of a URL:

```
    function output ()
    {
        echo "<object classid='clsid:D27CDB6E-AE6D-11cf-96B8-444553540000'
codebase='http://download.macromedia.com/pub/shockwave/cabs/flash/swflash.cab#version
=6,0,29,0' width='".$this->button['buttonWidth']."' height='".$this-
>button['buttonHeight']."'>";
        echo "<param name='movie'
value='flash_button.php?button=".urlencode(serialize($this->button))."'>";
        echo "<param name='quality' value='high'>";
        echo "<embed src='flash_button.php?button=".urlencode(serialize($this-
>button))."' width='".$this->button['buttonWidth']."' height='".$this-
>button['buttonHeight']."' autostart='false' quality='high'
pluginspage='http://www.macromedia.com/go/getflashplayer' type='application/x-
shockwave-flash'></embed></object>";
    }
}
?>
```

As you can see, all we are doing is writing out the standard HTML tags for embedding a Flash movie, except we are getting the `width` and `height` parameters from the `$button` variable, and we are passing the `urlencoded`, serialized `$button` as an argument to the `flash_button.php` script. As you may have guessed, `flash_button.php` is the script that builds the actual SWF. Let's take a look at it.

## flash_button.php

```
<?php
  function getRGB($hex) {
    $color = array();
    $r = hexdec(substr($hex, 1, 2));
    $g = hexdec(substr($hex, 3, 2));
    $b = hexdec(substr($hex, 5, 2));
    $color['R'] = $r;
    $color['G'] = $g;
    $color['B'] = $b;
    return $color;
  }
```

The first part of our script is a function to convert HTML hexadecimal color values into RGB values. An HTML hexadecimal color comes in the form of:

`#0033FF`

After the # symbol, there are six characters. These six characters are divided into three groups of two representing the values red, green, and blue. In the example above, the red value is `00`, green is `33` and blue is `FF`.

All our function is doing is using `substr()` to grab the relevant piece of the hexadecimal number and then converting it into a decimal with the `hexdec()` function. We then return an array of the RGB values.

The first thing we need to do is grab the information that we have been passed via the URL query and convert it back into the `$button` array.

13

First we URL decode the string that we've been passed; since it's got double quotes in it, PHP will escape them with slashes. We therefore have to pass the string to the `stripslashes()` function before using `unserialize()` to convert it back into its original form:

```
$button = unserialize(stripslashes(urldecode($_GET['button'])));
```

Now we can use the familiar format to build the button:

```
$movie = new SWFMovie();
$movie->setDimension($button['buttonWidth'], $button['buttonHeight']);
$movie->setRate(12);
$color = getRGB($button['buttonButtonColNormal']);
```

Before we set the background color of the button we need to pass the hexadecimal color value to the `getRGB()` function to return the individual RGB values.

```
$movie->setBackground($color['R'],$color['G'],$color['B']);

$font = new SWFFont('_sans');

$labelNormal = new SWFTextField(SWFTEXTFIELD_NOEDIT | SWFTEXTFIELD_NOSELECT);
$labelNormal->setFont($font);
$color = getRGB($button['buttonTextColNormal']);
$labelNormal->setColor($color['R'],$color['G'],$color['B']);
$labelNormal->addString($button['buttonLabel']);
```

As we have done before, we create the font and the text element, and set the font and the other text properties. The properties we grab from the `$button` array.

When we create the shape for the button, we'll create two of them – one for the normal state and the second one for the rollover:

```
$shpButtonN = new SWFShape();
$color = getRGB($button['buttonButtonColNormal']);
$shpButtonN->setRightFill($shpButtonN-
>addFill($color['R'],$color['G'],$color['B']));
$shpButtonN->movePenTo(0,0);
$shpButtonN->drawLineTo($button['buttonWidth'],0);
$shpButtonN->drawLineTo($button['buttonWidth'],$button['buttonHeight']);
$shpButtonN->drawLineTo(0,$button['buttonHeight']);
$shpButtonN->drawLineTo(0,0);

$shpButtonR = new SWFShape();
$color = getRGB($button['buttonButtonColRollover']);
$shpButtonR->setRightFill($shpButtonR-
>addFill($color['R'],$color['G'],$color['B']));
$shpButtonR->movePenTo(0,0);
$shpButtonR->drawLineTo($button['buttonWidth'],0);
$shpButtonR->drawLineTo($button['buttonWidth'],$button['buttonHeight']);
$shpButtonR->drawLineTo(0,$button['buttonHeight']);
$shpButtonR->drawLineTo(0,0);

$stageButton = new SWFButton();
```

Now when we add the shapes to the button, we add the first one for the 'up' and 'hit' states, and the second shape for the 'over' and 'down' states. This will create the rollover effect for the button:

```
$stageButton->addShape($shpButtonN, SWFBUTTON_UP | SWFBUTTON_HIT);
$stageButton->addShape($shpButtonR, SWFBUTTON_OVER | SWFBUTTON_DOWN);
```

When we create the action for the button, we'll use the ActionScript `getURL()` function – this navigates to the specified URL. The function takes a second optional argument which is the target window for the URL to open in:

```
$buttonAction = new
SWFAction("getURL('".$button['buttonURL']."','"".$button['buttonTarget']."');");
$stageButton->addAction($buttonAction, SWFBUTTON_MOUSEUP);

$handle = $movie->add($stageButton);
$handle = $movie->add($labelNormal);
```

We then add the two elements to the stage and output the movie:

```
header('Content-type: application/x-shockwave-flash');
$movie->output();
?>
```

In order to see it in action, we'll have to write a small PHP script to use the class.

### mkbutton.php

```
<?php
include_once('class_flashbutton.php');
$button = new FlashButton();
$button->output();
?>
```

This will create a Flash button with the default settings (a white button that turns gray when you move the mouse over it):

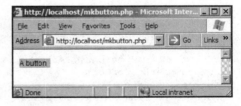

Of course we don't want to have a default button, so let's modify mkbutton.php to use our own settings:

```
<?php
include_once('class_flashbutton.php');
$button = new FlashButton();
$button->setDimensions(300,15);
$button->setButtonColors('#87C687','#CC3366');
$button->setLabel('Dreamweaver MX: Advanced PHP Web Development','#FFFFFF');
$button->setLink('http://www.glasshaus.com','_blank');
$button->output();
?>
```

13

This will give us a button labeled Dreamweaver MX: Advanced PHP that points to the glasshaus web site, and changes color when the mouse cursor passes over it:

# Creating a Flash Button Server Behavior

Now that we have our code, it would be nice if we could quickly insert it into our page. There are several ways that we can do that.

The first is by creating a code snippet for the code that is in mkbutton.php. However this is not the ideal solution because we will have to go and edit it each time we insert it. A much better solution would be to create a server behavior for this code with which Dreamweaver MX will prompt us for the relevant information.

In the *Application* panel, choose the *Server Behaviors* tab, drop down the menu and choose *New Server Behavior*. In the dialog that pops up, choose *PHP/MySQL* and the document type, and call it *Flash Button*. Click *OK* and you'll be presented with the Server Behavior Builder.

This is where we want to put the code from mkbutton.php. Click the + button and name this block *Main*. What you need to do now is replace all of the values that you would normally pass to the member functions with parameters. When you are done your code block should look something like this:

```php
<?php
include_once('class_flashbutton.php');
$button = new FlashButton();
$button->setDimensions(@@width@@,@@height@@);
$button->setButtonColors('@@Normal Color@@','@@Over Color@@');
$button->setLabel('@@Label@@','@@Text Color@@');
$button->setLink('@@Target URL@@','@@Target Window@@');
$button->output();
?>
```

Set the code to insert *Relative to the Selection*, *After the Selection*:

![Flash Button (PHP MySQL) - Server Behavior Builder dialog showing Code Blocks to Insert with Main block and Code Block text area containing PHP code]

Click *Next*, and set all the parameters to *Text Field,* except *Target URL* which can be an *URL Text Field*

Now when you insert the Flash Button server behavior, you will be prompted for the relevant information:

The only drawback is that you will have to manually insert the hexadecimal values for the colors yourself.

One option for changing this would be to alter the color options to be list menus containing color options. To do this, edit the behavior, and set the color fields in the dialog generator to be of type *List Menu*. Then you will need to edit the behavior's EDML file (stored in `Configuration\ServerBehaviors\PHP_MySQL`).

FlashButton dialog:

| width: | 300 |
| Over Color: | #00Ff0B |
| height: | 100 |
| Normal Color: | #2CB235 |
| Target URL: | glasshaus.php | Browse... |
| Text Color: | #72331C |
| Target Window: | _blank |
| Label: | glasshaus |

Open the file in Dreamweaver and it will look like this:

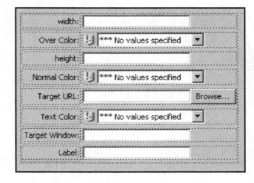

**13**

Now simply alter the list menus to contain labels for colors and hex values using the *Properties* inspector (that is, a menu option with the label Red and the value #FF0000). It should now look like this:

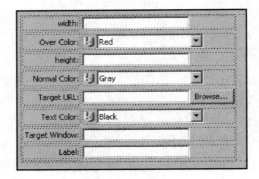

Save the file, and create a new PHP file in Dreamweaver. Insert a *FlashButton* behavior, and you will notice that the dialog now matches the page you designed.

Note, that if you wanted to use this server behavior in a site, you would have to move the relevant class files into the correct folder.

# Summary

In this chapter we have dealt with the various ways that we can integrate PHP and Flash. We began by looking at some traditional methods that are available to Flash and PHP programmers for programming interaction.

We then moved on to looking at the Ming library for PHP, which allows us to build our own Flash movies without the need for Macromedia Flash. Our tour of Ming started with some basics of Flash, moved onto animation, and finished off with adding some ActionScript interaction. To bring it all together we created a PHP class to create Flash buttons on the fly.

# Case Study 1

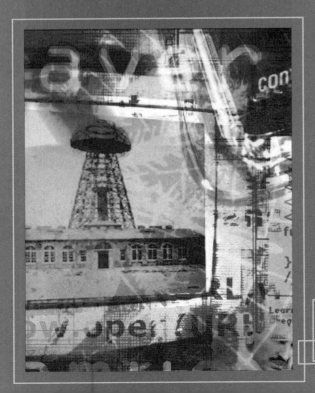

Author: Allan Kent

# Case Study: Personal Training Log

In this chapter we will be looking at how we can create a personal training log application in PHP. The application is basically a way of logging your progress across a number of different training scenarios. In this case we will be creating a training log for an endurance athlete, so the disciplines that will be covered are running, swimming, and cycling.

The aim of the chapter is not to show you in minute detail how to go about creating this application, but rather to provide general instructions in the process and focus on how we can take the skills we have learned in the rest of this book and apply them to a working example. We are also assuming you have a reasonable level of experience with using the PHP server behaviors in Dreamweaver MX.

The format of the chapter is as follows: we will start by providing a rough outline of what the program needs to do, and how we intend to provide that functionality. Any specific requirements for the program will be detailed. In this section we will also provide a list of components that we will be creating for the application.

We will then move on to creating each component, and look at the process and code for each of them. Each page will be described and once all the components are built we will look at the working application.

## Requirements

We will be logging data to a database, so you will need access to MySQL. Since we will be creating charts of our progress, we will need to have some way of generating graphics. You have already encountered the JpGraph plotting library in *Chapter 12*, so we will continue to use it here.

# Application Spec

The application is going to be fairly basic. We will have predefined disciplines within which the user can train. Each discipline, such as swimming or running, will have defined training types. A training type defines what the person was doing within that discipline.

There will also be a number of routes. A route describes an actual place that you would go to train and is linked to the training type.

The actual logging of the training will log the route you were training on (and therefore through their relationships, the training type, and discipline), the date of the training session, time spent, and distance covered.

The initial setup and occasional maintenance of the system will interact with the discipline, type, and routes tables, while the day-to-day training logs will be stored in the logging table.

We will therefore need a page within which we can maintain the disciplines, training types, and routes, and also their relationships with one another. We will also need a page to log daily training sessions. This page can also be used as a quick view into the current training cycle – showing recent training logs and progress.

The last page we will need is a page from which we can view reports of our progress in tables or charts.

## Database

The first step is to create our database. Here is a relationship diagram of the database:

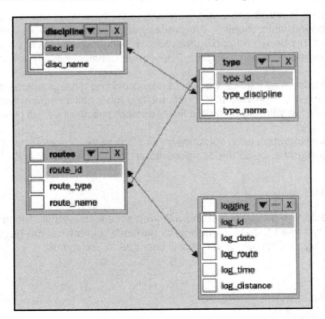

As we mentioned previously, the user will train within pre-defined disciplines, such as cycling, running, or swimming. Within each discipline there are different types of training that can be done. If we use running as an example, you could run on the road, you could do cross-country trail running, or you could run on a treadmill at the gym. We then define a set of routes that we would train along – each route is tied to a training type, and therefore a discipline.

I have provided a database script below that already contains some sample data:

```
CREATE DATABASE training;

USE training;

CREATE TABLE discipline (
  disc_id bigint(20) NOT NULL auto_increment,
  disc_name varchar(30) NOT NULL default '',
  PRIMARY KEY  (disc_id)
) TYPE=MyISAM;

CREATE TABLE type (
  type_id bigint(4) NOT NULL auto_increment,
  type_discipline bigint(20) NOT NULL default '0',
  type_name varchar(30) NOT NULL default '',
  PRIMARY KEY  (type_id)
) TYPE=MyISAM;

CREATE TABLE routes (
  route_id bigint(20) NOT NULL auto_increment,
  route_type bigint(20) NOT NULL default '0',
  route_name varchar(50) NOT NULL default '',
  PRIMARY KEY  (route_id)
) TYPE=MyISAM;

CREATE TABLE logging (
  log_id bigint(20) NOT NULL auto_increment,
  log_date bigint(20) NOT NULL default '0',
  log_route bigint(20) NOT NULL default '0',
  log_time bigint(20) NOT NULL default '0',
  log_distance bigint(20) NOT NULL default '0',
  PRIMARY KEY  (log_id)
) TYPE=MyISAM;

INSERT INTO discipline (disc_id, disc_name) VALUES
  ('1','Cycling'),
  ('2','Running'),
  ('3','Swimming');

INSERT INTO type (type_id, type_discipline, type_name) VALUES
  ('1','1','Road'),
  ('2','1','Trail'),
  ('3','1','Downhill'),
  ('4','1','Stationary'),
  ('5','2','Road'),
  ('6','2','Trail'),
  ('7','2','Stationary'),
  ('8','3','Pool'),
  ('9','3','Open Water');
```

## Components

The application will be made up of three main HTML files, and a file to handle the graphs:

- admin.php – this is the page that we will use to administer the support tables for the application. All disciplines and route information can be altered here.

- index.php – this is the main page that you will use for the application. It will contain a recent log of your training as well as a facility for you to log additional training sessions.

- reports.php – the reports page will allow you to generate reports and charts on your athletic progress.

- mkgraph.php – a script that is responsible for building the charts themselves.

# Application Development

Before we begin coding the application, we need to set up Dreamweaver MX for our new project. Create a new site called *Training*, and set PHP/MySQL as the server technology.

Once you have done this, you will need to create a page that we can use as our template. How you lay it out is up to you, but you will need three navigational elements: *Home*, *Admin* ,and *Reports*. These will link to index.php, admin.php, and reports.php.

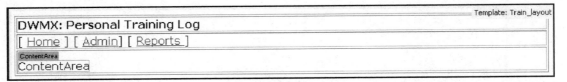

Make sure you define an editable region for the template and save it.

## admin.php

Since we will need to have some sort of data in the supporting tables of our application before we start logging training information, it makes sense that we create the admin page first. This page takes the form of a simple listing of each of the values in the tables disciplines, types, and routes respectively. We will also need to be able to delete entries and add new ones.

Because of the relationships in our database, we want to restrict users of the application from deleting records under certain conditions. If records exist in a related table that are linked to the record we are examining, then we must not allow the user to delete that record. If they could, there would be a number of records in the database that would become orphaned and data integrity would be lost. In order to do this we must somehow *not* provide a delete function for those records that have related records in the database. As we build the page we will pay particular attention to this.

Begin by creating a new page based on our template, and save the file as admin.php.

In the editable region we can create the basic skeleton of the page. Create the three headings for each of the tables that we will be providing an interface for: *Disciplines*, *Training types*, and *Routes*. Since we won't typically have hundreds of disciplines, types, and routes, we will display all the records on the same page.

We'll begin by working on the disciplines database table. First create an HTML table in which to display the records – two columns, two rows. The first row will eventually contain the headings, the second will contain the actual records from the database.

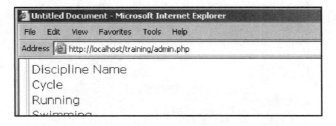

We will need a recordset for the disciplines, so first go to the *Database* tab and create a MySQL connection to the training database. Once we have that sorted out we can go to the *Bindings* tab and start creating recordsets. Call the new recordset `rstAllDisciplines`, drill down to the `disciplines` table and select both fields from the table. We will need the discipline name to display and the `disc_id` to identify this record for our delete function:

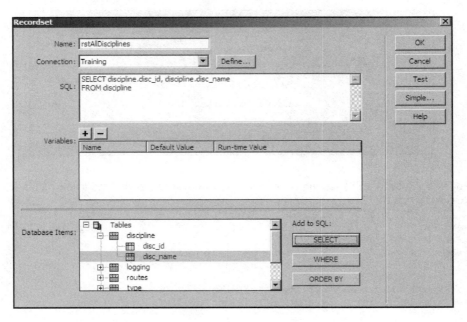

Personal Training Log

C1

Once we have our recordset, we add *Dynamic Text* to the second row of cells of the table.

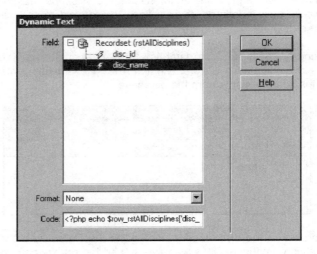

We'll be deleting a record, so we may as well go ahead and insert the *Delete Record* server behavior. We will pass the URL parameter delete to the function, as well as a parameter called discipline which will correspond to the disc_id primary key of the table.

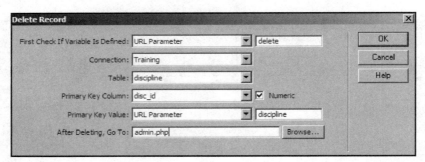

In the design view you won't see the code, but Dreamweaver has added the following piece of code to our document:

```php
if ((isset($HTTP_GET_VARS['discipline'])) && ($HTTP_GET_VARS['discipline'] != "") &&
(isset($HTTP_GET_VARS['delete']))) {
  $deleteSQL = sprintf("DELETE FROM discipline WHERE disc_id=%s",
                    GetSQLValueString($HTTP_GET_VARS['discipline'], "int"));

  mysql_select_db($database_Training, $Training);
  $Result1 = mysql_query($deleteSQL, $Training) or die(mysql_error());

  $deleteGoTo = "admin.php";
  if (isset($HTTP_SERVER_VARS['QUERY_STRING'])) {
    $deleteGoTo .= (strpos($deleteGoTo, '?')) ? "&" : "?";
    $deleteGoTo .= $HTTP_SERVER_VARS['QUERY_STRING'];
```

```
    }
    header(sprintf("Location: %s", $deleteGoTo));
}
```

There are a couple of things we need to keep in mind here: the first is that we will only be able to delete the record if a GET variable called discipline exists, if it is not blank, and if a variable called delete is set. In the link we create to delete this record, we will need to include all of this information.

The second thing we need to keep in mind is what's happening in the following code snippet:

```
if (isset($HTTP_SERVER_VARS['QUERY_STRING'])) {
    $deleteGoTo .= (strpos($deleteGoTo, '?')) ? "&" : "?";
    $deleteGoTo .= $HTTP_SERVER_VARS['QUERY_STRING'];
}
header(sprintf("Location: %s", $deleteGoTo));
```

The code is reconstructing the query string that was appended to the end of the URL and redirecting the page back to that with the PHP header() function.

If we had a URL such as:

*admin.php?delete=yes&discipline=6*

it would reconstruct the URL and redirect to it. Because delete is set to something, it will try to delete that same record again, reconstruct the URL, and redirect us off to the same page. We're in an internal loop – a bad thing. In the *Code View*, comment out the snippet of code:

```
/*
if (isset($HTTP_SERVER_VARS['QUERY_STRING'])) {
    $deleteGoTo .= (strpos($deleteGoTo, '?')) ? "&" : "?";
    $deleteGoTo .= $HTTP_SERVER_VARS['QUERY_STRING'];
}
header(sprintf("Location: %s", $deleteGoTo));
*/
```

Right. Now we need to construct the link to delete the record.

In *Design View*, click in the table cell to the right and choose *Hyperlink* from the *Insert* panel.

The link we want to create is to delete the current record. To do this we point to admin.php, but need to pass it the parameters it needs to delete the record. These are a switch to say that we are deleting a record and the ID of the current record. In the *Hyperlink* dialog, click the *Browse* button next to the *Link* entry and select admin.php. Then click the *Parameters* button to add the parameters we need. Add the delete with a value of yes, and then discipline with a value equal to the current ID. In this case it will be the disc_id field of the rstAllDisciplines recordset:

*This feature of the server behavior is such that you can redirect to a blank page with a message like "Record deleted" or something to that effect. By passing the query string along to this informational page, we would then have all of the information we needed to link back to the page we originally came from. In this example we are not doing that, which is why we have had to remove this functionality from the server behavior.*

**Personal Training Log**

C1

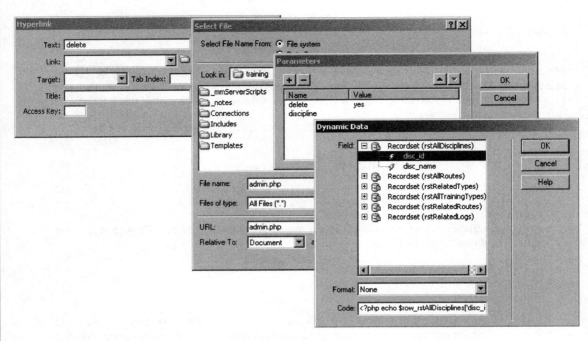

Click on *OK* to get back to the original dialog and *OK* to insert the hyperlink.

Let's preview this page now:

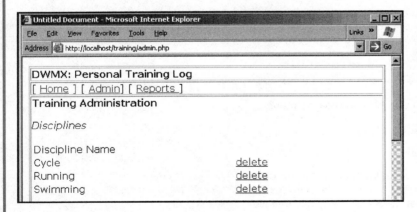

Notice the URL that it is pointing to. At the moment *delete* will be available at all times, which is not the behavior we wish to have. We only want it to appear if there are no training types related to this discipline. To do this we need to use a *Show If Recordset Is Empty* server behavior. So we'll need a recordset.

The recordset that we test against will have to be unique for each of the discipline records that we have. Remember the disciplines may have training types related to them, so for each discipline we will have to check if there are any related training types.

Create a new recordset, and switch to *Advanced* mode:

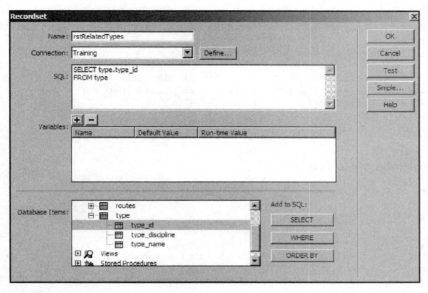

Add to the SQL code:

```
SELECT type.type_id
FROM type WHERE type.type_discipline = CurrentDiscipline
```

Then add a variable called CurrentDiscipline, by clicking on +.

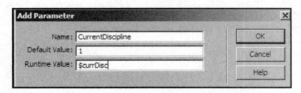

When the query runs it will use the PHP variable $currDisc to form the relevant portion of the WHERE clause. The following code is added to the top of the page:

```
$CurrentDiscipline_rstRelatedTypes = "1";
if (isset($currDisc)) {
  $CurrentDiscipline_rstRelatedTypes = (get_magic_quotes_gpc()) ? $currDisc :
addslashes($currDisc);
}
mysql_select_db($database_Training, $Training);
$query_rstRelatedTypes = sprintf("SELECT type.type_id FROM type WHERE
type.type_discipline = %s", $CurrentDiscipline_rstRelatedTypes);
$rstRelatedTypes = mysql_query($query_rstRelatedTypes, $Training) or
die(mysql_error());
$row_rstRelatedTypes = mysql_fetch_assoc($rstRelatedTypes);
$totalRows_rstRelatedTypes = mysql_num_rows($rstRelatedTypes);
```

C1

Now this recordset is getting created once for the page load, but we want it generated for each record in the `discipline` table. In *Code View*, cut that block of code and navigate down till you find the following bit:

```
    <tr>
        <td><?php echo $row_rstAllDisciplines['disc_name']; ?></td>
        <td><a href="admin.php?delete=yes&discipline=<?php echo
$row_rstAllDisciplines['disc_id']; ?>" title="Delete this
Discipline">delete</a></td>
    </tr>
```

We're going to alter this to read:

```
    <tr>
            <?php
                $CurrentDiscipline_rstRelatedTypes = "1";
                if (isset($currDisc)) {
                  $CurrentDiscipline_rstRelatedTypes =
(get_magic_quotes_gpc()) ? $currDisc : addslashes($currDisc);
                }
                mysql_select_db($database_Training, $Training);
                $query_rstRelatedTypes = sprintf("SELECT type.type_id FROM
type WHERE type.type_discipline = %s", $CurrentDiscipline_rstRelatedTypes);
                $rstRelatedTypes = mysql_query($query_rstRelatedTypes,
$Training) or die(mysql_error());
                $row_rstRelatedTypes = mysql_fetch_assoc($rstRelatedTypes);
                $totalRows_rstRelatedTypes = mysql_num_rows($rstRelatedTypes);
            ?>
        <td><?php echo $row_rstAllDisciplines['disc_name']; ?></td>
        <td><a href="admin.php?delete=yes&discipline=<?php echo
$row_rstAllDisciplines['disc_id']; ?>" title="Delete this
Discipline">delete</a></td>
    </tr>
```

What we need to do now is just make the variable `$currDisc` equal to `disc_id` of the current record. After the line that reads:

```
$CurrentDiscipline_rstRelatedTypes = "1";
```

add the following line of code:

```
$currDisc = $row_rstAllDisciplines['disc_id'];
```

Now the results of the `rstRelatedTypes` recordset will be determined by the ID of the current discipline type. All we need to do now, is switch back to design view and add the server behavior to hide the delete button. Select the delete link, add a new server behavior of the type *Show If Recordset Is Empty* and choose the `rstRelatedTypes` recordset.

Now we select the table cells, and tell PHP to repeat that row for each discipline in the database with a *Repeat Region* server behavior:

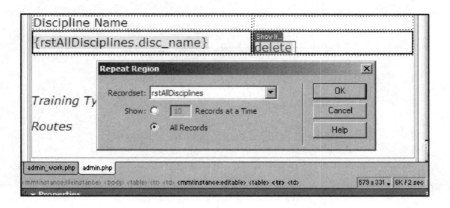

and we're all done. The resulting page will look like this:

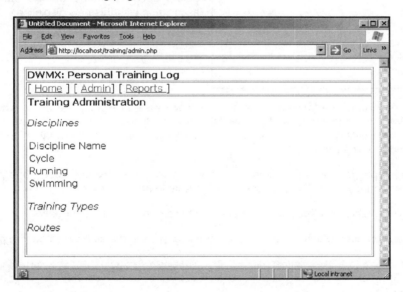

Notice that the delete option is not available for any of the disciplines, as all of them have associated training types – this was part of the sample data that was included with the SQL script.

Now we need to create a form that will allow us to create new disciplines; we'll place this under the existing disciplines (outside the repeat region). The form needs a single text element called `disc_name`, to hold the name of the discipline and a *Submit* button. Once we have that in place we can create a server behavior to insert the record:

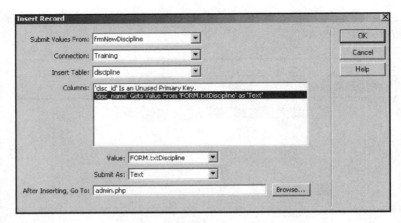

We can now test this, by inserting a new discipline, '*Resting*':

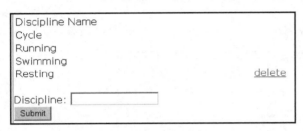

Notice how the `Resting` discipline has the delete option as there are no training types associated with this new discipline.

Right, let's move onto the training types now. This will work in exactly the same way as for the disciplines. We'll need to show all of the available training types, a form to add new ones, and an option to delete existing ones. We must only be allowed to delete an existing training type if there are no related routes for this type.

I'm not going to provide detailed instructions, only step you through this process, and point out the differences when they arise. The full code will be available at *www.glasshaus.com*.

Create an HTML table with three columns and two rows to display the information

Create a new recordset, which selects all of the training types and their associated discipline names:

```
SELECT 'type'.'type_id',     'type'.'type_discipline',     'type'.'type_name',
'discipline'.'disc_name',     'discipline'.'disc_id'
FROM 'discipline'
INNER JOIN 'type'
ON ('discipline'.'disc_id' = 'type'.'type_discipline')
```

Insert *Dynamic Text* for the *Discipline Name* and *Training Type*:

| Training Types | |
|---|---|
| Discipline | Training Type |
| {rstAllTrainingTypes.disc_name} | {rstAllTrainingTypes.type_name} |

Create a link to delete the record: as before, link to `admin.php` with `delete=yes` in the query string. We'll also need to pass the ID of the current training type, so insert the parameter type with a value of `type_id` of the current record in the `rstAllTrainingTypes` recordset.

Once again you will need to comment out the following piece of the code so that we don't get stuck in an internal loop:

```
/*

  if (isset($HTTP_SERVER_VARS['QUERY_STRING'])) {
    $deleteGoTo .= (strpos($deleteGoTo, '?')) ? "&" : "?";
    $deleteGoTo .= $HTTP_SERVER_VARS['QUERY_STRING'];
  }

*/
```

The next step in the process is to make it so that the delete link is not shown if there are related records in the database. In the case of a training type, a related record would be in the `routes` table. Therefore we must test to see whether this training type has any routes associated with it. Create the `rstRelatedRoutes` recordset:

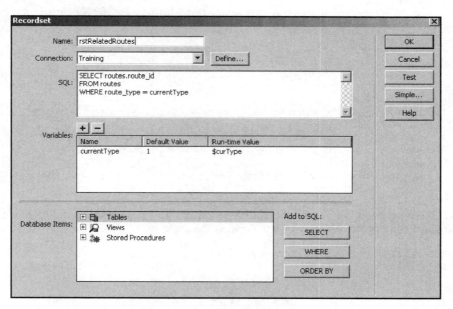

If you now go and hunt in the block of PHP code near the top of your page in the *Code View*, you will find the following block of code has been inserted into your page:

```
$currentType_rstRelatedRoutes = "1";
if (isset($curType)) {
  $currentType_rstRelatedRoutes = (get_magic_quotes_gpc()) ? $curType :
addslashes($curType);
}
mysql_select_db($database_Training, $Training);
$query_rstRelatedRoutes = sprintf("SELECT        'type'.'type_id',
```

```
'routes'.'route_id' FROM      'routes'      INNER JOIN 'type' ON ('routes'.'route_type'
= 'type'.'type_id') WHERE 'routes'.'route_type' = %s",
$currentType_rstRelatedRoutes);
$rstRelatedRoutes = mysql_query($query_rstRelatedRoutes, $Training) or
die(mysql_error());
$row_rstRelatedRoutes = mysql_fetch_assoc($rstRelatedRoutes);
$totalRows_rstRelatedRoutes = mysql_num_rows($rstRelatedRoutes);
```

You now need to move it so that it will be inside the *Repeat Region* code block. Find the following
lines of code:

```
<tr>
    <td><?php echo $row_rstAllTrainingTypes['disc_name']; ?></td>
```

and move the code in between them as follows:

```
        <tr>
        <?php
        $currentType_rstRelatedRoutes = "1";
        if (isset($curType)) {
            $currentType_rstRelatedRoutes = (get_magic_quotes_gpc()) ? $curType :
addslashes($curType);
        }
        mysql_select_db($database_Training, $Training);
        $query_rstRelatedRoutes = sprintf("SELECT      'type'.'type_id',
'routes'.'route_id' FROM      'routes'      INNER JOIN 'type' ON ('routes'.'route_type'
= 'type'.'type_id') WHERE 'routes'.'route_type' = %s",
$currentType_rstRelatedRoutes);
        $rstRelatedRoutes = mysql_query($query_rstRelatedRoutes, $Training) or
die(mysql_error());
        $row_rstRelatedRoutes = mysql_fetch_assoc($rstRelatedRoutes);
        $totalRows_rstRelatedRoutes = mysql_num_rows($rstRelatedRoutes);
        ?>
            <td><?php echo $row_rstAllTrainingTypes['disc_name']; ?></td>
```

The next thing we need to do is set the `$curType` variable to the ID of the current training type so
that the query returns the results we want. Change the lines:

```
$currentType_rstRelatedRoutes = "1";
if (isset($curType)) {
```

to:

```
$currentType_rstRelatedRoutes = "1";
$curType = $row_rstAllTrainingTypes['type_id'];
if (isset($curType)) {
```

Once we have that in place we can add the *Show If Recordset Is Empty* server behavior:

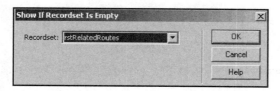

The last thing to do is select the entire row and add the *Repeat Region* server behavior to conclude creating the table of training types:

The next step is to create a form for adding new training types to the database. We first create the form `frmNewType` with a textbox for the Type name (`txtType`) and a select box for the discipline (`selDiscipline`).

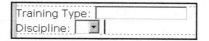

We'll make the contents of the menu dynamic and use the existing recordset `rstAllDisciplines`:

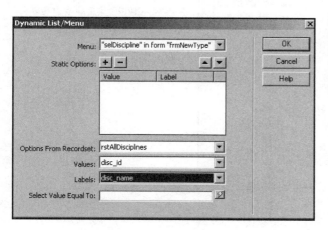

If you save and test this now you will see that the drop-down menu for *Discipline* is empty. This is because the `rstAllDisciplines` recordset has already been used, so the pointer is at the end of the recordset.

**C1**

Find the following piece of code:

```
do {
?>
          <option value="<?php echo $row_rstAllDisciplines['disc_id']?>"><?php echo
$row_rstAllDisciplines['disc_name']?></option>
          <?php
} while ($row_rstAllDisciplines = mysql_fetch_assoc($rstAllDisciplines));
```

and just before it add the following line:

```
mysql_data_seek($rstAllDisciplines,0);
```

What this function does is move the internal row pointer back to the beginning of the result set so that the records are displayed again.

Add a *Submit* button and then we can add a new *Insert Record* server behavior and link the `txtType` to the `type_name` field and `selDiscipline` to the `type_discipline` field in the `types` table. The `selDiscipline` should be set to *Submit as Integer*, since the `type_discipline` field in the database is an integer type. Dreamweaver will know this and should change it for you automatically.

With our current data we have a discipline of *Resting*, which has no training types associated with it. The delete link is therefore available, as it should be.

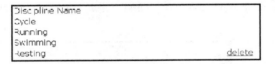

If we now go and add a training type of *Couch* that is linked to the *Resting* discipline, the delete option for the *Resting* discipline should disappear:

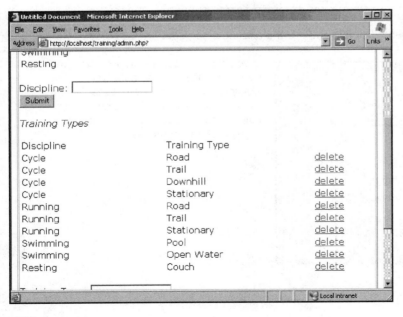

It has, so we can be confident that the code is working as it should.

In order to complete the admin page we have to go through the same exercise for the routes.

We're not going to go through it as it's the same process as we have just gone through for the disciplines and training types. What you do need to know is that the routes are linked to the logging table, so if a log entry exists for a route, then that route cannot be deleted.

The SQL for the recordset `rstAllRoutes` is as follows:

```
SELECT 'routes'.'route_id',    'routes'.'route_type',    'routes'.'route_name',
'type'.'type_name'
FROM 'type'    INNER JOIN 'routes' ON ('type'.'type_id' = 'routes'.'route_type')
```

When we create the dynamic contents of the drop-down menu for the training types we have the following code:

```php
mysql_data_seek($rstAllTrainingTypes, 0);
do {
?>
        <option value="<?php echo $row_rstAllTrainingTypes['type_id']?>"><?php
echo $row_rstAllTrainingTypes['type_name']?></option>
        <?php
} while ($row_rstAllTrainingTypes = mysql_fetch_assoc($rstAllTrainingTypes));
```

This only shows the *Training Type* as the label for the menu, but as you can see, there are duplicates:

We can get around this problem by including the discipline along with the training type. We do this by altering the PHP code above. The line:

```php
        <option value="<?php echo $row_rstAllTrainingTypes['type_id']?>"><?php
echo $row_rstAllTrainingTypes['type_name']?></option>
```

changes to:

```php
        <option value="<?php echo $row_rstAllTrainingTypes['type_id']?>"><?php
echo $row_rstAllTrainingTypes['disc_name'].' -
'.$row_rstAllTrainingTypes['type_name']?></option>
```

which results in:

Again, you can test that the logic in the page is working correctly by adding routes and checking that the delete option for the training type you have just created a route for is no longer available.

# index.php

The `index.php` page is the page that will be used on a day-to-day basis to log training sessions. This page will also serve to provide a snapshot of your current training cycle. To do this we will show the five most recent log entries. A form will allow us to enter new training data.

Create a new file from the template we created earlier and save it as `index.php`. The first thing we will create right at the top of the page is a form to add new training entries.

## Creating The Form

The logging table needs the route, the date of the training, the time taken, and the distance traveled.

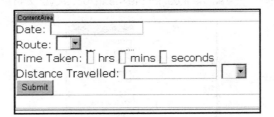

Our form fields are as follows:

| Form Field | Name |
| --- | --- |
| Date | txtDate |
| Route | selRoute |
| Time (hours) | txtHrs |
| Time (minutes) | txtMins |
| Time (seconds) | txtSecs |
| Distance traveled | txtDistance |
| Distance Type | selDistance |

We want the Date field to default to the current date, so set the initial value of the field to:

```php
<?php echo strftime("%d %b %Y",time()); ?>
```

Now we need to provide content for the Route drop-down box. We'll need to create a recordset for this. We'll want to provide full information about the route, so we'll also need to pull the training type and discipline for that route. The SQL for the query is:

```sql
SELECT 'routes'.'route_id',      'routes'.'route_name',      'type'.'type_name',
'discipline'.'disc_name'
FROM 'routes'
INNER JOIN 'type' ON ('routes'.'route_type' = 'type'.'type_id')
INNER JOIN 'discipline' ON ('type'.'type_discipline' = 'discipline'.'disc_id')
```

We can then bind the route_id as the value for the select menu and route_name as the label. We'll then need to manually add the extra detail. The code that is added for the select menu:

```php
do {
?>
          <option value="<?php echo $row_rstRouteInfo['route_id']?>"><?php echo
$row_rstRouteInfo['route_name']?></option>
          <?php
} while ($row_rstRouteInfo = mysql_fetch_assoc($rstRouteInfo));
```

needs to be altered to read:

```php
do {
?>
          <option value="<?php echo $row_rstRouteInfo['route_id']?>"><?php echo
$row_rstRouteInfo['route_name']?>
 (<?php echo $row_rstRouteInfo['disc_name']?> - <?php echo
$row_rstRouteInfo['type_name']?>)
</option>
          <?php
} while ($row_rstRouteInfo = mysql_fetch_assoc($rstRouteInfo));
```

The result is that the full information about the route is displayed in the menu:

The contents of the selDistance select menu will be list values of kilometers and meters. These are static options – which are the label of km with a value of km and a label of metres with a value of m:

```html
<select name="selDistance" id="selDistance">
  <option value="km">km</option>
  <option value="m">metres</option>
</select>
```

## Validate and Record

We should add a client -side *Form Validation* behavior to make sure that we are getting valid data from the form and then we can create our *Insert Record* server behavior:

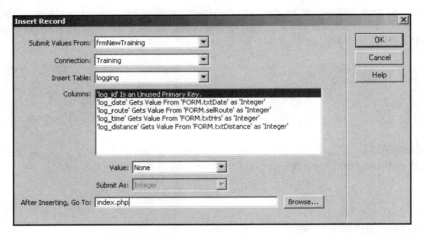

We will need to modify the code though, as we will need to convert the date into a standard format, calculate the total time spent from all three fields and convert the distance into a standard format as well.

This is the relevant code that the server behavior created:

```
if ((isset($HTTP_POST_VARS["MM_insert"])) && ($HTTP_POST_VARS["MM_insert"] ==
"frmNewTraining")) {
$insertSQL = sprintf("INSERT INTO logging (log_date, log_route, log_time,
log_distance) VALUES (%s, %s, %s, %s)",
                        GetSQLValueString($HTTP_POST_VARS['txtDate'], "int"),
                        GetSQLValueString($HTTP_POST_VARS['selRoute'], "int"),
                        GetSQLValueString($HTTP_POST_VARS['txtHrs'], "int"),
                        GetSQLValueString($HTTP_POST_VARS['txtDistance'], "int"));
```

We will be changing the code as follows:

```
$trainingDate = strtotime($HTTP_POST_VARS['txtDate']);
if (($trainingDate > 0) && (isset($HTTP_POST_VARS["MM_insert"])) &&
($HTTP_POST_VARS["MM_insert"] == "frmNewTraining")) {
  $totalTime = (GetSQLValueString($HTTP_POST_VARS['txtHrs'],"int") * 3600) +
(GetSQLValueString($HTTP_POST_VARS['txtMins'],"int") * 60) +
GetSQLValueString($HTTP_POST_VARS['txtSecs'],"int");
  if ($HTTP_POST_VARS['selDistance']=='m') {
    $totalDistance = $HTTP_POST_VARS['txtDistance'];
  } else {
    $totalDistance = $HTTP_POST_VARS['txtDistance'] * 1000;
  }
  $insertSQL = sprintf("INSERT INTO logging (log_date, log_route, log_time,
log_distance) VALUES (%s, %s, %s, %s)",
```

```
                    $trainingDate,
                    GetSQLValueString($HTTP_POST_VARS['selRoute'], "int"),
                    $totalTime,
                    $totalDistance);
```

The first thing to do is grab the string that the user has entered for the date and convert it into a Unix timestamp. I'm doing that before the `if` statement because we will use the `$trainingDate` variable in the `if` statement to make sure that the user has entered a valid date.

We then add `($trainingDate > 0)` to the `if` expression. If the user has entered an invalid date, `strtotime()` will return –1 and the rest of the query will not be executed.

Then we need to convert the total time in hours, minutes, and seconds into a standard format to store in the database. We can do this by converting it to its lowest common denominator, in this case seconds.

We then check to see if the user has entered their distance as kilometers or meters – if kilometers, then we convert it to meters to store in the database.

Once we have these values we can alter the line that builds the SQL statement to use our variables instead of the ones directly from the form.

We can then test the form. You will not see any results, as we have not yet added anything to display records from the logging table. To do that we add an HTML table with 6 columns – for the date, discipline, training type, route, time, and distance.

## Display results

In order to show results, we're going to need to retrieve that info from the database. Add a recordset to the page called `rstRecentAll`. We will grab the five most recent log entries for display. The SQL for the recordset `rstRecentAll` is:

```
SELECT 'logging'.'log_date', 'logging'.'log_route', 'logging'.'log_time',
'logging'.'log_distance', 'routes'.'route_name', 'type'.'type_name',
'discipline'.'disc_name'
FROM 'logging' INNER JOIN 'routes' ON ('logging'.'log_route' = 'routes'.'route_id')
INNER JOIN 'type' ON ('routes'.'route_type' = 'type'.'type_id') INNER JOIN
'discipline' ON ('type'.'type_discipline' = 'discipline'.'disc_id')
ORDER BY log_date DESC LIMIT 5
```

Add in *Dynamic Text* server behaviors to the second row of your table for the fields `log_date`, `disc_name`, `type_name`, `route_name`, `log_distance`, and `log_time`. Then select the entire row and add a *Repeat Region* server behavior for the `rstRecentAll` recordset.

If you look at the output on the screen you get the following:

| Date | Discipline | Training | Route | Distance | Time |
|------|-----------|----------|-------|----------|------|
| 1034805600 | Cycle | Trail | Tokai | 12000 | 2700 |
| 1034719200 | Cycle | Trail | Silvermine | 7000 | 2040 |

We'll need to convert the Unix timestamp into something readable by humans, the distance into kilometers or meters (depending on the distance) and the number of seconds taken into an hour, minute, second format.

The date is easy. We use the `strftime()` function and we can use the same format as we do in the date field of the form.

The distance is a simple matter of determining whether the distance is over a certain threshold – if it is then we convert it to kilometers, otherwise we leave it as meters.

The time is a tricky one. We could write an algorithm to convert seconds into hours, minutes, and seconds, but we can get around it by using the `gmstrftime()` function.

The current code to display the row is:

```
<tr>
   <td><?php echo $row_rstRecentAll['log_date']; ?></td>
   <td><?php echo $row_rstRecentAll['disc_name']; ?></td>
   <td><?php echo $row_rstRecentAll['type_name']; ?></td>
   <td><?php echo $row_rstRecentAll['route_name']; ?></td>
   <td><?php echo $row_rstRecentAll['log_distance']; ?></td>
   <td><?php echo $row_rstRecentAll['log_time']; ?></td>
</tr>
```

We'll change it to read as follows:

```
<tr>
   <td><?php echo strftime("%d %b %Y",$row_rstRecentAll['log_date']);
?></td>
   <td><?php echo $row_rstRecentAll['disc_name']; ?></td>
   <td><?php echo $row_rstRecentAll['type_name']; ?></td>
   <td><?php echo $row_rstRecentAll['route_name']; ?></td>
   <td><?php
        if ($row_rstRecentAll['log_distance'] > 2000) {
             echo ($row_rstRecentAll['log_distance'] / 1000).' km';
        } else {
             echo $row_rstRecentAll['log_distance'].' meters';
        }
        ?></td>
   <td><?php echo gmstrftime("%H:%M:%S",$row_rstRecentAll['log_time']);
?></td>
</tr>
```

The extra code means that the date is now formatted in a more human way. The distance is checked to see whether it is greater than 2000 meters – if it is then we return the distance in kilometers. Finally, we use `gmstrftime()` to produce the hour, minutes, and seconds.

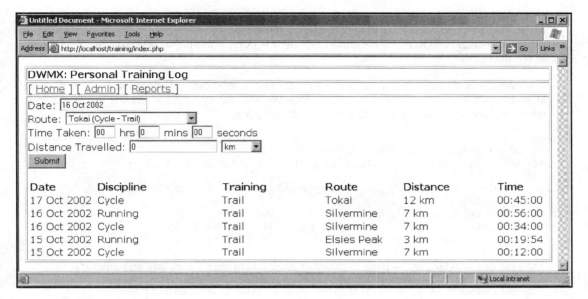

## reports.php

The last HTML page to create is the `reports.php` page. Here we will create some charts that you can use to monitor your progress from week to week.

As we mentioned in the *Requirements* section earlier in the chapter we will be using the JpGraph library to create our charts, so if you do not have it installed, you will have to do so before you continue. Instructions on installing JpGraph are included in *Chapter 12*.

For this section of the case study we're going to approach it a bit differently. Rather than stepping our way through the tasks involved in Dreamweaver, we'll be looking at the final code for the page and working our way through that.

Before we begin looking at it though, we should determine what we will be reporting on. We have logging information on a day-to-day basis, as a nice overview of how you're doing, and at the same time looking at some of the more advanced features of JpGraph, we'll be creating three pie charts that show the breakdown of your training by discipline for the last 7 days. Number of sessions, distance traveled, and time taken will be compared for each discipline.

The way that we will approach this is to create a recordset in the page that pulls together all the relevant information (distance covered, time taken, and number of sessions) for each discipline for the last 7 days, and then builds all of that information into an array. We'll then pass the array of data to a second script that will use that information to build the actual chart.

OK, on to the code itself.

```php
<?php require_once('Connections/Training.php'); ?>
```

**C1**

Within all of the pages that we created, Dreamweaver has included the `Connections/Training.php` script. This script contains all of the information that we need in order to connect to our database, as well as the code itself to make the connection. At this point in the page, we are already connected to our database.

The next piece of code is the result of a creating a simple recordset in Dreamweaver. The recordset is simply all the records in the `discipline` table. We will loop through the records in this recordset when we collect the logging information for each discipline.

```php
<?php
mysql_select_db($database_Training, $Training);
$query_rstAllDisciplines = "SELECT discipline.disc_id, discipline.disc_name FROM
discipline";
$rstAllDisciplines = mysql_query($query_rstAllDisciplines, $Training) or
die(mysql_error());
$row_rstAllDisciplines = mysql_fetch_assoc($rstAllDisciplines);
$totalRows_rstAllDisciplines = mysql_num_rows($rstAllDisciplines);
?>
```

Then the actual HTML of the page begins. We are working from a template and the code:

```
<!-- InstanceBegin template="/Templates/Train_layout.dwt.php"
codeOutsideHTMLIsLocked="false" -->
```

is used by Dreamweaver to determine which parts of the page are editable or not.

```html
<html><!-- InstanceBegin template="/Templates/Train_layout.dwt.php"
codeOutsideHTMLIsLocked="false" -->
<head>
<!-- InstanceBeginEditable name="doctitle" -->
<title>Untitled Document</title>
<!-- InstanceEndEditable -->
<meta http-equiv="Content-Type" content="text/html; charset=iso-8859-1">
<!-- InstanceBeginEditable name="head" --><!-- InstanceEndEditable -->
<link href="training.css" rel="stylesheet" type="text/css">
</head>
<body>
<table width="100%" border="1">
  <tr>
    <td><strong>DWMX: Personal Training Log</strong></td>
  </tr>
  <tr>
    <td>[ <a href="index.php" title="Main Page">Home</a> ] [ <a href="admin.php"
title="Administration Page">Admin</a>]
      [ <a href="reports.php" title="Reports and Charts">Reports </a>]</td>
  </tr>
  <tr>
```

This next area is where our editable region begins.

```
    <td><!-- InstanceBeginEditable name="ContentArea" -->
```

We're going to need to pass the script building the graph some sort of data to work with. In our case we need to pass quite a lot of information, so we will build an associative array of the information and pass that to the script. Like we saw in *Chapter 13* on Flash, we will encode the data so that it is passed correctly to the script building the actual chart. Since we want the contents of the $data array to remain intact for each iteration of the rstAllDisciplines recordset, we declare it at the beginning of the code block, before we begin looping through the rows in the recordset.

```php
<?php
    $data = array();
```

This do...while loop is stepping through the individual records in the disciplines table. Dreamweaver also created the portion of code immediately inside the loop, but Dreamweaver stuck it in at the top of the page where it normally keeps all the recordset code. This is the recordset that retrieves the distance and time information from the logging table. Since we will want to refresh the recordset for every record in the disciplines table, I have moved the code down to inside the loop and altered it to use the current discipline inside the WHERE clause. We did this on a few occasions in the admin page.

```php
do {
$currDisc_rstDiscLog = "1";
```

Set the $currDisc variable to the current discipline ID. $currDisc will be used later in our SQL query.

```php
$currDisc = $row_rstAllDisciplines['disc_id'];
if (isset($currDisc)) {
      $currDisc_rstDiscLog = (get_magic_quotes_gpc()) ? $currDisc :
addslashes($currDisc);
    }
$pastDate_rstDiscLog = "1";
```

We only want the last 7 days, so we use the handy strtotime() function to get the UNIX timestamp for a week ago:

```php
$pastDate = strtotime("-1 week");
if (isset($pastDate)) {
    $pastDate_rstDiscLog = (get_magic_quotes_gpc()) ? $pastDate :
addslashes($pastDate);
    }
mysql_select_db($database_Training, $Training);
```

Then we create the SQL query. The first portion of the SQL query is the SELECT clause. We are not interested in individual records here, we only want the totals. We're using the SQL SUM() and COUNT() functions to grab all the data for us in a single query. We'll grab the sum of all the time logged (in seconds), the sum of all the distances logged (in meters) and the number of times there were logs (using COUNT). At the same time that we SELECT them, we use the AS keyword to give the columns names that are easier to work with. This is not renaming anything in the database, it only applies to our current result set.

```
SELECT
  SUM('logging'.'log_time') AS 'totalTime',
  SUM('logging'.'log_distance') AS 'totalDiatance',
  COUNT('logging'.'log_id') AS 'totalSessions'
```

The next portion is where we are grabbing the data from:

```
FROM 'discipline'
```

and how this table is connected to the others. The `discipline` table relates to the `type` table, the `type` table relates to the `routes` table and the `routes` table relates to the `logging` table. By relating the tables together in the query we can limit the records returned from the `logging` table to only those that are within a specific discipline.

```
INNER JOIN 'type' ON ('discipline'.'disc_id' = 'type'.'type_discipline')
INNER JOIN 'routes' ON ('type'.'type_id' = 'routes'.'route_type')
INNER JOIN 'logging' ON ('routes'.'route_id' = 'logging'.'log_route')
```

Not only do we want to limit the discipline, but we want to also limit the records returned from the `logging` table to those logged within the last 7 days. The `%s` symbols are the placeholders for the PHP variables that store the current discipline ID and UNIX timestamp from 7 days ago. The entire SQL statement is built by the PHP `sprintf()` function in Dreamweaver and `%s` is the placeholder for a string.

```
WHERE   ('discipline'.'disc_id' =  %s)
AND   ('logging'.'log_date' >  %s)
```

Here is the code as it appears in the page:

```
        $query_rstDiscLog = sprintf("SELECT SUM('logging'.'log_time') AS
'totalTime', SUM('logging'.'log_distance') AS 'totalDistance',
COUNT('logging'.'log_id') AS 'totalSessions' FROM 'discipline' INNER JOIN 'type' ON
('discipline'.'disc_id' = 'type'.'type_discipline') INNER JOIN 'routes' ON
('type'.'type_id' = 'routes'.'route_type') INNER JOIN 'logging' ON
('routes'.'route_id' = 'logging'.'log_route') WHERE ('discipline'.'disc_id' =  %s )
AND ('logging'.'log_date' >  %s)", $currDisc_rstDiscLog,$pastDate_rstDiscLog);
        $rstDiscLog = mysql_query($query_rstDiscLog, $Training) or
die(mysql_error());
        $row_rstDiscLog = mysql_fetch_assoc($rstDiscLog);
        $totalRows_rstDiscLog = mysql_num_rows($rstDiscLog);
```

Now that we have the data, we can check to see whether there was anything logged for this discipline. If there are no sessions logged for this discipline, then we don't want to add it to the chart. The `totalSessions` column in the results will tell us this.

```
        if ($row_rstDiscLog['totalSessions'] > 0) {
```

Here is where we build the `$data` array.

The array will need to contain the time, the total distance covered, and the number of sessions trained for each discipline. We will also want to store labels for the slices of our chart as well as data for a legend for the charts.

The legend will be common for each of the pie charts, so this information can be kept at the top level of our array. We will then have three 'child' arrays – one for the time, a second for the distance, and the third for the sessions. Each of these arrays will contain the actual data, as well as the label.

The legend is made up of the current discipline:

```
                $data['legend'][count($data['legend'])] =
$row_rstAllDisciplines['disc_name'];
```

The `count($data['legend'])` syntax is simply determining how many elements are already in the array and then placing this entry as the next element.

The time portion of the array contains the time taken. For this discipline we add the total time to the data portion of the array and the label to the label portion. We create the label in the same way as we do on the index page, by using the `gmstrftime()` function to convert the seconds into hours, minutes, and seconds.

```
                $data['time']['data'][count($data['time']['data'])] =
$row_rstDiscLog['totalTime'];
                $data['time']['label'][count($data['time']['label'])] =
gmstrftime("%H:%M:%S",$row_rstDiscLog['totalTime']);
```

The distance portion of the array contains the total distance for this discipline and the label, built in the same way as the output on the index page.

```
                $data['distance']['data'][count($data['distance']['data'])] =
$row_rstDiscLog['totalDistance'];
                $data['distance']['label'][count($data['distance']['label'])] =
($row_rstDiscLog['totalDistance'] > 2000) ? ($row_rstDiscLog['totalDistance'] /
1000).' km' : $row_rstDiscLog['totalDistance'].' meters';
```

The sessions portion is simply the number of training sessions for that discipline, and the number can be passed as both the data and the label.

```
                $data['sessions']['data'][count($data['sessions']['data'])] =
$row_rstDiscLog['totalSessions'];
                $data['sessions']['label'][count($data['sessions']['label'])] =
strval($row_rstDiscLog['totalSessions']);
            }
        ?>
```

Once we are done with the first discipline, we loop around and go through that same process for the next discipline.

```
        <?php } while ($row_rstAllDisciplines =
mysql_fetch_assoc($rstAllDisciplines)); ?>
```

Now that the `$data` variable has been built, we can serialize it, URL-encode it and pass it as the argument to the `mkgraph.php` script.

```
            <img src="mkgraph.php?data=<?php echo urlencode(serialize($data)); ?>">
        <!-- InstanceEndEditable --></td>
    </tr>
</table>
</body>
<!-- InstanceEnd --></html>
<?php
mysql_free_result($rstAllDisciplines);

mysql_free_result($rstDiscLog);
?>
```

To illustrate what that code is doing, imagine it is using following data:

| Date | Discipline | Training | Route | Distance | Time |
|------|------------|----------|-------|----------|------|
| 17 Oct 2002 | Cycle | Trail | Tokai | 12 km | 00:45:00 |
| 16 Oct 2002 | Running | Trail | Elsies Peak | 3 km | 00:19:54 |
| 16 Oct 2002 | Cycle | Trail | Silvermine | 7 km | 00:34:00 |
| 16 Oct 2002 | Running | Trail | Silvermine | 7 km | 00:56:00 |
| 15 Oct 2002 | Cycle | Trail | Silvermine | 7 km | 00:12:00 |

We would have the following in our $data array:

- $data['legend'] will have two entries: Cycle and Running
- $data['time']['data'] will have two entries – the total time for cycling and the total time for running.
- $data['time']['label'] will have the two entries for the label of the slices – the formatted times from $data['time']['data'].
- $data['distance'] and $data['sessions'] are built in the same way.

You can see that the three cycling and two running sessions are correctly reported in the sessions portion of the array. If you add up the individual distances and times for each, you will see that they correspond as well. Now we can create the script to build the chart and we're all done.

## mkgraph.php

The first thing to do at the beginning of any script that is using JpGraph is to include the relevant files. We'll be building a pie chart, so we will need to include the base class jpgraph.php and the pie chart class jpgraph_pie.php. We put these classes into the Includes folder inside our site.

> *The details of these classes are all covered in the JpGraph documentation,*
> *which is available as a separate download from the web site:*
> *http://www.aditus.nu/jpgraph/jpdownload.php*

```php
<?php
include ("Includes/jpgraph.php");
include ("Includes/jpgraph_pie.php");
```

We then need to grab the data that has been passed to the script. We URL-decode it, strip out any slashes that PHP may have put in, and unserialize it. The `$data` associative array that we created in `reports.php` has now been reconstructed here.

```php
$data = unserialize(stripslashes(urldecode($_GET['data'])));
```

We can then create a new blank pie chart, and set some properties for it. We'll give it a drop shadow and a title so that we know what it is about.

```php
$chart = new PieGraph(600,300);
$chart->SetShadow();
$chart->title->Set("Training Breakdown by Discipline");
$chart->title->SetFont(FF_FONT1,FS_BOLD);
");
```

In this example we will be adding all three of the pie charts to the same image. Rather than create three separate images, it will be more efficient to put all three on the same chart.

When we create the plot of the time data, we pass the time data to the constructor function. In our case the data will be `$data['time']['data']`. We then create the legends and set the labels. All of this information has been passed through in the `$data` array. We will only need to set the legends once for all of the plots. To give the charts a nice earthy feel, we set them to 'sand'.

```php
$timePlot = new PiePlot($data['time']['data']);
$timePlot->SetLegends($data['legend']);
$timePlot->SetLabels($data['time']['label']);
$timePlot->SetTheme('sand');
```

We then set the size and center of the plot. The center is the important piece, and you will need to tweak this setting when laying out multiple plots in the same chart. Otherwise you may get plots overlapping each other.

```php
$timePlot->SetSize(0.2);
$timePlot->SetCenter(0.15,0.52);
```

We then set up the labels and captions for the plot:

```php
$timePlot->value->SetFont(FF_FONT1,FS_BOLD);
$timePlot->value->SetColor('black');
$timePlot->SetLabelPos(0.65);
$timePlot->title->Set('Time');
```

And explode the slices by 5 pixels:

```php
$timePlot->ExplodeAll(5);
```

and put a shadow on the plot itself.

```
$timePlot->SetShadow();
```

That's done for the time plot, we can now do exactly the same for the distance and sessions. We'll be setting similar information for these, but just grabbing the information from a different part of the $data array. The parts that will change are the settings for the center point of the graph.

```
$distPlot = new PiePlot($data['distance']['data']);
$distPlot->SetLabels($data['distance']['label']);
$distPlot->SetTheme('sand');

$distPlot->SetSize(0.2);
$distPlot->SetCenter(0.45,0.52);

$distPlot->value->SetFont(FF_FONT1,FS_BOLD);
$distPlot->value->SetColor('black');
$distPlot->SetLabelPos(0.65);
$distPlot->title->Set('Distance');
$distPlot->ExplodeAll(5);

$distPlot->SetShadow();

$sessPlot = new PiePlot($data['sessions']['data']);
$sessPlot->value->SetFormat('%s');
$sessPlot->value->Show();
$sessPlot->SetLabels($data['sessions']['label']);
$sessPlot->SetTheme('sand');

$sessPlot->SetSize(0.2);
$sessPlot->SetCenter(0.75,0.52);

$sessPlot->value->SetFont(FF_FONT1,FS_BOLD);
$sessPlot->value->SetColor('black');
$sessPlot->SetLabelPos(0.65);
$sessPlot->title->Set('Sessions');
$sessPlot->ExplodeAll(5);

$sessPlot->SetShadow();
```

Once we have created all three plots we can add them to the chart and output it to the browser.

```
$chart->Add($timePlot);
$chart->Add($distPlot);
$chart->Add($sessPlot);

$chart->Stroke();
?>
```

For our sample data that we looked at earlier the graph that the script will generate is:

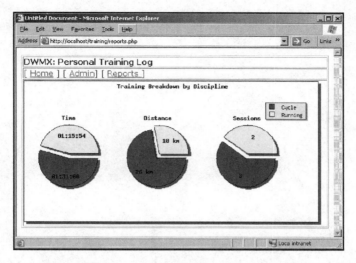

If we go and add another discipline, we should see the charts add that additional data:

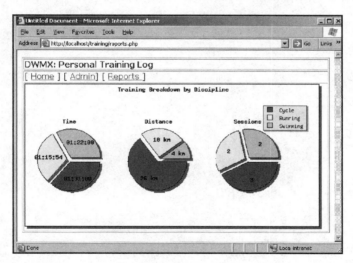

# Summary

In this chapter we have taken a look at Dreamweaver, MySQL, PHP, and graphing and how we can pull it all together to create an interesting application.

By combining elements of Dreamweaver MX templates, server behaviors, hand coding PHP, and third party classes, we saw how we could use them to complement one another in achieving our programming goal.

# Case Study 2

Author: Gareth Downes-Powell

# A Content Management System

In this case study, we create a custom Content Management System, that makes it easy to add, edit, and update web site content over the Internet through a standard web browser.

We examine the CMS structure, and look at creating different types of documents, for displaying different types of data. The whole web site is styled using CSS for both layout and formatting. An image upload function is included so that images can easily be added to the dynamic content via a web browser.

Although this is a complete, working system, it will be very easy for you to add your own custom information types or expand the system for your own purposes. Many of the functions and classes used in this case study will come in useful in similar projects, and the whole CMS System is created around PHP classes, meaning that the code can very easily be reused.

## A Content Management System (CMS)

A CMS allows you to easily organize information, such as the pages of a web site. Small web sites are easy to update: you create the new page, upload it to your server, and then manually add a link to the document in the main menu. Dreamweaver MX can ease this process, through the use of templates for the site, and the creation of site menus in library files, so if you make a change it's updated throughout the site automatically. However, when you work with a larger site, organizing the information and site structure can start turning into a real headache.

Another problem arrises if users want to update the site themselves. This can cause problems, as the user probably doesn't have a copy of Dreamweaver MX, and the editor they use could break the code or functionality of the site.

A good CMS solves all these problems, by separating the entire site content from the actual code that is used to display the pages. The data itself can be stored separately, and then when a page is viewed, the relevant data automatically inserted. As all the pages viewed by the users are dynamically generated, along with the site menu system, data can be easily added and changed, with the changes reflected instantly, and without having to re-upload all your pages.

Users can only change the data, and don't have access to the back-end code, so there's no chance of any accidents occurring. Alternatively, you may want to use the CMS for your own site. You can update your site from anywhere, using a standard web browser, and can keep your site up to date from your office, or using a public access PC in a hotel, for instance, without needing template files for the site, and so on.

# Defining the CMS

In this section we're going to plan the CMS, and set the goals that the system should achieve. Planning the site before we start helps to ensure that it will do everything we want it to do, and helps to keep continuity throughout the site.

- Dynamic Menu System – The Menu System will be completely dynamic, so that it can be easily altered, without having to change the actual page code or uploading the files again.

- Ease of Use – The system needs to be easy to use. Adding and editing content must be possible using a web browser, so the site can be edited from anywhere with web access available. Users should be able to add content as text and format it with basic HTML.

- Ready Adaptability – The CMS system needs to be easily adaptable. To do this we'll separate the back end totally from the front end. We're also going to make the system modular, using PHP classes. This means that, in the future, new sections can be easily "bolted on" to the existing site, with a minimum of code needed to link in the new section. CSS (Cascading Style Sheets) will be used for the layout and formatting, so that, in the future, the layout and formatting can be changed to give a completely different style to the site, without having to change the actual PHP code.

- Able to Handle Different Article Types – As this is a fairly simple example, we're going to create two different document types, which cover a multitude of different uses. We'll start with two types, one for news articles and one for full articles.

# Planning the CMS

The whole CMS is going to be constructed using PHP Classes, which we looked at in *Chapter 4*. This allows us to build the CMS in a series of modules, with each module consisting of a class that contains all the code necessary for that module. The modules can thus be easily reused in other projects, and also extended using extra modules in the future, with minimum adjustments to the existing code.

We will have a number of PHP pages that will contain the HTML forms necessary to input the data, and to display output from the PHP Classes. A diagram of the complete system is shown here:

As shown in the diagram above, there are two ends to the system, a back-end administration system to allow articles to be added and edited, and the front end which displays the dynamic information to the user. The shaded area of the diagram shows the PHP classes that are called by the front end and back end pages to generate the HTML for the dynamic pages.

A single page, `page.php`, is used to display the output to the end user, and displays the HTML generated by the PHP `createPage` class.

The front and back ends have separate stylesheets, so that the look of both can be totally different. This makes it clear to a user whereabouts they are in the system. For this example, the back end of the CMS will be styled in blue, and the front end of the site in green.

## The PHP Classes

There are two classes for each of the document types and for the menu, one to perform administration tasks, and the other to perform display tasks. At the hub of the CMS is the `Database` class. This contains a number of useful functions to allow us to connect to the database, and easily execute SQL statements with the minimum of code.

To save repetition of code, we define all the database functions in the `Database` class. All of the other classes that require reading or writing to the database will extend this class, so the database functions are available to the other classes without having to retype the same functions for each class, as each child class inherits the functions of its parent class.

We also have a `page` class, which coordinates all of the front end display classes, to build the correct HTML for the required page.

C2

387

# PHP Requirements

The only extra PHP library that we need for this CMS is Exif, the **Exchangeable Image File Format** extension, which allows the conversion of image files between formats. This needs to be compiled into PHP using the compile option `—enable-exif` if you're running PHP on Linux. We need `exif` so that we can use the `getimagesize()` command later on in the CMS. No libraries need to be installed, it just needs to be enabled. Exif is included in the Windows binaries, but is not enabled by default. To enable it, open your `php.ini` and uncomment the line that reads ";`extension=php_exif.dll`" by removing the semicolon from the start of the line.

The `getimagesize()` function will determine the size of any JPG image file and return the dimensions along with the file type and a `height` and `width` text string to be used inside a normal HTML `<img>` tag.

For more information see *http://www.php.net/manual/en/function.getimagesize.php*.

# Creating the Site Structure

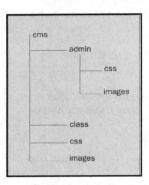

To start creating the site, create the following directories under a main `cms` directory, as shown in the diagram.

Next we'll create the database in which we'll be storing the dynamic data.

# Creating the New Database

Create a new MySQL database, called `glasshausCMS`. You can do this by using a MySQL administration tool such as PHPMyAdmin (*www.phpmyadmin.net*), or you can just add the new database using the MySQL client command-line application, using the command:

```
CREATE DATABASE glasshausCMS;
```

You can then switch to the new `glasshausCMS` database, using the SQL command:

```
USE glasshausCMS;
```

This makes our new `glasshausCMS` database the current database to be worked on.

You will also need to create a new user, who can connect to the `glasshausCMS` database using the host `localhost`. In this case study the user created is called `cms`. You need to be the root MySQL administrator in order to add this user. In MySQL Client, use the following commands:

```
USE MySQL;
```

This switches to the `MySQL` database, which contains all the MySQL user settings. Now enter:

```
insert into user (Host, User, Password, Select_priv, Insert_priv, Update_priv,
Delete_priv, Drop_priv) values('localhost', 'cms', password('password'), 'Y', 'Y',
'Y', 'Y', 'Y');
```

This command adds the new user called `cms` to the `user` table that MySQL employs to manage its users, with permission to connect to the MySQL host `localhost`, with the username `cms`, and the permission to execute all the necessary database operations. Change ('`password`') to the password you require for this user. Finally we tell MySQL to use the new user information with the command:

```
FLUSH PRIVILEGES;
```

## Creating the Database Table – tblmainmenu

As the menu will be generated dynamically, the data for the menu options are held in the database, in a table called `tblmainmenu`, which has the fields: `id`, `label`, `position`, and `link`.

| Field Name | Field Data Type | Extra Options |
|---|---|---|
| id | integer (8) | Auto Increment, Primary Key |
| label | varchar (50) | |
| position | integer (8) | |
| link | varchar (250) | |

This table can be created using a MySQL administration tool, or using MySQL Client with the following command.

```
create table tblmainmenu (id integer(8)  auto_increment primary key, label
varchar(50), position integer(8), link varchar(250));
```

## Creating the Database Table - tblnews

Our news table will have five fields, which are: `id`, `title`, `author`, `date`, and `body`. Create the fields with the following parameters:

| Field Name | Data Type | Extra Options |
|---|---|---|
| id | Integer (8) | Primary Key, Auto Increment |
| title | Varchar 150 | |
| author | Varchar 150 | |
| date | Date | |
| Body | Medium Text | |

To create the table using MySQL Client, you can use the following statement.

```
create table tblnews (id integer(8)  auto_increment primary key, title varchar(150),
author varchar(150), date date, body mediumtext);
```

Content Management System

389

## Creating the Database Table – tblarticles

| Field Name | Data Type | Extra Options |
|---|---|---|
| id | Integer (8) | Primary Key, Auto Increment |
| title | Varchar (150) | |
| author | Varchar(25) | |

The `id` is used to give each article a unique number, and is filled in automatically by MySQL. The `title` field holds the article title, the `author` field holds the author name, and the `date` field holds the article date. The `body` field holds the article itself. Finally we have the `menuID` field that is used to store the ID of the menu option the article is linked to.

To create the table using MySQL Client, you need to use the following statement.

```
create table tblarticles (id integer(8)  auto_increment primary key, title
varchar(150), author varchar(25), date date, body longtext, menuID integer(8));
```

# Creating the Database Class

As we mentioned above, the `Database` class is at the hub of the CMS, and almost all the other classes are extensions of this class.

Create a new PHP page, and save it in the class directory as `database.php`. Switch into *Code View* in Dreamweaver MX, and delete all the HTML code that Dreamweaver MX has automatically generated. As this is a PHP class, the file will only contain PHP code. The class is never displayed in a browser, so no HTML is needed.

## Creating the Database Class Structure

Add the following code to the page, to create the basic `database` class structure and save it in the `/cms/class/` folder.

```php
<?php
#####################################################
# CMS Database Class                                #
#####################################################

class Database {
    // Database Connection Variables
    var $dbName = "glasshausCMS";
    var $dbHost = "localhost";
    var $dbUser = "cms";
    var $dbPass = "password";

    function Database(){

    }
?>
```

This creates the basic structure for the `database` class, ready for us to populate with the actual functions.

We also assign a number of variables that contain the information needed to connect to the MySQL database, namely the database name, the MySQL host, user name and password. We can then refer to these variables from any of the functions in this class. Substitute the value you earlier assigned to your user `cms`, in place of the word "`password`", above.

Now that we have the basic structure we can start to populate the class with our functions, which will perform the database operations.

## DB_databaseConnect()

The first function that we use allows us to connect to the MySQL database, using the `mysql_connect()` function, using the user variables we set up in the `database` class structure. If the connection to the database fails, then the `die()` command is executed and the script stops and returns an error message. Once a connection is created to the database, we next use the `mysql_select_db()` command to set the active database as `glasshausCMS`. Again we use the die statement if the `mysql_select_db()` function fails, to stop the script from running.

The code for this function is shown below, and needs to be added into the basic class structure.

```
function DB_databaseConnect(){
    // Connect to the MySQL Server and Select the database
    $dbLink = mysql_connect($this->dbHost, $this->dbUser, $this->dbPass);
    if (!$dbLink)
        die ("Database Class: Couldn't connect to MySQL Server");
    mysql_select_db($this->dbName, $dbLink)
        or die ("Database Class: Couldn't open Database");
    return $dbLink;
}
```

Finally this function returns a value, `$dbLink`, which is the MySQL connection variable, and refers to the newly opened database connection.

## DB_executeQuery($query,$dbLink)

This function takes an SQL Query, for example "`SELECT * FROM myTable`", and the database connection variable returned from the `DB_databaseConnect()` function. It then executes the SQL query, and returns a pointer to MySQL result set obtained. If the SQL query fails, then we stop the script using the `die` command, and print an error message.

Add the function below to our class structure, below the `DB_databaseConnect()` function.

```
function DB_executeQuery($query,$dbLink){
    // Execute an SQL query passed to this function
    $dbResult = mysql_query($query, $dbLink)
        or die ("Database Class: MySQL Error: " . mysql_error() );
    return $dbResult;
}
```

## DB_getRecordID()

This function returns the ID number of the record that was last inserted into the database, using the `mysql_insert_id()` command. Add the code below to the class.

```
function DB_getRecordID(){
    // After a Record has been inserted, get ID number
    $id = mysql_insert_id();
    return $id;
}
```

## DB_getRecords($dbResult)

This function takes a pointer to a MySQL result set (as returned from `DB_executeQuery()`), and returns the number of records. Again, add the function below to the `database` class.

```
function DB_getRecords($dbResult){
    // Passed a MySQL result variable, returns number of records
    $rows = mysql_num_rows($dbResult);
    return $rows;
}
```

## DB_closeDatabase($dbLink)

This function takes a variable `$dbLink`, which is a reference to an open MySQL connection, and closes the connection to the database. Add the following function to the class.

```
function DB_closeDatabase($dbLink){
    // Close MySQL Connection
    mysql_close($dbLink);
}
```

## DB_date2mysql($date)

Although this function and the next one are not actually database commands, they are useful in this class, as they work with the date format that MySQL uses to store dates in the database.

This date function, converts a date in US Format (mm/dd/yyyy) into the MySQL date format (yyyy-mm-dd), which can then be stored in a MySQL date field. The code for the function is as follows:

```
function DB_date2mysql($date){
    // Change a date from US Format (dd/mm/yyyy) to MySQL format
    $temp = explode("/",$date);
    $date = $temp[2] . "-" . $temp[0] . "-" . $temp[1];
    return $date;
}
```

This function doesn't use any PHP date commands, instead we use the `explode()` function. Imagine that we have the date 12/03/2002, which is in the US date format. We can use the `explode()` function to split the date by the "/", and put the results into an array, `$temp`. We can now rebuild these parts of the date in a different order, and add a "-" to separate each part.

$date will now equal yyyy-mm-dd, which is 2002-12-03, which is a valid MySQL date format. If you need to convert a date which is in a different format, for example UK (dd/mm/yyyy), you can simply rearrange the elements of the $temp[] array in the appropriate order.

## DB_mysql2date($date)

This is the last function in the class. It does the reverse of the DB_date2mysql() function above, and converts a date from the MySQL date format to the US date format.

```
function DB_mysql2date($date){
    // Change a date from MySQL (yyyy-mm-dd) to US Format
    $temp = explode("-",$date);
    $date = $temp[1] . "/" . $temp[2] . "/" . $temp[0];
    return $date;
}
```

The function explodes the date into an array again, this time using the "-" separator that MySQL uses. It then rearranges the parts of the date, and rebuilds them into the US date format. We use this function to read a MySQL date from the database, and display it on the screen.

Save the class; we have now entered all the necessary functions. Don't forget to add a final brace to close the class.

## Using the database Class

Now we have the database class completed, we're going to look at how it can be used. As a simple example, take a look at the code below.

```
<?php
    require_once("database.php");

    $database = new Database();

    $dbLink = $database->DB_databaseConnect();
    $query = "SELECT * FROM users";
    $result = $database->DB_executeQuery($query, $dbLink);
    $numRecords = $database->DB_getRecords($result);
    $database->DB_closeDatabase($dbLink);
?>
```

First we include the class file database.php. We then instantiate a new Database object, referenced through the $database variable.

We then open a new connection to the database using the DB_databaseConnect() function, then we set up and execute a simple query, and store the result in the variable $result. Next, we execute the DB_getRecords() function, passing it the result from the previous query. $numRecords now contains the number of records returned by the select query. Lastly we close the database connection.

We can use this code to execute any SQL statement, be it a SELECT query, as shown above, or an INSERT query, to insert data into the database, or a DELETE query, to delete certain records. We will look at using these later on in the case study.

While this class forms the hub of this system, feel free to use it in your own projects, as it is very useful. It cuts down on the amount of code you need to access your database. You may wish to turn it into a Dreamweaver code snippet for this purpose.

# Administration Area CSS Styles

As well as styling the text, we also use CSS to lay out the web page. This separates the layout and look of the site from the code, so that it can be changed independently of the code in future.

## Creating the Layout Stylesheet

The first stylesheet we are going to create is the one that lays out the web site. This is very simple. Create a new CSS file, and enter the following code.

```css
/* Styles for the Document Body */
BODY {
    margin-bottom : 0px;
    margin-left : 0px;
    margin-right : 0px;
    margin-top : 0px;
    background: #ffffff;
}

/* Styles for the Main Header Bar */
#header {
    margin-left: 0px;
    margin-right: 0px;
    height: 80px;
    background-color: #6699cc;
}

/* Create the Left Column */
#leftColumn {
    position: absolute;
    left: 5px;
    top: 80px;
    width: 200px;
}

/* Creating the Main Content Area */
#mainContent {
    margin-left: 210px;
    margin-right: 20px;
    margin-top:10px;
    background : #FFFFFF;
    padding-left : 20px;
    padding-bottom : 10px;
    border-left : thin dotted #6699cc;
}
```

Save this file as adminLayout.css in the /cms/admin/css folder that we created earlier.

All of these styles (apart from the BODY style) are used with HTML <div> tags, which we'll see in the next section, when we actually start creating the administration pages. A blue header bar will contain the site logo. The leftColumn style creates a column running down the left side of the screen, in which we place the *Administration* menu. The mainContent style sets up the rest of the page, which will be used for displaying content. Since leftColumn is fixed at 200 pixels, the rest of the screen width is occupied by mainContent, which automatically expands to fill the screen.

## Creating the adminStyles Stylesheet

Now that we have our main page layout styles defined, we're next going to create another stylesheet, which is used for formatting rather than page layout. Create a new CSS file, and save it as adminStyles.css, in the /cms/admin/css directory we created earlier. Add the following styles to the file:

```css
/* Default Link Styles */
a {
    color: #6699cc;
}
a:link {
    color: #6699cc;
    text-decoration : none;
}
a:visited {
    color: #6699cc;
    text-decoration : none;
}
a:hover {
    color: #999999;
}
a:active {
}

/* Clear Styles */
.clear {
    clear: both
}

/*Admin Menu Styles */
#adminMenu{
    padding-top: 10px;
    padding-bottom: 10px;
    padding-left: 10px;
    padding-right: 10px;
    margin-left: 20px;
    margin-right: 20px;
    margin-top: 20px;
    margin-bottom: 20px;
    height: 60px;
    background-color : #E2ECF5;
}
.adminMenuLink{
    font-family : Arial, Helvetica, sans-serif;
    font-size : 12px;
}
```

```css
.adminMenuHeader{
    font-family : Arial, Helvetica, sans-serif;
    font-size : 12px;
    color : #000000;
}
/* Menu Styles */
#menu{
    padding-left:10px;
    background-color : #F4F4F4;
}
#menuSpacer{
    background-color : #F4F4F4;
    height: 20px;
}
#mainMenuRow{
    margin-top:10px;
}
#subMenuRow{
    padding-left:20px;
    margin-top:10px;
}

/* Content Border */
#editableContentBorder{
    border : thin solid #6699CC;
    height:100px;
}

/* Form Styles */
#formBorder{
    margin-left: 20px;
    margin-right: 20px;
    margin-top: 20px;
    margin-bottom: 20px;        }
#formLeft{
    text-align : right;
    float : left;
    width: 150px;
    height: 30px;
}
#formRight{
    float: left;
    height: 30px;
}
.formHeader{
    font-family : Arial, Helvetica, sans-serif;
    font-size : 12px;
}
.formText{
    font-family : Arial, Helvetica, sans-serif;
    font-size : 12px;
}
.formButton{
    padding-left: 10px;
    padding-right: 10px;
}
```

```css
/* News List Styles */
#newsListBlock{
    margin-left: 20px;
    margin-right: 20px;
    margin-top: 20px;
    margin-bottom: 20px;
    background-color : #F1F1F1;
}
.newsList{
    font-family: Arial, Helvetica, sans-serif;
    font-size: 10px;
    color: #6699cc;
    margin-left: 5px;
    margin-right: 5px;
}
.newsCurrentText{
    font-family: Arial, Helvetica, sans-serif;
    font-size: 10px;
    color: #000000;
}
/* Article Styles */
#articleMenuSelect{
    width: 400px;
    background-color : #E2ECF5;
    padding-top: 10px;
    padding-bottom: 10px;
    padding-left: 10px;
    padding-right: 10px;
}
/* Left Blue Menu Select */
#articleMenu{
    background-color : #E2ECF5;
    padding-top: 10px;
    height: 60px;
    margin-left: 20px;
    margin-right: 20px;
    margin-top: 20px;
    margin-bottom: 20px;
}
/* Left Gray Article List*/
#articleListBlock{
    margin-left: 20px;
    margin-right: 20px;
    margin-top: 20px;
    margin-bottom: 20px;
    padding-left: 10px;
    padding-top: 5px;
    padding-bottom: 5px;
    background-color : #F1F1F1;
}
/* Left Article listings */
.articleList{
    font-family: Arial, Helvetica, sans-serif;
    font-size: 10px;
    color: #6699CC;
}
```

All styles used for formatting blocks such as a menu are defined with a #, and are of the CSS ID type, for example #admin which creates a blue block, 60 pixels high. Styles which are defined with a ".", for example .articleList above, refer to formatting for text, and are the normal CSS class types.

The styles listed above are for all the *Administration* pages, and are split into sections for the menu, article and news sections of the back-end administration system.

Make sure you save the file before you continue, so that you don't lose the CSS styles you just defined. The screenshots below show how the styles defined above actually look in a browser:

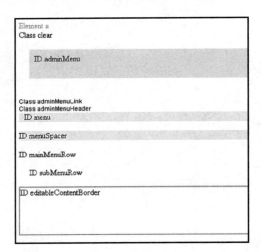
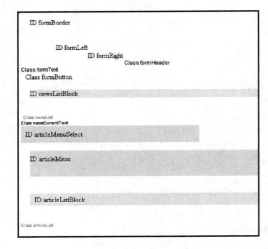

Now the stylesheets have been created, we can move on, and start to create the actual administration pages themselves.

# Creating the Menu Administration Section

It's logical to do the *Menu Administration* section first, as the other administration sections allow us to link the document types to the menu.

## Creating the Menu Administration Page

We're now going to create the page that the administrators will use to add and edit the menu items. This page is fairly simple, and contains the HTML form that the administrators use to add and edit the menu items, and HTML created by the PHP class that we're going to create next.

First, create a new PHP page, and save it as editAdminMenu.php, in the cms/admin/ directory. Alternatively, you can download the code from the accompanying web site. If you are creating the page yourself, enter the following code in *Code View*.

```
<? require_once("../class/adminMenu.php");?>
<?php $adminMenu = new adminMenu(); ?>
<!DOCTYPE HTML PUBLIC "-//W3C//DTD HTML 4.01 Transitional//EN">
<html>
<head>
<title>Update Site Menu</title>
<meta http-equiv="Content-Type" content="text/html; charset=iso-8859-1">
<link href="css/adminLayout.css" rel="stylesheet" type="text/css">
<link href="css/adminStyles.css" rel="stylesheet" type="text/css">
</head>
<body>
<div id="header"><img src="images/adminlogo.gif" width="220" height="80"
alt="logo"></div>
<div id="leftColumn">
  <?php echo $adminMenu->adminMenu; ?>
</div>
<div id="mainContent">
  <div id="editableContentBorder">
    <div id="formBorder">
      <form name="form1" method="post" action="<?php echo $_SERVER['PHP_SELF']; ?>">
        <?php echo $adminMenu->userMenu; ?>
        <?php echo $adminMenu->moveButtons; ?>
        <br>
        <div align="center">
          <div class="formHeader" >Menu Item Label:</div>
          <div>
            <input name="label" type="text" id="date"
            value="<?php echo $adminMenu->label; ?>" size="50" maxlength="50">
              </div>
          <br>
          <div class="formHeader">Menu Item Link:</div>
          <div>
            <input name="link" type="text" id="date"
            value="<?php echo $adminMenu->link; ?>" size="50" maxlength="250">
          </div>
        </div>
        <?php echo $adminMenu->adminButtons; ?>
      </form>
      <div class="clear"></div>
    </div>
  </div>
</div>
</body>
</html>
```

In the header `<div>`, we have inserted a logo that is 220 pixels wide and 80 pixels high. The width isn't too important, but the graphic height should match the height of the header section set in the `layout.css` stylesheet.

You will notice that there are a number of PHP functions in the HTML, to open the `adminMenu` class that we're going to create. The `adminMenu` class will set variables containing HTML that is displayed using the PHP commands above, to create the dynamic sections of the page.

Once you have added the code, switch back to the *Design View*, and it should be the same as the accompanying screenshot.

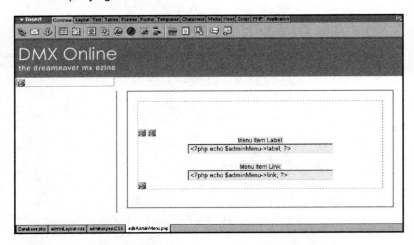

You can see that with a small amount of CSS code, we have laid out the entire screen, including the form-field and textfields where the site administrators will enter or edit the menu data.

Save this file. Next we'll create the actual PHP class that provides the back end that drives this page.

## The adminMenu.php Class

Open a new PHP page, switch to *Code View*, and then delete all of the existing HTML code, as we won't need it for this page. Save the page as `adminMenu.php` in the `cms/class/` directory. Again you can download this file from the accompanying web site, if you don't want to type all the code yourself.

Add the following to create the basic structure for the `adminMenu` class.

```php
<?php
require_once("database.php");
####################################################
# CMS Admin Menu Class                             #
####################################################
# Inherits
#     DB_date2mysql($date) : DB_mysql2date($date) : DB_databaseConnect()
#     DB_executeQuery($query,$Link) : DB_getRecordID()
#     DB_getRecords($Result)  :   DB_closeDatabase($Link)

class adminMenu extends Database{    var $menuLink;
    var $adminMenu;
    var $userMenu;
    var $moveButtons;
    var $adminButtons;
    var $menuArray;
    var $currentPosition;
    var $numRecords;
    var $label;
    var $link;
```

```
       function adminMenu(){
            $this->menuLink = $this->DB_databaseConnect();
            $this->performActions();
            $this->createAdminMenu();
            $this->createUserMenu();
            $this->createMoveButtons();
            $this->createAdminButtons();
            $this->DB_closeDatabase($this->menuLink);
       }

?>
```

This creates the basic structure for the class, and you will see that it extends the `database` class we created earlier. This means that all the functions we created in the `database` class, are also available to this class.

The function `adminMenu()` is the class constructor function, and is run when a new instance of the class is created. First the `adminMenu()` function creates a new connection to the MySQL database, using the inherited function `DB_databaseConnect()`. Once the database connection is open, we run a series of functions which we are going to create in the next sections, finally the database connection is closed using the inherited `DB_closeDatabase()` function. We store the pointer to the database link in the class variable `$menuLink`, so that we can refer to the database connection link in any of the class functions.

Before we start looking at the rest of the functions, have a look at the screenshot below, which is what the `menuadmin.php` page will look like when we're finished. By referring to this, you'll be able to see what the output looks like and what's being referred to as we create the functions we'll need.

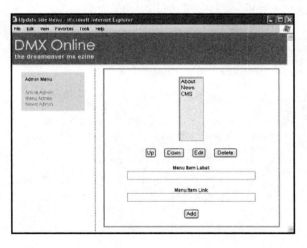

## performActions()
This is the first function to add to the `adminMenu` class. The code to add a menu item is shown overleaf.

```
function performActions(){
    if($_POST['Up']=='Up'){
        $this->changePosition("up");
    }
    if($_POST['Down']=='Down'){
        $this->changePosition("down");
    }
    if($_POST['Edit']=='Edit'){
        $this->editMenuItem();
    }
    if($_POST['Delete']=='Delete'){
        $this->deleteMenuItem();
    }
    if($_POST['Add']=='Add'){
        $this->addMenuItem();
    }
    if($_POST['Update']=='Update'){
        $this->updateMenuItem();
    }
}
```

This function is called by the constructor class, and checks to see if the form on the adminMenu.php page has been submitted. You can see in the previous screenshot of the final output, that there are a number of buttons. These are form *Submit* buttons, which have the same name as their label. Each one will post the form when clicked.

As only one of the buttons could be used to submit the form, we check the form data until we find the *submit* button that was pressed. We then run a particular function to process the form data, depending on which button was used to submit the form.

## createMenuArray()

The next function we're going to create reads in all the records from the tblmainmenu table we created earlier. Add the following code to the class.

```
function createMenuArray(){
    $query = "SELECT id,label,position,link FROM tblmainmenu ORDER BY position
ASC";
    $result = $this->DB_executeQuery($query,$this->menuLink);
    $this->numRecords = $this->DB_getRecords($result);
    for($count=1;$count<=$this->numRecords;$count++){
        $row = mysql_fetch_assoc($result);
        $this->menuArray[$count] = $row['id'];
            if($row['id'] == $_POST['menu']){
            $this->currentPosition = $row['position'];
        }
    }
}
```

First we create a SELECT statement to read in all records from the tblmainmenu table, ordered by the value of the position field, in ascending order. We then execute the query, putting the pointer to the MySQL result set in $result. Next we use the inherited function DB_getRecords($result) to find out how many records there are in the result set returned by the SQL query.

Now that we have the number of records, we use a `for` loop to cycle through every record returned by our SQL statement. At each cycle of the loop we put the complete record in an array, `$row`, where the index for each value is the field name, using the `mysql_fetch_assoc()` function, which we pass the pointer to the result set which is held in `$result`. Next we read the record `id` field from the `$row` array, and place it in a new global array called `menuArray`, using the current value of `$count` as its index. Next we see if the POST data (which is created when a form is submitted), contains a value for menu, which is the select box from where the user has chosen a menu option. If there is a value for menu, it will hold the `id` of the menu item that has been selected. We then compare this value to the current record `id`, and if it matches we set the global variable `currentPosition` to the position in the menu of the current record.

We now have the menu items in the correct order that they are to be displayed held in the array `$menuArray`.

## changePosition($direction)

This function is called when the user pushes the up or down buttons, to move a menu item up or down the menu list. First `performActions` checks to see if either of the buttons have been pushed, and if they have it calls this function, passing it the direction in which the menu item is to move that is, up or down. Add the following code to the class.

```
function changePosition($direction){
    $selected = $_POST['menu'];
    $this->createMenuArray();
    $currentPosition = $this->currentPosition;
    if($direction == "up"){
        $swapPosition = $currentPosition - 1;
    }
    if($direction == "down"){
        $swapPosition = $currentPosition + 1;
    }
    if(($swapPosition > 0) && ($swapPosition <= $this->numRecords)){
        $query = sprintf("UPDATE tblmainmenu SET position ='%s' WHERE id = '%s'",
                        $swapPosition, $this->menuArray[$currentPosition]);
        $result = $this->DB_executeQuery($query,$this->menuLink);
        $query = sprintf("UPDATE tblmainmenu SET position ='%s' WHERE id = '%s'",
                        $currentPosition, $this->menuArray[$swapPosition]);
        $result = $this->DB_executeQuery($query,$this->menuLink);
    }
}
```

First we read the value of menu from the PHP `$_POST[]` array. If this is set it will hold the ID of the menu item to move. Next we call the `createMenuArray()` function that we previously created, to populate the array `menuArray` with all the menu items in the `tblmainmenu` table in their correct order. The `createMenuArray()` function also populates the global class variable `$currentPosition` with the position of the currently selected menu item, which we copy into the `$currentPosition` variable.

We now check which direction to move the menu item, either up or down. If it's up (that is, towards the top of the screen) we subtract one from the current position to get its new position, and if the direction is down we add one to find the new position, which we store in the variable `$swapPosition`.

To explain how we move the item up or down, we'll look at an example $menuArray and imagine it contains the following data.

| menuArray index | Menu item id | Position ( for reference ) |
|---|---|---|
| $menuArray[1] | 3 ( About ) | 1 |
| $menuArray[2] | 5 ( News ) | 2 |
| $menuArray[3] | 6 (CMS) | 3 |

Now, if the currently selected menu item is 5, which is position 2 in the menu, and we wanted to move it up the menu, its new position will be 2 − 1 = 1. Now we know its new position, we perform an SQL UPDATE operation to set the position for menu ID 5 (*News*) to 1, and we perform another SQL Update to move the menu item that was at position 1 (*About*) to position 2. If we wanted to move *News* down the menu, we would set menu item 5 (*News*) to position 3, and menu item 6 to position 2. This moves the selected menu item up or down the menu.

Note that the expression for the if statement is:

```
(($swapPosition > 0) && ($swapPosition <= $this->numRecords))
```

If $swapPosition is zero, it means we have tried to move the menu item at position 1 up the menu. As it's already in the first position, we can't move it any further up, so we perform no action if this is the case. If $swapPosition is greater than the number of records stored in the global $numRecords variable, then it means the selected menu item is already last in the menu order, and so can't be moved down any more. We only perform the update operations if both expressions are True.

## editMenuItem()

This is another function that is called by performActions(), and is run if the form *Edit* button is clicked. Add the code below to the class:

```
function editMenuItem(){
    $selected = $_POST['menu'];
    $query = sprintf("SELECT id,label,position,link FROM tblmainmenu
                    WHERE id='%s'", $selected);
    $result = $this->DB_executeQuery($query,$this->menuLink);
    $row = mysql_fetch_assoc($result);
    $this->label = $row['label'];
    $this->link = $row['link'];
}
```

First, this function reads the menu value from the PHP $_POST array, which, if set, will hold the id number of the selected menu item from the menu listbox.

Now that we have the ID of the selected record, we use an SQL SELECT statement to read the record with the same id number from the database. We then read in the values of the label and link fields for that record, and put the values in the global class variables $label and $link, which we'll use later on in this class to set the values of the textfields on the form.

## updateMenuItem()

The `updateMenuItem()` function is used to update the menu item record held in the database, with the new values the user typed into the textfields on the form.

```
function updateMenuItem(){
    $selected = $_POST['menu'];
    $label = $_POST['label'];
    $link = $_POST['link'];
    $query = sprintf("UPDATE tblmainmenu SET label='%s', link='%s'
                     WHERE id = '%s'",$label,$link,$selected);
    $result = $this->DB_executeQuery($query,$this->menuLink);
}
```

First we find the selected menu item, and the value of the label and link textfields, by reading the form data submitted from the $_POST array. We then insert these values into an UPDATE query, which we then execute to change the required values in the database.

## addMenuItem()

This function adds a new menu item to the database:

```
function addMenuItem(){
    $query = "SELECT id,label,position,link FROM tblmainmenu ORDER BY position
DESC";
    $result = $this->DB_executeQuery($query,$this->menuLink);
    $row = mysql_fetch_assoc($result);
    $highestPosition = $row['position'];
    $nextPosition = $highestPosition + 1;
    $query = sprintf("INSERT INTO tblmainmenu (label, link, position) VALUES
                     ('%s','%s','%s')",
                     $_POST['label'], $_POST['link'], $nextPosition);
    $result = $this->DB_executeQuery($query,$this->menuLink);
    }
```

First we read the highest position number from the database. We do this with a standard SELECT query, with the records ordered by the position field in descending order. As the records are ordered in descending order, it follows that the first record in the resulting recordset will contain the highest position number. We then add 1 to this number to find the next position number. Lastly we write the new record to the database, using the data from the form fields in the $_POST array.

## deleteMenuItem()

This function, as the name suggests, deletes a menu item from the database.

```
function deleteMenuItem(){
    $query = "DELETE FROM tblmainmenu WHERE id='" . $_POST['menu'] . "'";
    $result = $this->DB_executeQuery($query,$this->menuLink);
}
```

All we need to do is to execute an SQL DELETE statement to delete the record where the id number matches the one submitted by the menu listbox on the form.

## createUserMenu()

This function creates the menu listbox, from which the user selects the menu item to update or delete etc. We execute this function after we have performed any database operations so that the menu listbox always displays the latest menu data.

```
function createUserMenu(){
    $userMenu = "<div align=\"center\">";
    $userMenu .= "<select name=\"menu\" size=\"10\" id=\"menu\">";
    $query = "SELECT id,label,position,link FROM tblmainmenu ORDER BY position
ASC";
    $result = $this->DB_executeQuery($query,$this->menuLink);
    while($row = mysql_fetch_assoc($result)){
        if($_POST['menu'] == $row['id']){
            $userMenu .= "<option value=\"{$row['id']}\" selected>" .
$row['label'];
            $userMenu .= "</option>";
        } else {
            $userMenu .= "<option value=\"{$row['id']}\">{$row['label']}</option>";
        }
    }
    $userMenu .= "</select>";
    $userMenu .= "</div>";
    $this->userMenu = $userMenu;
}
```

This is one of the functions that generates HTML that is displayed on the adminMenu.php web page. First we add the opening HTML for the menu listbox. We then execute an SQL SELECT query to pull all the records from the tblmainmenu table ordered by their position number in ascending order (so position 1 represents the top of the menu).

We then use a while loop which runs code for each record returned by the query, until the last record is reached. At each cycle of the loop we read the record from the database into an array $row, and then add the id and label from the $row array to the HTML code to create a new option in the listbox. If there is a value in the $_POST array for menu, it means that a menu item has been selected, and the form submitted by the user. $_POST['menu'] is equal to the record id of the record read in the current loop. We thus add "selected" to its option value, so that when the page loads the same menu item is selected for the user as they had selected previously. Finally, we place the HTML generated in the global variable $userMenu.

## createMoveButtons()

This function creates the *Up*, *Down*, *Edit*, and *Delete* buttons on the form.

```
function createMoveButtons(){
    $buttons="<br><div align=\"center\">";
    $buttons .= "<span class=\"formButton\"><input name=\"Up\" type=\"submit\"";
    $buttons .= " value=\"Up\"></span>";
    $buttons .= "<span class=\"formButton\"><input name=\"Down\" type=\"submit\"";
    $buttons .= " value=\"Down\"></span>";
    $buttons .= "<span class=\"formButton\"><input name=\"Edit\" type=\"submit\"";
    $buttons .= " value=\"Edit\"></span>";
    $buttons .= "<span class=\"formButton\"><input name=\"Delete\" type=\"submit\"";
```

```
$buttons .= " value=\"Delete\"></span>";
$buttons .= "</div>";
$this->moveButtons = $buttons;
}
```

This function is very simple, and just puts the HTML to create the buttons into a global variable $topButtons. We output the HTML held in $topButtons on the menuadmin.php web page.

## createAdminButtons()

This function creates the bottom set of buttons on the form, that is *New*, *Add*, and *Update*.
Because only certain buttons are needed at certain times, we use an if structure to show the correct buttons for the available actions. If there is no value held in the global variable $label, it means that the label textfield on the form will be empty, and so consequently it means that the only operation the user can perform is adding a new menu item to the database, and so we only show the *Add* Button.

If $this->label is not empty, it means that a user previously selected a record and pressed the *Edit* button. $this->label is then set by the editMenuItem() function, which is called by the

```
function createAdminButtons(){
    $buttons="<br><div align='center'>";
    if($this->label == ""){
        $buttons .= "<span class=\"formButton\"><input name=\"Add\"";
        $buttons .= " type=\"submit\" value=\"Add\"></span>";
    } else {
        $buttons .= "<span class=\"formButton\"><input name=\"New\"";
        $buttons .= " type=\"submit\" value=\"New\"></span>";
        $buttons .= "<span class=\"formButton\"><input name=\"Update\"";
        $buttons .= " type=\"submit\" value=\"Update\"></span>";
    }
    $buttons .= "</div>";
    $this->adminButtons = $buttons;
}
```

performActions() function when the *Edit* button submits the form. If the user pressed the *Edit* button, the label and link for that menu item will be displayed in the label and link textfields on the form, therefore the user can't add a new record, they can only update the existing data or request a blank form to add a new record, so we only display the *New* and *Update* buttons.

All the HTML needed for the relevant buttons is stored in the global variable $bottomButtons, and the HTML is displayed on the adminMenu.php web page.

## createAdminMenu()

This function generates the HTML for the administration menu, which takes the user to different administration pages. It's hard coded, as unlike the front end, the back end administration pages are unlikely to change location. If you wanted, you could store all of the URLs in your database, and generate this dynamically, but for simplicity's sake, we'll stick with this approach for now.

```
function createAdminMenu(){
    $adminMenu = "<div id=\"adminMenu\">";
    $adminMenu .= "<span class=\"adminMenuHeader\">Admin Menu</span><br><br>";
    $adminMenu .= "<a href=\"editAdminArticles.php\"";
    $adminMenu .= " class=\"adminMenuLink\">Article Admin</a><br>";
    $adminMenu .= "<a href=\"editAdminMenu.php\"";
    $adminMenu .= " class=\"adminMenuLink\">Menu Admin</a><br>";
    $adminMenu .= "<a href=\"editAdminNews.php\"";
    $adminMenu .= " class=\"adminMenuLink\">News Admin</a><br>";
    $adminMenu .= "</div>";
    $this->adminMenu = $adminMenu;
}
```

We store the HTML generated in a global variable $adminMenu, and we output this HTML on the editAdminMenu.php web page. The *News* and *Article* pages don't exist yet, but we'll be creating them in the following section.

This completes all the functions needed for the adminMenu class. Don't forget to add a closing brace and save the file before you move on.

# Creating the News Administration Section

Now that we've created the *Menu* administration page, we're now going to look at the *News* administration page. The adminNews Class allows us to enter smaller documents, which have a headline and body. They are then displayed x number of headlines at a time, as shown in the front-end screenshot below.

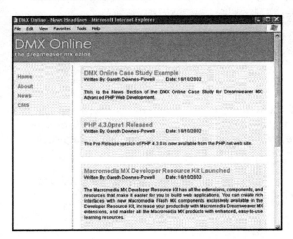

The *News* administration pages will allow us to create new news items, and edit and delete existing ones.

## Creating the editAdminNews.php Page

The editAdminNews.php web page is a front end for the adminNews class we are going to create in the next section. It contains a form with fields to allow the user to view and edit the news items, and displays HTML created by the adminNews class.

Open a new PHP page, switch to *Code View* and enter the following code:

```php
<? require_once("../class/adminNews.php");?>
<?php
$news = new adminNews();
?>
<!DOCTYPE HTML PUBLIC "-//W3C//DTD HTML 4.01 Transitional//EN">
<html>
<head>
<title>News Administration</title>
<meta http-equiv="Content-Type" content="text/html; charset=iso-8859-1">
<link href="css/adminLayout.css" rel="stylesheet" type="text/css">
<link href="css/adminStyles.css" rel="stylesheet" type="text/css">
</head>

<body>
<div id="header"><img src="images/adminlogo.gif" width="220" height="80"
alt="logo"></div>
<div id="leftColumn">
  <?php echo $news->adminMenu; ?>
  <?php echo $news->newsList; ?>
</div>
<div id="mainContent">
  <div id="editableContentBorder">
    <div id="formBorder">
      <form name="form1" method="post" action="<?php echo $PHP_SELF; ?>" >
        <div class="formHeader" id="formLeft">Title:</div>
        <div id="formRight">
          <input name="title" type="text"
          value="<?php echo $news->title; ?>" size="40" maxlength="150">
        </div>
        <div class="clear"></div>
        <div class="formHeader" id="formLeft">Author:</div>
        <div id="formRight">
          <input name="author" type="text" size="40"
          value="<?php echo $news->author; ?>">
        </div>
        <div class="clear"></div>
        <div class="formHeader" id="formLeft">Date:</div>
        <div id="formRight"><input name="date" type="text" id="date"
        value="<?php echo $news->date; ?>" size="10"></div>
        <div class="clear"></div>
        <div class="formHeader" id="formLeft">Text:</div>
        <div id="formRight">
          <textarea name="body" cols="60" rows="10">
          <?php echo $news->body; ?>
          </textarea>
        </div>
        <div class="clear">
          <input name="id" type="hidden" id="id"
          value="<?php echo $news->id; ?>">
          <input name="block" type="hidden" id="block"
          value="<?php echo $news->block; ?>">
        </div>
        <div id="formLeft"></div>
        <div id="formRight">
```

```
            <?php echo $news->buttons; ?>
          </div>
          <div class="clear"></div>
        </form>
        <div class="clear"></div>
        </div>
      </div>
    </div>
  </div>
</body>
</html>
```

Save the page as `cms/admin/editAdminNews.php`.

The following values in the PHP code are created by the `adminNews` class, and are inserted into the HTML when the code is viewed in a browser.

- `adminMenu` – contains the HTML for the Administration Section menu.
- `newsList` – contains the HTML for a list of news items, so that an administrator can pick one to edit.
- `title` – will contain the title for the current news item being edited.
- `author` – will contain the author for the current news item being edited.
- `date` – will contain the date for the current news item being edited.
- `body` – will contain the news body for the current news item being edited.
- `id` – will contain the ID number for the current news item being edited.
- `block` – will contain the current news block number.

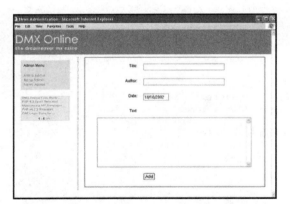

When we've finished the *News Administration* system, the page will look similar to the screenshot below when viewed in a browser.

## Creating the adminNews Class

Open a new PHP page, switch to *Code View*, and delete the existing HTML. Save the file as `/cms/class/adminNews.php`. Add the following code to create the basic structure for the `adminNews` class, again this class extends the `database` class we created earlier.

```php
<?php
require_once("../class/database.php");
###################################################
# CMS News Class                                  #
###################################################
# Inherits
#  DB_date2mysql($date) : DB_mysql2date($date) : DB_databaseConnect()
#  DB_executeQuery($query,$Link) : DB_getRecordID() : DB_getRecords($Result)
#  DB_closeDatabase($Link)

class adminNews extends Database{

    var $showNewsNumber = 5;
    var $newsLink;
    var $newsResult;
    var $totalRecords;
    var $startRecord;
    var $endRecord;
    var $title;
    var $author;
    var $body;
    var $date;
    var $id;
    var $block;
    var $adminMenu;
    var $newsList;
    var $buttons;

    function adminNews(){
        $this->date = date("m/d/Y");
        $this->newsLink = $this->DB_databaseConnect();
        $this->getVars();
        $this->showRecord();
        $this->performActions();
        $this->createNewsList();
        $this->createNavigation();
        $this->createButtons();
        $this->createadminMenu();
        $this->DB_closeDatabase($this->newsLink);
    }
?>
```

The variable $showNewsNumber, which is set to 5, determines the number of news items that are displayed on the page at once, and can be changed to a higher or a lower value if desired.

We're next going to create the functions called by the adminNews constructor function.

## testVars()

The first function that we are going to create is called testVars(). Unlike the adminMenu class which used only form POST data, on the adminNews.php web page data can either come from the form, which uses the $_POST array, or from the URL query string variables, which can be read from the $_GET array. This function checks both the POST and GET arrays to find a value, so the value is available to us whether it was posted by the form, or sent through the URL query string. Add the following code to the class.

```
function testVars($variable, $default){
    if(strlen($_GET[$variable]) > 0){
        $temp = $_GET[$variable];
    } elseif (strlen($_POST[$variable])>0){
        $temp = $_POST[$variable];
    } else {
        if(strlen($default)>0){
            $temp = $default;
        }
    }
    return $temp;
}
```

testVars() takes two parameters, the name of the variable to look for, and a default value which is returned if the value doesn't exist in either the $_POST or $_GET array.

First we check for the variable in the $_GET Array. If there is a value in there for our variable, then the length of the value will be greater than zero characters, so we know we have found the correct value. If we can't find a value in the $_GET array we next check the $_POST array, to see if there is a value for our variable in there. Finally if we still haven't found a value, if the default parameter is set then we return that value.

### getVars()

All this function does is call the testVars() function we just created.

```
function getVars(){
    $this->id = $this->testVars("id","");
    $this->block = $this->testVars("block",1);
}
```

We use this function to set the global class variables $id, which will be the ID of the current news item, and $block, which is the block that the current menu item exists in. Each block contains the number of news items specified by the global class variable $showNewsNumber, which in this example is set to 5. If we had 14 news items, we would have 3 blocks, the first with 5 records, the second with 5 records, and the third block with 4 records.

### performActions()

This function is similar to the performActions() function in the adminMenu class we created earlier in this case study. The function checks to see which *Submit* button was used to submit the form, and then calls the appropriate function to perform the action that matches the button clicked.

```
function performActions(){
    if($_POST['Add'] == "Add"){
        $this->addNewsItem();
    }
    if($_POST['Delete'] == "Delete"){
        $this->deleteNewsItem();
    }
    if($_POST['Update'] == "Update"){
        $this->updateNewsItem();
    }
```

```
    if($_POST['New'] == "New"){
        $this->newNewsItem();
    }
}
```

## addNewsItem()

The `addNewsItem()` function, as the name suggests, adds a news item entered in the form into the database table `tblnews`.

```
function addNewsItem(){
    $this->title = $_POST['title'];
    $this->author = $_POST['author'];
    $this->body = $_POST['body'];
    $this->date = $_POST['date'];
    $mysqlDate = $this->DB_date2mysql($this->date);
    $query = sprintf("INSERT INTO tblnews (title, author, date, body)
                        VALUES('%s','%s','%s','%s')"
                      ,addslashes($this->title)
                      ,addslashes($this->author)
                      ,$mysqlDate,addslashes($this->body));
    $this->DB_executeQuery($query, $this->newsLink);
    $this->id = $this->DB_getRecordID();
}
```

First we read the values that we've submitted with the form into the class global variables. We then use the inherited `DB_date2mysql()` function to convert the date from US to MySQL format.

Next we use an INSERT query to insert the data into a new record in the database. We then use the inherited `DB_getRecordID()` function to find the `id` number of the record we just inserted, and place it in the global class variable `$id`.

## deleteNewsItem()

This function is used to delete a news item from the database.

```
function deleteNewsItem(){
    $query = sprintf("DELETE FROM tblnews WHERE id = '%s'", $this->id);
    $this->DB_executeQuery($query, $this->newsLink);
}
```

Here we use an SQL DELETE statement to delete the record with the `id` which matches the `id` in the global class variable `$id`, which is set using the `getVars()` function.

## newNewsItem()

This function wipes all the global class variables that contain the record info, so that the user can enter a new news item.

**C2**

```
function newNewsItem(){
    $this->id = "";
    $this->title = "";
    $this->author = "";
    $this->body = "";
}
```

### updateNewsItem()

This function is called when the user edits an existing news item, and updates the record in the database with the new details entered.

```
function updateNewsItem(){
    $this->title = $_POST['title'];
    $this->author = $_POST['author'];
    $this->body = $_POST['body'];
    $this->date = $_POST['date'];
    $mysqlDate = $this->DB_date2mysql($this->date);
    $query = sprintf("UPDATE tblnews SET title = '%s', author = '%s', date = '%s'
                    , body = '%s' WHERE id='%s'"
                    ,addslashes($this->title)
                    ,addslashes($this->author)
                    ,$mysqlDate,addslashes($this->body),$this->id);
    $this->DB_executeQuery($query,$this->newsLink);
}
```

First we read the values of the form fields submitted, which are read from the $_POST array. We then execute an SQL UPDATE query to change the details stored in the database, where the id matches the value in the global class variable $id.

### createButtons()

This function simply creates the HTML for the *New*, *Update*, *Delete*, and *Add* form buttons.

```
function createButtons(){
    $this->buttons = "<br>";
    if(strlen($this->title)>0){
        $this->buttons .= "<input name=\"New\" type=\"submit\" value=\"New\">";
        $this->buttons .= "<input name=\"Update\" type=\"submit\"
value=\"Update\">";
        $this->buttons .= "<input name=\"Delete\" type=\"submit\"
value=\"Delete\">";
    } else {
        $this->buttons .= "<input name=\"Add\" type=\"submit\" value=\"Add\">";
    }
}
```

The HTML text is stored in the global class variable $buttons.

### createNewsList()

If you refer back to the screenshot at the start of this class, you'll see that this function creates the navigation menu on the left-hand side of the screen, which is enclosed in a gray box. It shows five news items records at a time, and allows the user to move backwards and forwards in steps of five records. When the user selects a record, the `id` of the selected record is passed in the URL query string.

```
function createNewsList(){
  $query = "SELECT id,title,author,date,body FROM tblnews ORDER BY id DESC";
  $this->newsResult = $this->DB_executeQuery($query,$this->newsLink);
  $totalRecords = $this->DB_getRecords($this->newsResult);
  $this->totalRecords = $totalRecords;
  $startRecord = (($this->showNewsNumber * $this->block) - $this->showNewsNumber) +
1;
  $this->startRecord = $startRecord;
  $endRecord = $this->showNewsNumber * $this->block;
  $this->endRecord = $endRecord;
  $this->newsList .= "<div id=\"newsListBlock\">";
  for($count=1; $count <= $totalRecords; $count++){
    $row = mysql_fetch_assoc($this->newsResult);
    if(($count >= $startRecord)&&($count<= $endRecord)){
      $title = stripslashes($row["title"]);
      $title = $this->trimString($title);
      $this->newsList .= "<a href=\"".$_SERVER['PHP_SELF']."?id=".$row["id"];
      $this->newsList .= "&block=".$this->block."\" class=\"newsList\">";
      $this->newsList .= $title . "</a><br>";
      }
  }
}
```

We start with a SELECT query that selects all the records in the news recordset, and then execute the query. Next we use the inherited `DB_getRecords()` function to find out how many records have been returned, and we store this value in the global class variable `$totalRecords`.

Now we use the `$block` variable to work out which is the first record in that block. For example if we have 18 records, we would have 4 blocks, the first three blocks containing 5 records, and the last block with just 3 records. If we wanted to find the record at the start of the second block, we use this formula:

```
$startRecord = (($this->showNewsNumber * $this->block) - $this->showNewsNumber) + 1;
```

For the second block, this would be:

```
$startRecord = ((5 * 2) - 5 + 1
```

So `$startRecord` would equal 6, and we have successfully found the first record in the second block.

Next, we find the last record in the selected block, using the formula:

```
$endRecord = $this->showNewsNumber * $this->block;
```

If we look at the example of the second block again, the formula would be:

```
$endRecord = 2 * 5
```

This means that the last record of the second block is 10. So we know that the second block consists of the records 6 to 10.

We then cycle through the records in the recordset checking the record number each time. For the above example when record 6 is reached its field values are added to the menu HTML, and we keep adding the records until we get to record number 10, we then ignore the rest of the records as we have the ones we need.

The HTML generated for the news list is now stored in the global class variable newsList, ready to output to the browser in the adminNews.php page.

## createNavigation()

This function creates the navigation buttons at the bottom of the menuList box, used for moving backwards and forwards between blocks, and to display the first and last record numbers of the current block.

```
function createNavigation(){
    $this->newsList .= "<div align=\"center\">";
    $previousBlock = $this->block - 1;
    $nextBlock = $this->block + 1;
    $lastBlock = ceil($this->totalRecords / $this->showNewsNumber);
    if($this->block >1 ){
        $this->newsList .= "<a
href=\"".$_SERVER['PHP_SELF']."?block=".$previousBlock;
        $this->newsList .= "\" class=\"newsList\">"."<<"."</a> ";
    }
    $this->newsList .= "<span class=\"newsCurrentText\">";
    $this->newsList .= $this->startRecord." - ".$this->endRecord."</span>";
    if($this->block < $lastBlock){
        $this->newsList .="<a href=\"".$_SERVER['PHP_SELF']."?block=".$nextBlock;
        $this->newsList .="' class=\"newsList\">".">>"."</a> ";
    }
    $this->newsList .= "</div>";
    $this->newsList .= "</div>";
}
```

First we calculate the previous block, and the next block. If the previous block number is greater than 1, we display a set of arrows to move to the previous block. We then check that we're not on the last block and if we're not, we display a set of arrows so the user can navigate to the next block.

We add the HTML text generated to the HTML which is already in the global class variable $newsList.

## showRecord()

Once a record has been selected from the news list created by the function createNewsList(), the menu item id is passed in the URL query string. This function checks to see if an id number is present. If it is, we read the record with that id from the database, and place the field data into global class variables which are used to populate the textfields on the adminNews.php web page.

```
function showRecord(){
    if($this->id > 0 ){
        $query = sprintf("SELECT id,title,author,date,body
                          FROM tblnews WHERE id = %s",$this->id);
        $this->newsResult = $this->DB_executeQuery($query,$this->newsLink);
        $row = mysql_fetch_assoc($this->newsResult);
      $this->title = stripslashes($row["title"]);
  $this->author = stripslashes($row["author"]);
  $this->body = stripslashes($row["body"]);
  $this->date = $this->DB_mysql2date($row["date"]);
    }
}
```

We convert the date from MySQL format to US format using the inherited `DB_mysql2date()` function.

## trimString()

Because the news headlines stored in the `$title` field can be fairly long, we use this function to display only a small part of the title.

```
function trimString($text){
    $maxTextLength=26;
    $aspace=" ";
    if(strlen($text) > $maxTextLength ) {
        $text = substr(trim($text),0,$maxTextLength);
        $text = substr($text,0,strlen($text)-strpos(strrev($text),$aspace));
        $text = $text.'...';
    }
    return $text;
}
```

This function returns the first 26 characters of the title string followed by "...", but we make sure that the text is actually cut off at the end of a word, rather than the middle of one.

## createAdminMenu()

The last function in this class is the same as in the `adminMenu.php` class and creates the menu which allows the user to move between administration pages.

```
function createAdminMenu(){
    $adminMenu = "<div id=\"adminMenu\">";
    $adminMenu .= "<span class=\"adminMenuHeader\">Admin Menu</span><br><br>";
    $adminMenu .= "<a href=\"editAdminArticles.php\" class=\"adminMenuLink\">";
    $adminMenu .= "Article Admin</a><br>";
    $adminMenu .= "<a href=\"editAdminMenu.php\" class=\"adminMenuLink\">";
    $adminMenu .= "Menu Admin</a><br>";
    $adminMenu .= "<a href=\"editAdminNews.php\" class=\"adminMenuLink\">";
    $adminMenu .= "News Admin</a><br>";
    $adminMenu .= "</div>";
    $this->adminMenu = $adminMenu;
}
```

Save the file. You can now upload the pages to your server, and check the *News Administration* page at: *http://www.yoursite.com/cms/admin/editAdminNews.php* (substituting the appropriate domain, of course).

# Creating the Article Administration Section

The last section in our *Administration* section is to add new articles to the CMS System. Articles can be longer documents than news items, and can also include images, which we allow the user to upload through their web browser. The actual article data will be stored in the database, and images will be stored in a separate directory for each article referenced by the article id number.

## Creating the Web Page editAdminArticles.php

This is the most complicated page of the CMS as it contains two parts. The first part is shown in the next screenshot, which shows the top of the page.

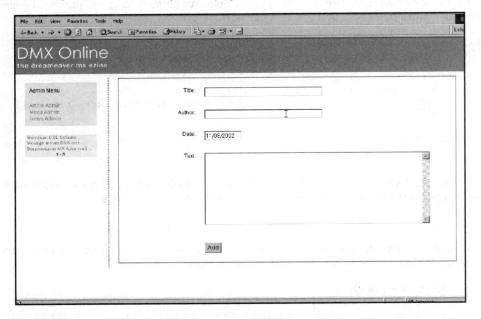

On the left-hand side of the screen, we first have our standard *Admin Menu*. Below that is a drop-down menu, which contains a list of the menu items in the tblmainmenu database table. When the user selects a menu item, any articles linked to that menu item will be displayed in the gray panel below. When the user clicks one of these article links, it passes the article id as a URL query string value, and the article is loaded from the database so that the user can update or delete it, etc.

On the right-hand side we have the main content area. Another drop-down menu displays the menu items again, this time so that the user can select one to link the article to the selected menu item. Below the content area we have the buttons to allow the user to add or update, etc.

The second part is still on the same page, but is below the main content area, and contains another form. This second part is shown in the following screenshot, and shows the bottom of the page.

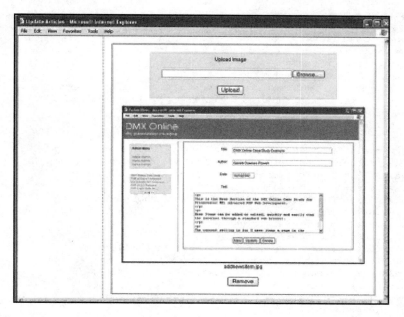

Here the user can select an image on their PC, and upload it. If the article `id` was `20`, then the image would be stored as `/cms/images/articles/20/imagename`. All the images which have been attached to the selected article are shown below the *Upload Image* block, along with the image name and a *Remove* button which when clicked will delete the image from the server.

Open a new PHP page, and save the page as `editAdminArticles.php` in the `cms/admin/` directory. Alternatively you can download the page from the accompanying web site. If you are entering the code yourself, add the following code.

```
<? require_once("../class/adminArticles.php");?>
<?php $articles = new adminArticles(); ?>
<!DOCTYPE HTML PUBLIC "-//W3C//DTD HTML 4.01 Transitional//EN">
<html>
<head>
<title>Update Articles</title>
<meta http-equiv="Content-Type" content="text/html; charset=iso-8859-1">
<link href="css/adminLayout.css" rel="stylesheet" type="text/css">
<link href="css/adminStyles.css" rel="stylesheet" type="text/css">
</head>
<body>
  <!- Part 1 !->
  <div id="header">
    <img src="images/adminlogo.gif" width="220" height="80">
  </div>
  <div id="leftColumn">
    <?php echo $articles->adminMenu; ?>
    <?php echo $articles->menuList; ?>
```

```html
    <?php echo $articles->menuArticleBlock; ?>
  </div>

  <div id="mainContent">
    <div id="editableContentBorder">
      <div id="formBorder">
        <form name="dataForm" method="post" action="<?php echo $PHP_SELF; ?>" >
          <div align="center">
            <div id="articleMenuSelect">
              <span class="formHeader">Link to Menu Option:</span>
                <?php echo $articles->menuLink; ?>
              </div>
            </div>
            <br>
            <div class="formHeader" id="formLeft">Title:</div>
            <div id="formRight"><input name="title" type="text" size="60"
             value="<?php echo $articles->title; ?>"></div>
            <div class="clear"></div>
            <div class="formHeader" id="formLeft">Author:</div>
            <div id="formRight"><input name="author" type="text" size="60"
             value="<?php echo $articles->author; ?>"></div>
            <div class="clear"></div>
            <div class="formHeader" id="formLeft">Date:</div>
            <div id="formRight"><input name="date" type="text" id="date"
             value="<?php echo $articles->date; ?>" size="10"></div>
            <div class="clear"></div>
            <div class="formHeader" id="formLeft">Text:</div>
            <div id="formRight">
              <textarea name="body" cols="70" rows="20">
              <?php echo $articles->body; ?></textarea>
            </div>
            <div class="clear">
              <input name="id" type="hidden" id="id"
               value="<?php echo $articles->id; ?>">
            </div>
            <div id="formLeft"></div>
            <div id="formRight">
              <?php echo $articles->buttons; ?>
            </div>
            <div class="clear"><br></div>
          </form>
        </div>
      </div>
    </div>
<!-- Part 2 !-->
    <?php if($articles->id > 0){ ?>
    <br>
    <div id="editableContentBorder">
    <div id="formBorder">
      <form action="<?php echo $PHP_SELF; ?>" method="post"
       enctype="multipart/form-data" name="uploadForm">
        <div align="center">
          <div id="articleMenuSelect">
            <p class="formHeader">Upload Image</p>
              <input name="filename" type="file" id="filename" size="50"
maxlength="200">
              <br>
```

```
                <input type="submit" name="Upload" value="Upload">
                <input name="MAX_FILE_SIZE" type="hidden"
                 id="MAX_FILE_SIZE" value="250000">
                <input name="id" type="hidden" id="id"
                 value="<?php echo $articles->id; ?>">
          </div>
        </div>
        <?php echo $articles->imageHTML; ?>
      </form>
      </div>
    </div>
  <?php } ?>
</div>
</body>
</html>
```

Save the file before you continue.

The PHP adminArticle class variables which are used on this page are:

## Part 1

adminMenu – Will contain the HTML for the Admin Menu
menuList – HTML for the drop-down menu in the left column.
menuArticleBlock – HTML for the article list in the left column
menuLink – HTML for the link to the menu drop-down in the main content
title – If an id is passed, contains the title of the article.
author – If an id is passed, contains author of the article
date – If an id is passed, contains the article date
body – If an id is passed, contains the article body
id – Contains the id if one is passed
buttons – Contains the HTML for the *Add / Edit* etc. buttons

### Part 2

id – Contains the ID of the article if one is passed
imageHTML – Contains the HTML which displays the images that are attached to the article if any

We only actually display part 2, which is the image upload section if an article id has been passed, as we need an article to be added to the database before we can attach images to it.

## Creating the adminArticles Class

Create a new PHP page, and then switch to code view and delete the HTML. Save this file as /cms/class/adminArticles.php. Alternatively download the file from the accompanying web site.

First add the following code to create the basic structure of the adminArticle class.

```
?php
require_once("../class/database.php");
####################################################
# CMS adminArticles                                #
####################################################
# Inherits
#  DB_date2mysql($date) : DB_mysql2date($date) : DB_databaseConnect()
#  DB_executeQuery($query,$Link) : DB_getRecordID() : DB_getRecords($Result)
#  DB_closeDatabase($Link)
class adminArticles extends Database{

    var $articleLink;
    var $articleResult;
    // Directory below should be changed to the correct path on your server
    var $mainImageDirectory = "/home/web/cms/images/articles/";
    var $adminMenu;
    var $menuPrimary;
    var $menuList;
    var $menuLink;
    var $menuArticleBlock;
    var $images;
    var $imageHTML;
    var $id;
    var $title;
    var $author;
    var $body;
    var $date;
    var $menuID;
    var $sideMenuID;

    function adminArticles(){
        $this->date = date("m/d/Y");
        $this->articleLink = $this->DB_databaseConnect();
        $this->getVars();
        $this->performAction();
        $this->showRecord();
        $this->getImages();
        $this->displayImages();
        $this->createArticleListBlock();
        $this->readPrimaryMenu();
        $this->createMenuLink();
        $this->createMenuList();
        $this->createButtons();
        $this->createadminMenu();
        $this->DB_closeDatabase($this->articleLink);
    }
?>
```

Next we are going to add the functions that make up the class.

## testVars()

This is the same as the testVars() function in the adminNews class. It hunts for a specified variable; first in the $_GET array, then the $_POST array. If the variable is still not found, we can assign an optional default value.

```
function testVars($variable, $default){
    if(strlen($_GET[$variable]) > 0){
        $temp = $_GET[$variable];
    } elseif (strlen($_POST[$variable])>0){
        $temp = $_POST[$variable];
    } else {
        if(strlen($default)>0){
            $temp = $default;
        }
    }
    return $temp;
}
```

## getVars()

This function calls the `testVars()` function above, to set the global class variables `$sideMenuId`, `$menuID` and `$id`.

```
function getVars(){
    $this->sideMenuID = $this->testVars("sideMenuID",1);
    $this->menuID = $this->testVars("menuID","");
    $this->id = $this->testVars("id","");
}
```

## showRecord()

This function checks to see if there is a valid `id` in the global class variable, `$id`. If there is then we use that value to select the record from the `articles` table with a matching ID. We then use the data read from the database to populate global class variables with the same names as the database fields, ready to be used later on in this class.

```
function showRecord(){
    if($this->id > 0 ){
        $query = sprintf("SELECT id,title,author,date,body,menuID
                          FROM tblarticles WHERE id = %s",$this->id);
        $this->articleResult = $this->DB_executeQuery($query,$this->articleLink);
        $row = mysql_fetch_assoc($this->articleResult);
        $this->title = stripslashes($row["title"]);
        $this->author = stripslashes($row["author"]);
        $this->body = stripslashes($row["body"]);
        $this->date = $this->DB_mysql2date($row["date"]);
        $this->menuID = $row["menuID"];
    }
}
```

## readPrimaryMenu()

This function reads all the records from the `tblmainmenu` table, ordered in ascending order by their position value. We cycle through the array and place each record's field values into an array, indexed by the field name. We then store this array in the main `$menuPrimary` array, again ready to display later on.

```
function readPrimaryMenu(){
    $query = "SELECT id,label,position,link";
    $query .=" FROM tblmainmenu ORDER BY position ASC";
    $result = $this->DB_executeQuery($query, $this->articleLink);
    $tempArray['label'] = "Root";
    $tempArray['id'] = 0;
    $this->menuPrimary[] = $tempArray;
    while($row = mysql_fetch_assoc($result)){
        $tempArray['label'] = $row['label'];
        $tempArray['id'] = $row['id'];
        $this->menuPrimary[] = $tempArray;
    }
}
```

### createMenuLink()

This function uses the $menuPrimary array created by the previous function and cycles through each of the elements. Each element's values are used to create the drop-down menu in the main content section, which allows the user to link an article to a menu item. As we loop through each element, we check to see if its id matches the id in global class variable $menuID, and if it is we add "selected" in the HTML for that option. This means that the $menuID is preselected after the form has been submitted.

```
function createMenuLink(){
    // Create Main Content Menu Link Menu
    $menuLink .= "<select name='menuID' id='menuID'>";
    foreach($this->menuPrimary as $menuItem){
        if($menuItem['id'] == $this->menuID){
            $menuLink .= "<option value=\"{$menuItem['id']}\"";
            $menuLink .= " selected>{$menuItem['label']}</option>";
        } else {
            $menuLink .= "<option value=\"{$menuItem['id']}\">";
            $menuLink .= "{$menuItem['label']}</option>";
        }
    }
    $menuLink .= "</select>";
    $this->menuLink = $menuLink;
}
```

### createMenuList()

createMenuList() creates the drop-down menu in the left column of the page. This drop-down lists the available menu items that the user can select to show the articles attached to that menu item.

The HTML includes form code, and when a new menu option is selected from the sideMenuID menu the form is submitted. We do this by adding the following JavaScript to the menu <select> tag.

```
onChange="menuForm.submit()"
```

menuForm is the name of the form. We then place the generated HTML in the global class variable $menuList, ready for display on the articleAdmin.php web page.

```
function createMenuList(){
    // Create Navigation Menu List
    $menuList = "<div id=\"articleMenu\" align=\"center\">";
    $menuList .= "<span class=\"formHeader\">Select Menu:</span>";
    $menuList .= "<form name=\"menuForm\" method=\"post\" action=\"";
    $menuList .= $PHP_SELF . "\" >";
    $menuList .= "<select name=\"sideMenuID\" id=\"menuOption\"";
    $menuList .= " onChange=\"menuForm.submit()\">";
    foreach($this->menuPrimary as $menuItem){
        if($menuItem['id'] == $this->sideMenuID){
            $menuList .= "<option value=\"{$menuItem['id']}\"";
            $menuList .= " selected>{$menuItem['label']}</option>";
        } else {
            $menuList .= "<option value=\"{$menuItem['id']}\">";
            $menuList .= " {$menuItem['label']} </option>";
        }
    }
    $menuList .= "</select>";
    $menuList .= "</form>";
    $menuList .= "</div>";
    $this->menuList = $menuList;
}
```

## createArticleListBlock()

This function creates the list of articles in the gray box in the left column, which allows the user to select an article to edit. We use an SQL SELECT query to select all articles with a menuID value the same as the one passed when a menu item is selected. We create each article as a link which passes the current menuID, and the article's own id number in the URL.

```
function createArticleListBlock(){
    // Create Article Listings for Navigation
    $query = sprintf("SELECT id,title,author,date,body,menuID
                    FROM tblarticles WHERE menuID = '%s'
                    ORDER BY id ASC",$this->sideMenuID);
    $result = $this->DB_executeQuery($query, $this->articleLink);
    $menuArticleBlock .= "<div id=\"articleListBlock\">";
    while($row = mysql_fetch_assoc($result)){
        $link = "{$_SERVER['PHP_SELF']}?sideMenuID={$this->sideMenuID}";
        $link .= "&id={$row['id']}";
        $menuArticleBlock .= "<a href=\"$link\" class=\"articleList\">";
        $menuArticleBlock .= "{$row['id']}{$row['title']}</a><br>";
    }
    $menuArticleBlock .= "</div>";
    $this->menuArticleBlock = $menuArticleBlock;
}
```

## createButtons()

This is a simple function which creates the various types of *Submit* buttons the user can use to submit the form and perform certain actions.

```
function createButtons(){
    $this->buttons = "<br>";
    if(strlen($this->body)>0 || strlen($this->title)>0 || strlen($this->author)>0){
        $this->buttons .= "<input name=\"New\" type=\"submit\" value=\"New\">";
        $this->buttons .= "<input name=\"Update\" type=\"submit\" value='Update'>";
        $this->buttons .= "<input name=\"Delete\" type=\"submit\"
value=\"Delete\">";
    } else {
        $this->buttons .= "<input name=\"Add\" type=\"submit\" value=\"Add\">";
    }
}
```

## performAction()

This function we've seen before in the previous classes. It determines which functions to run depending on which form submit button was pressed.

```
function performAction(){
    if($_POST['Add'] == "Add"){
        $this->addArticle();
    }
    if($_POST['Delete'] == "Delete"){
        $this->deleteArticle();
    }
    if($_POST['Update'] == "Update"){
        $this->updateArticle();
    }
    if($_POST['New'] == "New"){
        $this->newArticle();
    }
    if($_POST['Upload'] == "Upload"){
        $this->uploadImage();
    }
    if($_POST['Remove'] == "Remove"){
        $this->deleteImage();
    }
}
```

## addArticle()

This function reads the values that were submitted from the form, and inserts them into a new record in the `tblarticles` table. We then use the inherited function `DB_getRecordID()` to get the `id` number of the newly inserted article.

```
function addArticle(){
    $this->title = $_POST['title'];
    $this->author = $_POST['author'];
    $this->body = $_POST['body'];
    $this->date = $_POST['date'];
    $mysqlDate = $this->DB_date2mysql($this->date);
    $query = sprintf("INSERT INTO tblarticles (title, author, date, body, menuID)
                    VALUES('%s','%s','%s','%s','%s')"
                    ,addslashes($this->title)
                    ,addslashes($this->author)
                    ,$mysqlDate,addslashes($this->body)
```

```
                            ,$this->menuID);
    $this->DB_executeQuery($query, $this->articleLink);
    $this->id = $this->DB_getRecordID();
}
```

## deleteArticle()

This function deletes an article from the `tblarticles` table where the `id` number matches the `id` number of the currently selected article, which is held in the global class variable `$id`.

```
function deleteArticle(){
    $query = sprintf("DELETE FROM tblarticles WHERE id = '%s'", $this->id);
    $this->DB_executeQuery($query, $this->articleLink);
}
```

## updateArticle()

This function updates the articles in the database with the changes the user made in the submission form. First we read the submitted fields from the `$_POST` array, then we execute an SQL `UPDATE` query.

```
function updateArticle(){
    $this->title = $_POST['title'];
    $this->author = $_POST['author'];
    $this->body = $_POST['body'];
    $this->date = $_POST['date'];
    $mysqlDate = $this->DB_date2mysql($this->date);
    $query = sprintf("UPDATE tblarticles
                    SET title = '%s', author = '%s', date = '%s'
                    , body = '%s', menuID = '%s' WHERE id='%s'"
                    ,addslashes($this->title)
                    ,addslashes($this->author)
                    ,$mysqlDate
                    ,addslashes($this->body),
    $this->menuID, $this->id);
    $this->DB_executeQuery($query,$this->articleLink);
}
```

## newArticle()

This function simply sets the global class variable `$id` to zero. With the variable `$id` set to `0` the user is presented with a blank form so that they can add a new record.

```
function newArticle(){
    $this->id = 0;
}
```

## uploadImage()

This function is called by the second part of the `adminArticles.php` web page, which is the image upload section. First we set the main directory to the value stored in the global class variable `$mainDir`, which in this example is:

```
/home/web/cms/images/articles/
```

and should be changed as appropriate for your server. Note that we have to use the full server path to the directory, not the web path.

It's important to note that before images can be uploaded, the directory in $mainDir needs to have its permissions set to be writable by everyone, so that the image can be written to the directory, or any subdirectories beneath it.

On Windows, right-click on the folder icon in Explorer and set its permissions under Properties.

If you use a UNIX operating system, such as FreeBSD, OS X, or Linux, you need to execute the command chmod 777 <directory_name>.

The image is stored in a subdirectory under this main directory, where the subdirectory name is the same as the article ID to which the image is attached. So if a file called picture.jpg is uploaded and attached to an article with id of 26, the image would be stored in:

```
/home/web/cms/images/articles/26/picture.jpg
```

Next we read from the superglobal array $_FILES, which contains details of uploaded files, and we get the name of the image and its temporary name on the server.

We then use the substr() function to grab the last four characters of the filename, which will give us the file extension. We then check this is either .gif or .jpg, as these are the only two image formats we will allow. If the file extension is OK we check to see if an images directory already exists for the current article, and if not we create a new directory, setting its permissions to *775* on UNIX systems, so that the web server can read the images.

The last operation is to create a string which contains the full image path including the directory we created, and we use the move_uploaded_file() command to move the temporary image file to its new home.

```php
function uploadImage(){
    $mainDir = $this->mainImageDirectory;
    $uploadDir = $mainDir . $_POST['id'] ;
    $origFilename = $_FILES['filename']['name'];
    $tempFilename = $_FILES['filename']['tmp_name'];
    $fileExtension = substr($origFilename,-4);
    if($fileExtension == ".gif" || $fileExtension == ".jpg"){
        umask(0);
    if(!file_exists($uploadDir)){
        mkdir($uploadDir, 0775);
        chmod($uploadDir, 0775);
    }
    $newPath = $uploadDir . "/" . $origFilename;
    move_uploaded_file($tempFilename, $newPath);
    system("chmod 755 $newPath");
    }
}
```

## getImages()

This function is used to find any images that are attached to the selected article. We first create the directory path where the images for the current article would be stored for example: `/home/web/cms/images/articles/26/` if the current article `id` was `26`. We then check the directory exists, and if it does we open a handle to the directory using the `opendir()` command.

We then cycle through the directory, looking at a new file each cycle. When we have a valid file, we use the PHP function `GetImageSize()`, which creates an array containing the image's x and y dimensions. We place the filename and the x and y values in an array `$temp`, and place the `$temp` array in the global class array `$images`. We then close the handle to the directory with the `closedir()` command.

```
function getImages(){
    $mainDir = $this->mainImageDirectory . $this->id;
    if (file_exists($mainDir)) {
        $handle = opendir($mainDir);
        while (false !== ($file = readdir($handle))) {
            if(strlen($file) > 4){
                $temp['name'] = $file;
                $imageXY = GetImageSize($mainDir . "/" . $file);
                $temp['x'] = $imageXY[0];
                $temp['y'] = $imageXY[1];
                $this->images[] = $temp;
            }
        }
    closedir($handle);
    }
}
```

## displayImages()

This function uses the global class array `$images` we created in the previous `getImages()` function. We cycle through the array, and create HTML to display each image, using the filename and the x and y values stored in the array. We then place the HTML in the global class variable `$imageHTML`, ready for display on the `adminArticles.php` web page.

```
function displayImages(){
    if(is_array($this->images)){
        $count = 1;
        foreach($this->images as $image){
            $imageHTML .= "<br>";
            $imageHTML .= "<div align='center'>";
            $imageHTML .= "<form name='dataForm$count' method='post' action='" .
$_SERVER['PHP_SELF'] . "'>";
            $imageHTML .= "<img ";
            $imageHTML .= "src=\"../images/articles/{$this-
>id}/".$image['name']."\">";
            $imageHTML .= "width=\"{$image['x']}\" height=\"{$image['y']}\">";
            $imageHTML .= "<br>";
            $imageHTML .= "<span class='formHeader'>{$image['name']}</span>";
            $imageHTML .= "<br><br>";
            $imageHTML .= "<input name='imageName' type='hidden'id='imageName'
 value='{$image['name']}'>";
```

```
                $imageHTML .= "<input name='id\" type='hidden'id='id'value='{$this-
>id}'>";
                $imageHTML .= "<input name='Remove' type='submit' value='Remove'>";
                $imageHTML .= "</form></div>";
                $count++;
        }
    }
    $this->imageHTML = $imageHTML;
}
```

### deleteImage()

This function deletes the image selected in the submission form, using the `unlink()` command, which deletes the file from the server's hard disk

```
function deleteImage(){
    $filePath = $this->mainImageDirectory . $this->id . "/" . $_POST['imageName'];
    unlink($filePath);
}
```

### createAdminMenu()

This is the last function in the class, and is the standard function we use to generate the HTML for the administration menu.

```
function createAdminMenu(){
    $adminMenu = "<div id=\"adminMenu\">";
    $adminMenu .= "<span class=\"adminMenuHeader\">Admin Menu</span><br><br>";
    $adminMenu .= "<a href=\"editAdminArticles.php\"";
    $adminMenu .= " class=\"adminMenuLink\">Article Admin</a><br>";
    $adminMenu .= "<a href=\"editAdminMenu.php\"";
    $adminMenu .= " class=\"adminMenuLink\">Menu Admin</a><br>";
    $adminMenu .= "<a href=\"editAdminNews.php\"";
    $adminMenu .= " class=\"adminMenuLink\">News Admin</a><br>";
    $adminMenu .= "</div>";
    $this->adminMenu = $adminMenu;
}
```

Make sure that you save the class before you continue.

That completes the entire *Administration* section now, with three administration pages for the menu, news type, and article type. We're now going to start on the front end of the system, which displays the articles and news documents in the database to the web site's readers.

# Creating the CSS Stylesheets for the Front End

As before, the front end is laid out and formatted using CSS stylesheets, which we're going to create now. We use different stylesheets for the front and back end of the system so that users can easily distinguish between the two by their different formatting.

# Creating the layout.css Stylesheet

As with the administration system, the layout stylesheet defines the actual layout of the screen. There are three areas, a header bar, a left column, and the rest of the screen for the main content.

Open a new CSS file, and save it as `/cms/css/displayLayout.css`. Add the following CSS code:

```css
body {
    margin-bottom : 0px;
    margin-left : 0px;
    margin-right : 0px;
    margin-top : 0px;
    background: #ffffff;
}

/* Main Layout Styles */
#header {
    margin-left: 0px;
    margin-right: 0px;
    height: 80px;
    background-color: #5cad33;
}
#leftColumn {
    position: absolute;
    left: 5px;
    top: 80px;
    width: 150px;
}
#mainContent {
    margin-left: 160px;
    margin-right: 20px;
    margin-top:10px;
    padding-left : 20px;
    padding-bottom : 10px;
    border-left : thin dotted #5cad33;
    background : #FFFFFF;
}

/* Menu Layout Styles */
#menu{
    padding-left:10px;
    background-color : #F4F4F4;
}
#menuSpacer{
    background-color : #F4F4F4;
    height: 20px;
}
#mainMenuRow{
    margin-top:10px;
}
#subMenuRow{
    margin-left: -10px;
}
```

These styles are displayed in the following screenshot, which shows how they appear in a browser.

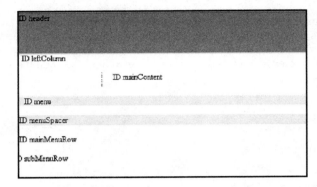

## Creating the mainStyles.css Stylesheet

Next we are going to create the `mainStyles.css` stylesheet, which contains the CSS that formats the information on the screen.

Open a new CSS file, and save it as `/cms/css/displayStyles.css`. Add the following CSS code:

```css
/* Redefine Default Link Style */
a {
    color: #5cad33;
}
a:link {
    color: #5cad33;
    text-decoration : none;
}
a:visited {
    color: #5cad33;
    text-decoration : none;
}
a:hover {
    color: #999999;
}
a:active {
}

/* Define Menu Styles */
.menuLink{
    font-family: Arial, Helvetica, sans-serif;
    font-size: 14px;
    font : bold;
    color: #5cad33;
}
.subMenuLink{
    font-family: Arial, Helvetica, sans-serif;
    font-size: 10px;
    color: #5cad33;
}
```

```
/* Define main content styles */
.mainContentHeading{
    font-family: Arial, Helvetica, sans-serif;
    font-size: 16px;
    color: #5cad33;
    font-weight : bold;
    margin-bottom: 20px;
}
.mainContentBodyText{
    font-family: Arial, Helvetica, sans-serif;
    font-size: 12px;
    text-align : justify;
}
.mainContentAuthor{
    font-family: Arial, Helvetica, sans-serif;
    font-size: 12px;
    color: #000000;
    font-weight : normal;
}
.mainContentDate{
    font-family: Arial, Helvetica, sans-serif;
    font-size: 12px;
    color: #000000;
    font-weight : normal;
    margin-left: 30px;
}

/* Define News Styles */
.newsHeadline{
    background-color : #F4F4F4;
    padding-left: 10px;
    padding-right: 10px;
    padding-top: 10px;
    padding-bottom: 10px;
}

/* Define Navigation Styles */
.navigation{
    background : #ECF8EC;
    padding-left: 10px;
    padding-right: 10px;
    padding-top: 10px;
    padding-bottom: 10px;
}
.navigationPrevious{
    font-family: Arial, Helvetica, sans-serif;
    font-size: 12px;
    font-weight: bold;
    padding-right: 50px;
}
.navigationNext{
    font-family: Arial, Helvetica, sans-serif;
    font-weight: bold;
    font-size: 12px;
    padding-left: 50px
}
```

```
.navigationBlocks{
    font-family: Arial, Helvetica, sans-serif;
    font-size: 12px;
    padding-left: 5px;
    padding-right: 5px;
}
.navigationLink{
    font-family: Arial, Helvetica, sans-serif;
    font-size: 14px;
    color: #5cad33;
    font-weight : bold;
}

.pictureLink{
    padding-top: 10px;
    padding-left: 10px;
    padding-right: 10px;
    padding-bottom: 10px;
}

/* Clear Styles */
.clear {
    clear: both
}
```

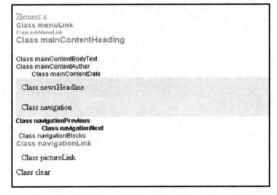

The result of these styles is shown in the screenshot to the right:

As with the back-end administration system, each of the document types, news, articles, and the menu, have its own PHP class, to generate the relevant code. We're now going to create these classes which read the data from the database, and format it correctly for display.

# Creating the Menu Class

The first class we're going to create generates the HTML for the dynamic menu, which takes its data from the `tblmainmenu` table in the database.

Create a new PHP page, and switch into *Code View* and delete the HTML. Save this page as `cms/class/displayMenu.php`. Add the following code to create the basic structure for the class:

```php
<?php
require_once("database.php");
#####################################################
# CMS Menu Class                                    #
#####################################################
# Inherits
#   DB_date2mysql($date) : DB_mysql2date($date) : DB_databaseConnect()
#   DB_executeQuery($query,$Link) : DB_getRecordID() : DB_getRecords($Result)
#   DB_closeDatabase($Link)

class Menu extends Database{

    var $menuLink;
    var $result;
    var $primary;
    var $secondary;
    var $menu;
    var $subMenu;
    var $selectedID;

    function Menu(){
        $this->menuLink = $this->DB_databaseConnect();
        $this->getVars();
        $this->getPrimaryMenu();
        $this->getSecondaryMenu();
        $this->createSubMenu();
        $this->createMenu();
        $this->DB_closeDatabase($this->menuLink);
    }

?>
```

The Menu class extends the database class to make all our custom database functions in the database class available. We're now going to create the functions that make up the class.

## getVars()

This function is very similar to the one in the admin classes. It populates the global class variables $type, which holds the document type (article or news), and menuID which is the menuID of the currently selected menu item. It does this by first checking for a value in the $_GET array and, if it's not found, checks the $_POST array.

```php
function getVars(){
    if(isset($_GET['type'])){
        $this->type = $_GET['type'];
    } elseif(isset($_POST['type'])){
        $this->type = $_POST['type'];
    }
    if(isset($_GET['menuID'])){
        $this->menuID = $_GET['menuID'];
    }elseif(isset($_POST['menuID'])){
        $this->menuID = $_POST['menuID'];
    }
}
```

## getPrimaryMenu()

This function reads in all the records in the `tblmainmenu` table, ordered in ascending order by the position value. As it cycles through each record, it puts the field values in an array, `$temp`, indexed by the field name. It then adds the `$temp` array to the main global class array `$primary`.

```
    $query = "SELECT id,label,position,link
                FROM tblmainmenu ORDER BY position ASC";
    $this->result = $this->DB_executeQuery($query,$this->menuLink);
    $temp['label'] = "Home";
    $temp['link'] = "?";
    $primary[] = $temp;
    while($row = mysql_fetch_assoc($this->result)){
        $temp['id'] = $row['id'];
        $temp['label'] = $row['label'];
        $temp['position'] = $row['position'];
        $temp['link'] = $row['link'];
        $primary[] = $temp;
    }
    $this->primary = $primary;
}
function getPrimaryMenu(){
```

## getSecondaryMenu()

If the current menu item is linked to an article, rather than a news type, and there is more than one article linked to the menu item, this function creates a submenu of the linked articles.

First we check that a menu item has been selected, and that the type is the article type. If both these conditions are met, we read all the articles from the `tblarticles` table where the `menuID` field value equals the currently selected menu item. We loop through each record returned, and place the values into an array `$temp`. We then add the `$temp` array to the global class array `$secondary`.

```
function getSecondaryMenu(){
    if($this->menuID > 0 && $this->type=="article"){
        $query = "SELECT id,title,author,date,body,menuid
                FROM tblarticles WHERE menuID='".$this->menuID."' ORDER BY id
ASC";
        $this->result = $this->DB_executeQuery($query,$this->menuLink);
        $numRecords = $this->DB_getRecords($this->result);
        if($numRecords > 1){
            while($row = mysql_fetch_assoc($this->result)){
                $temp['title'] = $row['title'];
                $temp['id'] = $row['id'];
                $this->secondary[] = $temp;
            }
        }
    }
}
```

## createSubMenu()

This function uses the global class array `$secondary` that we created using the previous `getSecondaryMenu()` function to generate the actual HTML for the article submenu.

We create each article in the submenu as a link, which passes the article ID menu, and the type value set to "`article`". We store all the HTML code that is generated in the global class variable `$subMenu`, ready for display later.

```php
function createSubMenu(){
    if(is_array($this->secondary)){
        $subMenu = "<div id='subMenuRow'><ul>";
        foreach($this->secondary as $menuItem){
            $extraLink = "?articleID={$menuItem['id']}&menuID={$this->menuID}" .
"&type=article";
            $subMenu .= "<li><a href=\"{$_SERVER['PHP_SELF']}" .
"{$menuItem['link']}$extraLink\" class=\"subMenuLink\">";
            $subMenu .= $menuItem['title'] . "</a></li><br>";
        }
        $subMenu .= "</ul></div>";
        $this->subMenu = $subMenu;
    }
}
```

## createMenu()

This is the last function in this class, and creates the HTML for the main menu. It loops through each menu item in the global class array `$primary`, and creates the menu item as a link, using the link data in `$primary` that came from the link field in the `tblmainmenu` table. If a menu item has already been selected, we insert the HTML for the submenu that we created with the `createSubMenu()` function above in the appropriate place. All the generated HTML is stored in the global class variable `$menu`, ready to display later.

```php
function createMenu(){
    $menu = "<div id=\"menu\">";
    $menu .= "<div id=\"menuSpacer\"></div>";
    foreach($this->primary as $menuItem){
        $extraLink = "&menuID=" . $menuItem['id'];
        $menu .= "<div id=\"mainMenuRow\">";
        $menu .= "<a href=\"".$_SERVER['PHP_SELF'].$menuItem['link'];
        $menu .= $extraLink."\" class=\"menuLink\">";
        $menu .= $menuItem['label']."</a><br></div>";
        if($menuItem['id'] == $this->menuID){
            $menu .= $this->subMenu;
        }
    }
    $menu .= "<div id=\"menuSpacer\"></div>";
    $menu .= "</div>";
    $this->menu = $menu;
}
```

Save the page before you move on to the next class.

# Creating the displayNews Class

Next we're going to create the class that displays the news items from the database. We use a similar technique to the adminNews class, showing a block of five news items at a time. When a user clicks on a news item's title, the whole news article is displayed on its own.

Create a new PHP page, and delete the HTML code. Add the following to create the basic class structure.

```php
<?php
require_once("database.php");
#####################################################
# CMS DisplayNews Class                             #
#####################################################
# Inherits
#  DB_date2mysql($date) : DB_mysql2date($date) : DB_databaseConnect()
#  DB_executeQuery($query,$Link) : DB_getRecordID() : DB_getRecords($Result)
#  DB_closeDatabase($Link)

class DisplayNews extends Database{

    var $showNewsNumber = 5;
    var $mainContent;
    var $pageTitle;
    var $block;
    var $title;
    var $author;
    var $body;
    var $date;
    var $headlineArray;
    var $totalRecords;
    var $startRecord;
    var $endRecord;
    var $newsLink;
    var $newsResult;

    function DisplayNews(){
        $this->getVars();
        $this->newsLink = $this->DB_databaseConnect();
        $this->processNews();
        $this->DB_closeDatabase($this->newsLink);
    }

?>
```

Save this page as /cms/class/displayNews.php. We'll now add the functions that make up the class.

## getVars()

First we have our standard getVars() function to retrieve the news item id if set, and the current block number (refer back to the adminNews class for the explanation of how the blocks are used).

```
function getVars(){
    if(strlen($_GET['id'])>0){
        $this->id = $_GET['id'];
    } else {
        $this->id = 0;
    }
    if(strlen($_GET['block'])>0){
        $this->block = $_GET['block'];
    } else {
        $this->block = 1;
    }
}
```

## processNews()

This function decides whether we display a whole news article or a block of headlines. If the global class variable $id is set it means that a news item had been selected, so we call functions to display the whole news item only. If the variable $id hasn't been set then we call functions to display the news headlines.

```
function processNews(){
    if($this->id > 0){
        $this->fetchNewsItem();
        $this->displayNewsItem();
    } else {
        $this->getNewsHeadlines();
        $this->displayNewsHeadlines();
    }
}
```

## fetchNewsItem()

This function is used to pull a single news item from the database, where the record id is equal to the value in global array $id, which contains the id of the selected news item. We place the field data into the global class variables that have the same name as the field they contain. We use this data later to create the HTML for the news item.

```
function fetchNewsItem(){
    $query = sprintf("SELECT id,title,author,date,body FROM tblnews WHERE id =
'%s'", $this->id);
    $this->newsResult = $this->DB_executeQuery($query,$this->newsLink);
    $row = mysql_fetch_assoc($this->newsResult);
    $this->title = stripslashes($row['title']);
    $this->author = stripslashes($row['author']);
    $this->body = stripslashes($row['body']);
    $this->date = $this->DB_mysql2date($row['date']);
}
```

## displayNewsItem()

This function takes the data stored in the global class variables by the fetchNewsItem() function above, and creates the HTML which will be used to display the news item. The HTML generated is stored in the global class variable $mainContent for use later on. At the end of the function we call another function addMenuLink() which adds a link to the news item, so that the user can go back to the previous block of news headlines.

C2

```
function displayNewsItem(){
    $this->mainContent = "<div class=\"mainContentHeading\">".$this->title."<br>";
    $this->mainContent .= "<span class=\"mainContentAuthor\">";
    $this->mainContent .= "Written By: ".$this->author."</span>";
    $this->mainContent .= "<span class=\"mainContentDate\">";
    $this->mainContent .= "Date: ".$this->date."</span>";
    $this->mainContent .= "</div>";
    $this->mainContent .= "<div class=\"mainContentBodyText\">";
    $this->mainContent .= $this->body;
    $this->mainContent .= "</div>";
    $this->pageTitle = "News - " . $this->title;
    $this->addMenuLink();
}
```

## addMenuLink()

This is the function called from the `displayNewsItem()` function above, which creates the HTML for a link back to the news headlines. It passes the `$block` variable, so that the user goes back to the same block of headlines that they were looking at before they selected a news headline to display.

```
function addMenuLink(){
    $start = "<div align=\"center\" class=\"navigation\">";
    $end = "</div>";
    $link = "<a href=\"".$_SERVER['PHP_SELF']."?type=news&block=";
    $link .= $this->block. "\" class=\"navigationLink\">";
    $link .= "Return to News Headlines";
    $link .= "</a>";
    $menuLink = "<br>" . $start . $link . $end;
    $this->mainContent .= $menuLink;
}
```

## getNewsHeadlines()

This function is used to read in the news headlines from the database. We use the same logic that we used in the `adminNews` class to work out the first and last records in the current block, and we store those records in the array `$tempArray`. Once we have the whole record in `$tempArray`, we place `$tempArray` in the global class array `$headlineArray` ready for use later.

```
function getNewsHeadlines(){
    $query = "SELECT id,title,author,date,body FROM tblnews ORDER BY id DESC";
    $this->newsResult = $this->DB_executeQuery($query,$this->newsLink);
    $this->totalRecords = $this->DB_getRecords($this->newsResult);
    $this->startRecord = ($this->showNewsNumber * $this->block);
    $this->startRecord -= $this->showNewsNumber + 1;
    $this->endRecord = $this->showNewsNumber * $this->block;
    for($i=1; $i <= $this->totalRecords; $i++){
        $row = mysql_fetch_assoc($this->newsResult);
        if(($i >= $this->startRecord)&&($i<= $this->endRecord)){
            $tempArray['id'] = $row['id'];
            $tempArray['title'] = stripslashes($row['title']);
            $tempArray['author'] = stripslashes($row['author']);
            $tempArray['date'] = $this->DB_mysql2date($row['date']);
```

```
            $tempArray['body'] = stripslashes($row['body']);
            $this->headlineArray[] = $tempArray;
        }
    }
}
```

## displayNewsHeadlines()

This function takes the data stored in the global class array $headline, set by the previous function getNewsHeadlines() and generates the HTML. Each news item has the title as a link which passes the headline's unique id number. We use the grabParagraph() function we'll create soon, to only display the first paragraph of the news item's body, as a short preview of the news item. The HTML generated is stored in the global class array $mainContent.

```
function displayNewsHeadlines(){
if(is_array($this->headlineArray)){
    foreach($this->headlineArray as $headline){
        $this->mainContent .= "<div class=\"newsHeadline\">";
        $link = $_SERVER['PHP_SELF']."?type=news&block=";
        $link .= $this->block."&id=".$headline['id'];
        $this->mainContent .= "<a href=\"$link\"";
        $this->mainContent .= " class=\"mainContentHeading\">";
        $this->mainContent .= $headline['title']."</a><br>";
        $this->mainContent .= "<span class=\"mainContentAuthor\">";
        $this->mainContent .= "Written By: " . $headline['author']."</span>";
        $this->mainContent .= "<span class=\"mainContentDate\">";
        $this->mainContent .= "Date: ".$headline['date']."</span>";
        $this->mainContent .= "<div class=\"mainContentBodyText\">";
        $this->mainContent .= $this->grabParagraph($headline['body']);
        $this->mainContent .= "</div>";
        $this->mainContent .= "</div><br>";
        }
    $this->pageTitle = "News Headlines";
    $this->displayNavigation();
    }
}
```

## displayNavigation()

This function creates HTML which is added to the bottom of the news headlines to allow the user to move backwards and forwards between blocks of news headlines. We use the same formulas we used in the adminNews class to calculate when the *Older Headlines* and *Newer Headlines* links should be displayed. These take the users to the previous and next blocks respectively.

```
function displayNavigation(){
    $previousBlock = $this->block - 1;
    $nextBlock = $this->block + 1;
    $numberOfBlocks = ceil($this->totalRecords / $this->showNewsNumber);
    $lastBlockNum = $this->totalRecords - (($numberOfBlocks-1)*$this-
>showNewsNumber);
    for($i=1; $i<=$numberOfBlocks; $i++){
        $startRecord = (($this->showNewsNumber * $i) - $this->showNewsNumber) +
```

```
1;
        if($i == $numberOfBlocks){
            $endRecord = $startRecord + $lastBlockNum - 1;
        }else {
            $endRecord = $this->showNewsNumber * $i;
        }
        $tempLink = "[$startRecord-$endRecord]";
        $middleBlocks .= "<span class=\"navigationBlocks\">";
        $middleBlocks .= "<a href=\"" . $_SERVER['PHP_SELF'];
        $middleBlocks .= "?type=news&block=$i\" class=\"\">$tempLink</a>";
        $middleBlocks .= "</span>";
        }
    if($this->block > 1){
        $leftLink = "<span class=\"navigationPrevious\">";
        $leftLink .= "<a href=\"" . $_SERVER['PHP_SELF'];
        $leftLink .= "?type=news&block=" . $previousBlock;
        $leftLink .= "\" class=\"menuLink\">Newer Headlines</a>";
        $leftLink .= "</span>";
    }
    if($this->block < $numberOfBlocks){
        $rightLink = "<span class=\"navigationNext\">";
        $rightLink .= "<a href='" . $_SERVER['PHP_SELF'];
        $rightLink .= "?type=news&block=".$nextBlock."\"";
        $rightLink .= " class=\"menuLink\">Older Headlines</a>";
        $rightLink .= "</span>";
    }
    $start = "<div align=\"center\" class=\"navigation\">";
    $end = "</div>";
    $this->mainContent .= $start.$leftLink." ".$middleBlocks." ".$rightLink.$end;
}
```

### grabParagraph()

This simple function is the last one in the class. When the administrator is creating the news body, paragraphs are marked using the HTML `<p>` tags. This function takes the body from the news item, and displays only the first paragraph.

We do this by looking for the first closing paragraph tag, and then use `substr()` to grab all the text up to and including the first closing paragraph tag found, and this is returned to the calling function. We've now completed the class, so save the page.

```
function grabParagraph($body){
    $end = strpos($body, "</p>");
    $end = $end + strlen("</p>");
    $paragraph = substr($body,0,$end);
    return $paragraph;
}
```

# Creating the displayArticle Class

Next we are going to create the `displayArticle` class, which creates the HTML to display an article from the database.

Open a new PHP page, delete the HTML, and save it as `/cms/class/displayArticle.php`. Add the following code to create the basic class structure.

```php
<?php
require_once("database.php");
##################################################
# CMS Display Article Class                      #
##################################################
# Inherits
#   DB_date2mysql($date) : DB_mysql2date($date) : DB_databaseConnect()
#   DB_executeQuery($query,$Link) : DB_getRecordID() : DB_getRecords($Result)
#   DB_closeDatabase($Link)

class displayArticle extends Database{

    // Change the directory below to the correct path for your server
    var $mainImageDirectory = "/web/cms/images/articles/";
    var $webImageDirectory = "images/articles/";
    var $articleLink;
    var $articleID;
    var $article;
    var $pageTitle;
    var $mainContent;
    var $body;
    var $title;
    var $author;
    var $date;

    function displayArticle(){
        $this->articleLink = $this->DB_databaseConnect();
        $this->getVars();
        $this->DB_closeDatabase($this->articleLink);
    }
}
?>
```

## getVars()

With the `displayArticle` class, all data variables such as the article id are sent through a URL query string only, so we only have to check the `$_GET` array in this class. If an article id is found, then we call the `readArticle()` function to read the article from the database. If there is no article id, we call the `findLinkedArticle()` function to find which article is the default for the chosen menu option.

```php
function getVars(){
    if(isset($_GET['articleID'])){
        $this->articleID = $_GET['articleID'];
        $this->readArticle();
    }else{
        $this->findLinkedArticle();
    }
}
```

### findLinkedArticle()

This is the function that we mentioned above, which is called if no article id is present. We perform a SELECT query to find all articles attached to the selected menu id, and grab the ID of the first record in the list, we then call readArticle() to read that article from the database. If no articles are found for the chosen menu item, we call the function pageNotFound() which creates the HTML for a *page not found* message.

```
function findLinkedArticle(){
    if(isset($_GET['menuID'])){
        $query = "SELECT id,title,author,date,body,menuID
                    FROM tblarticles WHERE menuID='".$_GET['menuID']."'";
        $result = $this->DB_executeQuery($query,$this->articleLink);
        $row = mysql_fetch_assoc($result);
        if(isset($row['id'])){
            $this->articleID = $row['id'];
            $this->readArticle();
        } else {
            $this->pageNotFound();
        }
    } else {
        $this->pageNotFound();
    }
}
```

### pageNotFound()

This is the function mentioned above, and creates the HTML for a simple "*Page Not Found*" message.

```
function pageNotFound(){
    $mainContent = "<div class=\"mainContentHeading\">";
    $mainContent .= "Error: Page not Found, return to <a href='";
    $mainContent .= $_SERVER['HTTP_REFERRER'] . "'>previous page</a>?";
    $mainContent .= "</div>";
    $this->mainContent = $mainContent;
    $this->pageTitle = "Error: Page not Found";
}
```

### swapImages()

When the user enters the text for the article body in the adminArticles.php page, they can include HTML tags for formatting. They can also enter a custom tag to display an uploaded image, using the format @@@image name:alignment@@@, where image name is the name of the uploaded image, and alignment can be left, center, or right, which controls where the image is placed.

Because the articles are dynamic and can have any article id number, and the images are saved in a directory with a name matching the corresponding article id, the user has no idea where the uploaded image will actually be stored. However, when you use an image tag you need to put the path to the image.

To get round this we allow the user to use the custom image tag above, and when an article is read this function checks for the presence of the tag, and if it finds one or more custom image tags it will automatically transpose the custom image tag to a normal image tag, creating the correct image path.

```
function swapImages(){
  $body = $this->body;
  while(strpos($body,"@@@") > 0){
    $first = strpos($body,"@@@") + 3;
    $second = strpos($body,"@@@",$first);
    $length = $second - $first;
    $imageTag = substr($body,$first,$length);
    $imageArray = explode(":",$imageTag);
    $image = $imageArray[0];
    $align = $imageArray[1];
    if(file_exists($this->mainImageDirectory.$this->articleID. "/".$image)){
      $imageXY = GetImageSize($this->mainImageDirectory.$this-
>articleID."/".$image);
      $x = $imageXY[0];
      $y = $imageXY[1];
      $imageLink = $this->webImageDirectory . $this->articleID . "/" . $image;
      $link = "<div class=\"pictureLink\" align=\"$align\">";
      $link .= "<img src=\"$imageLink\" width=\"$x\" height=\"$y\">";
      $link .= "</div>";
    } else {
      $link = "";
    }
    $replace = "@@@" . $imageTag . "@@@";
    $body = str_replace($replace, $link, $body);
  }
  $this->body = $body;
  if($_GET['menuID']>0){
    $this->createHTML();
  } else {
    $this->createRootDoc();
  }
}
```

First we look for the custom start tag marker, which is "@@@" (chosen because it's highly unlikely the combination "@@@" will be found in any normal document). We then use string-handling commands to extract everything between the opening and closing "@@@" symbols. This leaves us with some data in the format image_name:alignment.

We use the explode() function to split the text at the colon, so the first value in the resulting array will hold the image name, and the second value in the array will be the alignment option.

Next we check that the images do actually exist and are in the expected directory. If the images are not found, then we just ignore the custom error tag so we don't generate any errors. If the images are found, we use the GetImageSize() command to find the width ($x$) and height ($y$) for the image.

Now that we have the image filename, width, and height, we can generate the HTML code to display the image, aligned to the option set in the custom tag. We then replace the custom tag in the article body with the actual HTML code to display the image.

C2

Finally, if an `articleID` is present we call the `createHTML()` function to create the complete HTML for the article. If the article is not present, then we call the function `$createRootDoc`.

## readArticle()

This function selects an article from the database whose `id` matches the `id` in the global class variable `$articleID`. We then read the record from the database, and populate global class variables with the names of the fields that the data came from. We then use these variables later to create the HTML code to display the article.

```
function readArticle(){
    $query = "SELECT id,title,author,date,body,menuID
            FROM tblarticles WHERE id='" . $this->articleID . "'";
    $result = $this->DB_executeQuery($query,$this->articleLink);
    $row = mysql_fetch_assoc($result);
    $this->title = stripslashes($row['title']);
    $this->body = stripslashes($row['body']);
    $this->author = stripslashes($row['author']);
    $this->date = $this->DB_mysql2date($row['date']);
    $this->swapImages();
}
```

## createHTML()

This is the function mentioned above, which uses all the article data we have collected to create the final output HTML for the main content area, which is stored in the global class variable `$mainContent`.

```
function createHTML(){
    $mainContent = "<div class='mainContentHeading'>";
    if(strlen($this->title) > 0){
        $mainContent .= $this->title . "<br>";
        $mainContent .= "<span class=\"mainContentAuthor\">Written By: ";
        $mainContent .= $this->author . "</span>";
        $mainContent .= "<span class=\"mainContentDate\">Date: ";
        $mainContent .= $this->date . "</span>";
    }
    $mainContent .= "</div>";
    $mainContent .= "<div class=\"mainContentBodyText\">" . $this->body;
    $mainContent .= "</div>";
    $this->pageTitle = $this->title;
    $this->mainContent = $mainContent;
}
```

This function creates the document with a title, author, and date header at the top.

## createRootDoc()

This is the last function in the class, and is called if there is no actual article `id` present. If this is the case, we create slightly different HTML, without the author and date information.

```php
function createRootDoc(){
    $mainContent = "<div class=\"mainContentHeading\" align=\"center\">";
    $mainContent .= $this->title . "<br />";
    $mainContent .= "</div>";
    $mainContent .= "<div class=\"mainContentBodyText\">";
    $mainContent .= $this->body;
    $mainContent .= "</div>";
    $this->pageTitle = $this->title;
    $this->mainContent = $mainContent;
}
```

Save this file before you continue.

# The Page Class

This is the last class, and it ties all the other classes together. It acts as the "master control". It's also the simplest class, so we're going to list the whole class in one go. First open a new PHP page, and as usual delete the HTML code, and add the following.

```php
<?php
require_once("class/displayNews.php");
require_once("class/displayArticle.php");
require_once("class/displayMenu.php");
####################################################
# CMS Page Class                                   #
####################################################

class Page{

    var $type;
    var $mainContent;
    var $pageTitle;
    var $menu;

    function Page(){
        $this->getType();
        $this->createMenu();
    }

function getType(){
    if($_GET['type']==""){
        $link = $PHP_SELF . "?type=article&menuID=0";
        header("Location:" . $link);
    }
    if($_GET['type']=="news"){
        $this->news();
    }
    if($_GET['type']=="article"){
        $this->article();
    }
}
```

```
function createMenu(){
    $menu = new Menu();
    $this->menu = $menu->menu;
}

function news(){
    $news = new DisplayNews();
    $this->pageTitle = $news->pageTitle;
    $this->mainContent = $news->mainContent;
}

function article(){
    $article = new displayArticle();
    $this->pageTitle = $article->pageTitle;
    $this->mainContent = $article->mainContent;
}
}
?>
```

First we include the other classes (`displayArticle`, `displayMenu` & `DisplayNews`) so that they are all available to this class.

Next we check for the presence of the type variable, which will be in the `$_GET` array if it's set. If it hasn't been set then we set the type to `article`, and `menuID` to zero, which will display the root page for the site – equivalent to `index.html` on a static HTML site.

If the type is set, and is equal to "`news`", then we call the function `news()` which initiates the `DisplayNews` class, and shows the default set of news headlines.

If the type is set but contains "`article`" then we call the `article()` function to initiate a new instance of the `displayArticle` class.

This completes the `Page` class, so save it as `/cms/class/createPage.php`.

## Creating page.php

Create a new PHP page, and save it as `/cms/page.php`. This is the page that the user actually calls up in the browser. Add the following code.

```
<?php require_once("class/createPage.php");?>
<?php
    $page = new Page();
?>
<!DOCTYPE HTML PUBLIC "-//W3C//DTD HTML 4.01 Transitional//EN">
<html>
<head>
<title>DMX Online - <?php echo $page->pageTitle ?></title>
<meta http-equiv="Content-Type" content="text/html; charset=iso-8859-1">
<link href="css/layout.css" rel="stylesheet" type="text/css">
<link href="css/mainStyles.css" rel="stylesheet" type="text/css">
</head>
<body>
```

```
<div id="header"><img src="images/logo.gif" width="220" height="80" alt=""></div>
<div id="leftColumn">
   <?php echo $page->menu; ?>
</div>
<div id="mainContent">
    <?php echo $page->mainContent; ?>
</div>
</body>
</html>
```

First the page opens a new instance of the Page class, which controls the other classes that are called. There are three variables that are output to generate the complete HTML for the page. The classes initiated by the Page class populate these variables. Save the page.

We have now completed the design of the system, so make sure all your pages are saved, and upload them to your server.

# Setting Up the Content Management System

Now that we have the Content Management System complete, we can start to populate the system with some data. For this example we'll set up a small demonstration site for an imaginary e-zine DMX Online.

## Creating the Menu Options

The first stage in setting up the system is to create some menu options, so that we have some menu items we can link future articles to.

For this example we'll create three options:

- About – Which will display a single article about the site

- News – Which will link to the News Headlines

- CMS – Which will link to a number of different articles.

Open the editAdminMenu.php page in your browser:
*http://www.yoursite.com/cms/admin/editAdminMenu.php*

## Creating the About Link

Create the menu item with the following details:

| Menu Item Label | Menu Item Link |
| --- | --- |
| About | ?type=article |

All you have to do now is to add a new article selecting the *About* menu item as the item to be linked to, and then when the user selects "*About*", the linked article will load.

## Creating the News Link

| Menu Item Label | Menu Item Link |
|---|---|
| News | ?type=news |

Create a new item with the following details. When the user clicks on the *News* menu item the *News Headlines* are displayed.

## Creating the CMS Link

| Menu Item Label | Menu Item Link |
|---|---|
| CMS | ?type=article |

The CMS link will be used to display a number of articles about the CMS system. Add the menu item with the following details.

Now we can link a number of articles to the *CMS* menu option, and when the user selects that menu item, a submenu of the menu items will automatically be displayed.

After you have added a number of articles, if you want a specific article to be displayed on the *CMS* menu option instead of the first in the group, you can change the CMS menu details to:
where the `articleID` is the number of the article you want displayed by default, that is article ID 32 in the above example. You can see the article IDs on the `editAdminMenu.php` page, where they are displayed next to the articles in the article list.

| Menu Item Label | Menu Item Link |
|---|---|
| CMS | ?type=article&articleID=32 |

A screenshot of the `editAdminMenu` screen with the above menu items, with the CMS menu item selected for editing is shown below:

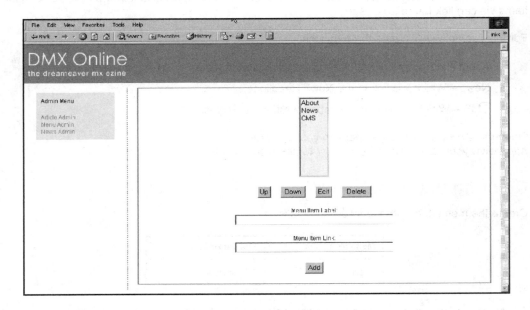

## Creating News Items

Next, browse to the *News Admin* page (*cms/admin/editAdminNews.php*). You can do that by selecting it from the *Admin Menu* of the `editAdminMenu.php` page. The news admin screen is shown below:

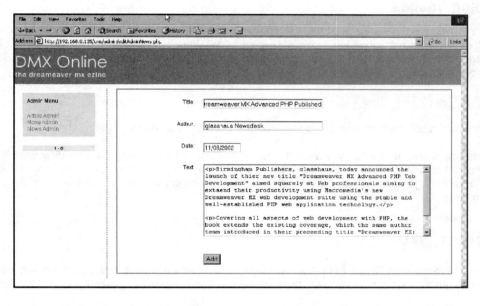

Adding and editing is pretty self-explanatory. The only thing you need to ensure is that in the news text you must have at least one set of HTML `<p>` and `</p>` tags, as this first paragraph is used in the news headline listings. It's a good idea not to make the first paragraph too long for this reason.

## Creating Articles

You can now go to the *Article Admin* page, and add some new articles. A screenshot is shown next:

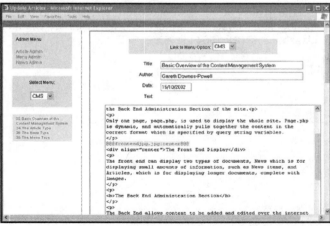

First we select CMS in the *Link to Menu* option, and we can then enter the article details. You'll notice in the *Link to Menu* options there's an additional option *Root*. This corresponds to the page which is shown when a user first views the site, and is equivalent to the `index.html` page on a static HTML site.

## Adding Images

Wherever you want an uploaded image to appear in the article, you can add the custom image tag, which uses the format: `@@@image_name:alignment@@@`, where `image_name` is the exact name of the uploaded image, for example `image1.jpg`. Alignment options can be `left`, `center`, or `right`. So for example, your custom image tag might look like:

```
@@@image1.jpg:center@@@
```

which would display an uploaded image called `image1.jpg`, aligned to center.

Update the article, and when you view it through the front end the image will be displayed in the location of the custom image tag. If you enter a custom image tag, and the image you wanted doesn't exist or the image name is typed incorrectly, the custom image tag will be stripped from the body and ignored.

# Summary

We now have our own Content Management System, with which we can easily add and edit data in the database through a standard web browser, so that the site can be updated across the Internet.

We used CSS for the page layout and formatting, which separates the formatting information from the code, enabling us to drastically change the look of the site in future, without having to make major changes to the back-end PHP code.

All back-end code is created in PHP classes so it can be easily reused in other projects, saving you from having to create the same sort of code over and over again for different projects.

Hopefully now we have whetted your appetite, and have got you interested in exploring Content Management Systems further. See, for instance, *Content Management Systems* (Addey, et al., glasshaus; ISBN: 190415106X).

# Index

## A Guide to the Index

The index is arranged hierarchically, in alphabetical order, with symbols preceding the letter A. Most second-level entries and many third-level entries also occur as first-level entries. This is to ensure that users will find the information they require however they choose to search for it.

# E

**N**

**O**

# personal training log, (Cont'd)

# S

# strings

Notes

Notes

**Notes**

Notes

Notes

# Notes

# Also from glasshaus:

Tools of the Trade

Dynamic Dreamweaver MX

Rachel Andrews, Omar Elbaga, Alan Foley, Bob Regan, Rob Turnbull

Overview of Dreamweaver MX fundamentals
Creating standards-compliant XHTML and CSS code using Dreamweaver MX
Accessibility features of Dreamweaver MX
Dynamic web page creation via server-side scripting
Using Server Behaviors to create advanced dynamic web applications with ease

glasshaus

## Dynamic Dreamweaver MX

**Rob Turnbull, Bob Regan, Omar Elbaga, Paul Boon, Rachel Andrew**

1-904151-10-8

US: $29.99

C  : $46.99

UK: £21.99

July 2002

This book gets you up to speed on using Macromedia Dreamweaver MX, the new version of Macromedia's premier visual web site design tool, to produce dynamic, creative, visually stunning sites that comply with web standards and accessibility guidelines. It gets straight to the heart of the matter so you spend less time reading, and more time building your site.

- **Rachel Andrew** is a member of the Web Standards Project's Dreamweaver Task Force, responsible for improving Dreamweaver's standards compliance and accessibility

- **Omar Elbaga** started out as a fine artist and moved to computer graphic arts. He is also a member of Team Macromedia

- **Alan Foley** is an Assistant Professor of Instructional Technology who teaches and consults on web accessibility and usability issues

- **Bob Regan** is the Senior Product Manager for Accessibility at Macromedia

- **Rob Turnbull** is also a member of Team Macromedia

# Also from glasshaus:

glasshaus

Tools of the Trade

**Dreamweaver MX:**
**PHP Web Development**

Gareth Downes-Powell, Tim Green, Bruno Mairlot

Overview of Dreamweaver MX, PHP, and MySQL
Site design
Interacting with the database
Hand coding and debugging in Dreamweaver

glasshaus

# Dreamweaver MX:
## PHP Web Development

**Bruno Mairlot, Gareth Downes-Powell**
**Tim Green**

**1-904151-11-6**

**US: $39.99**
**C  : $61.99**
**UK: £28.99**

**July 2002**

This book is all about making dynamic PHP web sites with Dreamweaver MX . It covers PHP, enough to get the reader up to speed with the technology, and how to use Dreamweaver MX to produce PHP code quickly and efficiently. It also covers site design and databases and SQL. It uses an example project, a hotel reservation system, that is built up through the chapters to demonstrate the concepts explained

Web Professionals have been calling for years for Dreamweaver/ UltraDev to support PHP, as it's the premier free open-source server-side scripting language. With Macromedia's landmark new release of Dreamweaver, PHP is fully supported in the familiar Dreamweaver visual environment.

It's is a no-fluff 400 pages, so you can learn enough PHP to make real dynamic web pages, spending less time reading and more time on the job.

Aimed at web professionals who want to use Dreamweaver MX to produce PHP web sites. It doesn't assume any knowledge of PHP, and it doesn't hold your hand when talking about Dreamweaver, so experience of Dreamweaver would be useful. It assumes knowledge of HTML and Web design.